Courtly Desire and Medieval Homophobia

ELIZABETH B. KEISER

Courtly Desire and Medieval Homophobia

THE LEGITIMATION OF SEXUAL
PLEASURE IN *CLEANNESS* AND
ITS CONTEXTS

Yale University Press
New Haven &
London

Copyright © 1997 by Yale University.
All rights reserved.
This book may not be reproduced, in whole or in part, including illustrations, in any form (beyond that copying permitted by Sections 107 and 108 of the U.S. Copyright Law and except by reviewers for the public press), without written permission from the publishers.

Set in Sabon type by Keystone Typesetting, Inc.
Printed in the United States of America.

Library of Congress Cataloging-in-Publication Data
Keiser, Elizabeth B.
  Courtly desire and medieval homophobia: the legitimation of sexual pleasure in Cleanness and its contexts / Elizabeth B. Keiser.
    p. cm.
  Includes bibliographical references and index.
  ISBN 0-300-06923-5 (alk. paper)
  1. Purity (Middle English poem). 2. Homosexuality—Religious aspects—Christianity—History—Middle Ages, 600–1500. 3. Pleasure—Religious aspects—Christianity—History of doctrines—Middle Ages, 600–1500. 4. Sex—Religious aspects—Christianity—History of doctrines—Middle Ages, 600–1500. 5. Christian poetry, English (Middle)—History and criticism. 6. Homosexuality and literature—England—History. 7. Civilization, Medieval—14th century. 8. Sodom (Extinct city)—In literature. 9. Courtly love in literature. 10. Homophobia in literature. 11. Gay men in literature. 12. Desire in literature. I. Title.
PR1964.K45 1997
821'.1—dc21   96-40206
                                                                             CIP

A catalogue record for this book is available from the British Library.

The paper in this book meets the guidelines for permanence and durability of the Committee on Production Guidelines for Book Longevity of the Council on Library Resources.

10 9 8 7 6 5 4 3 2 1

Contents

Acknowledgments   vii

Introduction   1

1 The Narrative Theology of *Cleanness* and the Aesthetic Ethics of Thomas Aquinas   17

2 Homophobic Wrath and Paradisal Pleasure   41

3 Educating Love: Nature as Sexual Norm in *Cleanness* and Alain's *Complaint*   71

4 The Sexual Ethics of *Cleanness* and Thomas Aquinas on Temperance   93

5 Revising the *Complaint:* Desire in the *Roman* as Context for *Cleanness*   113

6 Privileging the Feminine: Courtly Revisions of Masculinity   134

7 Homosocial Bondings with God and Christ   165

8 Theopoetic Coherence: *Cleanness* among Its Manuscript Companions   201

Notes   225

Selected Bibliography   273

Index   289

Acknowledgments

I dedicate this book to R. Melvin Keiser and Elizabeth D. Kirk, in love and gratitude for fidelity to me as a writer, tangible over decades of long listening, responding to innumerable drafts, editing, and proofreading. Besides their literary and theological acumen, they provide fare so fine that working together becomes a feast, from cauliflower soup to cappuccino. Even in a feminist academic tradition of collaboration, such an enabling partnership over thirty years is rare among three writers. May it flourish for as long as we live.

For all who have mentored me, I am grateful. I am grateful to Joe Elmore who, at Earlham College, introduced me to nominalists and realists, the question of whether God can be said to suffer, and the possibility of a theologically informed life. At Yale Divinity School, H. Richard Niebuhr nurtured my combined investigation of medieval theology and literature in the study of Dante. At Yale Graduate School, E. Talbot Donaldson taught me Middle English and launched my exploration of contrasting tones of voices in *Patience* and *Cleanness*. Marie Borroff, who directed my Yale dissertation, later believed this book into being by the authority with which she spoke of its importance and by her faith that I could and should write it. (The quixotic nature of my undertaking a book in the midst of so many other commitments was matched by the absolute seriousness with which she took my vow to meet her deadlines — and the unwavering patience with which she extended them.) I am grateful for her confidence as well as for her sound editorial suggestions and advice about translating *Cleanness*.

I am grateful to Derek Pearsall and Elizabeth Salter for broadening my horizons by their academic hospitality during a year spent at the Centre for Medieval Studies in York, England. I am grateful to Larry Benson and members of the seminar on "the Realism of Romance" he led at Harvard University and to Kevin Brownlee, Jeffrey Schnapp, Nancy Vickers, Peter Hawkins, and Rachel Jacoff, and to all my fellow-participants in the Dante Institute at Dartmouth College. I am indebted to the National Endowment for the Humanities for these professional gatherings where I gained a belief in the significance of continuing my research with an aim of publication. To Bonnie Wheeler and Judith Ferster I am grateful for their fostering of dialogue among medievalists from which I and many others benefit.

I am grateful to the many people who have improved the manuscript with their editorial suggestions. Helen G. Hole was an insightful and supportive early reader, as well as a model of what it meant to persevere to closure; I wish she were alive to comment on the results. Barbara A. Johnson assisted me greatly in several summers of shared work on our books. Gregory Gross usefully commented on the first half of the book in its final revision. Lee Johnson read it all and contributed much, especially to the end of chapter 6. An anonymous reader for Yale University Press offered salient criticisms of chapter 7, which I hope I have addressed. David Randall Teague was a close reader and discerning critic of every draft, as well as a tireless translator, typist, and research assistant. Eliza Childs's fine copy editing and remarkable patience made this a more readable and accurate book.

For thirty years, I have been teaching undergraduates as part of an innovative faculty, committed to learning with each other and our students how to think within but also beyond the boundaries that shape academic discourse. For that freedom of inquiry, and for the absence of pressure to publish, I am grateful to Guilford College. The college has generously assisted my writing with three study leaves, grants for travel expenses to many conferences, and research funds to defray the cost of manuscript preparation. To celebrate all those in the Guilford College community who have contributed significantly to my work and personal growth would fill another book. I must name here those who have been directly supportive of my writing this book because many would not otherwise know how much their confidence in me fueled my efforts: Linda Beatrice Brown, Jane Godard Caris, Martha and James Cooley, Ann Deagon, Carter Delafield, Judy Dwyer, Rebecca Gibson, Jerry Caris Godard, Claire Helgeson, Carol Hoppe, Jeff Jeske, Adrienne Israel, Lee and Alice

Johnson, Timothy Kircher, John Lamiman, Edward Lowe, Sarah and Jonathan Malino, Claire and Larry Morse, Betty Place, Sheridan Simon, Carol and John Stoneburner, Michael Strickland, Alice Vaughn, Adele Wayman, Carolyn Beard Whitlow, Robert Williams, Lisa Young, and Richie Zweigenhaft. I am grateful to alumni who have sustained me for many years by their unwavering belief that someday I would finish the book: thanks to David Jones, Robert and Syndee Lowdermilk Kraus, Martha Lang, Judy Whisnant and John Bell, Holly Fairbairn, Sandra Beer, Martha Wence Summerville, Laura E. Donaldson, and Mary Louise Bringle. For my students present and past, heartfelt thanks for the patience when my writing got in the way of grading papers, and my love to all, as though I named you.

In the scholarly community beyond Guilford College, there are several benefactors to whom I am indebted. Four summers of codirecting the Coolidge Colloquium for the Associates for Religion and Intellectual Life gave me access to the libraries of Harvard University and Episcopal Divinity School, and just as important, a community of inquiry and faith made up of Jews and Christians. The Procter Fellowship from Episcopal Divinity School and a fellowship as Friend in Residence at Pendle Hill (a Quaker center for study and contemplation) gave me the opportunity to write during my last study leave in stimulating and supportive communities.

Within and beyond these various academic settings, there are many, many people to thank. Again, the roll is too long to inscribe here and so must be called silently. I hope that my gratitude will be felt by each person who has encouraged me during the book's many stages. Yet I must name Roberta Ballard, who has communicated energy and determination for every challenge I have taken on since our friendship began while burning the candle at both ends as students at Earlham College, and Walter P. Blass, who exceeds the duties of devoted friendship in support for my writing and indefatigable assistance with multiple deadlines and details.

Megan Keiser and Christopher Keiser nourished this book by their love for me as mother, teacher, and author. As children, their sweet and smart strength gave me joy; as adults, they have become my good teachers. I am grateful for the hopes they inspire in me and others.

To all my kin and extended family and especially to my mother-in-law Marjorie H. Keiser, who gives me unconditional appreciation, I am grateful for enabling love and fidelity. Many other ancestors ask to be invoked as I close these acknowledgments. Two must be praised as paradigms of the good teaching I have been privileged to receive. Frances Kilmer, founder of Green Hedges School, put Latin and French into my mouth at an early age, and it tasted sweet; she helped me search for objects in the natural world with which to express wonder at the Incarnation; she opened her home to make a school, thus modeling a way to combine family and work. Charity James came to Guilford College, having had several careers, to teach adult students resuming their education; she was a model of lifelong learning, of outrageous joy and earnest playfulness in the midst of the hard labor of bringing ourselves to deeper trust in how we are taught by life, in and out of schools.

Introduction

In this book I shall argue that the poem *Cleanness*, when read comparatively with other medieval works that construct nature as a heterosexual norm, illuminates a formative stage of Western thought about the self and God, ethics and natural law, sexual differences, and gender ideals. It may seem puzzling that such cultural significance is attributed to a text anonymously authored some six centuries ago in a difficult dialect of Middle English, surviving into modern times in a single manuscript first published only in 1864. Even in its own time *Cleanness* was not influential, and it has received sustained critical attention from modern readers primarily because of its close affiliation with the three other poems from the late fourteenth century preserved in MS Cotton Nero A.x, Art. 3 in the British Library. This collection includes two unexcelled works of Middle English narrative art — *Sir Gawain and the Green Knight* and *Pearl* — and a homiletic paraphrase of the book of Jonah — *Patience* — that is a companion piece to *Cleanness*'s three lengthy exempla from the Old Testament. Too often the misleading connotations of modern English translations of its title, *Cleanness* or *Purity,* the sheer number of its biblical narratives and their cumulative length, and its narrator's announced emphasis on God's wrath against filth mean that this poem receives, relative to its manuscript companions, a cursory reading. Read as an innovative ethical vision in an original theopoetic mode, *Cleanness* is much more interesting than most of its modern audience has imagined. As Amos Wilder noted in commenting on the term *theopoetic,* which he used to title his exploration of theology and the religious imagination, the church's modifications of theological idioms requires the imagination's free play in fictional and poetic revisioning (Wilder 1–2). I argue that such freedom in resymbolizing the sacred is evident in *Cleanness.*

In addition to addressing readers who are already familiar with *Cleanness,* I have written for a broader audience who may never have read this or any other Middle English text but are interested in intellectual history and cultural critique of sexuality and gender. This book offers a close analysis of the sexual themes that are central to the poem, relating them to the dynamics of the sacred and profane that express the poet's inherently optimistic vision of divine order splendidly manifest in the Creator's aesthetic designs for his creatures. I argue that its sexual ethic is inextricably linked to its courtly model of the good life as the beautiful life in ways that are both beneficial and disastrous.

Cleanness includes one of the most powerful accounts of the joys of love in all of English poetry. The poet imagines that God intends a man and a woman to come together in a still, stolen moment; love's flame burns between them so intensely that it is virtually unslakable. This celebration of gratified sexual desire is ostensibly quoted verbatim from the Creator, and so it represents a religious endorsement of loveplay that is nothing short of astonishing for the medieval period or, for that matter, for any Christian poetry before the middle of our own century. If the unqualified divine approval of sexual passion as the sweetest of human sharings in the Creator's bounty were the only unique feature of this poem, it would be remarkable in its divergence from the received wisdom of Western ethical tradition that such pleasure is at best justifiable as a fitting means to ensure the activities required to perpetuate the species.

What is problematic, however, is that this frankly erotic discourse also justifies the homophobic wrath soon to be manifest in the fiery destruction of Sodom as it was previously evident in the waters of the Deluge. God utters his pleasure-affirming praise of passionate lovemaking just at the point in the poem where he is about to vent for the second time his unmitigated fury against men who indulge in what he calls "filth of the flesh." The Creator describes the game and play of love between men and women as his own invention—one that he prizes peculiarly and, indeed, so highly that his fury against the Sodomite males who take each other as sexual partners is rationalized as appropriately totalitarian in intensity and scope. His wrath against the Sodomites overflows in a catastrophic act of vengeance that destroys not only the offending sinners but entire populations, leaving the region forever defiled as a testimony to divine judgment evoked by unnatural deeds. Thus *Cleanness* dramatizes the seriousness of sexual deviance by depicting God's homophobic wrath, naturalizing that revulsion as an artist's rage for order. Any predilection for same-sex lovemaking strikes the poet as an intolerable slur on divine craftsmanship because heterosexual union is a part of the natural order which the Creator values uniquely for the paradisal pleasure it bestows.

Cleanness's legitimation of heterosexual desire is linked to, and to a degree depends logically upon, a rhetoric of intolerance against men who take each other for lovers. The poet vilifies them as boors who scorn the simultaneously ethical and aesthetic standard of nature's heterosexual norm. Such a rhetoric was already familiar to late medieval readers; *Cleanness* astonishes not by its harsh denunciation of same-sex love, but by its divergence from the procreative and patriarchal logic of compulsory heterosexuality as natural order. To conform sexually to the natural order and hence God's design in creation was to govern sexual relations by the aim of reproducing one's kind, while to indulge in sexual practices that could not result in procreation was to sin against nature. The conventional indictment of such unnatural alliances between men was that they perverted the symbolic gender hierarchy of male governing female which heterosexual union "naturally" established, giving themselves over to the sterile and death-dealing lust that was associated with Eve's original sin. Traces of this conventional interpretation may be found at points in *Cleanness,* where the symbolism of death and sterility alludes to what the medieval church taught was evil about sodomy—its disregard for both the literal fruits of intercourse in a legitimate family lineage and, allegorically, the spiritual fecundity of a virtuous life.[1] But the poet's attack on homosexual conduct, I shall argue, is not framed in these traditional terms. It is not the succession of the human species or the androcentric system of superior male acting upon inferior and submissive female which the poet celebrates as God's design revealed in the natural order. Rather, filth of the flesh practiced by males who couple with each other is defined as evil by their perverse refusal of the perfect delight bestowed by God himself in the loveplay of a heterosexual pair. This artful erotic activity epitomizes to the Creator his good craftsmanship and his bond to his creatures in the natural order.

By its preoccupation with the oppositional meanings of same-sex versus heterosexual pleasure, *Cleanness* illuminates the construction of social identities based on a dichotomizing classification of sexual desire in terms of preferring genital activity with partners of the same or opposite sex. The poem's logic, and its linkage of homophobic wrath and paradisal heterosexual pleasure, anticipate the dynamic interaction that modern feminist theory and queer theory trace between compulsory heterosexuality and the continuation of oppressive features of male-dominant culture. While differentiating the poem's analysis of the role of sex in culture from other models in the Middle

Ages and as well from modern models, I see in *Cleanness* a discourse of desire that illuminates the way contemporary Western consciousness continues to dichotomize sexual differences. Same-sex eroticism is still condemned as a perverse seeking for something better than the natural goodness of heterosexual pleasure, just as God in *Cleanness* denounces the inventiveness of the Sodomite men as a slur on his artistry. Gay and lesbian lovers are still condemned for contriving an artificial and elitist alternative to the more aesthetically fitting, because self-evidently natural, pursuits of the heterosexual majority. The poet shows the men of Sodom insisting upon initiating the visitors in their midst into their distinctive way of lovemaking, a regional custom that they denounce Lot for not appreciating. He does not share their taste because, they claim, he came to Sodom and prospered but remained an outsider, holding himself apart from their mores. This vignette suggests the poet conceived of the possibility of male same-sex coupling as a socially constructed preference, resulting in a recognizable and proudly displayed group identity which he denigrates as a boorish departure from the homosocial and heterosexual ideals defining courtly masculinity.

The connection between paradisal pleasure and homophobic wrath in *Cleanness* invites theoretical exploration that only recently has appeared in published commentary on the poem. While it may be that "most commentaries on *Cleanness* acknowledge the poet's use of sodomy" (Frantzen, "Disclosure" 462), not until the last decade have critics begun to map how sodomy in a literal sense (a term which is notoriously ambiguous in medieval moral writers and does not even appear in *Cleanness*) might apply to and help clarify the poet's often puzzling representations of what he calls the "filth of the flesh" that brought on God's uniquely harsh vengeance in the Flood and the destruction of Sodom. Literary critics ignored or downplayed the significance of the poem's sexual categories until 1988 when A. V. C. Schmidt and Michael W. Twomey each published detailed arguments focusing unprecedented attention on the meaning of filth of the flesh, which they explicated as homosexual relations between men. While these essays demonstrate conclusively how in both the stories of the Flood and of the destruction of Sodom and other cities on the plain God's wrath is evoked by this specific and literal deviance from the heterosexual norm of nature, neither critic probes the striking unconventionality of the poem's account of normative heterosexuality and its opposite.

Three recent critical analyses have initiated a scholarly discussion of *Cleanness*'s novel construction of homosexual pursuits in binary opposition to heterosexual loveplay.[2] Michael A. Calabrese's and Eric Eliason's "The Rhetorics of Sexual Pleasure and Intolerance in the Middle English *Cleanness*" provides an excellent introduction to the poem's surprising sexual claims, as well as a provocative account of the difficulties its celebration of the attractions of heterosexual intercourse should present for modern readers who recognize the connection between the rhetoric of praise and the rhetoric of revulsion. Calabrese and Eliason argue that instead of a rational appeal to nature's procreative purpose, *Cleanness* employs an affective rhetoric and evokes "feelings of physical revulsion to vilify" homosexual practices, and they assume their audience should and generally will feel antipathy to such a gratuitous vilification of same-sex lovemaking. They also note that many modern readers will like God's speech on heterosexual lovemaking, sympathizing with the absence of reference to procreative intentions and the presence of erotic imagery evoking joys usually condemned by moralizing works on sexual norms. They caution that an "innocent" sympathetic response to this hyperbolic praise of the bliss of making love in accord with God's design implicates readers in the poem's idealization of "otherwise questionable and ambiguous sexual behavior" (270). The absence of traditional negative imagery of defilement from this lyrical description of heterosexual lovemaking they interpret as part of a morally questionable "process of sanitization" (272) aimed at removing any taint from heterosexual pleasure in order to reinforce the association the poem makes with revolting filth and unnatural sexual activities. They warn that to praise the sanitized version of the good of heterosexual activity is to be complicit with the deplorable violence the poem depicts against the Sodomites whom it portrays as marauding homosexual purveyors of unspeakable filth. For Calabrese and Eliason, the poet's unusual religious legitimation of heterosexual joy apart from the usual requirements for procreative intentions in marital relations should not be seen as an intentional and programmatic revision of the church's repressive sexual theory; rather it is an accidental offshoot of the logically prior choice to construct sodomy in terms that stress its repulsive filthiness rather than its irrational sterility. The poet's unconventional approach to the evil of sodomy necessitates his emphasis on the unalloyed pleasures of heterosexuality, a rhetorical strategy which in turn issues in the amplification of Lot's offer of his daughters to rapists in which he stresses their appealing traits as bait offered to change the Sodomites' sexual preferences (273).[3] Calabrese and Eliason thus read *Cleanness* as primarily an unconventional attack on sodomy carried out by balancing the rhetoric of blame (a hyperbolic visceral condemnation based on sheer revulsion) with the rhetoric of praise (an equally hyperbolic visceral account of the attractions of heterosexual pleasure).

Central to the rhetoric of revulsion is the depiction of the revolting behavior of the Sodomites in the coarsest possible terms; as Calabrese and Eliason observe, "the language the poet uses to describe the dirtiness of the Sodomites pushes even the rich vocabulary of the alliterative revival to the limit" (264). In "Disclosure of Sodomy in *Cleanness*," Allen J. Frantzen focuses on the risks involved in this linguistic virtuosity; he senses "a certain glee on the part of the poet" (457) who, as he takes sides in the confrontation between the Sodomites and Lot, allows the villains to speak on their own behalf, which they do not in the biblical narrative, and discloses the precise nature of their sexual customs, left unspecified by scripture. Punning with excremental imagery and anatomical terms that in effect display the anus as the "chief sexual orifice of the Sodomites" (457–58), the poet narrows the definition of sodomy to homosexual male anal intercourse. By so graphic a representation of the evil which his warning against the sins of Sodom aims to suppress, *Cleanness* reproduces the risks priests took when they attempted to regulate the sexual lives of their parishioners. In preparing the sinner to confess and perform appropriate forms of penance for their misdeeds, the priest, on the one hand, had to say enough about the various forms of unnatural lust to "clarify acts that were obscured by conflation under the category of sodomy" (455); on the other hand, the clergy were warned against naming too concretely the illicit forms of intercourse lest such specificity prove alluring. Descriptions of forbidden activities could tempt their listeners to sins they would otherwise not feel drawn to commit or might not even otherwise know about. "By the time *Cleanness* was written and read, confession was a site of contradictory demands and impulses. The Church required priests to clarify acts that were obscured by conflation under the category of sodomy but also allowed priests to assume that penitents were familiar with 'generalities that everyone knows are sins'" (455). Frantzen argues that the *Cleanness*-poet shows none of the circumspection expected of late medieval clergy who were required to ferret out and suppress the unnameable sin — or sins — of sodomy, but the "poet's description of the forbidden acts of Sodom reproduces the moment of polyvalent risk of the confessor's inquiry" (455). While *Cleanness* denounces homosexual anal intercourse "in the most severe terms," the poet manages "at the same time to communicate almost salaciously the stimulus that draws men to one another" (457). Frantzen argues that it is in response to this verbal tour de force of boldly sexual innuendo with its risk of tempting the reader to homosexual wrongdoing that the poet denounces the sights, sounds, and smells of sodomy in such violently destructive images of Sodom's end. The city is reduced symbolically to the black hole of the hellishly excremental discharge of the Dead Sea, a stinking privy that resembles an anus (460–61).[4]

While the poet thus describes and damns anal intercourse in the most repelling terms, he also praises the delicate attractiveness, from a homosexual viewpoint, of angels who are so fair that they might be mistaken for women; these charming youths are meant by the poet to be thought about "bodily, sexually, as the Sodomites perceive them" — not as sexless heavenly androgynes, but "as men" (457). Even the clergy who should be risking closer surveillance of sodomy might be tempted as the admiring description draws the eyes "from the surface of the angels' clothes to the pretty flesh beneath" (457). Having risked making sodomy alluring, the poet must take a further risk in juxtaposing to the dangers of homosexual deviancy the safe and secure pleasures of the manner of intercourse God favors. Like Calabrese and Eliason, Frantzen argues that the poet's choices in defining and describing sodomy necessitate God's unusually "beautiful extended apology" (456–57); focusing as he does on the rhetorical virtuosity of the poet's disclosure of sodomy, Frantzen provides less detailed analysis than do Calabrese and Eliason of the surprising language God uses to legitimate the pleasures of heterosexual intercourse in terms of courtly loveplay.

The contrast between the licit and illicit forms of intercourse focuses for Frantzen on the poet's juxtaposition of the disclosure of sodomy, bringing the forbidden act of anal intercourse into full view, and his praise of heterosexual intercourse that takes place in privacy and darkness, safe from surveillance. God's explanation that he teaches heterosexual practices "derne" (secretly 697) strikes Frantzen as crucial to understanding the poem's endorsement of this form of sexual pleasure; although taking a risk in his praise of heterosexual intercourse, the poet does not provide detailed specification of what is permissible and what is forbidden in the manner of intercourse he commends. Literally, he keeps the acceptable act of heterosexual conjoining (presumably vaginal intercourse) "in the dark." So while readers are not only urged to exercise vigilance in watching out for unorthodox sexual practices among men who are drawn to each other bodily, but also invited to contemplate this form of unnatural lust by a risky rhetorical strategy of puns and other imagery that puts the "forbidden act in full view," no warning is issued against illicit forms of heterosexual intercourse (including anal intercourse between a man and a woman and other "unnatural acts" which, because they thwarted conception, were often also categorized as sodomy). The issue of whether God's speech, by omitting reference to the procreative possibility that defined "natural" heterosexual intercourse, subverts the orthodox sexual ethic is not addressed. From Frantzen's commentary on the imagery of darkness and from his emphasis on fertility as the antithesis to sodomy, I infer that he sees the poem's praise of heterosexual satisfactions in both God's and Lot's speech as congruent with the church's insistence on the reproductive aim as the sole redeeming motive which makes otherwise sinful pleasures acceptable in marital relations.

The *Cleanness*-poet's idealizing vision of heterosexual pleasure unaccompanied by the usual arguments for the good of procreation expresses, I shall argue, a more complex theological and ethical enterprise than what Calabrese and Eliason suggest is fundamentally a repressive demonstration of God's sexual squeamishness, or than what Frantzen suggests is a call for closer clerical surveillance of male homosexual anal intercourse. While the poem clearly urges vigilance against the slightest inclination toward homosexual practices, I think that the poet's concern to warn against such conduct is a response, at least in part, to the threat that the stigma attached to same-sex love posed to an ethic that merges virtue with pleasure and nature with artifice. The poem's vilification of homosexual practices strike me, as it strikes Calabrese and Eliason, as peculiarly nonrational because it omits the usual arguments about emasculation and failure to procreate, but my account of the poet's logic will at more than one point reverse theirs. Calabrese and Eliason interpret the symmetry between what they term *twin rhetorics* as caused by the poet's decisions about the rhetoric of blame which enable—or rather force—his decisions about the rhetoric of praise: since he "predicates his condemnation on disgust, he must predicate his praise on pleasure" (270). I also see the two rhetorics as intimately linked, but instead of subordinating the praise of gratuitous pleasure to the poet's primary commitment to a rhetoric of revulsion, I shall argue that representing homosexual deviance as perfectly loathsome provides a foil against which the poet can legitimate the way of life that he sanctifies as the manifestation of God's *clannesse* and his *clene* relations to the world. The rhetoric of revulsion I theorize as the rhetorical concomitant of the affirmation of pleasure as a foundational principle of the courtly Christian life. In the poet's aesthetic ethos, what is self-evidently desirable because pleasing to a cultivated sensibility is given priority over the usual utilitarian rationales for determining what is good and bad form in sexual matters. I think the poet depicts homosexual practices as the revolting invention of predatory brutes in order to maintain a reassuring boundary between licit and illicit and to remove from the courtly ideal of erotic artifice any taint of the stigma of effeminacy that usually was associated with heterosexual intercourse indulged in with no intention of procreation, but only for mutual delight.[5]

My book focuses on the poem's innovative redefinition of the normative eroticism which it depicts both as natural and as the product of aesthetic refinement; central to the life of all-encompassing virtue the poet praises as "clene layk" (proper play, noble practices) is the romantic masculinist ideal of a well-bred and properly nurtured courtier who is connoisseur and practitioner of the festive decorum which makes the good life imitate art. Carolyn Dinshaw's brief but incisive account of the poem's gender symbolics sketched from the perspective of modern theories of the interplay between matrices of gender and sexual desire, confirms my approach to mapping the interdependence of the sexual, the sacred, and the courtly in *Cleanness*. My reading of God's speech on the play of paramours agrees with Dinshaw's observation that it institutes courtly loveplay as the original, paradisal mode of heterosexual intercourse, thus naturalizing the art of love executed by the rules of secular aristocratic society which lack the boundaries of procreative intent crucial to the church's definition of normative heterosexuality. By representing the Sodomites' preferences as a strange practice for noblemen, a bad joke for any gentleman to play (861–64), *Cleanness* dispels, as Dinshaw implies, any suggestion of the "incommensurability of straightness and courtliness" showing instead that "Christian courtliness is in part constituted by the discourse of normative sexuality" ("A Kiss" 218, 220).[6] This potential incommensurability I view as the artifice of both courtliness and homosexual pursuits in conflict with the assumed naturalness of straightness, and I argue that it is partly to erase any stigma of impropriety from aristocratic refinements of sexual appetite that the poet depicts the Sodomites as revolting and uncivil in contrast to the courtly demeanor of Abraham and God, of Lot and the angels. The latter are all represented as friends whose homosocial bonds are graced by the erotic ethos of courtly romance; so far from threatening their masculine straightness, courtliness in this mode functions to contain and disinfect potentially disruptive homosexual yearnings.

One of the most fascinating resources *Cleanness* offers for the study of sex and gender is a series of exemplary male characters who are portrayed with particular attention to the kind of aesthetic sensitivity criticized by many clerical moralists in the High Middle Ages for its diminishment of the virtues prized in earlier monuments of masculinity. We may speculate that these tensions in the paradigm of male excellence are thrown into relief in the work of this poet precisely because of elements in the dynamic of the so-called Alliterative Revival, whose aesthetic was self-consciously concerned with relating the aristocratic romance ethos of the late Middle Ages to the heritage of Anglo-Saxon heroism. The conflict between the definition of male excellence as the warrior or as the courtier was in its advanced stage by the time *Cleanness* was written. The poet's celebration and interrogation of the ideals and sensibility of chivalric lordship and service dramatize the tensions in the masculine ideal in a culture that was still attempting to reconcile the mythologies of epic and romance.

In romance, the standard of social decorum governing external refinements of conduct and appearance is at once an ethic and an aesthetic. That courtly ethos is supremely represented, and interrogated, in *Sir Gawain;* what neither it nor any other romance provides that *Cleanness* does, however, is an explicit presentation of how aesthetic consciousness of the ethical order is theologically grounded in an image of God as artist, scrupulously concerned about the splendor of his creation and generously disposed to men and women who are his discerning collaborators. God's speech on the joys of making love shows the poet's theological concern to give positive religious significance to the erotic and the courtly. *Cleanness* celebrates human desire for relationships of intimacy and reciprocity between Creator and creature in the context of shared aesthetic values and appeals to its readers' urge to embody divine beauty and goodness.

In chapter 1 I introduce the poem from this theopoetic perspective, beginning with the poet's courtly definition of his theme by his creative fictionalization of God as courtly host. After the retelling of the parable of the wedding feast which introduces the poem's distinctive ethos of festive decorum, the poem's symbolic focus shifts to the sexual paradigms of desire and deviance that are central to defining God's generous but aesthetically scrupulous bond to his creation.

In chapter 2 I deal with the explication of "filth of the flesh," the circumlocution that I argue the poet uses to refer circumspectly to homosexual practices that brought on the Flood and the destruction of Sodom and the other cities of the plain. What is unconventional about the poet's claims for God's unique wrath against this particular form of sexual defilement is counterpointed against what is equally surprising about the poet's legitimation of passion between the sexes in God's speech on the play of paramours, which is analyzed in the context of the church's teaching about marital relations and homosexual deviations.

Whereas in chapter 2 I explore the poem's sexual themes against the backdrop of moralizing discourse of sermons and treatises for confessors, in chapters 3 through 5 I situate the poem in the more intellectually complex milieu of late medieval thought about nature as a sexual norm, drawing on three foundational texts from the late twelfth through the late thirteenth century. These precursor texts were widely enough read and easily enough available in late fourteenth-century English libraries for a poet with clerical education to be familiar with them. The resemblances and differences I trace between each of them and *Cleanness* are not, however, put forth as evidence in an argument about the poem's influences. This book is not a source study but a comparative reading; I draw attention to Alain de Lille, Jean de Meun, and Thomas Aquinas not to assert their various degrees of influence on the *Cleanness*-poet, but to provide a context that delineates a range of attitudes toward the dignity of pleasure within late medieval discourse of deviance and desire within the context of natural ethics.

Nature does not appear as a character in *Cleanness*, but the sway of natural law over the sexual lives of humankind and the animals is as evident there as it is in the medieval allegorical tradition which personifies nature as a benevolent but often outraged female authority. She first appears in this role in Alain de Lille's *De Planctu Naturae*, titled by translators either *Nature's Complaint* or *The Plaint of Nature*. This influential satire is discussed in detail in chapter 3 as one of *Cleanness*'s most important literary precursors. The *Complaint*'s repeated castigations of males making love with each other illuminate by both contrast and comparison *Cleanness*'s attacks on filth of the flesh. Despite the obvious generic differences between Alain's Latin allegorical vision and the poet's vernacular scriptural paraphrase, the two storytellers are narrative theologians; their comparably artistic reworkings of tradition articulate similarly homophobic visions of same-sex love as an archetypal deformation of cosmic order. Like Alain, the *Cleanness*-poet constructs an imaginative variation on traditional depictions of the centrality of sexual desire and deviance in the story of humankind's original goodness and eventual fallenness.

Alain's portrait of Nature, produced at the end of the twelfth century, provides Jean de Meun, writing about a hundred years later, with the basis for a character with the same name cast in a similar role but displaying radically diminished authority and a drastically different ethical norm in his portion of the *Romance of the Rose*. This extraordinarily popular allegory is the only text other than scripture explicitly cited in *Cleanness*. Jean's *Roman*, as I shall refer to it, satirizes the first portion of the courtly dream vision it builds upon and is as notoriously slippery in tone as Alain's Menippean masterpiece. We shall see in chapter 5 that Jean's liberalizing redefinition of Nature's norms differ dramatically from Alain's repressive ideals of marital coition for the sake of progeny, and we shall also see that these revisions are not to be taken without regard for the *Roman*'s multiple levels of irony. Still, I shall argue that Jean's assessment of pleasure as a salient ingredient in the naturally well-ordered sex act is more optimistic about the harmony between reason and appetite than is Alain's austere ethic of marriage.

A generosity toward the sensual appetites is even more striking in Thomas Aquinas, the theologian whose work on temperance is explicated in chapters 1 and 4 as a crucial component in the ideological genealogy of *Cleanness*. Writing in the latter half of the thirteenth century and contemporary with Jean's *Roman*, Thomas affirms sensual pleasure as part of the gratification of natural appetites which provides the bodily basis of human rationality. The virtue of temperance in the *Summa Theologiae* provides the occasion for Thomas's detailed consideration of sexual desire and deviance, as well as of many other aspects of the life of the senses. In praising the beauty of this virtue, he articulates his Aristotelian vision of the good life as the beautiful life with a generosity toward pleasure that is strikingly suggestive of the merging of aesthetic and ethical values in the *Cleanness*-poet's celebration of aristocratic ideals of decorum.

What makes these three texts particularly illuminating as a backdrop to *Cleanness* is the different definitions of nature's ordinances in each of them and the changing picture of pleasure that emerges when we read them sequentially. The dignity and value of heterosexual desire increases from Alain, writing at the end of the twelfth century, through Thomas and Jean in the third quarter of the thirteenth century, to the *Cleanness*-poet toward the end of the fourteenth. Against this backdrop, it becomes more obvious how the procreative aim of intercourse is downplayed in *Cleanness,* and how God's praise of love subverts the conventional patriarchal emphasis on male activism in a male-dominant marital union by making the intensity of the couple's mutual delight in and with each other peculiarly valuable to the Creator's design.

In chapter 6 I shall interrogate *Cleanness*'s investment in aristocratic culture's idealization of a feminized male and focus on issues of class and gender in medieval romance as these illuminate the poem's striking depictions of homosocial graciousness between men and of a similar bond of good taste between God and humanity. I argue that the poet's privileging of masculine homosocial pleasures contributes to his troubling elaboration of an already troubling biblical episode—Lot's offer of his daughters to the Sodomites in the hope of deflecting their sexual demands on his attractive male guests.

In chapter 7 I extend the exploration of overlapping matrices of gender and desire in *Cleanness* to a theological analysis of the poem's configuration of the sacred and the profane shaped by the paradigm of courtly masculinity. In a poem that presents God as the creative source of romantic ideals of courtesy and love and the homosocially companionable though fastidious patron of the arts of aristocratic living, it is not surprising to find Christ presented as the epitome of the genteel and loving courtier. There are, however, puzzling features in the poet's depiction of Christ as analogous to the beloved Rose in Jean's *Roman,* and an analysis of gender symbolics in this passage is needed to clarify why the poet omitted the Crucifixion from his account of incarnate cleanness. In this elision of the suffering required in the Creator's love affair with the creation, and as well in the depiction of penance as providing instantaneous and permanent conformity of human nature to Christ's pearl-like perfection, *Cleanness* minimizes to a remarkable—and theologically problematic—degree the costliness of the tension between God's sovereignty and his vulnerability enacted in the Incarnation and between divine order and finite subjectivity.

In chapter 8 I look at these theopoetic limitations with specific regard to the history of the vessels, focusing on the images that relate this final story to the sexual themes in the previous two Old Testament narratives while also analyzing the conflicting messages the poem delivers about the possibility of the Creator's order harmonizing with history's fateful dynamic. I will raise questions about the overall coherence of the poem's complex range of structuring ideas in concluding the exploration of *Cleanness*, assessing its cumulative impact in the context of what I argue is the more theologically complex and religiously satisfying artistry of *Patience, Sir Gawain,* and *Pearl*. While most of the issues in the debate over common authorship of these manuscript companions lie outside the scope of this study, I view the place of the courtly ethos in the theopoetic visions of the four poems as one of the most interesting pieces of evidence to be considered in examining the possibility that all are the product of one person.

Methodologically, a number of difficulties accompany this study. "Homosexuality" as such, in its various modern constructions, is not the subject of this study; yet *homosexual* is a term I will use throughout. I do not apply this adjective to people in groups or individually but use it to designate the sexual interaction between men that the poet condemns. Used in this way, *homosexual* seems a necessary term, despite its obvious anachronism and unclarity, for it generally functions in modern parlance to designate genital relations engaged in by partners of the same sex. So long as we are mindful of the wide range of meanings attached to that sexual sameness by the agents and their cultural contemporaries, *homosexual* is not a misleading adjective to apply to medieval same-sex desire and activities. No such term exists in Middle English or Latin to designate specifically the coupling of men with men and women with women, or their expressed desire for this activity. *Sodomy* often appears in medieval moral discourse as a term for the "unnatural" sins of lust, but it lacks specificity. Often it refers to such offenses in the aggregate and sometimes, by metaphorical extension, to nonsexual vices such as idolatry and heresy. Interestingly, the *Cleanness*-poet never uses "sodomy" or its related adjective; what he exemplifies by depicting the Sodomite men's proclaimed preference for making love with males is in fact far less precisely indicated for modern readers by "sodomitic vice" than by the admittedly anachronistic designation we are using instead, "homosexual relations."[7]

Equally problematic is the adjective *heterosexual* which I must use to designate sexual relations between a man and woman since there is no adjective in Middle English to restrict the denotation of lovemaking in terms of the partners' gender difference. The more recent and hence more obviously anachronistic term *heterosexism* or, as Adrienne Rich has put it, *compulsory heterosexuality,* I use in order to signal my dissent from discourse that speaks of heterosexual relations as normative in implied or explicit superiority to same-sex relations. The pejorative term names as oppressive dichotomies of desire as either natural or unnatural, normal or abnormal, licit or forbidden, when these distinctions are based on whether the relationship manifests sexual difference or sameness.[8]

Homophobia is a recent concept, often associated with Freud's notion of homosexual urges (universally present, but repressed or ambivalently expressed in the majority) as the starting point of prejudice, paranoia, and hatred some heterosexually inclined men show toward men who engage in genital relations with their own sex. Although *homophobic* may be used in a misleadingly narrow way to imply that individual psychosexual pathology must be the only explanation of why some people experience an extraordinary degree of fear and loathing of the Others who express openly homosexual desire, the word is used to theorize from other starting points about cultural processes that negate homosexual conduct and reinforce exclusively heterosexual social norms (Dynes, *Encyclopedia* I 552–54). The word itself appeared in dictionaries only in the last decade but has already achieved widespread currency, in part to describe the backlash against homosexuality associated with but not limited to AIDS. In the absence of any more suitable term, I use *homophobic* to designate a peculiarly intense hostility to same-sex love and what it represents; this intensity is evident when hatred and abject horror combine with fear of the Other and comes to literary expression in the rankling attacks of the "nature as sexual norm" tradition, where such authors as Peter Damian, Alain de Lille, and the *Cleanness*-poet (as well as their modern successors) vilify what they consider to be the uniquely defiling corruption of men making love with men.

For the general reader and for many academically specialized readers as well, translation is required for the four medieval texts this book explores in detail. *Cleanness* itself poses the most difficult linguistic problem. Even in its title, the poem is problematic, for in Middle English *clannesse* is a term that defies translation and is usually associated with the modern English terms *cleanness, cleanliness,* and *purity,* all of which have highly misleading connotations. Many of the key terms present similar difficulties, leading some translators and editors to substitute abstract terms for the concrete diction of the original, thus obscuring the metaphorical mode of the poet's ambitious cognitive inquiry. I have quoted in both modern and Middle English, therefore, and have given detailed glossings for terms crucial to the thematic inquiry.[9] The poet's freedom with syntax as well as vocabulary poses a challenge for a translation that aims simply to provide as literal a word-for-word "trot" as possible. He often changes verb tense, number, and mood within the sentence, and pronouns do not always agree in number with their subject; anacoluthons abound, as do abrupt moves in and out of direct speech. When dubious about which mistake to make in choosing between unsatisfactory modern English rough equivalents, I have consulted the poem's various editors and translators. I have drawn gratefully upon David R. Teague's unpublished translation, and I am most particularly indebted to Marie Borroff and Elizabeth D. Kirk who generously vetted translations in this book which they both read in its various stages. Quotations from the Middle English *Cleanness* and its manuscript companions are (with a few exceptions as indicated) from Malcolm Andrew's and Ronald Waldron's one-volume edition of the four poems in what they refer to as the "*Pearl*-manuscript."

For Thomas Aquinas, translations are quoted from the Blackfriars facing-page edition, for Alain's *Complaint* from James Sheridan, and for Jean's *Roman* from Charles Dahlberg. (The Blackfriars' Latin text for quotations from Thomas, Nikolaus M. Häring's Latin text for those from Alain, and Felix Lecoy's French text for those from Jean have been deleted from the endnotes in order to minimize the book's size and hence price.)

In the interests of reaching both a scholarly and a general audience, some points will be explicated in a more leisurely fashion than would be expected in a work addressed to one or the other. The notes have been kept to a minimum with no attempt to provide general bibliography for the various subjects and no attempt to recapitulate the surveys I have made of primary sources and scholarship as I have situated my claims in the pertinent scholarly conversations. I cite only those sources where my debt or disagreement is quite specific.

This book focuses primarily on the portions of *Cleanness* pertaining to its representations of sexual desire and deviance, gender symbolics, and the romantic idealism of its theopoetic strategy. Many other facets of this poem fascinate me, but as Lee Patterson has written: "Our daily lives are the only lives we have: there is no escaping from the historically specific and it is in terms of this specificity that we must decide what work to do and how to do it. Our scholarly activity, in other words, can never be guided by some impossible norm of correctness but only by the relation we want to establish to the social and political formation governing our own historical moment" ("Negotiating" 71). Writing about *Cleanness* has critical commentary on sexual themes in literature perpetuating the assumption that everyone is, or should become, or should wish they could become, naturally attracted to erotically charged intimacy with a person, or persons, of the other sex. The relation this book has helped me establish to the social and political formation of the historical moment in which I am writing is one of participating in a movement to liberate our own and future generations from that heterosexist bias. One piece of this emancipating work is rewriting the history of the desiring self with close attention to the dynamics by which heterosexual pleasure comes to be seen as exclusively and supremely good.

Mine is not a study premised on the belief that the poet's ideas in this strange work deserve to be influential. Quite the contrary: I will assert that the ethical difficulties and theological inadequacies he creates in articulating his unique views are revealing of blind spots in his thought and in medieval thought generally — as well as in ours. Reading the poem's appealing representation of the transcendental origin of romantic passion, one needs to temper a hermeneutic of desire with one of suspicion. Thus interpreted, the poem offers a welcome antidote to medieval religious culture's distrust of heterosexual pleasure; God's celebration of passion does not have to be read innocently in order to admire the daring theopoetic originality in the poet's assertion that erotically charged sexual relations between a man and a woman can be simultaneously natural, divine, artificed, and give supreme sensual and psychic mutual pleasure. Read critically, *Cleanness* also provides a modern audience an opportunity to resist the poet's heterosexual bias and his assumption that sexual passion intensely felt and mutually gratified must be the most paradisal experience on earth. As we reinvent the meaning of sexuality to cure modern culture's heterosexism and homophobia, we have to confront as well how consumerism constructs our erotic experience. We may be thus enabled to look critically not only at modern secular culture's continuing idealization of the heterosexual couple, but also at the notion of erotic fulfillment through sexual pleasure as the greatest joy.

To reconceive the value of sexual pleasure and its relation to the power of the erotic is a large order, pointing us toward a simultaneous reinvention of divinity and nature. As the *Cleanness*-poet did this in his fictional reworking of scripture, so I believe a critical and creative engagement with this poem and the other revisionary narratives of the Cotton Nero A.x, Art. 3 manuscript can and should foster our imaginative work of theopoesis. It will also, as my title suggests, illuminate the interactive dynamic between the evolution of the courtly ethos and the increasing homophobia of the hight and late Middle Ages.

I

The Narrative Theology of Cleanness *and the Aesthetic Ethics of Thomas Aquinas*

Cleanness's *Celebrative Ethic*

Cleanness presents the reader from the outset with two striking characteristics, each of which seems inherently contradictory. First there is its genre. It is most commonly considered a homily or a biblical paraphrase, yet nothing in either of these medieval traditions accounts for the poem's structure, for its kind and degree of narrative elaboration or for its close affinities with courtly romance. Second, the poem presents itself as a diatribe against the *fylþe* (filth) that is abhorrent to God, yet it is elaborately decorative and celebrates not the rigors of asceticism and self-denial but the earthly forms of graciousness, the amenities of life lived in accord with festive decorum. The major part of *Cleanness* is narrative, consisting of four main biblical exempla and a number of shorter vignettes, which recount superlative examples of God's anger; yet all of these events present themselves to the poet's imagination as *fayre formez,* so that his ostensibly negative didactic strategy is marked from the beginning as affirmative:

> Clannesse whoso kyndly cowþe comende,
> And rekken vp alle þe resounz þat ho by riȝt askez,
> Fayre formez myȝt he fynde in forþering his speche,
> And in þe contraré kark and combraunce huge. (1–4)[1]

17

18   Narrative Theology of Cleanness

> (Whoever could praise "Cleanness" in accord with her nature
> And reckon up all the considerations that are hers by right,
> Fair forms he might find to further his speech,
> And in attempting the contrary, enormous trouble and toil.)

Beauty simply works with the grain of the universe, and *fylþe* goes against it; it is as fitting to write a poem in support of cleanness as it is virtually impossible to write one against it. To reduce the poem to a warning against sin, supported by cautionary stories of the suffering of sinners in the hands of an angry God, is to miss the essentially celebrative impulse pervading *Cleanness* from its beginning to its close. In short, both in its genre and in its subject, the poem fuses two realms usually considered self-evidently antithetical — the aesthetic and the ethical — and presents them as being equally and inextricably linked with the splendor of the divine order.

A summary of *Cleanness* is required because this study is intended for both a specialized and a general audience, and even readers conversant with Middle English literature may not be familiar with the poem. After *clannesse* is introduced as a pleasing subject — personified as feminine — and an attribute of God himself, required in priests and all who serve him, Christ's authority is cited, promising (in a paraphrase of the sixth Beatitude, Matthew 5: 8) that the clean of heart will look upon God with a glad face (27–28). Typically, the poet then turns to God's inversely proportionate horror of all that is unclean, illustrated by analogy to the outrage a lord enjoying his seat of honor at a feast would feel if someone should approach him in disreputable attire (29–50). The same situation is then illustrated in the New Testament parable of the wedding feast where a guest is thrown out because he comes improperly dressed (51–160). The festive array required for the heavenly banquet is interpreted as the virtuous life required of the Christian who would maintain the *clannesse* bestowed sacramentally in baptism (161–77). A catalog of twenty-four vices that can hinder one's vision of God (177–92) provides the backdrop for the one sin he despises more than all others and punishes in unmerciful anger: *fylþe of þe flesch* (filth of the flesh) (193–204). The immoderate wrath this vice causes is contrasted to the judgments upon Lucifer and Adam and Eve (205–48), both made without anger and the second one displaying divine mercy.

Two biblical stories of genocidal vengeance follow, with a stress on how angry God has to be to act with such merciless malice; first the poet paraphrases the story of the Flood (249–544), and then, after a passage that unequivocally links the Deluge to the same evil that brought on the destruction of the cities of the plain, he tells the story of Sodom (601–1048). By the conclusion of these two Old Testament exempla, it is clear that the term *fylþe of þe flesch* refers to sexual relations between men.

The theme shifts away from God's homophobic rage back to the initial theme of his passion for *clannesse*, illustrated by three brief vignettes depicting Christ's life on earth as the example for all to follow who wish to see his face (1049–1148). To gain such integrity, the Christian must be like a pearl, restoring natural brilliance to the sullied soul by cleansing it sacramentally through penance.

This leads to one more story of God's vengeance, another Old Testament historical narrative. This one, however, is interpreted at the outset allegorically as an example of how angry God becomes if a soul consecrated to him by penance should again be defiled by sin. The final exemplum, nearly as long as the previous two combined, focuses upon the vessels made by Solomon for the temple, beginning with their capture when Jerusalem is destroyed because of Zedekiah's idolatry, leading to their safekeeping by Nebuchadnezzar, and concluding with their defilement by his idolatrous son, Belshazzar (1149–1804). The poem ends with a summary of how in three ways (presumably the three Old Testament exempla) God's love for cleanness and his hatred for its opposite have been demonstrated (1805–12), thus echoing the opening lines. The narrator offers a closing prayer, asking for grace to go "gay in oure gere" (elegantly arrayed and honorably outfitted 1811) to enjoy the unending solace of life in God's presence.

In spite of its obvious resemblances to a sermon rather than to a romance, *Cleanness*, like *Sir Gawain and the Green Knight*, mirrors the amenities of an aristocratic life typical of the households scholars associate with the Alliterative Revival.[2] Nothing yet permits us to locate the poet's social milieu precisely enough to settle the questions of patronage and affiliation, but there is no doubt that the refined aesthetic sensibility the poet represents in *Cleanness* would have been familiar to many contemporaries who would have appreciated his religious legitimation of the secular ethic of courtliness. To term the poem a homily in verse is somewhat misleading, since the narrative element far exceeds the exemplary materials provided by a sermon, even by literary examples of this genre; it is more accurately compared to scriptural paraphrase, where the impulse to connect the events in the text with contemporary ideals is evident in gratuitous description of food, fine clothes, and good manners.[3] The difference between the conventional elaboration found in paraphrases of biblical narrative and the attention the poet of *Cleanness* pays to these aspects of decorum may at first seem merely one of degree, not one of kind. Yet the more closely we read it and the more we compare it with its nearest medieval equivalents, the more we understand the poem's distinctively celebrative approach to its theme. As Derek Pearsall has put it, "the poet encourages us to read in a way that is appropriate neither to homily nor to the Old Testament" (*Old and Middle English Literature* 171).[4] His stance toward his materials is that of a craftsman whose boldly imaginative expansions of the Vulgate text attest to his confidence that he, like the Solomon he portrays in an account of the creation of treasures for the temple, should in the process of devising "vesselment . . . his Souerayn to loue" (vessels . . . his Sovereign to laud 1288–89) also fulfill earthly standards of excellence. Perhaps he hoped that his audience, upon contemplating the intrinsic splendor of the work he performed as a poet, would experience the same joy that led even his pagan king Nebuchadnezzar, admiring Solomon's artistry, to praise God:

> Bot þe joy of þe juelrye so gentyle and ryche,
> When hit watz schewed hym so schene, scharp watz his wonder;
> Of such vessel auayed, þat vayled so huge,
> Never ȝet nas Nabugodenozar er þenne.
> He sesed hem with solemneté, þe Souerayn he praysed
> Þat watz aþel ouer alle, Israel Dryȝtyn.(1309–14)
> (But the joy [he had] of the jewelry, so splendid and rich,
> Shimmering to his sharp wonder when it was shown to him!
> For of such vessels that had so huge a value,
> Never before had Nebuchadnezzar been informed until then.
> He seized them solemnly, he praised the Sovereign
> Who was noble over all, the Lord of Israel.)

The leisurely depiction of the beauty of these artifacts communicates the refined appreciation of aristocratic style basic to the life of virtue as the poet imagines it.

These liturgical objects are scarcely visualized in the scriptural sources, but through an extended ekphrasis (1441–92), even without having seen actual objects like those described here, a modern reader can grasp what George Henderson has called "the 'Bowre of Blisse' mentality . . . characteristic of the patrons and artificers of Gothic art" (*Gothic* 134). Luxuriating in his own verbally overwrought recreation, the poet has conflated a number of biblical passages with a fourteenth-century account of the palaces of the Great Khan and Prester John (Mandeville's *Travels*) to generate symbolically suggestive natural details. Between the branches of the golden candelabra, he imagines birds flying, of many colors and curious kinds, feathers aflutter as a wind lofts their wings. Within the branches and leaves embossed on the golden surface of the goblets are parrots and magpies, proud of having plucked pomegranates. Other fruits appear in abundance, formed out of pearls and a dozen other precious stones. The close attention to gems reveals the poet's jeweler-like mentality, and the alliteration and rhythm suggests his concern to set each word fitly into a composition that is itself a model of the decorative aesthetic embodied in the objects being described.[5]

Nowhere is his rhetoric more ornate, and nowhere are its effects more problematic for modern readers, even those who may defend his "massing together of details of rich materials and fine workmanship" (Davenport 71). The details the poet lavished on the vessels and other treasures of the temple significantly express his own distinctive idealization of God's *clannesse* embodied in earthly forms—both natural and artificed; such forms appeal to a courtly sense of entitlement to a life crafted in accord with an aesthetic ideal and lavishly adorned by the gratuitously decorative. The artifacts as they are verbally recreated embody an ideal of play basic to *Cleanness*'s legitimation of the aristocratic life—the sublimation of necessity and labor into a nonutilitarian experience of order.[6] Although modern readers may find themselves unpleasantly weighted down by the plethora of detail in the twenty-one lines devoted to the cups (1456–77) and the fourteen lines to the candlelabrum (1468), the rhetorical excess attests to the ideal of the fittingly magnificent that Thomas Aquinas endorsed in his discussion of temperance.[7] (In some cases, as we shall see, moderation calls for extremes—or as Mae West is credited with declaring, too much of a good thing is sometimes just enough.)

Elaborately ornate vessels were typical not only of the artifacts displayed on sacred altars but on courtly tables at feasts like the one in the parable that the poet retells to symbolize the simultaneous rigor and appeal of life in the kingdom of heaven.[8] Forecast in the opening lines' reference to *fayre formez*, the poet's aesthetic delight is indulged here in a playful but not irreverent response to the vessels' serious significance.[9] Implicitly, the decorative urges displayed in his own poetic style are legitimated by the clever fashionings of Solomon, whose *clene* and *curious crafte* he celebrates as an attribute of intimacy with God and collaboration with the divine wisdom of "þe Worcher" (the maker/creator 1501) of the world.

To celebrate, while it includes wit and verbal playfulness, is not to entertain in any trifling sense; to call attention to the poet's aesthetic intent is not to deny his didactic aims or minimize his fundamental horror at *fylþe* and its effects on God or humanity. Rather, it is to underline how the poem is constructed: it is not just an exhortation to virtue and a juxtaposition of rewards and punishments, but a ritualistic affirmation of the aesthetic and ethical values underlying aristocratic formalization of life. Thus the poem's elaborate detail is not simply authenticating realism intended to be captivating to a a socially elite audience, and not just the result of an extraneous hunger for refined standards of living. The aristocratic ethos epitomizes God's order, his very being. The idealized ordering of gesture and costume, splendid food and drink into a satisfyingly ceremonious meal, and the comparable refinement of sexual urges into a *kynde crafte* (natural craft) approaching heavenly joy—feasts, love, and sumptuous craftsmanship—epitomize the realm of God's goodness which presents itself to the poet's imagination as intelligible and splendid, unambiguously clear and compellingly attractive.

Throughout most of the poem a pervasively aesthetic frame of reference contains and transcends the violent energies of evil and their threatening consequences. Even the most dreadful acts of vengeance, issuing from a divine anger so intense that the earth is permanently scarred from its punishment of Sodom and Gomorrah, can finally be viewed as signs and tokens of God's passionate regard for the order of his own creation, the beauty of *clene layk* and *fre þewes*—two of the most distinctive terms used by the poet to describe what is in accord with God's sensibility. *Layk* itself means devices, practices, or even games, sports, and amusements that may be good or bad; God before the Flood is angered by the "lodlych laykez" (loathsome sports 274) of evildoers, but his court is rightly characterized by splendid ceremonies "with menske and with mete and mynstrasy noble, / And alle þe laykez þat a lorde aȝt in londe schewe" (with honor and with food and noble minstrelsy / And all the amusements that a lord ought to show in his country 121–22). The poet sums up what in God requires us to conform to his nature by saying "he louyes clene layk" (he loves noble practices/proper play 1053). Similarly, *þewes* refers to ordinances, customs, or manners that may be gracious or the reverse, but when the poet describes the degree of wrath God feels toward *fylþe*, he represents him as forgetting "alle his fre þewes" (all his noble customs or ways of acting 203) and unleashing sheer destruction.

This defining characteristic of the poem is embodied in its central word, *clannesse*, which has been seriously obscured by the changed associations of the modern word *cleanness*. The most ordinary sense of *clean* in modern English is "free from dirt or filth," and we have long ceased to think of being "clean" in this sense as a splendid luxury, central to the ideal of an aristocratic existence and the necessary condition of its beauty, something beyond the reach of most of society. As a result, we are initially prepared to think of cleanness as referring to the absence of something negative rather than as the presence of something profoundly delightful. And if we think of the poem under the more abstract title *Purity* given it by a modern editor (Menner), we are even more likely to transfer the negative notion of physical spotlessness to the figurative realm and assume the poet uses *clannesse* to refer to a life free of sinful pollution, a life as abstracted from earthiness, physicality, and immanence, as disembodied as ethical discipline can make it. Certainly the antithesis between God's love for *clannesse* and his hatred of filth—particularly certain forms of filth—is a central organizing motif in the poem. But the *clannesse* God loves is finally understood less as a matter of avoiding or removing filth than of affirming and participating in the more encompassing splendor of divine order.

The poet characteristically links *clene* with several terms that serve to remind us of the much broader range of meaning the Middle English word carried than its modern descendant does. The word is commonly juxtaposed with *clere* and *bryʒt*, whose meanings overlap with those of *clene*, underlining the element of clarity, radiance, and sheer brightness implicit in the word. The angels at the heavenly court are "enourled in alle þat is clene . . . , in wedez ful bryʒt" (adorned in all that is splendid . . . , in the most brilliant raiment 19–20), just as the hangings around Sir Gawain's bed at Bercilak's castle make a "bryʒt boure . . . / Of cortynes of clene sylk wyth cler golde hemmez" (bright bower . . . / Of curtains of shining silk with gleaming gold edges [*Sir Gawain and the Greene Knight* 853–54]). The term is also joined with *coynt* (wise, clever, skillful, well-dressed, ingenious), *fetys* (cleverly fashioned, neat, elegant), and *kyryous* (meticulous, fastidious, expert, intricate), all words denoting sophistication, elaboration and elegance of craftsmanship. Solomon's vessels for the temple, the "couered cowpes foul clene, as casteles arayed" (very fair covered cups, adorned like castles 1458) that dominate the poem's final exemplum, were made "wyth alle þe coyntyse þat he cowþe clene to wyrke" (with all the wisdom that he had, in fine workmanship 1287).[10] We may recall the Wife of Bath's comment that her fifth husband Jankyn "hadde a paire / Of legges and of feet so clene and faire / That al myn herte I yaf unto his hoold" (III, 597–99). A last eroded remnant of this meaning survives in the modern English phrases "clean-cut," "clean lines," and "a clean hit." In its Middle English richness, the term has recently been applied by Christopher Page to the a capella renaissance, in order to define "musical and stylistic qualities" often associated with this early music revival and in particular with the kind of performance valued in the English choral tradition: "As used in the 14th century by the English poet of *Sir Gawain and the Green Knight* (a man who knew the world of courts and chapels well), *clanness* is the quality of something that is pure (like a pearl) or of fine and precise workmanship (like an elaborate goblet). *Clanness* can characterize the vessels used in the Eucharist or the goblets which serve men and women of exalted dignity in their banquets; it blurs the edges of earthly things with a nimbus of heaven, in other words, and yet it can make what is celestial seem clearer to human sense" (467–68).

This convergence of earthly and heavenly qualities based on courtly values points to the way the poet uses *clannesse* to name the divine order of being itself. This order shapes his view of the world not as a synthesis of metaphysical concepts but as a moral absolute. This ultimate good, moreover, is grasped as inextricably interpersonal, an order that cannot be abstracted from the relationship between the Creator and his creatures who are ultimately responsible to him and to his designs. In one sense, of course, we would expect such a relational ideal of the good life to underlie any moral treatise in the Christian tradition and particularly one consistently showing God's wrath against evil. What is so striking here, however, is the poet's radically aesthetic grasp of humanity's relationship to the One who orders. His approach to the Good as the Beautiful makes it reasonable to write a poem about *clannesse* rather than to preach a sermon.

In spite of the homiletic framework and the initial reference to the various reasons to be reckoned up on behalf of cleanness, the poet addresses himself primarily not to his listeners' wills or intellects, but to their imaginations. *Clannesse* is defined not so much in terms of ethical mandates and doctrinal precepts as through stories and images illustrating the analogies between the *fayre formez* of decorum as the audience has known it in earthly settings and the perfect *clannesse* of the king of the heavenly court. Through eliciting their identification with an exalted standard of taste, the poet evokes his listeners' admiration and longing for the noble beauty of life shaped perfectly in accord with an aesthetic ideal. This didactic strategy differs from the usual attempt to turn aristocratic fastidiousness into spiritual scruple, as illustrated by Jill Mann's account of courtesy in Gautier de Coincy's advice to nuns; as courtly ladies adorn their bodies, so the female religious must adorn their souls, thus translating the role of the courtly heroine into the religious sphere (*Chaucer and Medieval Estates* 135–37). In contrast to this usual transferal of imagery from the romantic idiom into the devotional, the *Cleanness*-poet does not attempt to spiritualize and desecularize the class-specific behavior of his listeners. Rather, he incarnates the conception of the ethical and the divine in forms of life appealing to an aristocratic mentality.

This explains why the poet does not approach *clannesse* as a virtue to be conceptually defined, either in a broad or a narrow sense. He names it at the outset as his theme, and then immediately displaces this abstraction to embody it in the context of the sacerdotal order of the Mass and the requirements of courtesy and decorum laid upon priests by their participation in that order, arousing our revulsion at the very idea that someone should fumble awkwardly with, or lay dirty hands upon, the body of God:

> For wonder wroth is þe Wyȝ þat wroȝt alle þinges
> Wyth þe freke þat in fylþe folȝes hym after —
> As renkez of relygioun þat reden and syngen,
> And aprochen to hys presens, and prestez arn called;
> Thay teen vnto his temmple and temen to hymseluen,
> Reken with reuerence þay rychen his auter,
> Þay hondel þer his aune body and vsen hit boþe.
> If þay in clannes be clos þay cleche gret mede;
> Bot if þay conterfete crafte, and cortaysye wont,
> As be honest vtwyth, and inwith alle fylþez,
> Þen ar þay synful hemself, and sulpen altogeder
> Boþe God and his gere, and hym to greme cachen. (5–16)
> (For marvelously angry is the One who made all things
> With the man who in filth follows after him —
> Men of religion who read and sing
> And approach his presence, and are called priests,
> They proceed into his temple and belong to himself,
> Nobly with reverence they prepare his altar,
> There they handle his own body and use it, both;
> If they are enclosed in cleanness, they obtain great reward;
> But if they counterfeit craft and lack courtesy,
> As [those do who are] outwardly honorable and all filthy within,
> Then are they themselves sinful and they defile altogether
> Both God and his gear, and drive him to wrath.)

How graphic this image is can be brought home to us if we consider the emphasis placed in this period on the fact that a corrupt and unworthy priest does not lose his power to make the very being of Christ present, so that the vulnerability of God to human filth is underlined in the sexual connotations of the verbs "hondel" (handle) and "usen" (use) in line eleven.[11] Precisely what it means in line thirteen to "conterfete crafte" (counterfeit craft) — since both words refer to artifice vis-à-vis nature, one pejoratively and the other positively — and thus to lack "cortaysye" (courtesy) remains unclear; it suggests a lack of conceptual clarity about the difference between the good "crafte" of the harmoniously ordered aristocratic household and the bad "crafte" of the priest who, because he is not free from sin, is merely simulating in his external actions the wholehearted participation in God's order epitomized in the ritual of the Mass.[12] In any case, a hypocritical or slothful priest is denounced here not as dangerous to the sacerdotal order by which divine grace is given, but for the effect of the priest's shortcomings upon the Lord himself who is, in this image of the Mass, the central participant.

Clannesse is next associated with the quality God manifests in his heavenly household, and here again the abstraction is immediately replaced with a concrete image of a king who is "so clene in his courte" (17) that it would be impossible to imagine that he would not be "scoymus and skyg" (21), fastidious and disdainful of anything discordant with his *honeste,* his honorableness. In such a context, the abstraction is subsumed into the concrete picture of that *honeste* embodied in the service provided by the angels who surround him "enourled in alle þat is clene, / Boþe withinne and withouten in wedez ful bryȝt" (adorned in everything splendid, / Within and without in the most brilliant raiment 19–20). A. C. Spearing's comment on the poet's didactic strategy is worth noting in this connection: "Abstractions such as *clannesse* and *filthe* have no meanings except in so far as they are embodied in actual human situations; and the purpose of the poem is to create or re-create meanings for them by juxtaposing situations to which they can be applied" (*Gawain-Poet* 51). He sees the poem as consisting mostly of exempla from which "we learn not abstractly but concretely what *clannesse* is, how desirable and dear to God because part of himself." Spearing goes on to add "and still more, we learn what *filthe* is and how God shows his abhorrence of it" and to argue that this technique of recreating concrete meanings for moral abstractions is carried on more extensively with *filthe* and *unclannesse* than with *clannesse.*[13] The exempla emphasize primarily the value *clannesse* has for God, and this dramatic process of definition results in a constellation of meanings for the term which, while pointing to an ethical standard, have little direct, concrete reference to the actuality of moral experience but focus instead on aesthetic and social sensitivity.

Thus, when the poet first illustrates his theme, he counterpoints, in the passage quoted above, an attack on corrupt priests who exemplify those who wallow in filth with praise of those who are enclosed by *clannesse.* We are not given simply the negative image of hypocritical, inwardly corrupt "renkez of relygioun þat reden and syngen" (7) but the positive image of the priesthood at its aesthetically discerning best. *Clannesse* here suggests more than the all-encompassing purity of spirit which the counterfeiters of liturgical craftsmanship merely simulate. It includes as well all kinds of skills required for the proper performance of the Mass—accurate reading and singing, the correct preparation of the altar, the prescribed gestures in handling the eucharistic vessel and wafer. As God's servants, their interior disposition to him is expressed in their outward mastery of the forms which render his divine order tangibly present and accessible to the worshipers. Although the priest, in the ritualistic patterns of his calling, does not execute a design in the same sense that an artist does, in order to be *clene* he must satisfy in his work before the altar the same exalted standards as the craftsmanship displayed in the vestments he wears and the liturgical objects he uses.

As the poet initially illustrates the requirements of cleanness, we see his stress on the importance of both inner and outer; with his second, the image of the heavenly household, propriety of dress becomes an explicit image of the kind of self-presentation which mirrors rather than disguises the inner reality. The honor of the heavenly household is reflected in the retinue of angels who, in their livery and service, extend their lord's dignity. The anger God feels toward the priest who merely feigns such discerning compliance to the standards of the heavenly court is deduced by the poet from the perfection to which God is accustomed:

> He is so clene in his courte, þe Kyng þat al weldez,
> And honeste in his housholde, and hagherlych serued
> With angelez enourled in alle þat is clene,
> Boþe withinne and withouten in wedez ful bryȝt;
> Nif he nere scoymous and skyg, and non scaþe louied,
> Hit were a meruayl to much, hit moȝt not falle. (17–22)
> (He is so "clean" in his court, the King who governs all,
> And honorable in his household, and fittingly served
> By angels adorned in everything splendid,
> Within and without in the most brilliant raiment,
> If he were not scrupulous and fastidious and loved no evil,
> It would be a marvel so strange as to be beyond belief.)

Such *honeste* is like that of the well-bred servants and noble retainers of an earthly lord's household, in distinction from the mere obedience of the *garceouns,* or inferior servants, for it requires an identification with the noble ideal governing life in the lord's presence. The aristocratic custom of placing children in the service of neighboring lords and ladies, thus educating them in its standards of behavior while they developed their sense of identity as someone different from the household of their family, might well produce the sensibility the poet presents as essential to *clannesse*. Personal commitment and loyalty are fused with an understanding of what is fitting to the relationship and a devotion to carrying out these requirements to the complete satisfaction of the lord (see Mathew 110).[14] Richard Barber quotes a ninth-century letter from a lady to her son which articulates the psychology involved very well: "Since God as I believe, and your father Bernard have chosen you, in the flower of your youth, to serve Charles your lord, I urge you ever to remember the record of your family, illustrious on both sides, and not to serve your master simply to satisfy him outwardly but to maintain toward him and his service in all things a devoted and certain fealty of both body and soul" (27).

Like *clannesse*, *honeste* is difficult to translate; it has been obscured by its subsequent evolution into the modern English *honesty*, whose usage is restricted to a narrow ethical meaning as the opposite of lying and stealing. The *Middle English Dictionary* cites the usage of the term modifying God's household in line 18 as meaning "virtuous, upright, good." Yet other senses like "comely, rich, beautiful, delicious, magnificent, splendid" (which are cited for *honeste* when the poet uses it later to describe the robe required for the *halyday*) are equally applicable to the exalted status and standards embodied by the king in his heavenly court.[15] The angels' perfection depends upon their perception of the King's *honeste* in both the ethical and the aesthetic senses of that term. Their wholehearted devotion to the way of life his passion for *clannesse* both exemplifies and requires links them to the Lord in a bond of shared sensibility manifest in their own adornment.

As is made even more explicit in the detailed description of the boyish beauty of the angels sent as heavenly messengers to Lot, the angelic robe is not simply one of dazzling white, but it is elegantly suited in fit and cut to the wearer and the occasion. Of the angels visiting Lot, the poet writes:

> Wlonk whit watz her wede and wel hit hem semed,
> Of alle feturez ful fyn and fautlez boþe;
> Watz non aucly in ouþer, for aungels hit wern,
> And þat þe ȝep vnderȝede þat in þe ȝate syttez.(793–96)
> (Splendidly white was their clothing, and well it suited them,
> Of all features completely fine and also flawless.
> There was nothing unbecoming in either of them, for they were angels,
> And the alert man sitting in the gate understood that.)

The all-encompassing perfection the poet praises is like the adornment angels display to his imagination, whether they are this matched pair of envoys from heaven or the liveried retinue in attendance on the Creator in his court. Even more than the absence of dirt and a freshly laundered look, the poet emphasizes positive stylistic values of the attire he pronounces *clene*. Imagining the elegant clothes worn ceremonially by a noble lord or lady, or the vestments worn by the chaplain in an aristocratic household, we come closer to the idea of the poet's idea of lovely garments of the best quality, *schrowde of þe best* (170), than if we think of a simple shift, shapeless in cut and without adornment, that we are all too apt to envision as the symbolically apt equivalent of the purity required for heaven.[16] The point here is that the *clannesse* and the *honeste* the poet celebrates offer not mere cleanness in the modern sense of the term, but a splendor that is aesthetic as well. This is a quality of life in which there is no dislocation between inner and outer, but, instead, integrity and wholeness. In such a life, all of one's works become a garment, figuratively speaking, which is not only free of defiling sin but which answers to an ideal of formal excellence. The garment which is *honeste for þe halyday* must be *fetyse of a fayr forme*, comparable to the *fayre formez* which the poet's language must create to celebrate *clannesse* itself.

The Good as the Beautiful in Thomas Aquinas on Temperance

The ethos of a life in which outward conformity to an ideal issues from an inner appreciation of its beauty, and where there is consequently no distinction between inner and outer, rests on an optimistic assumption of harmony between what is pleasing to God and what is pleasing to humanity. This view of an essential congruity between the divine and human orders, between the realm of God's being in the heavenly court and the realm of society's values, had found its most eloquent spokesman in Thomas Aquinas a century before the poet wrote *Cleanness*, but had been under attack since a generation after his death. In the thinking of the poet's theological contemporaries, the idea that the whole of being reflected, and, according to its mode of creation, participated in the beauty of God's own being, had become highly problematic (see Knowles 258).[17] Yet something like this Thomistic sense of the beauty of the created order and its essential unity with God's own being is expressed through the poet's confidence in the various analogies by which he advocates participation by Christians in the cleanness which is not only God's but their own nature and delight. The various *formez* he finds *fayre* — the images befitting the commendation of cleanness — all appeal to the human aspiration to be part of a perfectly ordered whole; imaginatively participating in aesthetically arranged patterns of experience, the poet and his fictive audience transcend the transitory and utilitarian quality of life lived in the everyday mode. The chivalric aspiration to such formal perfection, and the closely related notion of the honorable as identical with the virtuous, remained alive, it would seem, in the aristocratic, artistic, and social milieu to which this late fourteenth-century poet belonged. While identification of the aesthetic and the ethical need not be attributed to the poet's familiarity with the *Summa Theologiae*, Thomas on temperance can help to illuminate the vision in *Cleanness* of a continuity between the beauty of the created and social orders and the nature of God himself. A comparison of St. Thomas's thought with that of the poet helps us grasp the rationale behind his theopoetic enterprise.[18]

As with "purity," it is well to discard modern preconceptions about temperance. We must distinguish temperance viewed principally as abstinence from excess — or, indeed, as in modern "temperance" movements, from any participation at all in certain activities—from the ideal of moderation as Thomas defines it. In chapter 4, when we explore Thomas's argument that the abundance of sexual pleasure in intercourse is not necessarily sinful, we shall see he is at pains to point out that the notion of a "mean" which he takes from Aristotle is a norm contrary to *excess*, in the sense of distortion toward qualitative extremes, but not contrary to *abundance* or to *intensity*. Thomas regards a sense of proportion as the most fundamental component of temperance and refers to it by the term *honestas*, cognate with the poet's term *honeste*, designating an aesthetic response to what is honorable rather than a volitional response to what is commanded.

The life of temperance is informed by a lucidity about ends and means and is thus luminous with a sense of order. Like *clannesse* as the poet defines it, temperance in the *Summa Theologiae* is akin to, and indeed manifests in human form, the divine beauty displayed in the material world of God's making. Thus Thomas relates *honestas* to *decorum* by citing Dionysius's claim that "God is named Beautiful because he is the cause of the consonance and clarity of the universe" (2a2ae. 145, 2). He continues his appeal to the imagination by noting how these same elements of fine proportions and brightness which create spiritual beauty give the human body its appeal to the eye: "So beauty of body consists in shapely limbs and features having a certain proper glow of color. So also beauty of spirit consists in conversation and actions that are well-formed and suffused with intelligence" (2a2ae. 145, 2).

The beauty of temperance affords a satisfaction that is valuable in two senses, intrinsic and instrumental, which Thomas takes care to distinguish. Since humanity's ultimate end is the beatific vision, nothing which appeals to reason can conflict with the path to this heavenly goal, and so temperance is of instrumental value as a virtue which leads to beatitude. Yet Thomas stresses as the major component of temperance a responsiveness to the value this virtue has *in itself*, apart from its usefulness as a means to an ultimately more valuable end. He argues that the virtues we know from experience are in fact more accessible to us than are God and beatitude, so that, although they are of less value finally, still they are appropriately to be grasped and delighted in by the mind as honorable—a thing of intrinsic worth (2a2ae. 145, 1).

While Thomas warns against confusing the appeal of visible beauty per se with the appeal temperance exerts (for there are many things lovely to the eye, he notes, which it would hardly be proper to call honorable), he clearly defines the idea of the honorable in terms of the aesthetic pleasure afforded by its intrinsic value. "The honorable," he says, "by its spiritual beauty becomes desirable" in a way that Thomas compares to an "object rousing the appetite," which apprehends it as good. So the good life, like the beautiful object, is "received as desirable and just right by the mind" (2a2ae. 145, 2). This is because human nature is rational, and thus men and women are created to realize within the very urges they share with other animals an order answering to the splendor of the cosmos; as part of the physical creation, in a uniquely honorable way they can reflect, like it, the lucid coherence of the Creator's own being. What Thomas defines as "the honorable" is a recognition of the spiritually beautiful, an aesthetic grasp of the fitting expressed in a life adorned with "conversation and actions that are well-formed and suffused with intelligence" (2a2ae. 145, 2).

This view of temperance provides a cheering contrast to the pessimistic dualism that polarized flesh and spirit, nature and grace, in much medieval ethical discourse. Such an Augustinian dichotomy is, of course, latently present even in Thomas's thought. As we shall see in chapter 4, his relative absence of mind-body split and his positive view of pleasure, including sexual pleasure, is obscured by the misogyny he derives from the tradition of supposed medical and scientific fact and his draconian restrictions on the conditions under which sexual activity is licit. His positive view of the relation between body and soul has been made still more difficult to apprehend by the role in which he has been placed since the Counter-Reformation, that of the authority for the Catholic Church's official position on sexuality and marriage. It is therefore difficult to appreciate how innovative and controversial it was for him to reorient the biblical and patristic tradition he inherited in order to ground it on Aristotle's anthropology. Here pleasure is by definition a sign that a creature or a person is doing what it is in its nature to do and is therefore, to that extent, not only happy but also, for human beings, virtuous.

In his praise for the honorable, the angelic doctor's confidence in the goodness of earthly forms of beauty resembles, and may have inspired, the *Cleanness*-poet's opening affirmation, where we have seen how he links the ethical and aesthetic inextricably with the splendor of divine order. Here Thomas similarly celebrates the aesthetic appeal of the honorable life to the rational appetite: "We have pointed out that a thing is called valuable in itself because of its beauty shaped by intelligence. To this shapeliness we respond because of what we are by our nature; each and everything delights in what matches it. Therefore a thing valuable in itself is naturally delightful to man; Aristotle proves this to be the case with the activity of virtue" (2a2ae. 145, 3).

In its specific sense, temperance is defined by Thomas as the virtue governing the most powerfully attractive pleasures of touch bound up with our physical preservation, namely food and sex: "Temperance takes on the strongest pleasures. Now since pleasure follows from congenial activity, the more natural the activity, the stronger its pleasure. Most natural for animal life are the activities that preserve the individual, by eating and drinking, and the species, by the coupling of male and female. Accordingly, the accompanying pleasures are the proper field of temperance" (2a2ae. 141, 4). Since pleasure is seen as the concomitant of appropriate activity, particularly in the spheres of eating and drinking and of sexual intercourse, Thomas's discussion of temperance affords a particularly interesting context for considering the poet's uses of the courtly norm of *honeste* governing feasting and love to evoke the readers' appreciation of the intrinsic value of *clannesse*.

For Thomas, along with the fundamental biological necessity served by sex and food, and the fundamental visceral gratification afforded in meeting these needs, there are secondary appeals which make these activities all the more enjoyable — the savor and aroma of meals, the beauty and adornment of women. The operation of temperance extends to these pleasures, and well beyond, governing less tangible and powerful human impulses as wrath, cruelty, pride, inquisitiveness, and play. Thus clemency, gentleness, modesty, humility, studiousness, good manners, well-turned wit — all are parts of the temperate life, striking a "common tone or measure" with the cardinal virtue to which they are allied (2a2ae. 161, 4). Arresting and repressing the rush of passion is one way in which all these parts of temperance reflect a common essence, but their more fundamental unity lies in the intelligent shaping of activities and feelings in accord with what is congruent to life's needs.

Thomas's attention to matters of taste and decorum in clothing makes his discourse on that part of temperance which he identifies as *modestia* (a term distorted and obscured by its English cognate, *modesty*) pertinent to *Cleanness,* whose author so obviously agrees that "grace of style goes with virtue, and it appears in how we are attired" (2a2ae. 169, 1). The parable of the wedding feast, first of the four major biblical exempla in the poem, illustrates this memorably. The poet forecasts its point in a question that resembles an anecdote about a squire's failure to conform to aristocratic dress code and may be based on either a French contemporary's account of an actual event or on his own experience.[19] Whether or not this passage alludes to the famous *Book of the Knight of the Tower,* the poet stresses the offensiveness of a careless lad's failure to observe courtly decorum and thus reinforces the relevance of contemporary aesthetic standards to the biblical story introduced by this vignette, phrased as a rhetorical question:

> For what vrþly haþel þat hyȝ honour haldez
> Wolde lyke if a ladde com lyþerly attyred,
> When he were sette solempnely in a sete ryche,

Abof dukez on dece, with dayntys serued?
Þen þe harlot with haste helded to þe table,
With rent cokrez at þe kne and his clutte traschez,
And his tabarde totorne, and his totez oute,
Oþer ani on of alle þyse, he schulde be halden vtter.(35–43)
(For what earthly lord who holds to his honor
Would like it if a lad came meanly attired
When he was placed solemnly on a rich seat
Above dukes on a dais with delicacies served?
Then [if] the lout should dash hastily up to the table
With leggings torn at the knee and his rags patched,
And his work shirt torn, and the toes of his shoes worn out,
Or any of these, he would be hauled outside.)

This exaggerated discrepancy between the noble occasion and the guest's hasty entrance clad in knavish shabbiness would constitute for Thomas a clear violation of temperance; to him as to the poet, "it is evident that our carriage and gestures come into the field of moral virtue." The reasonable standard of due measure in good manners, of which clothes are a crucial part, is twofold: to attend to "what is befitting," one must consider "first, the person, and second, the company, the business, and the place." The former requires "a *savoir faire* about decency in motion and dress"; the second "calls for an experienced discretion, a sense of occasion discerning differences of situation" (2a2ae. 168, l). The poet appeals to this socialized sense of "polish and tact," depicting the feast from the viewpoint of the host whose honor is on display as he sits "solempnely in a sete ryche, / Abof dukez on dece, with dayntys serued" (37–38). As he extends the vignette in his detailed retelling of the parable of the wedding feast, this point of view is further emphasized; although here the guest suffers still more terrible consequences upon entering the lord's presence in unsuitable garments, the poet still focuses on the affront dealt to the host's exemplary sensibility. The terse question asked by the noble host in the Vulgate narrative is expanded to elicit sympathy with the outrage any lord would feel when thus confronted with insulting failure in decorum.

Bot as he ferked ouer þe flor, he fande with his yȝe —
Hit watz not for a halyday honestly arayed —
A þral þryȝt in þe þrong vnþryuandely cloþed,
Ne no festiual frok, bot fyled with werkkez;
Þe gome watz vngarnyst with god men to dele.
And gremed þerwith þe grete lorde, and greue hym he þoȝt.
"Say me, frende," quoþ þe freke with a felle chere,

"Hov wan þou into þis won in wedez so fowle?
Þe abyt þat þou hatz vpon, no halyday hit menskez:
Þou, burne, for no brydale art busked in wedez.
. . . .
Hopez þou I be a harlot þi erigaut to prayse?" (137–42, 148)
(But as he moved over the floor, he perceived with his eye —
It was not [someone] honorably arrayed for a holiday —
A thrall thrust into the throng, unfittingly clothed,
In no festival frock, but all defiled by his labors.
The man was not appareled to have to do with good men,
And thereby the great lord was angered, and he thought to punish him.
"Tell me, friend," said the nobleman, with a baleful expression,
"How did you get into this place in such foul garments?
The clothes you have on do no honor to a holiday.
You, fellow, are dressed for no wedding feast.
. . . .
Do you think I am a boor, to praise your outfit?")

This sense of what festive decorum demands from a person's wardrobe is literally as well as figuratively central to the poet's vision of *clannesse*.[20]

Such an affirmation of displaying oneself at one's best in order to show honor to another surrounds the medieval ideal of *modestia*. As in Thomas's discourse on temperance, in *Cleanness* the virtuous ideal of conforming to aesthetic standards based on a reasonable sense of what honor requires is contrasted with self-centered modishness. In Belshazzar's banquet, the poet parodies the values of festive decorum he celebrates as a pre-enactment of the joys of the heavenly wedding feast. This kind of pretentiousness in matters of style Thomas clearly warns against; at the same time, he also encourages his readers to take care about manners and appearances for their souls' sake. He maintains that deficiency in style is itself a vice that presents itself in two ways: "First from negligence, as when a person fails to attend to and take due pains about dressing as he should. . . . Second, by seeking glory from your very lack of care about dress" (2a2ae. 169, 1). He dryly observes (quoting Augustine) "in bodily things not only dazzle and pomp but also dirt and drabness can be ostentatious" (2a2ae. 169, 2).

The Merchant of Paris, a fourteenth-century husband writing advice for his young wife, clearly agrees that there "can be virtue or vice in our style in dressing" (2a2ae. 169, 1). Like Thomas, he believes the virtuous wife must dress in accord with her husband's estate. She is not to claim to be so "diligent, hardworking and humble" that she does not care how she looks. Rather, honor requires that she pay appropriate attention to aesthetic details, displaying neither too much *nor too little* ostentation: "Have a care that you be honestly clad, without new devices and without too much or too little frippery. And before you leave your chamber and house, take care that the collar of your shift, and of your blanchet, *cotte,* and *surcotte* do not hang out one over the other, as happens with certain drunken, foolish or witless women, who have no care for their honor, nor for the honesty of their husband" (*Le Menagier* 9).

The poet of *Cleanness* offers similar counsel in warning his listeners that their attire must be "clene," not only in the sense of undefiled, but also "honeste for þe halyday" (165–66). He relies on the sense of *honeste* which dressing correctly expresses, transferring this appreciation of style to a feel for decorous conduct; this sensitivity itself is the costume which arrays the doer in honor or dishonor.

> Bot war þe wel . . . þy wedez ben clene
> And honest for þe halyday, lest þou harme lache,
> For aproch þou to þat Prynce of parage noble,
> He hates helle no more þen hem þat are sowlé. (165–68)
> (See to it . . . that your clothes be clean
> And honorable for the holiday, lest you meet with harm;
> For if you approach that prince of noble peerage —
> He hates hell no more than those who are soiled.)

The most developed explication of the clothing metaphor comes at the close of the parable of the wedding feast, when he admonishes those who would approach the noble Prince of heaven to adorn themselves in what Thomas describes as "conversations and actions that are well-formed and suffused with intelligence" (2a2ae. 145, 2). As he concludes the parable, and his introduction to the poem as a whole, the poet allegorizes attire that is *clene* and *honeste* for the holiday, equating it with *werkes* or actions that are both *wroȝt* and *lyued* (171–72).

> Wich arn þenne þy wedez þou wrappez þe inne,
> Þat schal schewe hem so schene schrowde of þe best?
> Hit arn þy werkcz, wyterly, þat þou wroȝt haucz,
> And ly[n]ed with þe lykyng þat lyȝe in þyn hert. (169–72)
> (Which are your garments in which you wrap yourself
> That will show them so bright, apparel of the best?
> They are your works, clearly, that you have wrought,
> And lined with the inclinations that lie in your heart.)

In the life he praises as *clene,* there is no difference between doing and being, for one's deeds have the vitality of "þe lykyng þat lyȝe in þyn hert" (172). In his edition of *Cleanness*, J. J. Anderson reads *lyned* instead of *lyued*, understanding the poet to refer to a literal lining of the garment as an apt metaphor for the "good disposition that may not be visible but which nevertheless underlies actions: 'and (which you have) lined with the good disposition of your heart'" (66–67).[21] Anderson illuminates the poet's typical freedom of movement between concrete and abstract meaning as he evokes the sensibility that adorns life with deeds which display their doer's beauty. The poet refers specifically to stylistic values such as the cut of the pattern, skillfully displaying the beauty of the wearer's own limbs, feet, and hands:

> Þat þo [one's works] be frely and fresch fonde in þy lyue,
> And fetyse of a fayr forme to fote and to honde,
> And syþen alle þyn oþer lymez lapped ful clene;
> Þenne may þou se þy Sauior and his sete ryche. (173–76)
> (That they [may] be comely and fresh, strive in your life,
> And well-fashioned in a fair form for foot and hand,
> And then all your other limbs elegantly draped—
> Then you may see your savior and his rich throne.)

Clearly the *Cleanness*-poet believes that outward apparel should manifest both the social status and the real state of mind of the wearer.

Such a sense of style making the man or woman sanctifies the aesthetic and moral values of a society where people honor each other by appearing at their best. The poet and Thomas agree; *honestas* includes sensitivity to the social context. The conformity of inner to outer Thomas holds up as a standard for the very motions of the body, which he calls the voice of the soul, expressing what is interior and, above all, the passions; the moderation of the exterior motions requires the moderation of the inward disposition (2a2ae. 168, 1). As we shall see in chapter 4, these passions, the appetites which move toward satisfaction, are themselves the instruments used by reason to create in a life of temperance the beauty Thomas praises as analogous to God's physical handiwork in the cosmos and in the human form. While sensitive to the social context, *honestas* is responsive as well, and even more fundamentally, to a norm reason discerns in nature, "whose likeness" is "the pattern for learning and the form for gracefulness" (2a2ae. 168, 1).

Problematics of an Aesthetic Ethic

The resemblance between Thomas and the poet with respect to the aesthetic appeal of temperance and *clannesse* throws into relief an even more critical difference between their two visions of virtue. For Thomas, the integral parts of the virtue of temperance are two complementary dispositions, both of them aesthetically sensitive: one is the sense of honor devoted to the beauty of temperance, and the other is a sensitiveness to shame, recoiling from anything squalid or against temperance (2a2ae. 143, 1). Sensitivity to squalor and the sense of honor do not, for Thomas, directly pertain to the divine nature and humanity's ultimate unity with it in beatitude, but to human behavior in the moral sphere. The appeal of "conversations and actions that are well-formed and suffused with intelligence" is not unrelated to one's enjoyment of the clarity and consonance of God's order in the universe, since all forms of beauty are delightful to the human mind because God has endowed it with rational intelligence. But the moral life affords satisfaction apart from this recognition of participation in a divine order and apart from the recognition that such a life leads humanity to its final destiny in the Creator's design. The continuity between the divine order and the realm of moral excellence seems so basic to Thomas that he takes it for granted, and so he can abstract the one sphere from the other. It is precisely this which the poet does not do.

As is already evident, the poet's *clannesse* and Thomas's temperance are concepts that do not function in a parallel way. The poet's view is always relational, attentive to the personal bond between the Creator and the created; Thomas's may or may not be. While Thomas conceives of a realm of secondary causality, within which actions may be judged as intrinsically worthwhile and appealing apart from their instrumental role as leading to humanity's heavenly end, the poet's concern for natural and social norms by which to shape one's life into a *fayr forme* cannot be abstracted from the sense of God's immediacy and the claims laid upon humankind's earthly conduct by the decorum of life in the heavenly household. Beginning with the Beatitude he quotes as Christ's word on cleanness—"Þe haþel clene of his hert hapenez ful fayre, / For he schal loke on oure Lorde with a leue chere" (Things happen beautifully to the man clean of heart / For he shall look on our Lord with a cheerful countenance 27–28)—the all-encompassing perfection of life the poem celebrates is always oriented toward recognition and intimacy in the relationship between God and humanity.

Characteristically he follows the citation of the Beatitude with the absolutist and concretely expressed corollary, foreshadowing the language he will use to describe the unwelcome guest at the wedding feast:

> As so saytz, to þat syȝt seche schal he neuer
> Þat any vnclannesse hatz on, auwhere abowte;
> For he þat flemus vch fylþe fer fro his hert
> May not byde þat burre þat hit his body neȝe.

Forþy hyȝ not to heuen in haterez totorne,
Ne in þe harlatez hod and handez vnwaschen. (29–34)
(That is to say, to that sight shall he never approach
Who has any uncleanness on, or anywhere about him,
For he who drives all filth far from his heart
Cannot endure that shock that it should come near his body.
Therefore do not hasten to heaven in torn clothing,
With the hood of a base fellow and unwashed hands.)

From this difference of perspective between the poet and Thomas, one might reasonably infer that the poet will be more theological and less worldly in his concerns, simply using metaphors drawn from aristocratic norms in order to win his listeners' approval for an otherwise daunting and unattractive standard of perfection. Yet, to the contrary, throughout, he displays a passion for matters of earthly decorum which are not allegorized in typological or moral terms. Indeed, he makes only two overt allegorizations in the entire poem: the first we have explored in the comments on the garment of the wedding guest; the second occurs when he introduces the sacred vessels that are desecrated at Belshazzar's feast in his third and last exemplum. Even in these two explicit uses of allegorical exegesis, he does not dissolve the literal, but instead merges it with moral precepts by the use of descriptive detail as metaphor.

For the form of the life he calls *clene* is finally intelligible not in terms of ethical mandates or rationally defined states of virtue or spiritual development, as it is in Thomas's ethics, but in terms of a bond between God and humanity based on an appreciation of the aesthetic possibilities to be enjoyed in the divine order of things. The vessels, not just in the workmanship which devised them nor simply in the worshipful use for which they were made, but in their very ornate splendor communicate the poet's vision of that order as akin to all that he and his listeners like best. Central to this positive ethical vision is a relationship between God and man which feels like that between lord and courtly servant, host and guest, as these are exemplified in the poem's opening vignettes and parable. The celebration and beauty surrounding a hierarchically shared life create an image of the moral life very different from that suggested by an ethics articulated in terms of negatives. Here the sacrilege committed by a priest who handles God's body unworthily or a guest who comes in a guise aesthetically discordant with the feast are alike violations of a self-evidently desirable and satisfying relationship whose forms are a gift mutually given and received and mutually delighted in. This delight in form and in reciprocity is at the heart of the poet's conception of *clannesse*.

Such a dramatization of a positive and aesthetic ethic, however, no matter how gripping and no matter how welcome as a corrective to the binary opposition of flesh and spirit endemic in traditional religious language, has a highly problematic undertow. Not only does it involve, obviously, an uncritical endorsement of a class-specific vision of life and an economically privileged elitism. It has more complex psychological implications as well in that it places revulsion or disgust in the place held by guilt and contrition in traditional Christian ethics as the motivation to recognize human deficiency and flawedness. Indeed, it renders the whole notion of evil difficult in new ways, since it offers no insight into why behavior and sensibilities that are presented as so self-evidently undesirable remain appealing to humanity. The result is a poetic vision in which revulsion, expressed in vividly personalized portrayals of God's violent wrath against *fylþe,* comes to dominate the structure of a text whose central dynamic is celebrative and relational. The same literal excess which is so richly positive when lavished on the creation of beauty, as in the description of the vessels, is proportionately disturbing in these accounts of God's wrath, as in the violence of the punishment inflicted on the ill-clad guest at the feast:

> Þen þe lorde wonder loude laled and cryed,
> And talkez to his tormenttourez: "Takez hym," he biddez,
> "Byndez byhynde, at his bak, bope two his handez,
> And felle fetterez to his fete festenez bylyue;
> Stik him stifly in stokez, and stekez hym þerafter
> Depe in my doungoun þer doel ever dwellez,
> Greuing and gretyng and gryspyng hard
> Of teþe tenfully togeder, to teche hym be quoynt." (153–60)
> (Then the lord spoke wondrously loudly, and cried,
> And talks to these torturers: "Take him," he bids them,
> "Bind behind his back both of his hands
> And fasten straightway fierce fetters on his feet,
> Stick him firmly in the stocks, and afterwards shut him up
> Deep in my dungeon where sorrow forever dwells,
> Grieving and weeping and hard gnashing
> Of teeth bitterly together, to teach him to be elegant.")

"Quoynt," indeed.[22] The familiar biblical language about the Last Judgment gleaming through this literal picture of the complete helplessness of any medieval peasant who has been so unfortunate as to irritate the man in power, so far from desecularizing this picture of gratuitous wrath and rendering it more palatable, assimilates the divine to the concrete reality of earthly hierarchy in a way that is more, rather than less, disturbing.[23]

William Davenport suggests that this contradiction in the characterization of the host's Janus-like nature, however troubling, is not unwitting on the poet's part. Rather, he thereby invites his audience to contemplate the opposites in the divine nature by bringing "two aspects of God together" (84) through combining two different versions of the same parable, one from Matthew which stresses the idea of exclusion, the other from Luke which stresses the idea of inclusion (81, 101). By amplifying the details from Luke to emphasize the generous reception shown to all, "no matter how poor, how base, how unclean," the poet ensures that the lord's sudden rejection of the guest whose clothes make him a blot on the festive landscape will seem at the realistic level "inhospitable, unfair, and contradictory" (82). If "the poet has confused the issues by entering energetically and imaginatively into amplification of the literal level of the story" (83), he does so precisely in order to show "the disparities in God's nature"(101).

This boldly expressed hunch about the simultaneous appeal for the poet of conflicting thematic elements he found in Matthew's and Luke's versions of the parable helps explain what makes *Cleanness* both so fascinating and so problematic when explored as an innovative ethical vision in an original theopoetic mode. Inclusiveness and exclusiveness, the opposing elements in God's *clannesse* portrayed parabolically in the poem's introduction, provide a similarly powerful antithesis in the two stories the poet retells to exemplify God's wrath against *fylþe of þe flesch*. The sexual ethic the poet develops in his versions of the history of the Flood and of Sodom and Gomorrah is inextricably linked to his vision of the good life as the beautiful life in ways that are both beneficial and disastrous. The pleasures of heterosexual loveplay, which epitomize the congruity between the Creator's designs and human desires, are depicted as a *kynde crafte* — a natural art — that enacts the very nature of God himself. Yet intrinsic to God's aesthetic appreciation of men and women's shared joy in the passionate play of love is an opposing element of exclusion, expressed as insanely violent revulsion against men who make love with other men. I will explore the implications of *Cleanness*'s linking of God's totally positive endorsement of heterosexual bliss with his equally intense homophobia, a linking unique in Western religious discourse, in the following six chapters, as I probe the poem's sexual themes of desire and deviance in the context of its literary and theological precursors.

2

Homophobic Wrath and Paradisal Pleasure

What Is Filth of the Flesh?

Cleanness takes a surprising turn from the general to the specific when, after the parable of the wedding garment, the poet introduces a sexual theme that is not forecast in the prologue. Up to this point, he has singled out no violation against divine *clannesse* as more important than any other, and he has said nothing directly suggesting his coming preoccupation with nature as a heterosexual norm. The transition is both explicit and oblique, for he singles out *fylþe of þe flesch* in contrast to every other conceivable offense against *clannesse,* but he only gradually discloses the meaning of such filth in the course of retelling the histories of the Flood and the destruction of the cities of the plain. While it is widely agreed that both narratives exemplify God's peculiarly intense wrath against violations of his designs in nature, what these unnatural acts consist of has not generally been specified by scholarly commentary on *Cleanness.* When *fylþe of þe flesch* is explicated, it tends to be identified with lust or with spiritual impurity in its most general form.[1] Editions from the last two decades note the poem's emphasis on unnatural sexual vice, but mostly they rely on the poet's circumlocutions without addressing specifically what nature as a sexual norm means in *Cleanness.* A. V. C. Schmidt published in 1988 a groundbreaking essay which focused on the "intensity of the poet's 'homophobia' as it would now be commonly regarded," his hatred of homosexual conduct, and "his unquestioning assumption that sodomy is gravely evil (the reason . . . that lies behind the hatred)" (Schmidt 109). In this first detailed consideration of the poem's sexual ethic, Schmidt argues (as Charlotte Morse did some years earlier) that the poet revises the order of events in Genesis 6 to establish a clear link "between unnatural sexuality among men and ultimate descent into intercourse with the devil," and then specifies (as Morse did not) that "the sin of the race before the Flood, no less than that of the citizens of the Plain, is at least initially *sodomy*" (106–7; italics in original).[2]

Michael Twomey's source study of *Cleanness,* also published in 1988, directly addresses the meaning of the acts that pre-diluvian men contrived against nature, arguing that the poet could reasonably allude thus to sodomy as the definition of the term *usus* (or *peccatum*) *contra naturam*, originally from Romans 1:26–27 and later one of the chief medieval designations for homosexuality, the traditional sin of Sodom" (205). He points out how unusual *Cleanness* is in defining sodomy as the sin leading up to the Flood and argues on this basis for the poem's dependence not just on Romans, but on an influential intermediary, the "putatively ancient and authoritative Christian prophecy, the pseudo-Methodian *Revelationes*" and on its successor, Peter Comestor's *Historia* and several other texts in the same tradition (208).[3]

My study of *Cleanness* similarly interprets the usually overlooked claim in lines 571–80 that the Flood was caused by the same evil that later destroyed Sodom and the other cities on the plain as equating *fylþe of þe flesch* with men taking men as sexual partners. What is at first ambiguous becomes definitively clear in these lines and in the subsequent passage when God explains the cause of his wrath against the Sodomites. To establish the meaning of *fylþe of þe flesch,* we must examine carefully the initial uses of the phrase and then trace how it is given specificity. Reiterating the counsel of perfection with which he began to praise *clannesse,* the narrator catalogs some twenty-six specific ways one might fall short of the holistic standard articulated allegorically in the image of the garment required for the heavenly feast (177–90). At the conclusion of his list of "feler fautez" (more faults 177) to be avoided, he states that the summary is not exhaustive; clearly there are more "such vnþewes as þise" (vices such as these 190) equally disastrous to the Christian who aspires to the "myrþe þat much is to prayse" (the mirth that is much to be praised 189). Abruptly, he shifts from a series of sins, where each seems to be of equal gravity with every other, to a contrastive and then a superlative structure of comparison. A complex sentence of twelve lines grammatically underscores the unequalled seriousness of *fylþe of þe flesch* by two adversative constructions and a sequence of four contrary-to-fact clauses, thus emphasizing through repetition the claim that God's displeasure with sin in general differs qualitatively from his vulnerability to one sin in particular, and to this sin only. In listening to clerics and reading moral discourses himself, the narrator claims to have learned that however angry God grows over every single point that tends to harm his order, never does he respond in totalitarian vengeance except when confronted with the usages of fools who defile their flesh.

> *Bot* I haue herkned and herde of mony hyȝe clerkez,
> And als in resounez of ryȝt red hit myseluen,
> Þat þat ilk proper Prynce þat paradys weldez
> Is displesed at vch a poynt þat plyes to scaþe;
> *Bot neuer* ȝet in *no* boke breued I herde
> Þat euer he wrek so wyþerly on werk þat he made,
> *Ne* venged for *no* vilté of vice *ne* synne,
> *Ne* so hastyfly watz hot for hatel of his wylle,
> *Ne neuer* so sodenly soȝt vnsoundely to weng,
> As for fylþe of þe flesch þat foles han vsed;
> For, as I fynde, þer he forȝet alle his fre þewez,
> And wex wod to þe wrache for wrath at his hert. (193–204; italics added)
> (*But* I have hearkened and heard from many learned clerics
> And also in discourses about righteousness read it myself
> That the same noble Prince who governs paradise
> Is displeased with every detail that tends to evil.
> *But never* yet in *any* written book have I heard it declared
> That he ever acted so fiercely against the work he made
> *Nor* took more revenge for *any* vileness of vice or sin
> *Nor* was so hastily enflamed because of the anger of his will
> *Nor ever* so suddenly sought fatally to take vengeance
> As for filth of the flesh that fools have practiced,
> For there, as I find, he forgot all his gracious customs,
> And grew furious for vengeance, because of the wrath in his heart.)

Here God is thoroughly distraught and so beyond himself that he forgets his noble qualities. Indeed, in venting his wrath that has invaded his very heart, the Prince who presides over paradise loses his propriety, acting instead like a man possessed by madness. Thus to describe the Creator behaving like an irrational person who has utterly lost his self-composure in the throes of indignation contradicts traditional understandings of the scriptural accounts of God's acts of vengeance.

That such an unorthodox reading of biblical history is contexted by so heartfelt a claim to hermeneutic credibility is worth pondering, for it calls attention to the poet's activity as an interpreter of what he has read and heard on the subject of God's sensitivity to evil. Referring to both oral and written discourse, the poet asserts his membership in an interpretive community of scripture readers; by implication, while attending to what others say about scripture, he is himself as fully entitled to deduce God's attributes and values from biblical texts and exegetical commentaries as are the learned clerics to whom he has hearkened and the authors whose expositions of right conduct he has read. This defensive self-representation of the narrator's status as a reliable reader, both of scripture and its glosses, suggests the poet's assumption that at least some of his listeners may find unorthodox the unique claims about God's anger and his sexual designs for humanity's pleasure in the biblical narratives of the Flood and the destruction of Sodom that *Cleanness* will set forth.

As part of his untraditional claim put forth here about the intensity of God's wrath, the poet interprets the sin that evokes such merciless vengeance as men having sexual relations with men, but this part of his innovative approach to these two stories emerges only gradually. In connecting them as exempla of *fylþe of þe flesch* and introducing them by contrast to the merciful judgments displayed in God's response to Satan's rebellion and Adam and Eve's disobedience, the poet heightens the distinction between this newly articulated extreme form of filth and every other form of defilement that is opposed to *clannesse*.[4] Despite the personal conviction and urgency that informs his shift from the all-encompassing standard of *clannesse* to the ethically specific focus on one form of filth, however, the poet's ample introduction to his new theme leaves oddly undefined this peculiarly offensive evil that seems to threaten God's very nature. In fact, not until after the Flood narrative and well into the second extended paraphrase from Genesis—in a speech where God explains why the usages of the Sodomite men infuriate him—does the poet name precisely the sin of males conjoining sexually with other males as the evil of *fylþe of þe flesch*.

Before this moment of unequivocal clarity, we are kept guessing about the circumlocution's meaning. From the outset, *fylþe of þe flesch* undoubtedly connotes some form of bodily defilement, most probably through sexual wrongdoing. But precisely what sexual act, or acts, must be avoided? The phrase can refer denigratingly to heterosexual intercourse, as in this warning against the descent from virginity to the marriage bed: the thirteenth-century author of *Hali Maidenhad* advises that sexual pleasures lead into "filth of the flesh, into the manner of life of a beast, into thralldom of a man . . . to cool thy lust with filth of thy body, to have delight of thy fleshy will from man's intercourse" (quoted in Bullough 66–67).[5] In *Cleanness*, however, the blazing delights of a man and his mate are not seen as defiling. This significant departure from the usual homiletic warnings against the flames of lust may explain why the poet does not mention sexual vice at all in the catalog of evils that provides the transition from the parable of the wedding garment into the portion of the poem warning against one form of filth. Although he does cite several violations of good order in marital relations (disinheriting and depriving widows of their dowries, marring marriages, maintaining shrews 185–86), lust per se is not one of the vices he warns against.

Besides their sexual denotations, both *fylþe* and *flesch* are often used in clerical discourse to refer to the carnality inherent in the fallen human condition, the incapacity of the disordered soul to resist evils of all sorts.[6] Yet the phrase cannot be reasonably construed at this level of generality in *Cleanness*. From the outset of this transition into the stories told to exemplify God's wrath against *fylþe of þe flesch*, the poet clearly indicates his concern with a fleshly defilement even more explicitly sexual than the body's tendency to sin because he includes the verb *used* in his initial identification of the evil as "fylþe of þe flesch þat foles han vsed" (202). This word *used* clearly suggests sexual practices.[7] More to the point, the context clarifies that the sin in question is being contrasted to, rather than blamed on, Adam's disobedience, and so concupiscence per se is too broad a reading of what *fylþe of þe flesch* means in *Cleanness*.

Sixty lines later, in the story of the Flood, the sexual definition of the fools' usages referred to in line 202 is made fully explicit in the phrase "And controeued agayn kynde contraré werkez, / And vsed hem vnþryftyly vchon on oþer" (And contrived works contrary to nature, / And indulged themselves dissolutely each with the other 266–67). Yet even in this passage, the reference to usages of each other contrary to nature might still be understood as condemning not only males uniting sexually with males, but an entire gamut of sexual practices, both hetero- and homosexual, which conventional moral discourse categorized as unnatural lust.

>Þer watz no law to hem layd bot loke to kynde,
>And kepe to hit, and alle hit cors clanly fulfylle.
>And þenne founden þay fylþe in fleschlych dedez,
>And controeued agayn kynde contraré werkez,
>And vsed hem vnþryftyly vchon on oþer,
>And als with oþer, wylsfully, upon a wrange wyse. (263–68)
>(There was no law laid down for them except to observe nature
>And keep to it, and all its course cleanly fulfill.
>And then they found filth in fleshly deeds

And contrived deeds contrary to nature
And indulged themselves dissolutely each with the other,
And also with others, willfully, in a wrong way.)

While the poet has not yet unequivocally named the antediluvian sin as male homosexual coupling and will never refer to this or the sin of Sodom as sodomy (a term that does not appear in *Cleanness*),[8] later he will clearly state that this first human contrivance against *kynde* which brought on the Flood is the very same sin that subsequently brought God's judgment against Sodom, where the unnatural practices are specified as homosexual relations between males as a matter of general preference: "vch male matz his mach a man as hymseluen" (each male makes a man like himself his mate 695). In the transition that links his lengthy narratives of the two singularly cataclysmic dooms of the Flood and the destruction of Sodom, the poet blames both events on one particular form of evil. By repetition of the word *ilk*, or same, he leaves no doubt that he understands that the identical sin is exemplified in both of these eruptions of God's vengeance against whole populations:

> Wheder wonderly he wrak on wykked men after,
> Ful felly for þat *ilk* faute forferde a kyth ryche,
> In þe anger of his ire, þat arȝed mony;
> And al watz for þis *ilk* euel. (570–73; italics added)
> (Yet he took vengeance wonderfully on wicked men thereafter,
> Most fiercely he destroyed a rich country for that *same* fault,
> In the anger of his ire that terrified many,
> And all was for that *same* evil.)

Although at that point he doesn't name the city of Sodom and so we are left to wonder what exactly was the evil deed that twice led to such unequalled vengeance, the poet finally equates *fylþe of þe flesch* with men conjoining sexually; God describes the behavior of the Sodomite males who, taking each other as mates, have thus discovered in their flesh what is from the Creator's viewpoint the worst of all faults.

> Þay han lerned a lyst þat lykez me ille,
> Þat þay han founden in her flesch of fautez þe werst:
> Vch male matz his mach a man as hymseluen,
> And fylter folyly in fere on femmalez wyse. (693–96)
> (They have learned a practice that ill pleases me,
> Which they have discovered in their flesh, of faults the worst,
> Each male makes his mate a man like himself,
> And [they] tangle foolishly together in the fashion of females.)

It is only when God himself confides to Abraham the motivation for taking such fierce vengeance on *fylþe of þe flesch* that the poet finally specifies what this evil deed is. He dramatically extends his scriptural sources to represent God declaring sexual conjoining of two males to be the worst of all faults to be found in the flesh. Although the poet's judgment of sexual relations between men as a uniquely horrible vice conforms in general terms to medieval moral theology, his emphasis on God's immoderate wrath and explanation of why he is so angry are astonishingly untraditional.[9]

The Flood and Sodom Stories: Two Exempla of the Same Sin

In linking the Flood with Sodom and Gomorrah, the poet follows biblical precedent. Among several references to the parallel fates of those who drowned in Noah's generation, those who perished in the destruction of the cities of the plain, and those who will be found unprepared for the day of doom, there is a passage in 2 Peter (2:4–10) which resembles *Cleanness*'s sequence of exempla. Similarly, the apocryphal Wisdom of Solomon links Noah to Abraham and Lot as figures delivered by Wisdom.[10] However, neither these two possible sources for the poem nor any of the other scriptural linkings of the Flood and Sodom single out a specific form of fleshly defilement as the cause; instead, the point in the biblical passages is to warn against carnal sins in general, as they elicit divine punishment on an apocalyptic scale.

To associate the threat of coming judgment upon contemporary society with these massive destructions in the past is a conventional moralizing rhetorical move in clerical warnings against lust. Chaucer's Parson, for example, blames lechery for God's punishment of the world in the Deluge and the subsequent destruction of the five cities of the plain (X, 835). But he does not specify, as the poet does, the particular sexual sin that awakens such vengeance.

More similar to the poet's claim, Jean Gerson (writing early in the fifteenth century and so not long after *Cleanness*) links the same two biblical events to support his argument about God's special judgment upon sexual deviations from the natural order: "On account of this detested sin the world was once destroyed with a universal flood and the five cities of Sodom and Gomorrah were burned with a celestial fire so that their inhabitants descended live into hell" (quoted in Tentler 188). Gerson goes on to warn that this evil—presumably the whole class of sexual practices contrary to nature—continues to call "forth divine vengeance" against whole populations, so that "famines, wars, plagues, epidemics, floods, betrayals of kingdoms, and many other disasters come more frequently, as Holy Scripture testifies" (quoted in Tentler 188).

Unlike the *Cleanness*-poet, however, Jean does not clarify what the "detested sin" is which elicits such horrifying consequences; as Tentler observes, "the principal characteristic of [Gerson's] attack on sins against nature is not its clarity but rather its tough words. He seeks to terrify" (187–88). The poet of *Cleanness* also demonstrates how "those who recklessly pursue their perverted inclinations" (Tentler 188) must face unusually intense vengeance in the hands of an angry God. While not unprecedented, the judgment the poem pronounces about homosexual deviation from natural law as the cause of both the Flood and Sodom significantly departs from the dominant exegetical traditions.[11] As Twomey argues, the poet may have depended upon a phrase in Peter Comestor's *Historia* that describes males catching fire from males before the Flood, or he may have been influenced by another text in the same tradition that descends from the *Revelationes* of pseudo-Methodius. What is even more striking than the poet's unusual but not distinctive blaming of the Flood and Sodom on the same specific evil of men conjoining sexually with men is his reshaping of the Old Testament accounts in order to support an unprecedented assertion: this deviation from the natural order, unlike any other evil, renders God himself vulnerable to anthropomorphically cruel indignation.

> When he knew vche contré coruppte in hitseluen,
> And vch freke forloyned fro þe ryȝt wayez,
> Felle temptande tene towched his hert.
> As wyȝe wo hym withinne, werp to hymseluen: (281–84)
> (When he knew each country corrupt in itself
> And each fellow strayed from the right ways
> Cruel afflicting anger touched his heart.
> Like a man sorrowful within, he spoke to himself:)

The poet's emphasis on the destructive effects of homosexual sins is made all the more extreme by this unorthodox assertion that God's fury against this defilement uniquely devastates his own nature, canceling the capacity for divine mercy that normally mitigates his judgments of evildoers.

Prophetic Threats of Temporal Doom in an Aristocratic Milieu

The emphasis on God's extreme wrath against homosexual conduct locates *Cleanness* in a prophetic tradition of warnings that such offenders risk bringing down upon themselves and upon their world apocalyptic vengeance. We have seen how Jean Gerson sought to terrify his French contemporaries guilty of unnatural lust; warnings of the temporal judgment of God upon sexual corruption were common as well in the poet's England. For example,

Thomas Brinton, archbishop of Rochester, blamed the decline of English success in the war with the French on moral decay (Barnie 28, 117).[12] But the poet's specific focus on the wrath of God evoked by homosexual practices most strikingly resembles the diatribes of two earlier reformers, Peter Damian from the eleventh century and Peter the Cantor from the twelfth. The former attempted, unsuccessfully, to mobilize the church to purge itself of all varieties of homosexual relations (relations which he claims are widespread among the clergy); in doing so, he sounded a blast against same-sex liaisons that the poet's hyperbole seems to echo: "Truly, this vice is never to be compared with any other vice because it surpasses the enormity of all vices" (63). Peter Damian argues that a man who has had sexual relations with a male remains unworthy to perform ecclesiastical duties, citing a papal prohibition against laymen who have been the vessels of homosexual vice handling the sacramental implements, and denouncing "those who were once the vessels of vice" as unworthy to handle the divine mystery" (62).[13]

Even more striking are the resemblances between *Cleanness* and the diatribe against sodomy issued by Peter the Cantor, who like the poet sees God's hasty and thorough vengeance as evidence for the eclipse of the nobler qualities of his nature: "When the Lord assigns the punishments to be inflicted for various sins, he seems to abandon his native patience and kindness with this one, not waiting for the Sodomites to come to justice but, rather, punishing them temporally with fire sent from heaven, as he will ultimately exact justice through the fires of hell." We may note, however, that Peter the Cantor hedges here by saying that the Lord "seems" to lose his gentler qualities. His depiction of the Dead Sea terrain transformed as a sign of God's anger foreshadows the poet's more developed meditation on this symbolic scene: "In his contempt for this sin God even turned against the land. . . . There are trees bearing fruit which crumbles at the touch into dust and ashes" (Boswell, *Homosexuality* 377). Drawing mainly on details from Mandeville's *Travels*, the poet expands on the medieval tradition of this ruined landscape for an additional forty lines, culminating in a vividly specific description of the ashy fruit that still blooms where Sodom once flourished:

> Þer þe fyue citées wern set nov is a see called,
> Þat ay is drouy and dym, and ded in hit kynde,
> Blo, blubrande, and blak, vnblyþe to neȝe;
> As a stynkande stanc þat stryed synne,
> Þat euer of smelle and of smach smart is to fele.
> . . . .
> And þer ar tres by þat terne of traytoures,
> And þay borgounez and beres blomez ful fayre,

50 Homophobic Wrath and Paradisal Pleasure

> And þe fayrest fryt þat may on folde growe,
> As orenge and oþer fryt and apple-garnade,
> Also red and so ripe and rychely hwed
> As any dom myȝt deuice of dayntyez oute;
> Bot quen hit is brused oþer broken, oþer byten in twynne,
> No worldez goud hit wythinne, bot wyndowande askes.
> Alle þyse ar teches and tokenes to trow vpon ȝet
> And wittnesse of þat wykked werk, and þe wrake after
> Þat oure Fader forþrede for fylþe of þose ledes. (1015–19, 1041–51)
>
> (Where the five cities were set is now called a sea
> Which is always turbid and dim, and dead in its nature,
> Dark, burbling, and black, dismal to go near;
> Like a stinking pool [is] that destroyed sin
> Which ever of scent and of odor is bitter to the smell.
> . . . .
> And there are trees by that lake of traitors
> And they burgeon and bear blooms full fair
> And the fairest fruits that may grow upon earth,
> Such as oranges, and other fruit, and pomegranates,
> As red and as ripe and as richly hued
> As delicacies any judgment whatsoever might conceive of
> But when it is bruised or broken, or bitten in two,
> [There is] no earthly good within, only winnowing ashes.
> All these are signs and tokens to believe in yet,
> And witness to that wicked work, and the retribution after
> That our Father carried out for the filth of those men.)

This harsh punishment of Sodom (where unlike the earth which is renewed after the Flood, the landscape is permanently scarred by God's wrath) was conventionally recounted throughout the Middle Ages as a rationale for stricter precautions against sodomy and other sexual practices contrary to nature. Did the *Cleanness*-poet, like Peter Damian and Peter the Cantor, fear that the alleged homosexual practices of some of his contemporaries could jeopardize not only the allegedly guilty parties but an entire population? Of course, the poet's description of the odors rising from the Dead Sea and the bitter fruits growing by it, commonplace throughout the Middle Ages, does not in itself link *Cleanness*'s rhetoric of sexual intolerance to a tradition of this polemic used to warn against the disastrous effects of homosexual practices in the church or society at large.[14] Still, in one part of the homiletic framework of *Cleanness*, in commenting on the story of the Flood and introducing the story of Sodom, the poet does sound a similarly prophetic warning against the particularly hasty punishment that will be dealt anyone who commits the shameful deeds that brought on God's wrathful vengeance in these two events. If we were to take lines 581–99 out of context in the poem as a whole, we might be tempted to surmise that, if not influenced by earlier jeremiads, *Cleanness* shares a common didactic purpose with them. In this one passage the two biblical exempla of God's extreme wrath against homosexual practices are interpreted to suggest a theological rationale for more stringent punishments for this particularly dangerous form of vice:

> Bot of þe dome of þe douþe for dedez of schame —
> He is so skoymos of þat skaþe, he scarrez bylyue;
> He may not dryȝe to draw allyt, bot drepez in hast. (597–99)
> (But as to the judgment of men for deeds of shame —
> He has such repugnance of that sin, he is provoked immediately;
> He cannot bear to hold back, but strikes down in haste.)

A few lines earlier (581–92), the narrator addresses male listeners still more directly, admonishing them to consider whether or not the God who has created human sight and hearing can be blind or deaf to what men try to keep secret. Even before a man can himself consciously think about his sexual longings, the all-knowing God is aware of, and offended by, shameful inclinations to the sort of conduct that brought on the Flood and the destruction of Sodom.

This part of *Cleanness* might reasonably, though reductively, be read as a warning against the disastrous effects of the corruption of society in general, and the clergy in particular, by homosexual perversions of the natural order. Recalling the warning against clerical corruption in the opening vignette of the priest whose inward filth dishonors God's body at Mass, late fourteenth-century readers might logically have taken the poem to be an attack on the homosexual relations that Lollards and other reforming groups alleged were prevalent among clergy who took vows of celibacy.[15] Impressed with the *Cleanness*-poet's impassioned version of traditional polemic against same-sex liaisons, a pious official could have been inspired to take up the righteous cause of expelling from his realm of influence anyone guilty of such defilement. The hatred the poem communicates for same-sex liaisons would strike a sympathetic response with anyone concerned with ostensibly celibate monks' or priests' indulgence in these forbidden comforts. A secular lord, John, Duke of Bedford, who was a lay brother of the neighboring monastery, expresses such antipathy and fear in a letter written in 1422. He is distressed lest the honorable reputation of the order (and by implication therefore, his own honor) be blighted by their lax treatment of one of the monks who had recently been found guilty of "the horrible synne of sodomye." (Contrary to the tradition that designates sodomy as a sin better not named, here there seems to be no hesitancy to specify the offense in question). Writing to the bishop of Durham, the duke notes that the said monk had escaped from his imprisonment, and requests that the prior now seek out the villain and punish him still more sharply (Storey 196). Such a vignette, suggesting a tension between the sexual codes of an aristocratic layman and the monastic community may tempt us to speculate on possible scenarios which could have provoked the poet or his patron to imagine the need for dramatizing the gravity of the threat posed by homosexual conduct. However, even if we were able to reconstruct with scholarly specificity some local situation, like the one described here, that might have influenced the production or reception of *Cleanness,* we would still not be justified in reading this poem simply, or even primarily, as a prophetic warning against the sexual practices it attacks. The horror of homosexual relations *Cleanness* communicates is part of a far more complex theopoetic enterprise.

The passage quoted above where the poet admonishes his audience to recognize God's power to discern and punish instantly even the slightest tendency to same-sex desire (597–99) is exceptional, for nowhere else does the poet evoke the imminence of divine vengeance like that which befell the sinners of Sodom. More typical of his didactic strategy is the way he finally interprets the unpleasant imagery of the story of Sodom less as a warning than as an encouragement to respond sensitively to God's passion for beauty. The loathsome sea, the deadly soil, the fruit which promises satisfaction but is inedible — these "teches and tokenes" (signs and tokens) when read correctly not only attest to God's anger aroused by sinners like the Sodomite men, but also, and even more fundamentally, they signify God's positive identification with those who honor the order he created.

> Alle þyse ar teches and tokenes to trow vpon ʒet,
> And wittnesse of þat wykked werk, and þe wrake after
> Þat oure Fader forþrede for fylþe of þose ledes.
> Þenne vch wyʒe may wel wyt þat he þe wlonk louies;
> And if he louyes clene layk þat is oure Lorde ryche,
> And to be couþe in his courte þou coueytes þenne,
> To se þat Semly in sete and his swete face,
> Clerrer counseyl con I non, bot þat þou clene worþe. (1049–56)
> (All these are signs and tokens to believe in yet,
> And witness to that wicked work, and the retribution after
> That our Father carried out for the filth of those men.
> Then each may well know that he loves the pure;
> And if he who is our glorious Lord loves noble practices/proper play,

>   And to be known in his court you desire then,
>   To see that seemly one in his seat, and his sweet face,
>   I can [give] no plainer counsel know I none but that you become clean.)

The poet shapes his account of the bitter fruits growing by the Dead Sea to make them tokens not only of the Creator's wrathful vengeance (their conventional significance, as we saw in Peter the Cantor), but also of the heavenly joy that awaits all who conform to the *clene layk* (noble practices, proper play) he prizes. Included in this standard of divine *clannesse* is delight so intense that paradise itself might prove no better. On the morning of Sodom's destruction, Abraham sees a pit filled with pitch where once there was a prosperous city in a most delightful part of the earth.[16] His memory of the natural beauty of this place that resembled paradise must call to mind the impassioned account God gave him of the paradise of paramours who learn the art of love as a natural craft. Seen from this perspective, the ruin of Sodom teaches readers not only how abhorrent homosexual practices are to God, but also how much he values sexual practices that conform earthly creatures to their Creator's refined aesthetic sensibility.

The inseparability of the poet's warning against *fylþe of þe flesch* and his legitimation of heterosexual pleasure as God's most prized design makes *Cleanness* unique in the tradition of polemic against men having sexual relations with men. By polarizing heterosexual and homosexual desire, this extraordinary praise of pleasure the poet adds to the story of Sodom removes any doubt that the sexual appetite, and its satisfaction, is of God's handiwork one of the most purely delightful achievements.[17] As much as we would like to know what in his contemporary milieu might explain the poet's fixation on men taking each other as sexual partners, so we would like to be able to specify the social location which might account for his departure from the ascetic vein of clerical discourse in general and of homophobic jeremiads in particular. The unclarity that shrouds the anonymous poet's identity and his situation, along with our uncertainty about who read or listened to *Cleanness* when it was first written, makes it impossible to discover what topical significance, if any, there could be to the combined attack upon the evils of same-sex relations and praise of heterosexual pleasures. Still, it seems reasonable to hypothesize from God's openness to the *play of paramorez* (700) that this poem was written not for a clerical audience but for an elite secular household, where the poet's listeners — even if provincial and not of noble rank — were aristocratic in taste and disposed toward courtly romantic idealizations of sexual passion. A clerical audience, posited by Frantzen ("Disclosure of Sodomy" 452), seems to me improbable, for the pleasures of lovemaking between a man and a woman are endorsed with a religious optimism about humanity's entitlement to earthly fulfillment of erotic appetites that would make even secular clergy fidget. Purporting to use God's own words, *Cleanness* legitimates both the private pleasures of paramours and the public pleasure of a text that depicts as exquisite divine craftsmanship the capacity for sexual intensity fostered by courtly love play and the gratification of each others' passionate longings achieved by men and women who practice these erotic acts. God's speech echoes the vocabulary of courtly romance, and his representation of good and evil resembles the plot dynamics of this genre more than the conflict between flesh and spirit in orthodox depictions of marriage. However, the sources of villainy in romance — a possessive and unattractive old husband, jealous gossips — are replaced by another self-evident evil that serves as a foil to heighten the beauty of the *play of paramorez*. *Cleanness* portrays men who practice sexual intercourse with other men as the opponents of romantic passion as God designed it, and hence as his archenemies.

Medieval and Modern Reluctance to Name the Unnameable Sin

While we must be tentative and speculative in reconstructing the poet's motive, his textual precursors, and his topical resonances, there can be nothing hypothetical about the poisonous effects of *Cleanness*'s message on readers who identify, as the poet invites us to, with God's homophobic viewpoint. Yet how confident can we be that a medieval audience would have discerned God's hatred of *fylþe of þe flesch* as referring to homosexual practices? Might not they have been disposed to construe this *fylþe* more abstractly as the propensity of the flesh to lead fallen humankind into defilement, and especially into such sins of carnal appetite as lust and gluttony? A system of moral control taught medieval Christians to categorize many forms of heterosexual intercourse as usages contrary to nature; how would they distinguish these practices from what I am claiming is the poet's attack on homosexual practices which he ultimately alleges to be the cause of both the Flood and the destruction of Sodom?

Granted that, unlike modern commentators, most of the poet's audience probably did not have the incentive to reread — or perhaps the opportunity to read just once — the various passages which gradually add up to this claim. Still, even if they heard the poem performed instead of reading it thoughtfully, they could hardly have missed the distinction the poet draws between this filth which angers God uniquely and every other form of uncleanness.

More to the point, they would have been familiar with the predominantly homosexual connotation of "[werkes] controeued agayn kynde" ([works] contrived against nature 266), and thus this phrase would have alerted them, more than it does many modern readers, to the poet's subsequent equation of the unnatural usages of the pre-diluvian men with the worst of all sins discovered by the men of Sodom in their practice of homosexual intercourse.[18]

But the most significant feature of a fourteenth-century audience's understanding of sexual terms unfamiliar to many modern readers is their likely recognition that homosexual usage in violation of nature is the sin that it is better to leave unnamed. It is precisely the poet's adherence to the familiar decorum of circumlocution and ambiguity that allowed *Cleanness* to reveal to its medieval readers and listeners as much as it veils to modern readers in its initially indeterminate references to *fylþe of þe flesch*.[19] To his contemporaries, the poet's delay in specifying the sin he is referring to as *fylþe of þe flesch* would have made more sense than it does to us. Indeed, they might have instead been shocked at the poet's explicit account of males using each other sexually, a practice which religious discourse conventionally represented as literally unmentionable, something "of which it is best to say nothing, which it is a shame even to think of" (Heyworth 186). In penitentials from the twelfth century on, it is evident that vagueness about sodomy is to be employed in order to "avoid public disclosure of sins unknown to the innocent" (185), creating a rhetoric of reticence still evident in Chaucer's Parson who describes the act against nature as "thilke abhomynable synne, of which that no man unnethe oghte speke ne write" (X 909; see Heyworth 187).[20]

Such a counsel to avoid publicizing precisely what is meant by "the sin against nature" did not prevent, of course, open attacks on men having sexual relations with men; in the period of *Cleanness*, sodomy was hardly an unfamiliar accusation — as P. L. Heyworth concludes, it was a "popular commonplace . . . cropping up in literary satire, religious polemic, and political manifestos" (192). Yet as predictable a theme as homosexual vice is in "the strident anti-clericalism of the late fourteenth and fifteenth centuries" (192), the taboo forbidding public discussion of sodomy is equally predictable. The sin and the prohibition against naming it are both referred to in the Lollards' Twelve Conclusions, nailed to the doors of Westminster Hall and St. Paul's during the Parliament of 1395, a document that is particularly interesting because it blames the prevalence of clerical sodomy on the requirement of celibacy, a mandate it claims is based on prejudice against women. The Lollards charge that "þe lawe of continence annexyd to presthod þat in preiudys of wimmen was first ordeynid inducith sodomie in al holy chirche" and go on to cite the Bible as their authority for ignoring "þe suspecte decre þat seyth we schulde not nemen it" (45).[21] The "suspicious decree" from which this denunciation of sodomy deviates was not simply one particular document forbidding mentioning the sin by name, but a textual tradition of at least three hundred years. Doubtless the *Cleanness*-poet knew that preachers who took up the topic of men's sexual relations with each other were apt to be criticized for their imprudence.

A century or so later, a preacher in Strasbourg became notorious for his outspokenness against sexual sins; Jean Geiler records that after he had explicitly condemned sodomy in a sermon, even his friend observed, "Dear doctor, it is enough." (It seems unlikely that any such expressions of displeasure dampened the zeal of this late medieval crusader against unnatural lust; apparently he preached the offending sermon with reference to two individuals who, "because they had slept together and left their wives," had been publicly burned in Strasbourg early in 1506.) In response to another critic who asked if he would never cease preaching upon such shameful topics, Geiler responded, "I will cease when you no longer sin" (C. Schmidt 439; my translation).[22]

The verbal sense of decorum Geiler lacked seems to have been part of the rhetorical constraint the poet of *Cleanness* felt was binding upon his ostensibly homiletic text, if not by an ecclesiastical decree against naming sodomy, at least by the clerical habit of circumlocution for sexual relations between men. Even after equating the violations of nature explicitly with the practices of men who use each other for their sexual pleasure, the poet himself employs a variation of the rhetorical formula which identifies homosexual practices by claiming to keep silence about things "which ought not to be named." Exclaiming over the defiling effect of the language used by the Sodomites who uttered their homoerotic desires, he exhibits the taboo mentality against naming same-sex love that we have seen was longstanding and widespread in the church:[23]

> "Ʒete vus out þose ʒong men þat ʒore-whyle here entred,
> Þat we may lere hym of lof, as oure lyst biddez,
> As is þe asyse of Sodomas to seggez þat passen."
> Whatt! þay sputen and speken of so spitous fylþe,
> What! þay ʒeʒed and ʒolped of ʒestande sorʒe,
> Þat ʒet þe wynd and þe weder and þe worlde stynkes
> Of þe brych þat vpbraydez þose broþelych wordez. (842–48)
> ("Send out to us those young men who recently entered
> So that we may teach them of love, as our pleasure decrees
> As the custom of Sodom is to men who pass through."
> Why, they uttered and spoke together of such hateful filth!

Why, they shouted and boasted of frothing muck
That the wind and the weather and the world still stink
From the breach that those vile words brought up!)

Perhaps it is from circumspection that the *Cleanness*-poet avoids altogether the word *sodomy* and only very gradually discloses that *fylþe of þe flesch* is epitomized by the same-sex predilections of the Sodomites. Yet what the poet seems to hide he paradoxically here discloses. In this passage, which ostensibly criticizes the naming of the most loathsome of evils, the poet puns on the anal associations of the specific sin he uses the Sodomites' words and deeds to exemplify, complaining that "the world stinks from the rump that the vile words raised up" (þe worlde stynkes / Of þe brych þat vpbraydez þose broþelych wordez 847–48).[24] If we translate *brych* as referring to buttocks as well as to a breach of moral law, the bizarre reversals of natural properties evident still in the Dead Sea and its surroundings clearly mirror the sexual designs the Sodomites proposed to teach Lot's visitors. The men of Sodom in effect name the unnameable sin in more explicit terms than the narrator will do; thus the poem breaks the barrier against uttering defiling sounds, even while it comments upon, and in a literal sense still conforms to, the taboo against referring to anal penetration or even naming sodomy as such.

Something resembling the medieval reluctance to speak of same-sex eroticism has until recently characterized most modern critical discourse about this poem. The predominant approach to *Cleanness* translates its sexual themes into more abstract meanings that elide the specific peculiarities of its construction of deviance and desire; such a move by modern readers "away from the earthly details" of the poem "and towards its divine implications" (Calabrese and Eliason 251) attests in part to a recognition that the poet is typically medieval in addressing sexual ethics as part of a broader and much more complex theological vision of the good. Granted, the men who desire other men sexually, and by this deviance from the natural order thus arouse God's wrath, serve a theopoetic function in *Cleanness* beyond any literal warning their doom might convey. Yet by translating sodomy into its more general categories of sin, such as lust or pride, or into its exegetically conventional equivalents (idolatry or sacrilege, sterile speech of false teaching and bad preaching), we miss what *Cleanness* has to teach us about the theopoetic logic of both homophobia and heterosexism, not only in the late Middle Ages but in the cultural legacy we have inherited from that formative period. While my analysis of God's hatred of *fylþe of þe flesch* explores, and indeed emphasizes, a broad range of meanings for defilement, this book is primarily concerned with the significance of the poet's literal denunciation of same-sex lovemaking and, inseparable from this, his literal affirmation of heterosexual pleasure. To understand these themes, we must think about the poem in a wide range of contexts, medieval and modern, that can help us clarify its social and psychological as well as its theological and ethical assumptions about sex and gender. The poem's polemic against males taking other males as their sexual partners could not be more forceful, and the association of its warning against such deviance with so unusual a theological legitimation of heterosexual pleasure invites sustained comparisons with late medieval literary and theological works where nature became a powerful concept for the shaping of heterosexist social and religious norms.

It is worth noting here two hermeneutical risks. One is that our account may unintentionally reinscribe the poem's damning representations of homosexual desire by explicating poetic images and formulations which, as one critic has stated, "truly have the effect of a revelation of God's inner feeling and thought" (Davenport 61). While Calabrese and Eliason may be correct in assuming that *Cleanness*'s unpopularity results in part from its modern readers' aversion to God's violence against men who take other men as sexual partners, in the published commentary about the poem's sexual themes little is said that registers such "sensitivity to violence (against homosexuals in particular)" (247). Recapitulating the logic of the poem's claims about what is sexually licit and what is therefore forbidden, critical discourse written from an ostensibly neutral point of view generally provides tacit endorsement of the continuing belief that sexual interaction between two males is an aesthetically and morally repugnant distortion of the paradisal bliss of love ordained by "the rule of Nature" (Davenport 61). This book aims to interrogate rather than to extend the poem's rhetorically seductive heterosexist bias.

The determination to avoid reinscribing the religiously legitimated heterosexism of *Cleanness* should not obscure an opposite hermeneutical risk, that of understating all that is extraordinary about the affirmation of sexual pleasure in the poet's vision of *kynde crafte*. It is true that men who enjoy sexual intimacy with other men were and are a persecuted, shamed, and marginalized minority in Western society; one of this book's agendas is to place *Cleanness* in the continuum of Christian constructions of deviance and the church's polemic against homosexual lovemaking, with the hope of helping to dismantle the persisting stereotypes and taboos still perpetuating that oppressive tradition. But it is also true that in the poet's time, and for many centuries before and after he wrote, the majority of Christian society were also shamed, stunted, and marginalized by religious denigration of their desires for heterosexual pleasure. The fundamentally sensual act of intercourse was antithetical to the ascetic ideal of rational self-control that shaped Christianity and was reemphasized in medieval monastic and clerical reforms that privileged celibacy. The ecclesiastical constraints surrounding any sexual activity—even in marriage—remained very much in evidence through the late Middle Ages, although the naturalism evident in the ethics of Thomas Aquinas and several other thirteenth-century theologians lessened to some degree the pejorative language about the enjoyments of conjugal rights. Those members of the contemporary audience of *Cleanness* who were heterosexually active were in the majority, sexually speaking, but they were nonetheless oppressed by the continuing sense of uncleanness and mortal sin in sexuality promulgated by the church's moral teachings.

Ecclesiastical Constraints on Marital and Same-Sex Intercourse

To be married within the medieval church was to learn that this sacramental bond "permits carnal intercourse without sin" only so long as it is "practised for the getting of children, not for the pleasure of the flesh" (Alan of Lille, *Art of Preaching* 164). Even homilists celebrating the dignity of marriage stress the danger to the spirit posed by the passionate energies of physical desire. In a model sermon to the married (from which the above quotation is taken), the husband is taught to see himself symbolically as a conjugal union of masculine and feminine. He must maintain self-control through reason ruling appetite in a spiritual hierarchy just as he maintains social control by ruling his wife in the literal hierarchy of marriage: "Let a man observe a spiritual marriage between the body and the soul, that the flesh, like a woman, may obey the spirit, and the spirit, like a man, may rule his flesh as if it were a woman" (164). Implicit within this hierarchical bonding of spirit and flesh is the male fear of losing control when faced with the tempting allurements of the feminine epitomized in the objectified female body. For the celibate clerics who engendered this conventionally discouraging view of sexual pleasure, women embody and evoke the aspect of human nature that an ascetic ethos had long denigrated as corruptly carnal. The flesh is seen as feminine, defiling and always on the verge of disobeying the spirit, which is seen as masculine in this patriarchal dualism of the divided self. Permissible in marriage under certain conditions, sexual desire always poses a threat to holiness; unless it is rigorously governed, the marriage bed itself becomes the site of spiritual adultery: "Let there be . . . fidelity to the marriage-bed; lest the flesh refusing to be ruled by the spirit, commit adultery with the world, or the reason, itself tempted by the allurements of the flesh, commit fornication with them: for it is said that he who loves his wife too passionately is an adulterer" (164). Christian marriage was represented in clerical discourse as reaching its ideal perfection when it became a sphere of masculine dominance, where the rational spirit demonstrated its control of the fleshly appetites.[25]

Given the homiletic framework within which the poet sets forth his argument, sermons on marriage like Alain de Lille's exemplar, as well as sermons on other subjects that include a portion on marriage, can amply document the ecclesiastical pessimism which makes *Cleanness*'s generous sexual ethic so surprising. Searching through printed collections for more generous affirmations of conjugal pleasure I must agree with G. R. Owst's appraisal; this genre, both in the vernacular and Latin, is discouragingly negative: "In no sphere, perhaps, does the sheer, overwhelming pessimism of the pulpit show itself more clearly than in its treatment of the theme of matrimony" (378).[26] While not all preachers approached the biblical texts on marriage through the austerely spiritual hierarchy of meanings that produced the usual allegorical glosses, in general the exegetical tradition evident in sermons illustrates the dualistic opposition between flesh and spirit which produced deep ambivalence toward marriage in the medieval church. Moderating the pleasures of intercourse was represented as a necessary and daunting discipline.

In shaping the sexual ethos of Western Europe, priests played a more intimate role with their parishioners than simply preaching to them, although the influence of the pulpit may be underestimated unless we recall how limited an exposure many people had to any other form of public discourse. From 1215 on, when confession became mandatory for every Roman Catholic communicant, the parish priests were responsible for instructing the laity in how to identify deadly sins in their lives individually in order to confess, repent, and thereby be absolved from evildoing. This task required that the clergy be provided with handbooks which amplified the categories of lust specifically pertinent to the married; drawing on such texts, modern historians have reconstructed the patterns of restraint and permission created by the church's teachings on sex as mediated by the sacrament of penance. Thomas Tentler's account of the guidance provided to confessors before the Reformation reiterates how persistently priests were encouraged "to suspect and decry the sexual pleasure of married people" (186). To what degree husbands and wives were taught the detailed constrictions on pleasure articulated in the guides for confessors we can only guess; to what degree the married internalized whatever degree of culpability their confessors attributed to them, we can similarly only speculate.[27]

Since confession normally was a yearly exercise for most lay Christians in preparation for communion at Easter, these guides do not dictate that confessors instruct penitents to account for the aim pursued in every act of conjugal intercourse performed in the preceding year (223–24). Clearly, however, married Christians were taught constant vigilance regarding their motives for sexual relations. For a sexual act to be legitimate, it is a necessary but not sufficient cause that by its nature the union can result in conception, and that the partners be married and intending to raise their offspring in the Christian faith. These motives were crucial, since desire for pleasure is condemned as morally unjustifiable and corrupting; only a good that transcends selfish enjoyment can excuse the sensual indulgence of the conjugal act.

Within these constraints, however, one other good motive can legitimate marital intercourse. When performed in order to prevent incontinency or fornication, sexual relations in marriage are excusable. Indeed, paying this "debt" when the spouse demanded it was taught to be no less obligatory than pursuing the procreative end of such relations. A spouse is duty-bound to provide sexual intimacy when asked, even if the request is made during a holy season or in a holy place; to refuse payment of this debt is itself a mortal sin for which confession and penance were required. Authorities differ about the degrees of sinfulness for which the spouse might be culpable who seeks payment of the debt as a way to avoid incontinence or fornication; they differ less about the blamelessness of payment made in order to help the spouse who asks for intercourse in order to avoid temptation. For most guides, whenever the conjugal act is undertaken for any reason except a desire for children, there is always some sin, but even Augustine concedes that if the motivation is to render the marital debt to one's spouse so that his or her incontinency is remedied, the transgression is slight enough to be remitted through the daily petition for forgiveness in the Lord's prayer. Most guides teach confessors that paying the debt was not to be judged as sinful, and generally they excuse as a mere venial sin seeking for the debt to be paid.

Only a few of the less rigorous late medieval authorities consider marital intercourse for the sake of avoiding one's own infidelity to be a positively virtuous act. Many might go so far as to affirm that the "exercise of conjugal rights with the proper motives and informed by the love of God" is "not merely excusable but honorable," but it is unusual that a guide dignifies as "meritorious" the request for payment of the marital debt from one's spouse in order to avoid one's own adultery (224–25). One interesting exception to the clerical tendency to dichotomize body and spirit appears in the fourteenth century in the commentary on the wedding of Cana by the liberal and influential married canonist John Andreae. He uses Christ's miracle on that occasion not only to commend marriage as a sacrament, but explicitly to dignify the pleasures of lovemaking: "Marriage is of such power that it transforms water, that is, corporal delight, into wine, that is, a good work, which is sometimes meritorious" (Kelly 257). The "sometimes meritorious" element John Andreae discerns in the corporal delight enjoyed by the married refers, most likely, to the payment of the marital debt, as distinct from asking for such payment. It certainly would apply to the begetting of children which, even if not the couple's primary aim, must always be possible in any legitimate sexual act, and which makes "what would otherwise be sinful, not to be a sin" (Kelly 257 — and here John is quoting a Cardinal Hostiensis). But even though it may be exculpated or (in John Andreae's own more poetic words) "transformed," carnal pleasure per se is neither celebrated by him as a good work nor explicitly allowed to be a legitimate intention for conjugal intercourse. To engage in sexual relations for the sake of pleasure is deemed to be sinful — always at least venially, and usually mortally — whether or not the couple is united in marriage.[28] Medieval orthodoxy draws the moral boundaries of matrimony narrowly enough to exclude any conscious seeking of its sensual delights.

Given the fundamentally sensual dynamic that can make intercourse so satisfying, excluding conscious considerations of pleasure from the motivations for conjugal relations seems a hopelessly hypothetical goal. Indeed, "marriage, given as a remedy for the temptations of concupiscence, is a serious source of sexual temptation" (Tentler 230). Tentler points out this paradox, and cites Jean Gerson's comment on it as illustrative of the clerical belief that chastity is more easily maintained in celibate life than in marriage: "Complete abstinence from carnal acts — as in virgins and widows — is often easier than exercising conjugal rights, just as a fever by drinking, a fire by blowing, and an itch by scratching, ultimately becomes more inflamed" (quoted in Tentler 231). The celibate clergy who conceived of a moral system enjoining husbands and wives to subordinate their desire for pleasure to unselfish aims in intercourse believed at the same time that even sexual relations in marriage must necessarily fan lust's flames.

To satisfy desire within the bounds of matrimony established by the orthodox theological ethic meant constant vigilance not only with regard to motive, but also with regard to the degree of physical passion permitted. When preaching to the married, the clergy were typically counseled to address husbands, warning each of them against being "too ardent a lover of his wife" and teaching him that to be wise, he should "love his wife with judgement (*judicio*), not with passion (*affectu*), so that the impulse of pleasure should not govern him, so that he be carried headlong into intercourse" (Guibertus de Tonaco, quoted in d'Avray and Tausche 100). More technically minded ethicists responsible for instructing confessors define the prohibited degree of ardor by specifying a distinction between normal sexual arousal and deliberately awakened desires for intercourse or for more intense pleasure in the marital act. Most authorities taught that in order to diagnose whether desire had trespassed the boundaries of marital moderation, a husband should decide whether he had so passionately desired his spouse that he would have done what he did even if she had not been his wife, or even perhaps would have done it with someone other than his wife, if she happened not to be available to pay the marital debt. Recommending such an intricately hypothetical self-examination, one (presumably celibate, straight, and straight-faced) writer concedes regarding the verdict: "this is difficult to determine" (180). Nevertheless, the conundrum we have seen in Alain de Lille's sermon to the married, that "whoever loves his wife adulterously is an adulterer," is habitually referred to throughout the medieval literature of sexual ethics.[29] As Pierre Payer states, "The standard formulaic explanation for sex outside the limits was sex with one's wife regardless of whether she was one's wife" (*The Bridling of Desire* 122). Jean Gerson's clarification made this formula easier to apply. Instead of asking what the husband might have done if the circumstances were different, the confessor should ask the husband what in fact he did or, more specifically, who in fact did he think about when having sexual relations with his wife. To think of someone else as the object of the act was to seek pleasure beyond the limits of matrimony (Tentler 180).

All these constraints, if taken to heart, dilute the enjoyment of sexual intercourse with a wariness, if not downright terror, of trespassing the moral boundaries protecting conjugal rights from deadly sin. Excluding the motive for pleasure from the justifiable reasons to engage in intercourse reflects Augustine's view that the morality of sexual activity depends on the ability to direct it rationally toward external unselfish goods (168). The literature on confession and forgiveness of sexual sins varies in rigor throughout the Middle Ages, but the Augustinian framework means that even when authorities talk about "excusing" the marital act, they must imply that having intercourse with one's spouse in order to satisfy one's own desire for pleasure is necessarily wrong and mortally sinful.[30]

Given that the legitimating motives for intercourse are primarily procreation and secondarily the dutiful performance of the marital debt to prevent fornication or adultery, same-sex relations were logically unjustifiable because they allow the force of sex unbridled play in disregard of the limits set for marriage. Joan Cadden states concisely the principle that links medieval condemnation of sinful heterosexual and homosexual intercourse: "chastity did not permit the pursuit of sexual pleasure for its own sake, a prohibition that covered marital intercourse as well as sexual interaction between persons of the same sex" (219).[31] John Baldwin's survey of a variety of discourses on sexuality and gender in northern France around 1200 (including medical treatises) found that "only on one conclusion were the five voices unequivocal in agreement: that homosexual and bestial expressions of desire are totally reprehensible" (818).

Clerical attacks on expressions of same-sex desire condemn its violation of natural and social order, evidenced in both the absence of the intention to procreate and the distortion of the proper order of marriage where male must govern female. When two men engage in sexual relations, they necessarily disobey God's command to be fruitful and multiply, and thus they are accused of breaking this law. Besides the failure in literal obedience, however, same-sex union also exemplifies allegorically the failure to produce wide-ranging fruits of a virtuous life which are "begotten as if they were children when there is a proper intercourse and copulation of the flesh and the rational spirit" (Alan of Lille, *Art of Preaching* 163). This idea of virtue as the proper governance by male formative and active reason of the female amorphous and passive flesh, expressive of Platonic dualism and pervasive in the allegorizing mentality of most exegetical commentaries on scripture, must exclude by definition same-sex coupling, for such a pair subvert the gender hierarchy of marriage crucial to orthodox conceptions of both the social and spiritual order. Moreover, the union of male and male is sterile, a sodomitic waste that was symbolized traditionally by the trees that bear bitter fruit in the ruined landscape around the Dead Sea. Homosexual unions can produce neither literal children nor the allegorical fruitfulness of virtue. And same-sex desire between males epitomizes the deadly effects of the Fall, where the conjugal bond that unites the soul to God has been disrupted through a perverse lust for novelty and artifice in place of the rational order of nature (see chapter 3).

In a variation on this allegorical thematizing of gender roles in marriage, Kelly and Irwin interpret the poet's emphasis on *fylþe of þe flesch* as condemning a "direct perversion of the ideas of cleanness, marriage, and authority.... Lust by misusing the sexual drive outside of marriage does not produce the family unit and the father-child relationship and so undermines the very image of God's authority in this world—fatherhood" (240). They argue that the reason why Lucifer's and Adam's sins of disobedience do not merit God's full destructive wrath, while the sin of lust does, is because it "strikes at the very possibility of obedience" (240). Viewed in this framework, the poet's addition of the detail of Lot's wife disobeying her husband makes richly symbolic moral sense. She is turned into a pillar of salt as punishment, not only for disobeying God (when she looks back at Sodom during their flight from destruction), but also for previously disobeying her husband (when she serves forbidden salted and leavened bread to her angelic guests): "It is now a sin which strikes at the authority of the father in the family unit as does the sin of lust; it is not simply disobedience but rather the attempt to overthrow the fundamental principle of authority. Like lust it strikes at that authority through a process of material corruption (the fermentation of the salt and the leavening in the bread) which offends the spirit (the angels)" (241). The sin of Lot's wife and that of the Sodomites merit "the same treatment" because both threaten the male-dominant family unit which "is a portrayal of God's own nature" (242–43).

Extending Kelly's and Irwin's use of this traditional patriarchal hermeneutic, the Sodomites' deviant practices could be condemned as disrupting the *conjugialum spirituale* whereby the feminine flesh is married to the masculine spirit in a union of opposites brought into harmony by obedience of the former to the latter. The sexual union of male with male was considered by definition to demote at least one of the men into the female role, and as such it exhibits the spectacle especially abhorrent to patriarchy of a member of the superior class betraying, from within, the order on which male supremacy is based. (Compare the extreme disdain of the British Raj when one of their members has gone "native.") The poet's construction of the same-sex relations of Sodom has God describing both partners as acting "on femmalez wyse" (*Cleanness* 696).[32] Yet as God explains his motives for anger against these practices, nothing suggests either the "father-child authority motif" that Kelly and Irwin see as central to the poet's symbolizing imagination or the male-dominant paradigm of marriage prescribed by orthodox clerical discourse.[33] Instead of God viewed as the patriarch whose rules must be obeyed in the social and biological sphere governed by these conventionally misogynous teachings, he is represented as an aesthetically sensitive Creator who teaches the art of love in the privacy of a romantic tryst; here, at a quiet and secret meeting, a man and a woman experience between them a blazing delight that is the closest they can come to the joys of paradise. It is in contrast to this idyllic standard of consummate mutual pleasure that the poet represents the same-sex predilections of the Sodomites. While their habits are depicted as a gross diminishment of masculine dignity, their sin is theologically constructed by the poet neither as a failure to gain masculine supremacy by establishing fatherly dominance over a wife and family, nor as a failure to govern the appetites conventionally symbolized by a woman's sensual appeal and subversive nature.

Natural and Illegitimate Artifice in Love

Cleanness represents as God-given, natural, and completely honorable the erotic intensity fostered in romantic ideals of lovemaking and contrasts such loveplay with the unsavory sexual sport of the Sodomites. Celebrating pleasure as God's point in devising the *play of paramorez* and calling it his most valued design, the poet positively values the very preoccupation with sexual gratification that religious discourse generally attacked as the sinful pursuit of males softened by courtly artifice and tempted by the lure of feminine charms. Doing so in metaphorical terms, the poet legitimates secular romance's construction of mutual delight as an intrinsically virtuous aim in sexual intercourse. In contrast, he condemns the Sodomites for their illegitimate sexual contrivance — an aesthetic violation of nature's law, not because they fail to subordinate pleasure to the procreative aim, but because they are insensitive to the appeal of lovemaking taught as a divine art.

The extraordinary intellectual and imaginative feat represented by the poet's break with the body-denigrating worldview so dominant in the medieval religious tradition can hardly be overstated. In our exploitatively consumerist and voyeurist society, the very ease of conceiving of sensual passion as different from psychological love makes it difficult to appreciate the originality of the poet's claim that passion with love in it is the most exquisite of earthly goods, a direct expression of the Creator's delight in what gives joy to his creatures. Clearly, an artist's erotic joy and sense of accomplishment in his own making is at stake as the poet imagines God as a craftsman of human desire, angry on behalf of the form of loveplay he himself "portrayed" to teach men and women what he values most dearly:

> I compast hem a kynde crafte and kende hit hem derne,
> And amed hit in myn ordenaunce oddely dere,
> And dyȝt drwry þerinne, doole alþer-swettest,
> And þe play of paramorez I portrayed myseluen,
> And made þerto a maner myriest of oþer:
> When two true togeder had tyȝed hemseluen,
> Bytwene a male and his make such merþe schulde co[m]e,
> Welnyȝe pure paradys moȝt preue no better;
> Ellez þay moȝt honestly ayþer oþer welde,
> At a stylle stollen steuen, vnstered wyth syȝt,
> Luf-lowe hem bytwene lasched so hote
> Þat alle þe meschefez on mold moȝt hit not sleke.
> Now haf þay skyfted my skyl and scorned natwre,
> And henttez hem in heþyng an vsage vnclene. (697–710)
> (I devised for them a natural craft, and taught it to them secretly,
> And esteemed it in my ordinance uniquely dear,
> And placed love within it, the very sweetest gift,
> And I myself portrayed the play of lovers,
> And made for it a kind of behavior which is the most delightful of all;
> When two faithful [ones] have tied themselves

Between a male and his mate such pleasure should come
That well-nigh pure paradise might prove no better;
So long as they honorably could use each other
At a quiet, private appointed time, unguided by sight,
The flame of love would blaze so hotly between them
That all the evils on earth would not be able to quench it.
Now they have altered my design and scorned nature
And adopted for themselves in contempt an unclean usage.)

The concluding two lines underscore the poet's appeal throughout this passage to what he assumes is his audience's appreciation of artifice — the legitimate artifice of *kynde crafte* in contrast to the Sodomites' shocking alteration of God's design in nature.

Before exploring further this fascinating albeit illogical endorsement of true as opposed to false art in making love, let us inventory the many equally interesting departures in this passage from the usual religious ideology about sexual relations practiced in accord with the natural order:

1. Sexual intercourse is not justified by procreation; while perhaps implicit, it is simply not mentioned.
2. Marriage, implicit in "a male and his make" and "two true togeder have ty3ed hemseluen," is not explicitly named.
3. The union of two lovers who have chosen to honor each other is not legitimated publically by patriarchal family roles but is sacralized privately, in the dark seclusion of intimacy.[34]
4. Mutuality of erotic power and excitement is affirmed, with no suggestion of male phallic conquest or control of resistant passive female. In fact, except for the phrase "a male and his make," the couple are not defined in terms of gender difference; each acts on the other.
5. Tactility and the darkness of carnal knowledge are affirmed without appeal to the beloved's visible attractiveness or to the traditional pejorative contrast between the night of lust and the light of reason and its control of passion.[35]
6. The Creator-creature relationship is characterized by intimacy and reciprocity, as God secretly teaches the *play of paramorez,* and as they — made male and female in his image — emulate his nature by engaging in what he himself portrays.[36]
7. Courtly, passionate language is sacralized, but not allegorized, as God is intensely interested in the paramours' literal and, as such, spiritual pleasures, artfully whetted through loveplay.
8. God's language endorses a romantic idealization of intercourse, combining

sexual passion with mutual devotion to what is honorable (*honeste*) as the superlative form of the natural sexual relationship.
9. Sexual desire is not referred to as dangerous or defiling, to be rationally restrained, but is defined by mutual "mirth" of exquisitely intense sharing, unsurpassed except (perhaps) in paradise.

All nine points pertain to what is meant by lovemaking as a *kynde crafte* in *Cleanness*, but the last three bear most directly on the poet's construction of a standard of honorable artifice in opposition to the counterfeit contrivances of the Sodomites who scorn nature. What God has designed as a "natural craft" requires education, and he represents himself as personally teaching each *male and his make* the roles played by *paramorez*. The intensification of delight in loveplay is not condemned, nor is it to be carried out with an eye on the future good of offspring; God's lessons focus on the present good of pleasure, a gift given and taken. Evoking the secrecy of a love tryst — or as Schmidt aptly puts it, "forbidden amours" (118) — the poet imagines the couple discovering in secluded darkness the supreme rewards of *drwry*. Using this term *drwry* to denote sexual intimacy, the poet not only emphasizes the mutual expression of affection in intercourse (Morse, *Pattern of Judgment* 173) but establishes aristocratic culture's rituals of love talk as God-given. As Dinshaw observes, "love talk between Gawain and the lady in the bedroom sounds just like this . . . in fact; the 'play of paramorez' instituted by God can be nothing other than courtly love games and the roles of courtly men and women" ("A Kiss" 218). To participate in God's heterosexual scheme, the lovers must actively collaborate in cultural artifice. Unlike the dubious interplay of the lady and Gawain, in *Cleanness*, at least at this point, the class-specific dimensions of courtly loveplay do not appear here as detrimental to *honeste* bonds; rather, the poet legitimates erotic artifice in the name of the Creator and thereby subverts the biological and social roles associated with religious definitions of the patriarchal family as a reflection of nature's order. As the *paramorez* enter into the courtly game and play of love, each wields power over the other; doing so honorably entitles them to the mutual bliss which is the sweetest of earthly pleasures.

The law of *kynde* is equated here with the cultural standard of *honeste*, which we have seen the poet constructing from the outset as an ideal of ordered reciprocity that is simultaneously ethical and aesthetic. The poet transfers the enjoyment of the bounty and beauty in the festive decorum evoked in the introductory parable of the wedding feast into a banquet of sense enjoyed in the private erotic sphere of the bedchamber. Just as at a courtly feast food becomes more than a way of answering the body's needs for nourishment, so as *a male and his make* enter into the sublime rituals of loveplay, pleasures are discovered that transcend the realm of physical means and ends. This *kynde crafte* produces a festive state of gratuitous order where the sexual appetite is legitimated in its own right as the medium for executing God's design, rather than being practically justified by its reproductive utility. Love as this passage idealizes it is a form of artifice, something that is consciously and collaboratively made; all the refinements that embellish the sexual hunger for physical gratification with the cultural superstructure of erotic desire, God himself secretly teaches. To say that not only is this taught by God but that in so doing he teaches the lovers something about himself is simply astonishing.

Heterosexual lovers who learn this craft are represented here as conforming to nature, but not because they engage in intercourse with the rational aim of procreating offspring, nor even because they come together physically in a way that allows procreation to take place whether or not that is their primary intention. Their natural craft is shaped not (as Schmidt claims) by "what God teaches . . . through the Natural Law accessible through man's reason or *skyl*" (123) but by what God teaches through communicating *drwry*, a cherished design for lovers giving each other exquisite pleasure. Their mutual enjoyment is legitimated not as a secondary part of God's purpose, a means to a higher end, but as the very essence of his plan.[37]

To deviate from this heterosexual norm is to violate nature, as was clear from the account of the sins of Noah's generation who were given no other law but "loke to kynde" (observe nature) and instead "controeued agayn kynde contraré werkez / And vsed hem vnþryftyly vchon on oþer" (contrived works contrary to nature / And indulged themselves dissolutely each with the other 263, 266–67). Having been given all the "blysse boute blame þat bodi myȝt haue" (bliss without blame that a body might have 260), they chose rather to use each other willfully in a wrong fashion. Specifically what is wrong about the antediluvians' sexual uses becomes explicit when, in the second exemplum, God explains his rage against the Sodomites who are guilty, according to the poet, of the same filth that evoked God's wrath in the Flood. Men who scorn the natural law are condemned because, preferring each other as sexual partners, they disdain and mar the heterosexual *play of paramorez* which is the masterpiece of God's entire oeuvre as a designer.

Cleanness shows no concern to warn women against this particular form of sexual defilement that so offends the Creator's sensibility. God does condemn the Sodomite men as behaving in a womanly way when they conjoin sexually with other males, but this does not invite us to infer that these sinners learned their homosexual tricks from women who invented same-sex love.[38] In fact, God indicts these men as having discovered in their own flesh the fault of which they are guilty (694). Nowhere does the poet equate flesh with female sexuality; the reference to the womanly way in which the Sodomites tangle together, insulting as it is to male homosexual practices, should not be read as a version of the traditional blame attached to women as daughters of Eve and hence as "mothers of lust" (Brundage 533–34). While the poet blames Eve for eating an apple (241), he makes no allusion to the idea that her transgression is symptomatic of the feminine appetite for pleasure and, indeed, assigns primary responsibility to Adam for having disobeyed in touching forbidden fruit (237, 245).[39] One fourteenth-century commentary blames the Flood on the transgressive female sexuality of evil women who got on top of men during intercourse in order to experience more intensely the pleasures of the flesh, but the *Cleanness*-poet shows no inclination to warn women against this or or any other of the various sexual activities categorized by the church as evil because violating nature's procreative aim (Tentler 191–92).[40] Nor is he concerned with men's temptation to any other violation of the Creator's order in nature, such as masturbation or bestiality — both classified as unnatural lust and often conflated under the term *sodomy*.

It is specifically the men desiring and using each other as sexual partners that the poet depicts as the repugnant antithesis to lovemaking within the courtly play of paramours God legitimates as the path to naturally perfect joy. The kind of play God himself designs, teaches to lovers, and holds "oddely dere" (peculiarly valuable) is a naturally artful form of life. This standard of beauty, revealed in the very nature of humanity as God creates it, is scorned in the ugly, because artificial, inventions of the Sodomites, who "han founden in her flesch of fautez þe werst" (have discovered in their flesh the worst of faults 694). Men who follow their corrupting example similarly mar the order of nature and trigger God's violent revulsion.

Critical discourse should distinguish the poem's liberating vision of *kynde crafte* from what appears to be the inevitable undertow of homophobic hatred that comes in the wake of such idealization of heterosexual passion.[41] To resist an ethos of "compulsory heterosexuality," it is useful to see how it is already under construction in *Cleanness*. When God himself is represented as legitimating the intrinsic value of intercourse in terms of paradisal pleasure, his language invokes not procreative imperatives but the experiential quality of sexual relations between two people. However, to enjoy the experience of paradisal pleasure God intends, these two must not only intend to use each other honorably and therefore to tie themselves together truly, but they must be two of different sex, a male and his female partner. To dwell imaginatively in this image of creation where sexual desire is designed by a skillful Creator for the mutual consummate pleasure of lovers who know how to share power and to deal honorably with each other comes at a cost; this study delineates the devastating shadow *Cleanness*'s heterosexist ideals cast on men who discover such bliss in loving each other.

3

Educating Love: Nature as Sexual Norm in Cleanness *and Alain's* Complaint

By viewing *Cleanness* against the horizon of expectation three influential works had created by the end of the fourteenth century, we can discern the logic of the poet's innovative account of what is licit and what is forbidden in sexual desire. These texts—Alain de Lille's *Complaint of Nature*, Thomas Aquinas's treatment of sexual pleasure and homosexual vice in the *Summa Theologiae*, and Jean de Meun's *Romance of the Rose*—will be explored in the next three chapters.

The literary context for the poet's polemic against homosexual deviance begins in the last quarter of the twelfth century, about one hundred years earlier than Thomas Aquinas's *Summa Theologiae*, with the prolific and influential French theologian Alain de Lille, whose sermon on marriage we have already encountered in chapter 2. His *Complaint of Nature*, a satire in Latin prose and verse, heaps abuse on men who deviate from Nature's rule in order to enjoy sexual relations with other men. Alain did not invent Nature as an allegorical character, but he cast her into a new and major role as the injured but powerful advocate of the endangered values of the patriarchal family— reproductive heterosexual relations for the good of the species and marriage as the male-controlled basis of the harmonious society.[1] Nature's complaints (which constitute the bulk of the text) focus on heterosexual as well as homosexual deviations from her norm of "marital coition with its lawful embraces"

(Moffat 50) and extend to many vices beyond sexual transgressions against her reproductive purpose. Still, Nature's anger is repeatedly directed to same-sex unions between men, which she represents as fundamentally crass, hideously defiling the original splendor of the natural order, and deserving judgment on a cosmic scale.

The *Cleanness*-poet and his contemporary readers would very likely have been aware of Alain's vision of Nature as a divinely constituted overseer of the reproductive sexual labors of all living species, for as the personification of the generative aim of sexuality she became a recurrent presence in later medieval dream visions. The *Complaint*'s themes of nature, art, and love as expressions of cosmic splendor are as boldly rewoven into the *Cleanness*-poet's imaginative recasting of scriptural history as they are into Chaucer's mythopoetic vision *The Parliament of Fowls,* where they are explicitly linked with Alain, and where a courtly audience's familiarity with Alain's goddess-like figure of Nature is assumed as a matter of course.[2] Unlike the allegorical landscapes of the *Parliament,* the biblical terrain of *Cleanness* cannot logically accommodate the female personification of Nature who, as the archvicar of God, governs the created order, nor can it admit such mythic protagonists as Hymen, Venus, Cupid, and Genius. And unlike Chaucer, the *Cleanness*-poet makes no direct allusion to Alain or to the *Complaint.* Yet he would have been at least as interested as Chaucer in Alain's visionary account of the place of heterosexual union in the natural order, and more concerned than Chaucer seems to have been with Alain's horror of the harm homosexual liaisons inflict on society and nature. The *Cleanness*-poet does in fact cite Alain's direct literary descendant Jean de Meun, and Jean's witty revision of the *Complaint of Nature* in the *Roman de la Rose* may well have inspired this ironic citation of the *Roman* in *Cleanness*.[3]

Alain's text influenced the literary tradition of polemic against males having sexual relations with males as well as the social climate of intolerance within which the *Cleanness*-poet reconstructed biblical history in order to depict homosexual desire as a singularly monstrous and unconscionable vice.[4] The extant manuscripts of the *Complaint* include fifteen produced in the fourteenth century or earlier in England, attesting to this work's popularity and availability in the poet's time and place.[5] Whether or not the *Cleanness*-poet knew the *Complaint,* he certainly could have, but its usefulness as a precursor text for our study of the sexual themes in *Cleanness* depends more on the extent to which Alain's influential text defined the horizon of expectations for fourteenth-century audiences. The *Complaint* has much to contribute to modern readers interested in the range and development of Western attitudes toward sex and gender. Establishing how the *Complaint* mythopoetically reproduces and revises orthodox sexual ethics sheds light, by contrast as well as by comparison, on both the conventionality and the originality of *Cleanness*'s approach to its sexual themes.

Both the *Complaint* and *Cleanness* suggest that what is sexually normative in the natural order is, for humans at least, an art acquired through education. But the two writers differ significantly in their vision of why and how that artful norm is taught. Like the *Cleanness*-poet, Alain characterizes God as a cosmic craftsman whose artistry, displayed in the splendor of the universe, provides an aesthetic standard for human conduct. Unlike Alain, however, the *Cleanness*-poet imagines this cosmic craftsman as intimately implicated in guiding the erotic pursuits of all honorable lovers, whose delight in sexual intercourse is one of the clearest signs of the Creator's immanence in his creatures' experience. The fictional world of the *Complaint* differs theopoetically from the scriptural history fictionalized in *Cleanness* insofar as the Creator is only occasionally referred to by Alain in his mythic account of a Neo-Platonic diversity of forces mediating between the uncreated source of being and the material world. As chief artisan, God has distanced himself from matter by assigning to Nature the task of supervising the reproductive process. Apparently free to redefine her role, Nature, too, prefers to live "in the delightful palace of the ethereal region" (146)[6] and so delegates her mundane work of making copies of the various exemplars of living things to a subartisan, Venus, who must be taught to conform precisely to Nature's male-dominant standard of heterosexual union.[7] Nature's teleological concept organizes sexual intercourse exclusively by the utilitarian and materialistic goal of reproducing the human species in a patriarchal marriage. Her magisterial ordering of sexual relations to her procreative and phallocentric end throws into sharp relief the gentler pedagogy of God in *Cleanness,* which valorizes mutuality and pleasure. Here, perhaps uniquely among medieval texts, heterosexual intercourse is not justified instrumentally by its reproductive aim; rather, it is intrinsically valued as a paradisal interplay of divine and human creativity.

These stories of educating love are both angry accounts told by teachers whose efforts have been foiled by rebellious students. *Cleanness*'s depiction of God as a craftsman indignant over the Sodomites' rejection of the design he taught them owes nothing to the Vulgate narrative and could well have been inspired by Alain's imaginative impersonation of an outraged Nature. Her narrative of frustrated pedagogy brings to life a mythical maker who speaks authoritatively, and passionately, of cosmic aesthetic standards for intercourse. Both texts remythologize the Fall in terms of deviation from the original heterosexual ideal, and in this mythic context they probe the causes and consequences of males enjoying sexual relations with males. Their theories of what the heterosexual order is and how its purpose is threatened by homosexual deviance, however, diverge radically. Different in genre, in ethical aim and logic, and in tone, these works repay comparison because each naturalizes the heterosexist norm; speaking through the imagined voice of nature's maker, both Alain and the *Cleanness*-poet borrow divine authority to dignify heterosexual intercourse as cosmically fitting and to vilify homosexual pleasure as an archetypally disruptive force.

Educating Venus

The *Complaint* opens on a shrill note of homophobic wrath as the narrator condemns a catastrophic and massive sexual transformation that corrupts many of his fellow men:

> I see that the essential decrees of Nature are denied a hearing, while large numbers are shipwrecked and lost because of a Venus turned monster, when Venus wars with Venus and changes "hes" into "shes" and with her witchcraft unmans man.... Nature weeps, moral laws get no hearing, modesty, totally dispossessed of her ancient high estate, is sent into exile. The active sex shudders in disgrace as it sees itself degenerate into the passive sex. A man turned woman blackens the fair name of his sex. The witchcraft of Venus turns him into a hermaphrodite. (67–68)[8]

While Nature weeps because men who deviate from her procreative aim defeat her mission of continuing the species in an unbroken succession, it is more than just the loss of procreative efficiency which she laments. Nature is revulsed by the dissolution of sexual boundaries that she holds sacred. She tells the story of Venus's failed education to explain to the narrator the origin of what he and Nature both lament as an instability in male sexual identity that has reached epidemic proportions. Venus's defection has resulted in a confusion of gender patterns; defying Nature's phallocentric logic that should ensure masculine control of the feminine, men come together sexually in monstrous combinations (136). Nature's rules dictate not only that males have sexual relations exclusively with females but that in doing so, the man exert control over the woman by placing the "part that is a specific mark of the male sex . . . in the prestigious position" (158). This insistence on the correct positions of man as active and superior, and woman as passive and inferior, in intercourse is figured in grammatical terms, some of them very opaque to a modern reader.[9] What they add up to is clear enough, however. First, there is an essential opposition between the two sexes (as Sheridan observes, "Manhood and womanhood can make contact, but they are mutually exclusive"

16on20), and male must control female. Patriarchal society depends upon maintaining, in both speech and action, a barrier between masculine and feminine identity and upon awarding the dominant position to the masculine. Second, heterosexual intercourse as a natural process requires men to maintain a dominant posture, thereby expressing their privileged status: "Lady Nature's first precept is that in sexual coupling the man should mount the woman, not vice versa; no tampering with the process is to be countenanced" (Ziolkowski 37).

Given her reproductive aims, Nature's exclusively heterosexual criterion for what is a fitting union makes sense, and given the widespread assumption that conception was most likely when intercourse took place with the woman on her back, under the man, it also makes sense that Nature warns against variations from what theologians in the next century would officially define as the ordinary or natural position. What is puzzling is why Nature assumes that so "outlandish and unpardonable" an impropriety as the "bond and union" of the same genders can exert such a compelling attraction for Venus, requiring repeated and stern exhortations against it (157). Nature addresses her student with "secret warnings and mighty, thunderous threats" lest Venus permit same-sex unions; the teacher obviously fears that without harsh external sanctions, her assistant cannot "concentrate exclusively in her connections on the natural union of the masculine and feminine gender" (157). Apparently, same-sex union is thought to be so desirable that only the severest threats and combinations can deter the human male from finding it preferable to heterosexual intercourse.

All of these categories Nature attempts to teach Venus in order to ensure the correct union of opposite sexes, and thereby to maintain the continuity of paternal lineage protected by marriage. Nature's curriculum metaphorically mandates masculine supremacy and sexual force in coital union as Venus is taught to guide the powerful tool of the male organ toward its passive female counterpart. The genitals are tools which, under God's supervision, Nature originally designed for one purpose, and for that purpose exclusively. The potential errors in logic, grammar, and rhetoric Venus must avoid are all ingenious circumlocutions for the failure to connect the male to the female sexual organ in accord with Nature's view of the active, dominant role required of men in procreative intercourse.

Alain's entire view of sex is epitomized by his dominant metaphor for intercourse, that of a (male) hammer striking the hard, flat surface of a (female) anvil. Inexplicably, there is an apparent engineering flaw in the hammer, for which Venus is taught to compensate with great effort and concentration. An inherent tendency of hammers to prefer another hammer in place of an anvil, or for a hammer to prefer taking the anvil's place, is obviously on Alain's mind, as Nature repeatedly warns Venus to be vigilant against such failures to connect the masculine with the feminine. In a variation on the theme of the hammer which threatens to stray from its correct anvil, Nature warns Venus that when producing copies of manuscripts, "the unusually powerful pen" must not be suffered to "wander in the smallest degree" from "suitable pages which called for writing by this same pen" (156). Thus, while there is no instruction about repressing phallic energy, the admonitions to apply the hammer forcefully to the anvil and to write firmly with the pen on the tablet present a vision of sex which lacks all erotic zest and seems completely violent and unpleasurable for either party. It is a fundamental and very significant point about this text (and pertinent to its odd assumption that homosexual deviation is to be regarded simultaneously as loathsome and as almost irresistibly attractive) that Nature's panoply of images for sexual intercourse are curiously insentient, repetitive, and unalluring, not to say brutal. The intense mutual pleasure that sexual union can provide is canceled by the pseudographic description of the female anatomy as an impervious, impenetrable surface. In fact, these metaphors seem calculated to evoke the male's responsibility for reproduction without evoking the pleasure of arousal, much less the cumulatively intense stimulation of penetration and ejaculation.[10]

Although she alludes metaphorically to the differences between the male and female organs whose conjunction Venus must accomplish, Nature does not even hint that a man and a woman thus conjoined might become one flesh through the complementarity of their bodies. The procreative force is so entirely masculine that there is no image of union, or even of insemination, for to speak of depositing sperm would require recognizing the womb as receptive vessel. The physical images of generativity as a process of reproducing images are almost comically misleading, depicting in the case of the hammer and anvil the bang, bang, bang of one hard insentient object against the unyielding surface of the other. This violent, percussive, and unpleasurable process provides a perhaps intentionally ironic contrast to conventional references to heterosexual intercourse as irresistibly attractive—positively so in secular lyrics praising love, negatively so in ecclesiastical polemic condemning lust.

Because Nature's rules for the sexual act do not refer to pleasure at all, the moral danger of the husband's too ardent pursuit of pleasure (so dwelt upon in Alain's own sermon on marriage and in medieval clerical discourse on sex generally) does not tarnish the ideal of marriage in the *Complaint*. The quest for ease and novelty that taints all pleasure-seeking is constructed as essentially alien to marriage, rather than as an inherent part of its dynamic. Nature warns the narrator about the tendencies of desire to overflow its boundaries, but this sensual corruption takes place extramaritally in all of her examples. Venus's rebellion is figured in a story of adultery and concubinage; it is her departure from her husband as well as her deviation from Nature's teaching that foster both homosexual and heterosexual deviance from the marital standard of procreative intercourse.

The energies of physical passion and the pleasures of lovemaking are conspicuously and tellingly absent in the marriage Alain imagines Nature arranging for Venus. Given the patriarchal assumption evident throughout the *Complaint* that the female must be guided by the male, it is not surprising that Venus would need to be married in order to perform her task, and given Alain's patriarchal view of the natural order, it is not surprising that he envisions Hymen, god of marriage, as Nature's brother and her idea of a perfect husband for her pupil Venus. However, given the symbolic suggestiveness of the figure of Venus and of her offspring Cupid, it is striking that Alain makes no reference to erotic desires in Nature's account of preparing this apprentice to carry out the reproductive work in the cosmos. Venus neither reproduces nor nurtures pleasure.[11]

Without any pleasurable incentive, eventually the solemn responsibility for sexual relations in conformity to Nature's rules becomes, from Venus's point of view, mere busy work. Despite the "active aid" of both son, Cupid, and husband, Marriage, Venus finds intolerable the drudgery of the reproductive tasks Nature delegated to her (146). Nature's story of Venus's defection displays a surprising moment of empathy with the failing student, implicitly acknowledging that this task, like any monotonous assignment, carries within it the potential for alienation: "Since a mind, that from birth has been disgusted by the cloying effect of sameness, grows indignant and the impact of daily toil destroys the desire to continue a task to the end, the frequent repetition of one and the same work bedeviled and disgusted the Cytherean and the effect of continuous toil removed the inclination to work" (163). Despite this apparent insight into how boredom creates sloth and how diversion is sought as an antidote to inertia, Nature sees no connection between her own choice to move away from this fatiguing job to an easier way of life in more pleasing surroundings and her apprentice's urge for recreation. Nature condemns Venus's retreat into self-indulgence and accuses her of abandoning a noble life as procreatrix in order to pursue childish and sensual pleasures: "Accordingly, desiring to live the soft life of barren ease rather than be harassed by fruitful labor, disliking the strain of continuous work, enervated by thoughts of slothfulness and excessive ease, she began to wanton with childish indiscretion" (163). Rebellion is blamed on the student's mental and moral limits; no deficiency is diagnosed in either the pedagogy or the aims of education.

The alienated Venus turns to a rival teacher who addresses her desire for novelty and recreation. Before we follow this myth of female transgression to its predictable end, where Venus's adulterous rebellion is figured as the root cause of the disordered state of human nature and society in general, and of the particularly horrifying confusion of gender displayed in male homosexual relations, let us compare the role of desire in the pedagogies of Alain's Nature and *Cleanness*'s God. Where, in the *Complaint*, Nature gives Venus control over the genitals to be used strictly as instruments for a utilitarian end, and then leaves the scene, God, in *Cleanness*, creates a design of intrinsic beauty which realizes desires that are essential to both divine and human beings. In her initial explanation to the narrator of the oppositions harmonized in the cosmos, Nature represented lust as fundamental to humanity's ordered being, issuing in a conflict that is as natural as its resolution. The victory of reason in this struggle is ensured by Nature as one of her "gifts" to humankind—albeit one that is "purchased by toil," and hence one that "bring[s] more honour and delight than all gifts given gratis" (120). As I have already noted, in the story she tells about educating Venus, Nature says nothing of the power—whether for good or ill—generated by the dynamic opposition between lust and reason that is built into human creatures, and she certainly communicates nothing about her gift to humankind of a natural harmony between the two forces. In fact, the topic of lust, the pleasure-driven appetite for sexual relations, is altogether and tellingly absent from Venus's education. Instead, Nature appeals only to Venus's capacity for endurance by sheer will. Venus must "exert herself" that she might "tirelessly maintain" (146) the work Nature herself wearied of doing. No wonder, then, that the routine of strict conformity to patterns becomes intolerably repetitive. Uninvigorated by passion, pleasure, or play, Venus is inevitably a prey to boredom and sloth. Given the absence of any suggestion of connubial bliss, not only Venus but most readers of the *Complaint* would imagine her production of the endless series of reproductions a tiresome task indeed.

In contrast, God's speech in *Cleanness* depicts an education focused on desire, with the means provided to bring it to consummate satisfaction: "Bytwene a male and his make such merþe schulde come, / Welnyȝe pure paradys moȝt preue no better" (Between a male and his mate such mirth should come, / That well-nigh pure paradise might prove no better 703–4). Through his daring revision of the biblical speech justifying the destruction of Sodom, the poet optimistically guarantees that the orgasmic capacity of both men and women aroused by loveplay fulfills a pattern that is personally valued by the Creator. By teaching his pupils how to interact sexually in this "maner myriest of oþer" (the kind of behavior which is the merriest of all 701), the Creator fulfills his own playful desires. Speaking to Abraham of the amorous delight which is *oddely dere* in the divine ordinance, God represents himself acting like a lover, bestowing his sweetest gift of *drwry* in secret (698–99). Since God states that he portrays the *play of paramorez* himself, we may understand both that he is the designer of such refined erotic behavior and that he enacts it personally as a teacher whose own creativity issues out of desire for loving interaction. Since the lovers' play is the medium of the divine design, their activities express not only their natures but the very mind and being of the Creator.[12]

This idea of a representation informed by the identity of its maker inevitably must call to a medieval Christian reader's mind both the trinitarian dynamics (where the Holy Ghost is the love between the Father and Son) and the Genesis 1:26 account of man created by God in his own image, male and female. It is the latter which seems to be alluded to most obviously, since the *play of paramorez* God portrays is designed by him exclusively for a man and a woman. The spirituality of heterosexual love in *Cleanness* resembles the teaching of Jewish mysticism about the Tetragrammaton where "the fires of passion that unite man and woman are seen as receptacles for the letters of the Divine Name, and hence, for the masculine and feminine elements of the Divine Essence" (Kaplan 156).[13] Heterosexual intimacy is so intense a pleasure not only because human beings are thus drawn to reproduce the species, but "on a much deeper level, . . . because it allows man and woman together to emulate the divine nature." Thus the heterosexual couple "can both realize that through their union they are creating an 'image of God'" (157). Although *Cleanness* is not explicitly concerned with the recognition lovers may have of themselves emulating the divine nature, God's very nature is represented in this poem as implicated intimately in the dynamic of heterosexual intercourse. By depicting God as the inventor and teacher of such delights, *Cleanness* raises sensual appetite imaginatively to new religious significance; the lovers' erotic longings, although certainly spiritual, are not figured as intellectual or contemplative, but fully sensual, coming to fulfillment in the embodied intensity of mutual sexual pleasure: "At a stylle stollen steuen, vnstered wyth syȝt, / Luflowe hem bytwene lasched so hote" (At a quiet, private encounter, unguided by sight, / The flame of love would blaze so hotly between them 706–7). The resulting joy is so nearly heavenly that paradise itself might prove no better, and "alle þe meschefez on mold moȝt hit not sleke" (all the evils on earth would not be able to quench it 708). The *Cleanness*-poet locates "doole alþerswettest" (the sweetest of all sharings 699) in the very night of desire which Nature, in Alain's text, warns the narrator against, since it "removes the light of the mind by the dark night of concupiscence" (119).

Sexual and Rhetorical Pleasure

The pleasure-seeking mentality that Nature's curriculum leaves unaddressed drives Venus to an adulterous passion that is blamed for the outbreak of homosexual relations lamented by both Nature and the narrator at the outset of the *Complaint*. Venus turns to a new instructor who teaches her the erotic arts missing from Nature's pedagogy and Hymen's husbandry. The novel aesthetic standards of discourse, and of intercourse, that she learns here energize the formerly bored and listless Venus. The seductive villain in this allegorical drama Alain calls Antigamus (AntiMarriage) — or in other manuscripts, Antigenius — who is a rake of low birth.[14] Nature blames her student's deviation from the heterosexual norm on the bad grammar Antigenius teaches Venus in place of Nature's precepts of the trivium and the forge: "Trapped by the deadly suggestions arising from her own adultery, she barbarously turned a noble work into a craft, a work governed by rule into something ruleless, a work of refinement into something boorish, and studiously corrupting my precept, she dispossessed the hammers of fellowship with their anvils and sentenced them to counterfeit anvils" (163–64).[15] When the love of novelty and ease displaces commitment to conformity and duty, the strict control Venus was taught to exercise over the male organ is subverted. The transgressive urge Nature represented to Venus as inherent in male sexuality, making the penis prone to deviate from strictly procreative connections, is here associated with the recreative impulse that made Venus leave her marriage to Hymen to unite with Antigenius in a life of "excessive fornications" (164; Pr. 5.144: "fornicariis excessibus") and endorse the fatal illogic of same-sex love. From Venus's pointless self-indulgence in the newly discovered pleasures of love issue sexual perversities which dissolve the reproductive logic of love and deform the language of lovers. Venus's bastard son is Jocus (Mirth or Sport), named, as George D. Economou comments, "as if by antiphrasis, for he is characterized by the absence rather than the presence of that disposition" (*Goddess Natura* 88).

This illegitimate offspring is a kind of verbal counterfeit, a parodic upstart who holds sway in place of the legitimate Cupid and thereby robs lovers of the natural meaning of sexuality in the patriarchal family. Venus's adultery is disastrous not only for Nature's procreative project of maintaining the continuity of paternal lineage but for the strictly rational discourse she considers the sole medium for the truth about sexual difference. The natural order of sexual difference required for biological reproduction not only guarantees the reproduction of male dominant forms of social organization, but also production of discourse that is judged as true and beautiful in terms of its correspondence to Nature's phallocentric standard of logic, grammar, and rhetoric. Ignoring Nature's rational rules and limits, Venus has played so freely that she conceives rhetorical absurdities. Transgressing the phallocentric logic of reproducing exact copies, her image-making energies go permanently awry, as she keeps "turning her art into a figure and the figure into a defect" (164). Jocus is brought forth as the product, and agent, of Venus's metaphorical self-destruction, a "trope gone awry" (Ziolkowski 39) whose deceptive name of Mirth or Sport suggests the illusory creativity of a sensual fascination with the novel possibilities of language. In her linguistic orgy Venus has made an erotic travesty of the trivium, "destroying herself with the connections of Grammar, perverting herself with the conversions of Dialectic, discolouring herself with the colours of Rhetoric" (164).

Nature's warning to beware lest the male organ deviate from its proper relation to the female that we have looked at in the metaphors of forge and scriptorium are evident as well in the metaphors of the trivium. Here the appeal of same-sex relations between males is even more explicitly denigrated as irrational, a failure in clarity of thought and expression: "If the masculine gender, by a certain violence of unreasonable reason, should call for a gender entirely similar to itself, this bond and union will not be able to defend the flaw as any kind of graceful figure but will bear the stain of an outlandish, unpardonable solecism" (157). Metaphorical deployments of rhetoric, grammar, and dialectic do not merely allow Nature to skirt the indecencies of straight talk about sexual organs.[16] Beyond their cosmetic purpose, the linguistic metaphors in Nature's curriculum point to language as itself a major theme in the *Complaint*, and one of such complexity that critical controversy surrounds the issue of what—if anything—this involuted work teaches about allegory, rhetorical artifice, and truth. Ironies abound, since the *Complaint*'s author "revels in every device of Rhetoric, . . . tortures the Latin language to such an extent that one is reminded of some of Joyce's English," and "so interweaves the ordinary, etymological and technical specification of words that, when one extracts the meaning of many a section, one despairs of approximating a satisfactory translation" (Sheridan, 33). Just as Nature trespasses beyond the very rhetorical limits she wants the narrator to learn to stay within, so Alain's own gratuitous elaboration of figurative speech conspicuously exceeds Nature's strict regulations.

In contrast to the aesthetics of the *Complaint* itself (which all critics acknowledge as verbal tour de force and some see as a Menippean satire, a self-destructing artifact par excellence), Nature's account of her stylistic norm inhibits creativity both in sexual conduct and in literary production. Most pertinent for our purpose is R. Howard Bloch's comment on her association of poetic and sexual indeterminacy: "It is, ultimately, the mobility of poetic language and of sexual identity that represents for Nature the most potent threat to the *straightness*—correctness, regularity, orthodoxy—of grammar and to the continuity of lineage. A lack of definition—and it should be remembered that the grammar of this early period was based upon the *rectitude* of definition—is tantamount to the dissolution of paternal relations and the transgression of nature's and society's most sacred taboo" ("Silence and Holes" 88; italics in original). Verbal and body language alike must be constantly measured and balanced to conform with Nature's predefined, strictly utilitarian ends. As Bloch notes in an earlier commentary on Alain, "In order to ensure genealogical succession, [Nature] endowed her handmaiden Venus with two instruments of rectitude—*orth*ography, or straight writing, and *orth*odox coition, or straight sexuality" (*Etymologies and Genealogies* 133; italics in original). The urge for imaginative embellishment must be controlled lest it carry the author beyond rational boundaries of unpretentious art. Although Nature admits the need for figures of rhetoric to provide an ornamental cloak for otherwise distasteful or mundane subjects, she cautions against figurative discourse unjustified by cosmetic necessity. Elegance and urbanity are permitted, but her definition of straight writing excludes self-indulgent novelty.

Alain treats the paradoxical language of courtly romance and lyric with particular suspicion, as Nature warns the narrator against the tendency of sensuality to exceed the rational boundaries she has established in both the language of bodies in the act of sexual reproduction and in verbal discourse aimed at truth that conforms to reality. Yet, after the changes wrought by Venus's adultery, Nature's own representation of the world becomes equally paradoxical; as Quilligan puts it: "primal cosmic order has become almost impossible and she must necessarily resort to the conventional oxymorons to describe [the fallen] Cupid's chaotic 'love'" (202). Nature produces a flood of courtly clichés (nearly fifty oxymorons) and justifies this indulgence on her part in the rhetoric of love as a pedagogical ploy. She parodically mirrors for the narrator the irrationality of his youthful discourse, when early in the *Complaint* he had juxtaposed homophobic diatribe with troubador lyricism, praising a life-transforming death through love.[17] Nature claims she displays her familiarity with conventional idioms of romance only to awaken him to the absurdity of longing for a fruitful life to be enjoyed through a maiden's kiss.[18] Nature is unresponsive to the renewing pleasure of either sexuality or textuality that overwhelms boundaries, where sensuality carries the imagination across the limits of a strictly rational logic. Renewal in the natural order is the reproduction of the species, not making love but making new and truthful copies of an original exemplar through a sexual act; her phallocentric logic excludes the romantic ideal of psychic generativity in the shared bliss of sexual consummation. Warning the narrator against falling under the sway of the enthralling false Cupid, she condemns the paradoxicality of lovers who inhabit his "strange dominions": "Here reasonable procedure is to be without reason, moderation means lack of moderation" (152–53).

Here the contrast between the *Complaint* and *Cleanness* becomes especially striking. Nature considers the hyperbolic claims of courtly lyric falsifying and associates them with love divorced from the procreative logic of patriarchal marriage. Yet the very style of language she condemns is precisely the language the *Cleanness*-poet portrays God as speaking in his praise of heterosexual pleasure. The Creator glorifies the *play of paramorez* in just the sort of figures that Alain's Nature blames on the perverting influence of the fallen Cupid who operates by "*antiphrasis* so that words lose their normal associations" (Wetherbee, "Function of Poetry" 108). God celebrates such wordplay by unapologetically identifying his own creativity with the erotically charged figures of speech in which lovers playfully array themselves. We might say, adapting Wittgenstein's phrase, that to engage in the *play of paramorez* is to imagine both a language and a form of life (par. 19). God's account of designing and teaching the art of love as it should be made draws out the nonobjectifying potential of figurative language. His images differ from the controlled similarities in the figures employed in Nature's discourse of desire. The kind of control Nature advocates in intercourse approached as a phallic domination of male over female is analogous to the kind of control she dictates of reason over metaphor in discourse generated by phallocentric logic.

Cleanness connects the refined erotic mentality of romantic discourse with the intensely sensual satisfaction enjoyed by the lovers in orgasmic union; both forms of pleasure are attributed to the Creator's aesthetic ingenuity in creating and teaching love as a *kynde crafte*.[19] The poet's distinction between the false artifice of the Sodomites' ways of talking about and making love and God's *kynde crafte* differs radically from the *Complaint*'s distinction between false and true art. Alain condemns erotic playfulness by associating it with the false arts Venus learned from Antigenius in her quest for pleasure and novelty denied under Nature's strict aesthetic standards. Divine *clannesse* sets an aesthetic standard for both erotic discourse and heterosexual intercourse that endorses nonrational paradox and metaphorical embellishments which soar beyond the bounds of logic. The Creator, speaking of the lovemaking he portrays as a form of play that men and women have the skills to enact, displays poetic virtuosity of the kind Nature disavows. Andrew and Waldron point out that in God's reference to his gift of "drwry" as "doole alþer-swettest" (699) the primary sense of "doole" is probably "sharing, intercourse," but there is also a possible pun, alluding to "do(e)l" which means "grief, lamentation," and thus a reference to the conventional idea of lovemaking's sweet sorrow (141; see also *OED* s.v. *dole* sb. 1, sense 7).

The most incontrovertibly gratuitous wordplay occurs in the remarkable final claim God makes for the mutual delight in their physical union that bonds the lovers to each other: "Luf-lowe hem bytwene lasched so hote / Þat alle þe meschefez on mold moȝt hit not sleke" (The flame of love would blaze so hotly between them / That all the evils on earth would not be able to quench it *Cleanness* 707–8). The uncontrollable heat released by love's flames is evoked as an intensely positive sensual experience, subjecting lovers to a burning that, doctrinally understood, would signify the corruption of love by ungovernable lust and, literally understood, would evoke pain rather than pleasure. This burning sensation that was paradoxically experienced as delightful rather than distressing is featured in various medieval discourses of desire, from moral to medical to fabliau and romance.[20] In the poet's imagination, the metaphor of love's flame undergoes another stage of positive transformation, so that this burning is seen now under the aspect of celestial thermodynamics, since nothing on earth can quench it. The poet thus describes elemental passion as an elevating force; when their sexual excitement gives rise to such heat, the lovers' pleasure transports them to a sphere beyond the mundane. The corruption or diminishment that ordinarily threatens earthly goods cannot touch it. At a factual level, of course, sexual pleasure this intense is, of all the joys of life, the one that is not only most momentary, but most vulnerable to the vagaries of circumstance. Yet by asserting that this love flame is so hot that it cannot be quenched by all of the *meschefez on molde* (708), the *Cleanness*-poet transports his reader beyond logic and carries the transitory perfection of sexual consummation to the farthest metaphysical remove from death and suffering.

To Alain's Nature, such high-flying hyperbole — affirming consummate sexual pleasure as a spiritual force and preserving it in the pure bliss of a paradisal forever — would seem like the contagious nonsense of the poetry the narrator wrote in his dangerously love-crazed youth. Because it is not reasonable to talk about enjoying something beyond the bounds of reason, Nature maintains the supremacy of her moralizing logic. For her, the erotically charged impulse to convey the multiple aspects of love in a dazzling display of rhetorical colors is inseparable from moral turpitude and sexual deviation. Venus's overthrow of the strictly patriarchal sex/gender system of grammatical order produces bad art and evil morals; she simultaneously corrupts both the aesthetic and sexual principles upon which Nature's sense of the Good as the Beautiful depends.

When Venus subverts the male-dominant order, allowing males to forsake the anvils or sheets of parchment that Nature defines as their female counterpart, the product of their powerful hammers and pens is aesthetically diminished. What should be a work of refinement becomes boorish, and the noble art becomes a mechanized craft (163–64). The desire for same-sex love is thus traced by Alain to an archetypally feminine, and essentially immature, impulse for novelty. Gay eroticism is degraded as it is equated with a loss of aesthetic bearings that must occur whenever carefree pleasure is pursued apart from the rationality that should control the process of generativity in human discourse and intercourse in accord with natural principles. The implication is that the feminization effected upon males by homosexual acts degrades the natural beauty they once had; as in Venus's deviation from the standards of art that Nature taught her, their conversion of hammers into counterfeit anvils is an illegitimate, because unnatural, form of artifice.

For Alain, both male homosexual partners are degraded from their rational dignity as men, but differently: the "passive" partner because he is *physically* assuming the woman's role, the "active" partner because his rejection of the fitting female object for his aggressive sexuality constitutes the adoption of a *psychically* female role, which subverts rationality through a thirst for novelty, by substituting an ugly artifice for a legitimate art. This view depends on a hierarchical power dynamic which makes male choice of a male sexual object asymmetrically wrong for the two parties.[21] What is particularly striking is that Alain's polemic does not, as so many mythologies about male sexual roles do, regard the passive partner as more degraded than the active one. (Some such mythologies, indeed, including those of several modern subcultures, do not regard the active partner as having lost his male dignity and standing at all.)

By contrast to these gender dynamics in the *Complaint,* the *Cleanness*-poet attributes to the Sodomites, as I shall argue in chapter 6, not female passivity, but female appetite for male erotic partners in the play of love. God's version of normative male and female complementarity does not define the required sexual difference in a conventional dominant male, passive female hierarchy, as Nature's grammar and rhetoric so clearly do in Alain's *Complaint*. The sex difference essential to the Creator's design he articulates not in terms of active versus passive gender roles but of the creation of a mutual attraction between male and female in which "ayþer oþer welde" (exercise power/control over each other 705). *Cleanness* assumes that both male and female have erotic desires, and that through divine pedagogy, they are taught naturally to fulfill desire through intercourse with a partner of the other sex. In God's indictment of them, the Sodomites are guilty of an inexplicable failure to appreciate and collaborate with the Creator in using erotic desire, as God taught them, to make heterosexual love. It is in their discovery of the attractiveness of each other's maleness and their consequent preference for mating with each other sexually that they exert a perverse artistic autonomy, rather than—as in the *Complaint*—in their refusal to restrict their creativity to the disciplined phallic reproductive labors Nature assigns to masculine sexual energy. The *Cleanness*-poet's view of homosexual activity is no less homophobic than Alain's and possibly even more so; but the point is that it rests on a fundamentally different view of gender distinction and gender hierarchy.

Eros Vindicated?

Alain is recognized by many of his modern interpreters for his idealistic evaluation of the natural order and of culture as the perfection of nature. Such readings of Alain are important to this study because their analysis of Nature's sexual ethics diverges revealingly from the pervasive dualism I argue is central to the *Complaint*. John Boswell's and Winthrop Wetherbee's interpretations of the *Complaint* are of particular interest because, coming from different perspectives, they both focus on themes of gender and sexuality that make Alain's text a relevant literary precursor to *Cleanness*. Boswell sees Alain's idealism negatively as epitomizing late-twelfth-century Christianity's increasing intolerance of sexual nonconformity. For Boswell, the literary image of Nature as goddess, into which Alain incorporated his own and his society's heterosexist prejudices, provides a new and formidable authority for popular hostility toward men who desire other men sexually. Alain caters to an audience hungry both for authoritative confirmation of their intolerance of same-sex love and for a nonderogatory view of heterosexual pleasure missing in religious discourse. Boswell thus implies that a widely renowned clerical author wrote the *Complaint* from the deliberately nontheological perspective of Nature in order to confirm secular idealizations of love and to enforce an emerging view of homosexual conduct as the unnatural antithesis of the idealized erotic passion foremost "in the fantasies, if not the realities, of the heterosexual majority" (*Homosexuality* 310–12). Locating Alain intellectually amidst his Platonist contemporaries in the twelfth-century "renaissance," Wetherbee also interprets the *Complaint* as evocative of a paradisal world of eros fulfilled. His interpretation shows Alain participating in an emerging theological conception of God's restoration of fallen humanity as returning the redeemed to a renewed Edenic state, and so closely linking the *opus restaurationis* to the original work of creation. This perspective on the Fall theorizes the possibility of renewing the divine likeness and thus recovering the ideal relation between the sexes that was lost, according to Nature's account, when Venus's unlawful sexual passion disrupted the natural order. Even though Nature does not teach theological truth and has no glimpse of the renewal of human nature by a second birth, she participates herself dramatically in a theopoetic resolution to the depravity she laments throughout the *Complaint*.

Boswell's interpretation is suggestive for this study because he focuses on the literal significance of the *Complaint*'s vilification of men who engage in sexual relation with other men, and because he places the text socially in what he argues is a climate of increasing intolerance toward same-sex relations, expressed by a heterosexual majority seeking a moral legitimation of their own erotic passion. Since he presents this view of Alain only briefly and hypothetically in the course of a survey of a wide range of other authors, he supplies no textual evidence for it. My study of the *Complaint* finds little to support his hypothesis that Alain's Nature legitimates erotic passion and has an idealized view of heterosexual union akin to his literary contemporaries whose romances were whetting the aristocratic appetite for a secular sexual ethic. When Nature condemns homosexual deviance as a threat to her order, she does so within the conventional moral framework of sensuality threatening reason. Thus she reinforces the clerical distrust of all erotic passion, regardless of whether it is expressed in same-sex or heterosexual relations.

Yet Boswell's speculation that Alain catered to the hunger of a heterosexual majority looking for a more generous view of erotic passion than orthodox ethics provided provokes reflection on how remarkable this text is in its naturalization of marriage and its legitimation of virility employed on behalf of the succession of the paternal line. Although Nature does not legitimate eros, Alain uses what Boswell points out is her innovative moral authority to glorify man's procreative force as a good which is not undercut by the usual unflattering clerical comparisons to celibacy. Admittedly by this time the clergy, although required to be celibate, had idealized matrimony as an Edenic blessing not removed by Adam and Eve's sin. This notion, indeed, came to be incorporated in the marriage service itself. Yet clerical discourse still ranked marriage as a poor second best to celibacy; in a hierarchy of supernatural and natural ends, to take a wife served an aim much inferior to that imitation of Christ achieved through the grace of celibacy. In the solely natural order delineated by the sexual ethic of the *Complaint*, marriage is relieved of this inferior status.

When Nature warns the narrator about the inevitable tendencies of desire to overflow its boundaries, she is warning him to abstain from love — marriage is not at issue. When Hymen reappears at the end of the narrator's vision, he does so as the god of marriage, accompanied by the virtues personified as attractive young women named Chastity, Temperance, Humility, and Generosity. He wears a marvelous robe on which "tales, told in pictures, showed, as in a dream, the circumstances connected with marriage" (197). The narrator discerns in these images four values familiar from sermons on marriage: "faithfulness proceeding from the sacrament of matrimony, the peaceful unity of married life, the inseparable bond of marriage, the indissoluble union of the wedded parties" (197).[22] Yet the pictures of married bliss, though legible, have almost been "forced . . . to fade out" by the "black paint of age" (197), and if we think of Hymen as the husband from whom Venus defected in adultery, there is further irony in the positive vision of marriage projected on his robe. Forced by humankind's bestiality to return to his heavenly home, Hymen takes the virtues away with him. In deference to his somber state, the musicians who accompany this god of marriage (and would normally be playing sweet sounds of the kind the narrator reads about on the robe) have muted their instruments and instead of melody produce moans. But negative as all this is, one simple and strong impression that this scene and the rest of the *Complaint*'s formidably complex ending leaves us with is that there is nothing dirty, dangerous, or second class about being married. Rather, matrimony—or more accurately, patriarchal marriage—is an inherently valuable and even cosmically correct institution. When "hammers" are "dispossessed of fellowship with their [natural] anvils" (164) in coital union, the resulting sexual and social disorder is the archetypally evil negation of an absolute good symbolized by the nuptial union and the patriarchal succession of generations.

With Alain's celebration of the literal good of marriage in mind, let us consider an account of its allegorical meanings in the *Complaint*'s "dramatization of the psychological experience of fallen man" which Wetherbee sees giving rise to a concluding affirmation of man's redeemed "intellectual, moral, and sexual participation in the life of the cosmos" ("Function of Poetry" 125). The most powerful image of such a spiritual renewal occurs in the narrator's early expression of longing; he wishes that he might enjoy the kisses of maidens' spurned by their erstwhile lovers, who prefer homosexual liaisons instead (70–71). Wetherbee notes both the implied dignity of the narrator's heterosexual "desire for sexual fulfillment" and "the sense that a psychic and moral failure has rendered this area of experience inaccessible" (*Platonism and Poetry* 204–5). Nature's rebuke of the narrator-dreamer's erotic longing for renewal through a maiden's kiss "localizes the sexual, psychological and intellectual aspects of the problem in the dreamer's own mind and will" ("Function of Poetry" 104–5). By the end of the *Complaint,* man's sexual nature as it had existed before the Fall is imaginatively reconstructed in the appearance of Hymen and the virtues; this optimistic view of the restorative force of marriage becomes clear in the characterization of Genius as Nature's consort. Responding to Nature's appeal for help, Genius comes to share in judging all who violate her laws. In the final scene of the *Complaint,* he excommunicates all who are alienated from Nature's integrating power, but still more important to his priesthood is the cosmically creative role he plays as he administers the mystical union of form and matter. As Nature's Lover, he is "the bearer of the *calamus* whereby a formative pattern impresses itself in her pliant *subjecta materia*" ("Function of Poetry" 114). She calls him "her other self," describing herself as his "alter ego by the likeness of Nature that is reflected in you as a mirror" (206–7). On Genius's arrival, she offers "kisses not corrupted by the poison of lawless Venus, but symbolic of the caresses of epicene attraction and even indicative of harmony of mystic love" (219). He delights in the opportunity to share with Nature their mutual grief at the state of humankind, so that even though his mind "straitened by man's disgusting vices travels down to the hell of gloom and knows not the paradise of joy, yet the seedlings of delightful joy" send him their fragrance because he sees that Nature joins in "sighs of longing for due punishment" (219). Read typologically, this heartfelt reunion of Genius and Nature signifies for Wetherbee the renewal of divine likeness in the proper relations of male and female and the restoration of the original integrity of creation through grace. By an earlier kiss, they have generated Truth, a daughter who (along with Falsehood, of undisclosed parentage) accompanies Genius. Typologically, Genius's fruitful union with Nature is analogous to the wedding of soul and body accomplished in the creation of humanity. Whereas for Ziolkowski, the reunion suggests a domestic drama, with the male spouse bringing equilibrium to his distressed wife ("Genius, like a good husband, restores poise to Nature, who was in a tumult at the beginning of the work" 44), for Wetherbee, the encounter evokes more the erotic joy of courtship that leads to the bliss of the well-mated couple. Before Genius's "anathema of expulsion" ends the narrator's vision, he has witnessed the reunion which for Wetherbee provides a hopeful premonition of a romantically happy ending; here Genius reassumes true masculine authority, and Nature responds joyfully as a courtly lady would to her lover. With this "cosmic reestablishment of right relations between male and female, the poem reaches a tentative resolution" (*Platonism and Poetry* 204–5).

Alain associates Genius with two levels of creativity, drawing on Bernard Silvestris who first elevated the late classical figure of the god of generation into an allegorical figure of the mediating agency by which the ideas eternally present in divine mind become embodied ("Function of Poetry" 112). Thus the procreative urge in man that guarantees the succession of the species emulates the cosmic generation of form uniting with matter through the impress of divine rationality. This complex figure confers cosmic and even theological dignity on male sexual energy by representing it as inherently generative and expressive of the union of form and substance by which incarnation is achieved. This procreative virility symbolized by Genius is credited by Wetherbee with providing an image of life's renewing force in both the biological succession of the generations and in the ontological continuity between creation and redemption (*Platonism and Poetry* 209).[23]

In his profoundly creative capacity, Genius evokes for Wetherbee the possibility of masculine erotic longing brought into harmony with cosmic purpose. In this allegorical scheme, the procreative impulse is dictated by man's higher nature, even though the act of intercourse by its "sensual and mindless animality" threatens to undermine this upward thrusting dynamic. In Bernardus's treatment of Genius, Wetherbee sees "the power of the innate 'genial' impulse to fulfillment which somehow still survives" in man, directing his sexual desires into the channel of procreation that transmits human form from one generation to the next" ("Function of Poetry" 112–13). However, one must embrace Alain's clerical misogyny to see Genius as an effective figure of the vestiges of an original perfection in "human nature," evoking the possibility of a paradise regained through the restoration of priestly male authority, joyfully accepted by the otherwise distraught female. What Wetherbee describes as giving dignity to sexual energy really only dignifies the phallic as such, since the sexual urge directed toward the "channels of procreation that transmit human form from one generation to the next" which Genius symbolizes is exclusively male. When Wetherbee states that Genius is Alain's representation of "man's link with Paradise, the element in his nature which, albeit subliminally, recalls and seeks to regain his original perfection" (*Platonism and Poetry* 209), I infer that "man" means male impelled by procreative impulse to seek intercourse with a female. Here, as in the *Complaint* generally, the reproductive process is defined as immense phallic force applied to a female blank; the feminine is entirely defined by its availability to the male as a passive page upon which the potent masculine signifier inscribes meaning.

Within my hermeneutic of feminist suspicion of and resistance to patriarchal symbolic structures, there is still room for a sympathetic reading of masculinist and heterosexist erotic poetry, as is evident by the joy I feel when reading God's endorsement of the *play of paramorez* in *Cleanness* even when I recognize its homosocial context and its homophobic underpinnings. I do not respond with comparable enthusiasm to the reproduction of male power in Alain's *Complaint,* and I find the ending particularly problematic when reading Wetherbee's account. How does the coupling of Nature and Genius present even an incipient resolution to the conflict between the narrator's initial longing for sexual fulfillment through heterosexual desire and the problems of love Nature explains to him? Sensuality is erased from the union that Wetherbee interprets as Alain's poetic type of the *opus restaurationis* that returns fallen humanity through grace to the Edenic state ("Function of Poetry" 121, 125; *Platonism and Poetry* 208). The harmony of mystic love between Nature and Genius may have been an apt figure of spiritual truth born from the fruitful acts of marital intercourse that Alain envisioned as the natural fulfillment of man's sexual potency. Yet every trace of sensual desire appears to me to have been excised from the transcendentally chaste kisses of Nature and Genius, which express so epicene and mystical an attraction as to lack any relevance to humanity's bodily participation in the incarnating life processes of the cosmos. Neither physical passion nor phallic force have any place in so spiritualized an image of heterosexual union and generativity.

Although it never vindicates eros, Alain's text does contribute to what might be termed the mystique of heterosexism as cosmically ordained. The *Complaint* privileges patriarchal marriage in a wide variety of images and might inscribe on a receptive reader's imagination the importance of celebrating and admiring the sexual act through which the paternal lineage is transmitted. This persuasive effect, however, comes about in spite of, rather than because of, Nature's images for the conjoining of sexual difference required for the generation of offspring, for as I have noted, those are so exclusively oriented toward male phallic reproductive effort that the pleasures afforded to either male or female by coital union are extraneous to her principles. We have to look beyond the images of hammer and anvil, pen and parchment, and the trivium to see how this text newly privileges the idea of marriage per se, apart from the gratifying possibilities of erotic desire and fulfillment. One of the most persuasive of Alain's rhetorical strategies is Nature's symbolic contrast of the well-born father and son, on the one hand, and, on the other, the villainous fornicator and his bastard son. Yet the sexual desires of the former two are never mentioned, while the deceptive attractiveness of the other villains is blamed for the corruption of Venus and, through her, human society. Nature's class-specific appeal to family values is made in her most sensually poetic terms; she legitimates her aristocratic model of patriarchal marriage by metaphors that celebrate its Edenic quality. Cupid dwelling amidst shady glades and glittering fountains evokes the cool pleasures appropriate to rational sex performed with procreative intent; in contrast, the desolate attractions of Jocus lure illicit lovers beyond the pale of Cupid's *locus amoenus* into a wilderness fraught with images of sterility (165).[24]

In summary, while Alain shields the nuptial union from the usual aspersions cast by orthodox discourse focused on concupiscence, we have to ponder the cumulative effect of so many passionless images of coition. They leave me wondering if there were, as Milton later argued, legitimate reasons for divorce in a marriage like Venus's to Hymen, where intercourse seems more of a grinding necessity than a delight. The ever-powerful attraction of subversive patterns, both homoerotic and heterosexual, is the clearest subliminal message of this curious text. I shall consider further Alain's bizarre construction of what is unnatural about both homosexual deviance and heterosexual desire when I explore the ambiguities of nature as a sexual norm in the the *Complaint*'s enormously influential direct descendent, Jean de Meun's *Roman de la Rose*.

Nature, who gained popularity in Alain's twelfth-century literary work, was theologically developed in thirteenth-century scholastic discourse. Before placing *Cleanness* in the literary context of Jean's transformation of the *Complaint*, however, we need to see how between Alain and Jean a major change occurs in the ways the natural order was conceived of in relation to the heavenly. Diverging from the tradition of Jean and Alain, the *Cleanness*-poet provides an unequivocal religious affirmation of the goodness of heterosexual pleasure as a privileged part of God's design for his creatures. Such an affirmation is a landmark in medieval ethical thought, but it invites comparison to Thomas Aquinas's unusual openness to the natural pleasures inherent in bodily life in general and in sexual intercourse in particular.

4

The Sexual Ethics of Cleanness *and Thomas Aquinas on Temperance*

In my introductory comparison of the concepts of *clannesse* and of the honorable in Thomas's definition of temperance, I noted how similar, as well as how different, their optimistic approaches to the Good as the Beautiful are. Now I return to Thomas on temperance in order to use this reliably orthodox, systematically developed theological ethic of sexual activity to assess the heterodoxy of *Cleanness*-poet's praise of pleasure as part of the natural order that is clearly "desirable and just right" (2a2a. 145) from the Creator's point of view.

In his Aristotelian conception of the reasonable life as inseparable from the bodily life of feeling and sensation, Thomas approaches sexuality disposed to show its potential worth to the life of virtue. Explaining how temperance regulates the basic sensual gratification that sexual activity, as well as eating, provides, Thomas repeatedly ponders what nature can teach humankind about these "pleasures common to us and beasts" (2a2ae. 141, 7). Yet even as he thus admits our necessary and natural commonality with other creatures, Thomas acknowledges that honor and beauty are especially associated with temperance "less because of the excellence of its own goodness than because of the baseness of the evil it keeps us away from by ruling pleasures common to us and the beasts" (2a2ae. 141, 8). Temperance is said to be the most beautiful of the virtues because the potentially degrading pleasures of touch are precisely what it can refine and temper by reason (2a2ae. 145, 4). As a virtue, it is located in "motions far removed from reason," where it can protect us from enslavement by our animal appetite for pleasurable objects (2a2ae. 141, 7). While more generous toward the sensual appetites than are most ethical thinkers of his time, he is nevertheless predictably ambivalent about what he refers to as "the lower levels of human life, namely those of our animal nature" (2a2ae. 141, 2). Overall, however, Thomas seems remarkably less squeamish than we would expect of a thinker labeled the "angelic" doctor; as Thomas Gilby aptly comments, appetite is not per se evil or good for Thomas, and *sensualis* is not an ugly epithet.[1] On the one hand, he does occasionally disparage what we have in common with other creatures as a threat to our nobler nature of rational humanity, a threat especially presented by what are "most indecent and ugly in human beings, namely brutal pleasures" (2a2ae. 145, 4). Yet on the other hand, he acknowledges that the pleasures of touch are "profoundly natural to us."

Of course, it is because such pleasures are "highly needful for human life" that the desire for them is so hard to moderate. Nevertheless, however hard it is, moderation is not impossible, and the claim of temperance to be a cardinal or principal virtue rests on its enabling power, making reason "capable of swaying far-flung desires and pleasures" (2a2ae. 141, 7). We recall that Thomas defines temperance as a virtue that in its broadest sense shapes a wide range of actions into what "is received as desirable and just right" (2a2ae. 145, 2) through "a certain temper and control given by intelligence to human activities and feelings" (2a2ae. 141, 2). More specifically, it is the "pleasures of touch bound up with our physical preservation" (2a2ae. 141, 4–5) which temperance controls, and these are most especially the visceral pleasures experienced in "activities that preserve the individual, by eating and drinking, and the species, by the coupling of male and female" (2a2ae. 141, 4). Throughout Thomas's entire discussion of temperance shines an optimistic assumption that by means of attraction to the honorable and sensitivity to squalor—the two components of this virtue—a person's sensual appetite for pleasurable objects can be so ordered that its aim is rationally congruent with the needs of this life (2a2ae. 143, 1). Even the most powerful desires for pleasures of touch, those involving sexual appetite, can participate rationally in the order of nature, and not simply by restraint imposed by the will. Thomas declared at one point in his early writings that God "put delight in copulation" in order "to impel man to the act" (*On the Sentences,* quoted in Noonan, *Contraception* 354). Sexual desire is justified in the discussion of temperance as not only necessary for the natural preservation of the species but as itself "a seat of human virtue" (1a2ae. 56, 4).

The *Cleanness*-poet's ethic resembles this optimistic view of nature as a sexual norm which should be enjoyably fulfilled by human creatures as well as by the other animals. The poet's view that nature's law is generously disposed to the bodily pleasures, evident in several additions to both scriptural exempla illustrating *fylþe of þe flesch*, is most winsomely manifest in God's attention to the sexual satisfaction of the beasts aboard the ark during the Flood. He instructs Noah to mingle the males with their female counterparts, not only to preserve the procreative potential of each species, but to assure that each couple enjoys mutual pleasure of each other's company on the voyage:

> Of vche best þat berez lyf busk þe a cupple,
> . . . .
> For to saue me þe sede of alle ser kyndez.
> And ay þou meng with þe malez þe mete ho-bestez,
> Vche payre by payre to plese ayþer oþer. (*Cleanness* 333, 336–38)
> (Of each beast that bears life, prepare for yourselves a couple
> . . . .
> In order to save for me the seed of all different kinds;
> And always mingle the males with the fitting she-beasts —
> Each pair by pair, that either one may please the other.)

By this and still more explicit references to the natural order, the poet alludes to an ethical concept not found in his Old Testament sources. The ideal of natural law as a divinely ordained pattern manifest in the desire for heterosexual union is central to the poet's dramatization of God's wrath against *fylþe of þe flesch*. Thus, in its attacks on this form of defilement as peculiarly serious because contrary to *kynde*, and in its celebrations of the blamelessness of bliss to be enjoyed in intercourse practiced as a *kynde crafte*, this section of the poem invites further comparison to Thomas on temperance, and specifically to his naturalistic understanding of sexual virtue and vice.

We shall see how Thomas confronts directly the conventional moral judgment that intercourse, because of the intensity of the pleasures it affords, must inevitably be sinful. Arguing against this traditionally pessimistic assessment, he provides a cogent legitimation of the abundance of pleasure in a well-tempered sex act and even defends passion so intense that it must extinguish for a time the light of reason. Ultimately, the naturalistic logic by which Thomas legitimates too much of a good thing being sometimes just enough differs very significantly from the praise uttered for love's pleasures in *Cleanness*'s account of the *play of paramorez* the Creator himself portrays and teaches secretly as a *kynde crafte*. Of the various theologians who can provide an orthodox ethical framework within which to ponder *Cleanness*'s vision of heterosexual attraction as a sacred expression of God's own being in the created order, Thomas on temperance affords not only the most significant resemblances but, for that very reason, the most telling contrasts as well.

Temperance and Unnatural Lust

The bodily pleasures that temperance regulates are tied up with the preservation of our physical nature; because the appetites for food and sex have to do with survival, they are the strongest. Augustine stated that what food is to the individual's health, intercourse is to the species' health; yet his emphasis, like the other early church fathers, fell more on the "rectitude the procreative purpose conferred on the sexual act, rather than on the result achieved" (Noonan, *Contraception* 298). Thomas shifts the emphasis significantly, albeit slightly, toward the naturally positive value of the preservation of the species resulting from the exercise of these appetites for their natural ends. Augustinian pessimism sees an otherwise deadly sin excused when a married couple turn the subjectively selfish pleasures of intercourse into something good because done selflessly for the sake of raising Christian offspring. Thomas's somewhat more optimistic perspective legitimates the sexual appetite by emphasizing its natural end; since preserving one's own nature is self-evidently the aim of intercourse, both the intense pleasures and the reproductive consequences of the sexual act are rationally desirable.[2] Margaret Farley, in an apt characterization of Thomas's ethics, states that "the fundamental inclinations of persons provide the material content of natural law" (141).[3] That is to say, "through reason, the very being of a person breaks through at a conscious level and speaks to itself a moral imperative," so that the person is dynamically oriented toward his or her end, which is "what is pointed to by tendencies of the person's being" (140). This of course assumes that the desire for engendering offspring through heterosexual union is an essential aspect of every man's and woman's being.

Thomas's definition of natural law, based on the discussion of the third-century Roman jurist Ulpian, explicitly stipulates a procreative union as a natural norm common to all living beings, which is distinguishable from the range of laws humankind legislates to govern sexual relations in various societies. The generative principle that defines nature itself as a sexual norm observable in all animals makes it impossible to consider intercourse and insemination apart from its larger aim, which was assumed by Thomas (as by Ulpian) to include not only conception and birth, but also the care by parents who share the responsibility for nurturing their offspring (Boswell, *Homosexuality* 313).

We have seen Thomas use "animal nature" pejoratively; he obviously believes that behaving like animals can be unnatural for reasonable human beings. One example is his characterization of a particular mode of copulation as a sexual aberration in that it models human behavior on that of dogs; this mode of copulation violates the rational norm of the positions of man and woman in intercourse that Thomas considered "the fit way instituted by nature."[4] Clearly human reason must be called upon in deciding whether what animals do is a part of the natural order and hence binding upon humankind. In his naturalistic (but hardly exhaustive) observation of other creatures, for example, Thomas claims to have found evidence based on the mating patterns of birds that the matrimonial bond is a natural requirement for lawful human sexual relations:

> We observe in all animals where the bringing up of the young requires male and female that their mating is not promiscuous but of male with determinate female, one or several, as is the case with all birds. It is otherwise with animals where the female alone suffices to rear offspring, and intercourse is promiscuous, as with dogs and so forth. Now it is evident that the bringing up of a human child requires the care of a mother who nurses him, and much more the care of a father, under whose guidance and guardianship his earthly needs are supplied and his character developed. Therefore indiscriminate intercourse is against human nature. The union of one man with one woman is postulated. . . . Being committed to one woman is called matrimony, and is held to be of natural law. (2a2ae. 154, 2)

In a broad sense, then, sex in conformity to this concept of natural law based on idealized animal behavior requires not only a procreative union of male and female, but marriage. Yet even though fornication and adultery violate the marital norm of nature, Thomas makes a distinction between these sins and other forms of heterosexual lust which he categorizes as more gravely offensive because they are "sins against nature."

Thomas emphasizes this difference between forms of sexual activity he considers natural, since they involve insemination in the proper vessel and can therefore lead to conception, and the forms of sexual activity from which, because of the kind of acts they are, it is impossible that generation can follow. Not all natural sexual activity that fulfills the reproductive aim of intercourse is good, even though it is thereby natural. We recall that temperance is the virtue which orders appetites in accord with reason; obviously, reason may be at odds with sexual activity that conforms to the law of nature. In the broadest sense, every lustful act and indeed every sinful act is unnatural for human beings, since it violates the natural end of humanity, which is to live in accord with reason. Thomas considers a variety of ways in which lust may violate the good of people involved, and even be condemned as a "bestial" distortion of the reasonable order that temperance creates in human nature, and yet not be "unnatural" in a strict sense of that term.[5]

In his exposition of temperance, Thomas resembles the *Cleanness*-poet in singling out sexual sin that is contrary to nature as a uniquely serious moral offense, but he provides a clearer explanation of its peculiar threat to the created order, and in the process he defines unnatural sex-acts both more broadly and more precisely than does the poet. Unlike *Cleanness*'s gradual disclosure of what activities are signified by *fylþe of þe flesch*, the *Summa*'s definition of this special category of unnatural vice explicitly focuses on failure to ejaculate male seed correctly into the appropriate female vessel. For Thomas, this proper placement of semen is what is meant by the "coupling of male and female" which is the most fundamental law that "nature teaches to all the animals."[6] Before we look more closely at where homosexual intercourse ranks in the graded categories of the various sins of this unnatural form of lust, we should explore a bit further Thomas's emphasis upon the sacred "givenness" of the act of insemination which he regards to be self-evidently the natural purpose of sexuality (Noonan, *Contraception* 292).

Nature, and specifically its generative heterosexual norm, is revered by Thomas as an order even more valuable than the order created by human reason. He distinguishes the order shared by all animals as primary, in contrast to the secondary status of the order of conduct rational animals can construct upon this natural foundation. People use their reason to build moral codes on the patterns they see in nature; prior to this human activity are the underlying principles these patterns reveal. "The lines along which our minds work are those consonant with the nature of things; the fundamentals have been laid down for us by nature, we have to start with these, the presuppositions which our later development must respect. This is true in matters of both theory and practice" (2a2ae. 154, 12). In one sense, Thomas conceives of natural law as including the human love of God and neighbor, but these are obviously precepts that only rational beings can understand and act upon; hence matters of justice and honoring the rights of others in sexual activity belong to the order of reason, to be distinguished as secondary, in contrast to the primary givenness of the order of nature (Noonan, *Contraception* 291–92).

This basic natural foundation upon which human reason must operate is presumed by Thomas to be evident in the exclusively procreative, exclusively heterosexual activities of animals lacking reason. To deviate from that fundamental norm of nature which should govern sexuality contaminates the very source of truth in human conduct by corrupting the order providing the presuppositions upon which rational thought and action depend. "A mistake in our thinking about the inborn principles of knowledge goes to the very bottom, and so does a practise opposed to the pattern set for us by nature. Since then unnatural vice flouts nature by transgressing its basic principles of sexuality, it is in this matter the gravest of sins" (2a2ae. 154, 12).

Thomas's appeal to an order in nature prior to human laws, an order that provides the basis for human reason to arrive at ethical principles, resembles the picture in *Cleanness* of the idyllic life before the Flood when there was no law to be obeyed except "loke to kynde, / And kepe to hit, and alle hit cors clanly fulfylle" (observe nature, / And hold to it, and wholly fulfill all its course 263–64). Noah is praised by God as having reigned in reason, in contrast to those who behave foolishly. In the evil times that the poet portrays as leading up to the Flood, homosexual practices do irrevocable violence to that physical and social harmony which the Creator intended. The pattern nature should provide for human fulfillment is corrupted, and there arises instead a political travesty where order is based on might rather than right.

The clear contrast Thomas constructs between unnatural lust and other forms of lust makes sins violating nature archetypally evil; as in *Cleanness*, such evil threatens all the reasonable orders of life humans should create in their moral and political conduct. Yet unlike the poet, Thomas does not explicitly cite unnatural sexual relations as the cause of God's vengeance against a dissolute world in the Flood; nor does he portray the particular sin of same-sex intercourse as the most gravely offensive of all the mortal sins, or even as the absolutely worst form of unnatural lust, a superlative degree of distinction he awards to intercourse with other animals. What is even more crucially different is that *Cleanness* makes no explicit allusion to the generative principle of nature which is central to Thomas's definition of unnatural lust; moreover, instead of defining *fylþe of þe flesch*, the poet simply exemplifies it, first in the story of the evils that brought on the Flood, and then more concretely in the story of the Sodomites' homosexual unions.

Thomas's analysis of unnatural lust as a peculiarly dangerous form of intemperance thus differs from the poet's attack on *fylþe of þe flesch* by being both more theoretically unified and more specifically diverse. Earlier in the *Summa* Thomas states that "nature of man" may be spoken of as "that which is common to man and other animals, according to which certain particular sins are said to be against nature, as intercourse between males (which is specifically called *the* vice against nature) is contrary to the union of males and females natural to all animals" (1a2ae. 94, 3).[7] That passage is echoed by the poet's emphasis on same-sex union of males as the sin which epitomizes unnatural practices. In the context of temperance, however, Thomas does not lay such singular stress on same-sex unions between males but enumerates this, along with same-sex union among females, as one of several other sorts of sins against nature. Thomas includes in the category of unnatural lust diverse activities that do not, from a modern ethical perspective, logically pose a common threat to a fundamental standard of human value. Yet from Thomas's point of view, they can be perceived as sharing a family resemblance insofar as they all exhibit an "especial ugliness making sex-activity indecent" (2a2ae. 154, 11).

The critical variable uniting all types of unnatural lust is that they are "in conflict with the natural pattern of sexuality for the benefit of the species" (2a2ae. 154, 11). Thomas enumerates four kinds of deviant sexual behavior, ranking them from the most to least grave (2a2ae. 154, 12): bestiality, sodomy (defined as intercourse between males or between females),[8] and two forms of violation of the due mode of intercourse, either, more seriously, by depositing the seed outside the female vessel or by improper positioning. Thomas is cited along with Albertus by several authorities in support of the view that deviations from normal positions are sometimes acceptable in excusing conditions, so long as the organs are properly joined; indeed, if it is only the position that is in question, and no other way is possible, what might be unnatural in one situation could be without sin in another (Tentler 192–94). As stated in the *Summa*'s discourse on temperance, however, Thomas's judgment that the wrong position is a form of unnatural lust is unqualified by exceptions; in any case, his contention that the positions assumed by a couple in intercourse constitute a moral issue of enormous gravity must have contributed to the ongoing clerical "distrust if not downright condemnation" of any mode outside of the missionary position when undertaken to increase pleasure (Tentler 192).[9]

While doubtless aware of this aspect of orthodox ethical teaching, the *Cleanness*-poet exhibits no concern over sexual practices of a man with his (female) mate that the church condemns as contrary to nature. Where Artesanus (an early fourteenth-century writer of a manual for confessors) claims that when the woman is on top, "the intention of nature is totally frustrated" and goes on to cite both Pseudo-Methodius and Peter Comestor as enumerating that sin as "among the causes of the Flood," the poet gives no indication at all that this is one of the acts against nature that the antediluvians practiced upon each other (Tentler 191–92). Instead, *Cleanness* resembles other passages from Pseudo-Methodius and Peter Comestor where the blame for the Flood is placed solely on men who came together homosexually (Twomey 205–8). In the description of *kynde crafte* the poet attributes to the Creator, any conventional stigma of unnatural lust is removed from the playful urges of lovers to do something for the sake of increasing pleasure. Heterosexual intercourse is commended when it is made in a manner merriest of any other, merriest not because it creates offspring (which it might or might not — proper insemination never is suggested as a criterion for proper play) but because the couple experience the most intense pleasure known outside of paradise.

By ignoring unnatural sins of lust men and women might commit with each other, the poet's warnings against *fylþe of þe flesch* underscore his bold legitimation of heterosexual pleasure in God's speech about *kynde crafte*. Yet this generosity toward heterosexual pleasure, however subversive of the church's norms, is the basis for the revulsion God expresses toward same-sex eroticism. Nature divinely ordered offers paradisal bliss in the *play of paramorez,* but when men like the Sodomites take delight in coupling with other males, divine inclusiveness is transformed into a fatality vastly broader than the extent of the offense which incites apocalyptic vengeance. The massive destruction of the cities of the plain and life in the surrounding landscape is the prototype of what, borrowing Louis Crompton's term, we might refer to as *gay genocide* (Sedgwick, 128). Eve Sedgwick describes "the array of sanctioned fatalities" in Sodom as part of "a fantasy trajectory, utopian in its own terms, toward gay genocide [that] has been endemic in Western culture . . . not clearly distinguishable from a broader trajectory toward something approaching omnicide" (128).[10] To grasp the ostensible logic of so thoroughgoing a rejection of same-sex love, we are looking at the poet's dramatization of God's homophobic wrath in the context of Thomas's influential rationale for condemning homosexual relations, along with other unnatural acts, as a singularly grave offense against the self, nature, and the Creator.

There is a startling objectivity to the logic by which Thomas perceives the sexually generative order of nature to be humanity's most definitive bond to the world of which it is a part. This can be seen in his claim that, along with marital intercourse carried out in unusual positions, masturbation is worse than fornication or adultery or even incest.[11] Extending the objection Thomas raises to his own claim that any form of unnatural vice is worse than lust which does not violate nature, we might ask why "self-abuse" which injures no one else should be condemned as morally worse than procreative intercourse which wrongs the child born out of marriage or than incest which defiles someone "to whom we owe love"? Thomas's answer is that an "individual within a nature is more bound to that nature than to any other individual of that nature; therefore, so much the worse are the sins committed against it" (2a2ae. 154, 12). Some forms of lechery do harm to others and transgress the rules adopted by right reason but are nevertheless less serious than masturbation because they do not flout what is for Thomas the most basic principle of nature, the generative aim of sexuality.

In *Cleanness* there are passages similar to Thomas's construction of an individual's bonds to an objective order that determines his (or her — although the poet exclusively, and Thomas mainly, addresses male homosexual conduct) own most fundamental identity. *Fylþe of þe flesch* is condemned by the poet not only as scorning of nature (709) but as dishonorable harlotry because it is scorning oneself (*harlottrye vnhonest, heþyng of seluen,* 579). But as we shall see, the concepts of both nature and self that homosexual desire threatens are inseparable from the awareness of the Creator's bond to the human subject's sexual inclinations. The nature to which humanity is bound is less objectively portrayed in *Cleanness* because the poet is not working, as Thomas does, with two levels of causality, the natural and the supernatural. In the *Summa*'s ethical system, natural virtue does not require any revealed knowledge of God acting in history, but only the use of reason in reflecting on nature as divinely ordered for the common good, which is the conservation of the species.

Nevertheless, Thomas's definition of unnatural lust as a particularly grave form of intemperance includes many references to God's will revealed in biblical history, including a claim about God's wrath against the Sodomites that bears striking resemblance to *Cleanness*. Because the order of nature is directly from God, while the order of reason is from humankind, Thomas argues that even lust that abuses what is for God's worship is not as serious an act of dishonor to God as lust that violates nature. This startling judgment that sacrilege is less offensive to God than is homosexual behavior, or even masturbation, is based on the fundamental premise that "the order of nature is more basic and stable than the order of reason we build upon it" (2a2ae. 154, 12). For Thomas, the givenness of the generative order of sexual reproduction in the natural world reflects the Creator's nature more directly than what men make and do in the sacerdotal rituals that exalt his honor. God is more intimately associated with the physical creation than with the order of his worship. As Noonan observes, "in Thomas' mind the gravity of sexual offenses depends on the injury to the welfare of the species, and the person who is specifically offended is God," who is for Thomas (as for Augustine, whom he quotes here) "the principal master of our body" (*Contraception* 297).[12] All illicit forms of pleasure wrong the temple of God — which is what the Christian's body is, or at least is becoming; however, to defile nature in sexual usages contrary to its procreative principles is to contaminate the basic pattern upon which human minds must work in order to arrive at moral truth, and even more seriously, to do graver injury to God himself than if a church or holy vessels had been desecrated by an act of lust from which generation could take place. The Creator has a personal stake in the bodies of his creatures and therefore in the right uses of the seeds of the species he formed: "The developed plan of living according to reason comes from man; the plan of nature comes from God, and therefore a violation of this plan, as by unnatural sins, is an affront to God, the ordainer of nature" (2a2ae. 154, 12).

Thomas's vision of the supreme importance the Creator of the universe places on how males deposit their sperm in the fitting vessel and of how he is personally offended when their use of each other sexually violates this pattern he ordains in nature resembles the *Cleanness*-poet's portrait of the intimate identification God makes personally with his design for human sexuality, and his consequent vulnerability to its misuse in men's homosexual practices contrary to nature: "Felle temptande tene towched his hert. / As wyȝe wo hym withinne werp to hymseluen" (Cruel tempting anger touched his heart. / Like a person inwardly anguished, he spoke to himself 283–84). Of course, Thomas's mode of scholastic argument differs from the poet's dramatic insistence on the anthropomorphism of God's vulnerability to passion. With regard to anger, Thomas clearly asserts that God is passionless because he "judges with tranquillity."[13] Yet Thomas supports his conclusions on unnatural lust as directly and uniquely damaging to the Creator by appealing to Augustine, who argues that the sins of Sodom are universally detestable and gives as evidence the defilement of the divine-human bond by men's sexual abuse of one another. Augustine writes: "These foul offenses against nature should be detested and punished everywhere at all times, such as were those of the people of Sodom, which, should all nations commit, then would all stand guilty of the same crime by God's law, which has not made men that they should so abuse one another. For then the very intercourse [*societas*] which should be between God and us is violated when that same nature, of which is he the author, is polluted by the perversity of lust" (2a2ae. 154, 12; citing Augustine's *Confessions* III, 8). Here is an idea of nature that resembles the *Cleanness*-poet's vision of its importance as the medium for divine-human intimacy; this intercourse (*societas*) or intersubjective unity is disrupted whenever the order God designs for lovemaking is polluted by men who abuse each other by the same homosexual practices that brought divine judgment upon Sodom.

Despite fundamental differences in their definitions of what is natural, the poet would have found appealing and may have been influenced by several of Thomas's rationalizations for homophobic rage. What could the poet have found in the *Summa* on temperance that might support *Cleanness*'s unusual affirmation of sexual pleasure?

Pleasure within the Bounds of Temperance

Thomas unequivocally legitimates the intensity of sexual pleasure within a virtuous life of well-tempered sensuality. Like the poet of *Cleanness*, he imagines the sexual appetite to be educable, and not by a pedagogy stressing the intellect or will. They both avoid a model of virtuous sexuality where the higher faculties are expected, however inadequate to the task, to arrest the natural momentum of the passions or diminish the intensity of pleasure toward which the bodies' energies drive. Intercourse is clearly, for Thomas, one of the occasions where the "civilly governed" appetite must be given its own motions by which it can suspend rational activity. It is fascinating that Thomas praises temperance as a virtue which works from within the desires for bodily pleasure, so that sexual appetite is rationally governed with a civil rather than a despotic control, "as free men are ruled who have in some matters a will of their own" (1a2ae. 56, 4). The appetites are not strictly subjected to a traditional model of soul-body, male-female hierarchic dualism, where their movement is wholly subordinated to reason's initiative. The desires for bodily pleasures are not to be ruled as the soul rules the body, with their entire movement attributed to reason; rather, in Thomas's Aristotelian analogy to the body politic, justice requires that "they have their own proper movements, by which at times, they go against reason" (1a2ae. 56, 4).

It is striking that for Thomas, not only is pleasure a good, but being overwhelmed by sensual passion is not always an evil; at times it is wholly fitting that the vision of intellect be obscured by the intensity of the sensory appetite. Thus he observes, "the abundance of pleasure in a well-ordered sex-act is not inimical to right reason" even though "the reason's free attention to spiritual things cannot be simultaneous with pleasure." There is nothing contrary to virtue when reason thus suspends its activity according to right reason; otherwise (and here we see the engaging pragmatism of the angelic doctor) "it would be against virtue to go to sleep" (2a2ae. 153, 2).

While temperance has, in all its forms, to do with "arresting and repressing the rush of passion" (2a2ae. 161, 4), being taken over by passion is sometimes precisely what moderation calls for, since "the virtuous mean lies in agreement with right reason, not the amount of material" (2a2ae. 153, 2). Classifying anger as one of the operations of concupiscence regulated by temperance, Thomas argues that while "it may somewhat clog [reason's] performance," spontaneous anger does not necessarily impede right relations; instead, too much rational reflection is as problematic as too little: "The intermission of conscious deliberation in well-advised activity does not militate against its quality of virtue; over-deliberateness can hold us up when we should be getting on with the job" (2a2ae. 158, 1).[14] Furthermore: "The passion of anger, like other motions of the sensory appetite, is useful in helping the prompt execution of the dictate of reason. Otherwise for a man to have a sensory appetite would be pointless. In fact, however, nature does nothing groundless" (2a2ae. 158, 8).

This principle of emotional spontaneity in the life of temperance is maintained in Thomas's surprising affirmation of sexual pleasure. In direct opposition to traditional Christian ethics, he maintains that despite the uncontrollable nature of sexual passion, the intense pleasures of sexual intercourse can be enjoyed without sinning. For Thomas, what is reasonable in regard to sexual appetite may *look* excessive, either positively or — in the case of virginity — negatively.[15] The moderation of sexual pleasure (like all other pleasure) is to be achieved by adherence to the central identity and purpose of an act: "We have already said that the virtuous mean lies in agreement with right reason, not in the amount of the material. Consequently the abundance of pleasure in a well-ordered sex act is not inimical to right reason" (2a2ae. 153, 2). Too little is as much a vice as too much — and we have seen in the first chapter's discussion of temperance and its parts how Thomas makes some striking criticisms of deficiencies of various sorts. With regard to sex, the extreme opposite to lasciviousness he names as the vice of "unfeelingness . . . found in those who so dislike intimacy with women as not even to be fair to their wives." (He observes that we do not frequently encounter this vice since "most of us are very prone to pleasure" [2a2ae. 153, 3].)

While Thomas's affirmation of the value of sexual pleasure is in a very different mode of discourse from the *Cleanness*-poet's lyrical praise of *kynde crafte*, they are similarly optimistic about the possibilities of ordering earthly life, including its sensual delights, in accord with the Creator's own perfection. And they both envision that perfection in terms of the Good known and enjoyed as the Beautiful. The poet seems to adhere to Thomas's idea that according to its mode of creation, each aspect of being participates in the Creator's own perfection; natural and spiritual beauty are thus complementary and analogous. Such complementarity is fundamental to the ethics of *Cleanness* and stands in sharp contrast to the pessimistic dualism generally evident in moral discourse of the period. This pessimism is concisely articulated by his contemporary John Gower's condemnation of sumptuous fare, fashionable dress, and pleasures of the bed he associates with feasting and its aftermath. In *Vox Clamantis*, he observes of the prelates who sponsor such occasions: "If they please the world and furnish things according to the flesh . . . the virtue of the soul will rarely be pleasing" (Gower 119). Within a more affirmative Christian ethics, virtue — whether it is temperance for Thomas or *clannesse* for the poet — does not have to be alienated by sensual desires for pleasures of touch and their associated refinements, but can instead make these desires harmonious with divine order displayed both in heaven and on earth.

We can see the optimism of Thomas's naturalistic ethic even more clearly by contrasting its assumptions about the nature of God to a fourteenth-century nominalist's denial of an inherent and absolute order among secondary causes. William of Occam's affirmation of God's absolute power makes the idea of natural order extraneous to ethics. Instead of reason participating in feeling, tempering and refining the appetite in accord with a sense of honor, the will alone is stressed by Occam as the determinative variable in good and bad acts. Rather than a natural process of the self developing its potential, executing every action with an intelligent and aesthetic regard for the context, immediate consequences, and ultimate end, the good life was seen by Occam as one of sheer obedience to God's divinely revealed will. The affirmation of God's absolute power meant that within the present dispensation, he has ordained certain acts as good; he could, because he is utterly unconstrained by anything except his own nature, decree differently, so that acts which are now good or bad need not have been so ordained and their opposites might have been required or forbidden instead. The question of what God's nature ("potentia absoluta") is as distinct from his explicitly expressed will ("potentia ordinata") is beyond human knowing (see Oberman).

By these contrasts, we can better appreciate the lofty rationalism of Thomas's location of temperance in the sensible appetite rather than the will, and the generosity of his comparison of the concupiscible powers to instruments well fitted for the action which reason, as a skilled craftsman, shapes. The habitual conformity of the sensible appetite to reason is distinguished by Thomas from the checking of passion through volitional choices. Control through conscious will power he defines as continence, one of the secondary parts of temperance; it stands in relation to the cardinal virtue as the unripe does to the fully mature (2a2ae. 155, 4). The superiority of temperance lies in its reaching past the will to the emotions where it brings what is potentially unruly into participation with reason itself. Thus, "its very name tells of the refining and tempering of base desires by reason" (2a2ae. 145, 4).

Procreative End versus Present Bliss: Insemination and Orgasm as Theological Rationales

The poet's approach differs importantly from Thomas's understanding of nature as a realm of secondary causality, and from the consequent emphasis on procreation for the good of the species as the rationally justifying aim of heterosexual pleasure. It should be noted, however, that *Cleanness* witnesses to the importance of childbearing in the providential acts of God in history, not only in the birth of Jesus but in the foreshadowing of that miracle in the covenant with Abraham and the reminder that Sarah, though barren, would yet bear the promised son. Moreover, the blessing and promises God gives to the human survivors of the Flood explicitly link the restored and enduring order of the cleansed creation to the sexual reproduction necessary to replenish the earth.

> "Bot waxez now and wendez forth and worþez to monye,
> Multyplyez on þis molde, and menske yow bytyde.
> Sesounez schal yow neuer sese of sede ne of heruest,
> Ne hete, ne no harde forst, vmbre ne droȝþe,
> Ne þe swetnesse of somer, ne þe sadde wynter,
> Ne þe nyȝt, ne þe day, ne þe newe ȝerez,
> Bot euer renne restlez: rengnez ȝe þerinne." (521–27)
> ("But increase now and go forth and become many
> Multiply on this earth, and may honor befall you.
> Seasons shall never cease for you, of seed nor of harvest,
> Nor heat nor hard frost, shade nor drought,
> Nor summer's sweetness nor the painful winter,
> Nor the night, nor the day, nor the new years
> But ever [they shall] run without rest — reign ye therein.")

This passage is the closest the poet comes to stating that human love made in accord with nature must conform, in its potential for procreation, to the divine mandate given to humankind in Eden to increase and multiply. Procreation, essential to Thomas, is altogether, and astonishingly, absent from the poet's later definition of *kynde craft* the Creator teaches to lovers. Not reproduction but the present joys of the man and *his make* united sexually is the aspect of the natural order he believes God holds peculiarly valuable.

For Thomas, while intense pleasure is naturally fulfilling and permissible, what God holds sacred about heterosexual intercourse is what nature teaches all animals, namely the generative act of insemination and its procreative results. Thomas contrasts the exclusive interest animals have in pleasures of touch with humankind's more refined appreciation of sight and sound.[16] The human propensity for detaching the basic pleasures of touch from the other sensual pleasures surrounding it is problematic for Thomas; exploring his distrust of artifice will further clarify the contrast between his affirmative ethic and the *Cleanness*-poet's. The human capacity for refinement can become the occasion for ingenious cultural overlays that are aimed not at achieving the procreative and therefore "natural" aim of the sexual appetite, but at turning the attendant pleasures of sensuality into an end in themselves. Thomas observes: "As for the specific things that nature requires, the natural desires themselves are no great cause of sin. . . . The main trouble arises from the incentives to concupiscence contrived by human ingenuity, for instance oversophisticated dishes and women's fashions" (2a2ae. 142, 2). Here are clear echoes of the traditional clerical suspicion of courtly artifice; however, we should note that Thomas is condemning excesses of refinement and not fashion as such. This attitude toward excess is also discernible in *Cleanness*, when the poet satirizes the newest styles in clothing displayed by Belshazzar's concubines and mocks the ornate presentations of food at his feast.[17] The contrast between the poet's and Thomas's attitudes toward gratuitous cultural inventions creating style should not be exaggerated. As we have seen, Thomas includes in his analysis of the operations of temperance many goods which, though not inconsistent with physical preservation of life, are not strictly necessary to it. When he takes up the question of women's attention to fashion in the context of modesty, he concludes that they may "lawfully adorn themselves, whether to maintain the amenities of their station or to please their men by gilding the lily" (2a2ae. 169, 2). Similarly, he states that women are permitted well-styled adornment in order to please their husbands (thus keeping them from the occasion of sinning with other women), and even cosmetics may be called for (2a2ae. 169, 2).[18]

Yet, keeping in mind the similarity between the poet's and Thomas's affirmations of the importance of honorable physical appearances (see chapter 1), we should also consider their fundamentally differing attitudes toward the creativity that transforms animal sexual rhythms into the conscious dance of human eros. By adopting the language of courtly romance for God's praise of love as a *kynde crafte*, the poet choreographs sexual attraction into a sustained work of art, where the lovers are creating an erotically charged form of life as well as a climactic moment of deliberate intensity. For Thomas, such willed pleasure — even in a heterosexual act of intercourse which fulfills the generative order of nature — is antithetical to the beauty of temperance, where the rational aim controlling the appetite is never focused on pleasure as an end in itself. Although the sensual ecstasy of intercourse may fittingly suspend reason temporarily, the appetite for pleasure must ultimately be so ordered by temperance that all enjoyment is rationally congruent with the needs of this life. The game and play of love is not, for Thomas, one of life's necessities; hence his condemnation of what he considered the unnatural manner of intercourse, novel positions adopted in order to intensify pleasure.

Another way of grasping the fundamental difference between Thomas's and the poet's generosity toward sexual pleasure focuses on their respective uses of natural law in a teleological mode of ethical thought. John Noonan's analysis of Thomas's rehabilitation of pleasure as a positive value is instructive in this regard. His early commentary *On the Sentences* was influenced by Aristotle's analysis of pleasure in the *Nichomachean Ethics*. Thomas echoed Aristotle in saying "Delight is the perfection of operation" and represented pleasure as the subjective sense accompanying performance of acts. A pleasure is good or bad depending on whether it accompanies a good or bad act, and since marital intercourse is good, so is the pleasure experienced in it (*Contraception* 354).[19] In *On the Sentences*, Thomas goes beyond Aristotelian principles in stating that God "put delight in copulation" to give incentive to perform this act for the good of the species. We might well ask, as Noonan does, "If pleasure was good, if sexual pleasure in particular was good, why was it not lawful to seek such pleasure? Why was it, according to Thomas, at least venial sin to seek pleasure" (*Contraception* 354)?

For Thomas to recognize pleasure as sometimes itself a need was apparently not possible with his logical framework. The idea of undertaking an activity for the sake of pleasure departs from the Aristotelian principle that pleasure itself is always attendant upon some act. The closest Aristotle comes to questioning whether pleasure might not itself sometimes be a necessity is with respect to amusement, which Thomas (in commenting on the *Nichomachean Ethics*, 10.9) translated as *ludus* or game and noted that "a game or rest is not the end, because rest is for operation, so that a man after it may work more vigorously" (Noonan, *Contraception* 355).

In his analysis of temperance in the *Summa*, Thomas transfers this idea to the subject of delightful things which can be sought for the sake of health or for the sake of a sound condition of the body. But he holds to the Aristotelian principle that one acts virtuously toward a worthy—that is, a rational—end, and the pleasure follows. Although the temperate person will experience pleasure while pursuing the necessities of his or her nature, he or she will not make pleasure a goal. Thomas could not logically endorse the poet's legitimation of *drwry* (the French loan word for courtly erotic play that God himself claims to have put into the *play of paramorez*); the closest concession in the *Summa* to such gratuitous embellishments of natural urges comes in the account of playfulness as a human impulse controlled by temperance. Arguing that too little play is a vice, Thomas maintains that "those who lack playfulness are sinful, those who never say anything to make you smile, or are grumpy with those who do" (2a2ae. 168, 4). Playful words and deeds afford recreation for the person who, intent on the works of reason, inevitably wears himself (and here the pronoun is clearly gender-specific) out psychologically as well as physically by pushing beyond "the attractive objects of sense." But Thomas could not logically extend this idea of playfulness as healthful relaxation for men of intellectual habits to the enjoyments sought in loveplay.

Similarly, he does not extend to pleasure per se the value that he acknowledges some delightful things have for the temperate person, even though they are not enjoyed simply for the sake of physical or psychological health.

Temperance governs "needs" that "go beyond purely physical requirements and extend to the befitting ownership of external things, thus wealth and a dignified profession and, what is more important, the right to be honoured and respected." Thomas supports this idea with Aristotle's view that the "objects which a temperate man takes pleasure in are not confined to those not inconsistent with a healthy and well-adjusted personality but cover as well those not beyond good, that is the decencies, or our substance, that is our means" (2a2ae. 141, 6). Nothing resembling the *play of paramorez* is included in the amenities and decencies of human living that temperance governs. To have recognized the recreative value of sexual play, or to have acknowledged the intrinsic value of pleasure per se, would have imperiled Thomas's requirement of a procreative purpose for rationally tempered sexual activity, as well as his assumption that any lawful sexual act had to be potentially procreative (Noonan, *Contraception* 355).

While God is intimately affected by human sexual violations of the created order in Thomas's theology, his sexual ethic always distances Creator from creatures in distinguishing primary from secondary causality. The latter, the realm of nature, can be known through reason, apart from any intimate disclosure of the Creator. God is not personally invested in teaching the art of love and has no stake in the quantity or quality of pleasure experienced by human creatures conforming to the natural order, except (and this early statement drops out of the sexual ethics of the *Summa*) as an inducement to performing the act whereby the species is reproduced.

Moreover, the self is distanced from its own desires through emphasis on the natural aim of reproduction, even though pleasure is necessarily instrumental to this goal. Natural order as the norm for virtuous sexual activity is extrinsic to the sensually desiring self, despite Thomas's distinction between continence (which is the will constraining the appetite) and temperance (which is a virtue located in the appetite itself). Learning about and attaining virtue is a rational activity; although based on the senses, it requires intellectual abstraction from bodily experience to arrive at conceptual clarity about pleasure as a means to a rationally desirable end. It is this biological end which presents itself as fitting, just right, appealing to the sense of *honeste* which is the component of temperance as a virtue controlling the otherwise unruly appetites from within.

In contrast to Thomas's natural law theory, the poet anticipates modern preconceptions of natural law in terms of an "ideal personal community."[20] The poet orients his readers toward such a community in the reciprocity he envisions as the divine teacher educates *a male and his make* in the space of a romantic tryst. As they open themselves to a sensual experience of mutual creativity, the Creator takes a proprietary delight in the mirth that comes when the flame of love blazes between them.

While Thomas does argue occasionally from biblical history — such as in his use of Augustine's reflections on the story of Sodom — natural virtue does not require any revealed knowledge of God acting in history, but only the use of reason in reflecting on nature as divinely ordered. Thus the *Summa*'s arguments about unnatural sexual relations are abstract, representing the sexual norm as an extrinsic and static law of nature. In contrast, this section of *Cleanness* teaches its readers to empathize with God's point of view. What he feels and how he acts in response to the historical violations of the natural order with which he is so intimately identified must be grasped affectively in order to live in accord with his creative sensibility. The response the poet depicts in his stories of God's wrath is, therefore, daringly different from traditional religious discourse; this drastic representation of the radical immediacy of the Creator's collaboration with *a male and his make* is really quite remarkable.

Though ostensibly writing in a homiletic mode and depending entirely on scriptural authority, the poet has fictionalized his sources to create an original theopoetic vision of sexual ethics. Unlike Thomas and also unlike the preachers whose rhetorical persona he borrows in the commentary that links his biblical narratives into a quasi-homiletic whole, this author is not concerned to clarify moral specifics, but to evoke contrasts between two ways of life, each portrayed as an all-encompassing ethos. The contrasting forms of sexual conduct he represents as conforming to, or deviating from, nature. Each expresses a different orientation to the order of the creation and its Maker: one participates in the cleanness the poem celebrates, the other pollutes and even threatens to obliterate the divine splendor.

Thus we understand his bold exercising of imaginative freedom in leaving unstated what was usually the most important definitive element between right and wrong, natural and unnatural, forms of sexual relating: procreation. Instead of focusing on reproduction, his praise of paradisal pleasure thematizes "alle þe blysse boute blame þat bodi myȝt haue" (all the bliss without blame that anybody might have 260) as a manifestation of the divinely created, aesthetically ordered, mutuality he calls *clannesse*. God's immediacy in devising and teaching his plan to the lovers relocates nature as the sexual norm in the sensual sphere of pleasurable interaction leading to orgasmic consummation, not insemination for the sake of future reproduction of the species. In this context, *fylþe of þe flesch* seems to be a foil against which the poet can legitimate pleasure, transmitting in religious narrative the romance ethos of sexual bliss. Since *Cleanness* provides no explicit reference to the necessity for justifying sexual pleasure by the reproductive aim, there is no logical requirement of sexual difference within this *play of paramorez*. The premise, however, is that only a male and his female mate can practice the play of paramours; "the maner myriest of [any] oþer" (701) is designed by God exclusively for heterosexual partners. For males to find a way in their own flesh to achieve this sexual interaction in *femmalez wyse* is, from the perspective of the Creator, not so much an insult to their masculinity as a scornful slur on his aesthetic masterpiece. Why this should be so raises a major question central to my study. Can a poet capable of such an extraordinary breakthrough about the legitimacy of pleasure in one kind of gratuitous sexual activity not see that it applies equally to the other? And why is he not only unable to see it but actually seems to need the rejection of the other in order to achieve the breakthrough on the first — so that the homophobia whose very basis he has just exploded seems necessary to the dynamic of his affirmation of heterosexual pleasures.

This issue will be probed as we explore further the originality of the poet's literary methods and ethical and theological vision of sexual deviance and desire within a context afforded by the *Roman de la Rose*. Reading the poem's representations of sexual deviance and desire as a continuation of the literary dialogue begun by Jean de Meun's revision of Alain de Lille's portrayal of Nature will further illumine the religious significance of the medieval romantic idioms considered here.

5

Revising the Complaint:
Desire in the Roman *as Context for* Cleanness

The poet's unique allusion to Jean de Meun and the thematic relevance of his continuation of the *Roman de la Rose* to *Cleanness*'s concerns about the role of sexuality in the good life compel us to look at Jean's text as central to the fourteenth-century poet's literary tradition. The reasons to read *Cleanness* in the context of the *Roman* are at once more evident and more elusive than the reasons to relate *Cleanness* to Alain's *Complaint*. The most evident reason is that in *Cleanness*, and indeed in the entire corpus of works closely associated with it, the *Roman* is the only nonbiblical text to which the poet explicitly alludes. The more general reason is the pervasive influence exercised by this extraordinarily popular text's range of perspectives on desire and, specifically, its radical revision of Alain's attack on deviance.

The *Cleanness*-poet's citation involves not only an allusion to Jean as author of the *clene Rose* (1057) but an actual paraphrase of a specific passage in the *Roman* which he employs in so elusive a way that I will take up its puzzles at greater length in chapter 7 when I consider its function in the poet's meditation on Christ's exemplary *clannesse*. The poet introduces his meditation on the Incarnation by paraphrasing counsel given to the Lover in the *Roman*; in so doing, he identifies his source as the *clene Rose* written by "Clopyngnel" (1057) — a mode of reference with a number of significant implications, one of which pertains to the *Cleanness*-poet's recognition of Jean de Meun's ironic representation of himself in the *Roman* as the divinely appointed successor to Guillaume de Lorris, its initial author.

When Jean inscribes his name as author in the *Roman* and clearly indicates the boundaries of his portion of the work, he refers to himself both by last name and by birthplace. The God of Love prophesies that "Jean Chopinel" (10535), who "will be born at Meung-sur-Loire" (10537), will finish Guillaume's unfinished romance, starting at the point where the Lover says of the Rose, "And perhaps I have lost it. At least I do not despair of it" (187–88; 10565–66).[1] The God of Love says that Jean will continue writing it to the end, where the Lover will finally take possession of his long-sought treasure, the Rose.[2] The name "Chopinel" for Jean de Meun occurs only in this passage where the second author of the *Roman* names himself in such explicit distinction from the first author. That the *Cleanness*-poet alludes to the "Rose" as written by "Clopyngnel" suggests he grasps its double authorship and indeed that he is prompting a courtly audience familiar with the *Roman* to receive *Cleanness* in the context of Jean's revisions of the Lover/Narrator Guillaume had constructed in the first portion of the allegorical narrative.[3]

The *Cleanness*-poet calls Jean's portion of the *Roman* Clopyngnel's "clene rose" (1057); that laudatory epithet has puzzled readers of *Cleanness* at least since its first editors. Jean's continuation of the first person account of a Lover's pursuit of a Rose has a strikingly different character from the unfinished work of Guillaume de Lorris it engulfed, producing an alliance of opposites suggestive of a Jane Austen novel completed by the author of *Tristram Shandy*. The massive additions transform Guillaume's carefully differentiated personae of a younger self as Lover and an older self as narrator into foils for Jean's ironic sophistication, encyclopedic learning, bawdry, satire, and weighty intellectual debate. The *Roman* circulated in a huge number of manuscripts (250 or more survive) and was translated, interpreted, and adapted both in transmission by scribes and in clearly separate works which bear the mark of its inspiration and influence.

No sooner was it completed by Jean than it gave rise to many interpretations, delighting some and disturbing others, and sometimes leaving the same reader simultaneously an admirer and a detractor. In the mid-fourteenth century, for example, Guillaume Deguilleville's *Pélérinage de la Vie Humaine* showed the influence of the *Roman* while criticizing Jean from a religious and moral perspective by having Venus declare that he was her ally (Luria 60). At the end of that century, not many years after the composition of *Cleanness*, Christine de Pisan's and Jean Gerson's attacks on the *Roman* made its problematic moral impact and misogyny a matter of public literary debate in Paris.[4] The poem was maligned and defended with equal fervor. This debatability of the *Roman*'s didactic aims and effectiveness has remained a central feature in its popularity throughout the history of its reception, and its complicated layers of irony continue to defeat critical consensus concerning its teaching on sexual pleasure. The power of Jean's text to generate controversy did not begin with modern scholars and does not derive from a latter-day loss of some hermeneutic key he could assume his medieval clerical audience possessed. Nor is this debatability the anachronistic creation of our own period's privileging of indeterminacy; rather, it demonstrates the absence from the poem's structure and rhetoric of any single unambiguously and overtly controlling moral standard.

The fact that such ambiguity could exist in so widely an influential work compels our recognition that medieval poets and their readers were willing to engage in original and subtle evaluation of the issues of sexual desire I have identified as central to the theopoetic ethics of *Cleanness*. Therefore, the citation of the "clene rose" of "Clopyngnel," rather than serving as evidence that a fourteenth-century poet of conventional views approved of Jean's poem as morally orthodox, as has been argued,[5] may with at least equal credibility signal the *Cleanness*-poet's self-conscious entry into dialogue, perhaps even playful and ironic dialogue, with a literary tradition where nature is dramatized as a sexual norm. It is hard to explain the allusion without assuming that he is appealing to a courtly audience which was as familiar as modern critics of the *Roman* with the debates and counterdebates staged in Jean's text, including his re-evaluation of crucial aspects of both Guillaume's and Alain's visionary narratives. Any such moderately well-informed courtly reader of the late fourteenth century would certainly have wondered if the poet's use of the crucial and complex "clene" as a laudatory epithet for the "rose" of "Clopyngnel" were a deliberate conundrum, a riddling comment on an already controversial, albeit extremely popular, work.

In examining the general applicability of certain themes in the *Roman* to the concerns of the *Cleanness*-poet in this chapter and the next, it is not my purpose to provide an overall survey of this giant compendium, nor to propose solutions to the conflicting perspectives explored.[6] Rather, I will display as much of the poem's dazzling array of discourses on desire, some directly borrowed and drastically revised from Alain's *Complaint,* as will provide a context for the treatment of these themes in *Cleanness*. After looking at how Jean legitimates desire, I will delineate a continuum of homophobic intensity evidenced in the literary tradition that constructs nature as heterosexual norm, comparing the polemics against deviance from this norm in Alain's *Complaint*, Jean's *Roman*, and *Cleanness*.

The portions of the *Roman* on which I shall focus occur at the beginning and at the end of Jean's text. The pleasures of heterosexual desire, which played so minor a role in Alain's *Complaint,* are here variously legitimated by several of the major characters in the *Roman:* Reason, Nature herself and Genius, her priest, Venus, and the Lover-Narrator. The moral credibility of these discourses varies from speaker to speaker; each is problematic to a degree, and Jean further qualifies their affirmations of sexual pleasure by the conflicts he constructs between their differing points of view. Deciding what the *Roman* is likely to have taught the poet of *Cleanness* or his readers about the value and danger of sexual pleasure enjoyed in accord with Nature's norm is not the point of my comparative study of these speeches. Rather, I shall establish the tensions within Jean's work to the extent required to display the inherent debatability of the subject of desire and then show the implications of such indeterminacy for assessing the *Cleanness*-poet's startling theopoetic account of sexual ethics. Seen against the backdrop of Alain's and Jean's widely known allegories, the poet's departures from traditional renderings of nature as a sexual norm are revealed, on the one hand, as part of an already established pattern of variations on conventions of love, art, and nature and, on the other, as all the more surprising in God's speech that discards procreation and male dominance as the legitimizing elements of what is "natural" about heterosexual pleasure.

Reason's Teachings on Pleasures of Natural Love

The opposition between reason and love which was already a standard motif in romance by the time Guillaume staged the Lover's first encounter with Reason is central to Jean's continuation of the allegory; this female personification dominates the first 3,000 lines of his text. A reader entering the *Roman* where Jean's revision of Guillaume de Lorris's poem begins (91; 4029) hears the Lover in despair because of the imprisonment of Fair Welcoming, the personified aspect of the Rose's psychology who can respond positively to his quest for her love. Jean emphasizes the continuity between his protagonist's quest and Guillaume's by letting the Lover recollect Reason's lessons from which he failed to profit previously; at the same time, Jean signals a possible shift in the text's moral perspective by letting the Lover reconsider his rejection of what she had previously taught him. Yet, having momentarily re-evaluated his previous hasty rejection of Reason's council that he should abandon the service of Love, the Lover again wavers and quickly reaffirms his loyalty to the God of Love in opposition to Reason. If Jean is going to dramatize the Lover's moral conversion, he must feel more immediately the force of Reason, and so she is brought back on the scene, ready to seize this teachable moment in her formerly resistant pupil.

The continuity in Reason's first appearance in Guillaume's text and her reappearance in Jean's is reinforced by the Lover's recognition of her as she enters again from the same tower from which she had initially descended: "I saw fair Reason coming straight back to me; as she descended from her tower she heard my complaints" (93; 4195–98). Jean, however, endows Reason with added authority, volubility, and verve.

One source Jean has obviously drawn from to enlarge Reason's discourse is Alain de Lille's characterization of Nature. Very early in Reason's resumed effort to change the Lover's mind, she launches a diatribe on the terrible paradoxicality of love which echoes Nature's memorable tour de force in the *Complaint,* similarly aimed at curing a foolish narrator of his ill-founded service to Love: "Love is hateful peace and loving hate. It is disloyal loyalty and loyal disloyalty, fear that is completely confident and despairing hope. It is reason gone mad and reasonable madness." (94; 4263–70). After dozens of these borrowed oxymorons, we hear (just as we did from Nature in Alain) that "There is no one, however high his lineage nor however wise he may be found, of such proved strength, bravery, or other good qualities, who may not be subjugated by the God of Love" (95; 4305–10). No one, that is, except those who, like Alain's narrator, are among the educable and, fortified by Reason, can learn to flee from Love's times and places. The reader of the *Roman* who recognizes this allusion to the *Complaint* might wonder if Reason will succeed, as Nature seems to in Alain's text, in teaching the narrator the origins of love's corrupting force and thence converting him to a life based on reason.

As teachers, both Jean's Reason and Alain's Nature construct natural heterosexual union as a normative pattern of behavior founded on the necessity to overcome death by ongoingly reproducing new copies of the species. The reproductive consequences of sexual union are generally downplayed, if not ignored altogether, in the courtly romance, both by the advocates of love and by its detractors, and so it is not surprising that this emphasis upon procreation is missing entirely from Guillaume's earlier portrayal of Reason's attempt to dissuade the Lover from his service to the God of Love. The influence of Alain's Nature on Jean's Reason is evident when she focuses on the Lover's lack of interest in the procreative aim as the symptom which shows the pathology of his desire for the rose. Taking "no account of bearing fruit" (96; 4357), he instead strives simply for the delight of bodily union.

This pursuit of delight as an end that is valuable in itself rather than as a means to progeny is Reason's definition of love "par amors" (96; 4362):[7] "A lover so burns and is so enraptured that he thinks of nothing else; he takes no account of bearing fruit, but strives only for delight" (95–96; 4347–58). She condemns such ungoverned desire as the "root of all evil" (96; 4389).

Yet heterosexual pleasure per se is not condemned by Reason. Indeed, the explicit attention she pays to the appropriate place of pleasure between men and women in the love she defines as natural provides the most striking contrast between Reason's teachings in the *Roman* and those of her precursor Nature in the *Complaint*. Whereas Alain's Nature never mentions delight as an incentive to the correct use of the sexual parts she teaches Venus to oversee, Reason teaches the Lover that Nature uses this "subtle means" to her reproductive end: "Nature has implanted delight in man because she wants the workman to take pleasure in his task . . . , for there are many who would never make a move toward it if there were no delight to attract them. Thus Nature uses this subtle means of gaining her end" (96; 4382–91). Is this Jean's implied rebuttal of Alain's peculiarly repellent representation of Nature's tedious assignment that the masculine be correctly connected to the feminine? Reason makes it amply clear that from her point of view, Nature's heterosexual requirements are never sheer repetitive drudgery, as Venus found them to her displeasure, but predictably joyful in the doing.

However, Reason also predictably clarifies and repeatedly stresses the rational limits to be observed when enjoying Nature's ample rewards. Adding to this emphasis on begetting offspring she insists: "whoever lies with a woman ought to *wish with all his might* to continue his divine self and to maintain himself in his likeness" (96; 4374–81; italics added). In contrast to Alain's preoccupation with correct physical joining of male and female sexual parts, Jean makes Reason stress correct intentionality with regard to such a union. Pleasure as Nature's lure into sexual activity is justified rationally when, and only when, the lovers' powers are consciously bent toward a procreative outcome.

In contrast both to Nature's pessimism about the pleasures of intercourse in the *Complaint* and to Guillaume's initial representation of Reason's attempting to dissuade altogether the Lover from his desire, Jean uses Reason to give voice to a powerful normative endorsement of heterosexual pleasure as an essential ingredient in love made in accord with nature. Generously, she explicitly enjoins that both male and female lovers, without regard to their age, are entitled to their share of the pleasures Nature has built into the procreative act: "whoever wants to enjoy love, without fail, man or woman, whether lady or girl, should seek its fruit, although they should not deny their share of delight" (98; 4516–20). The traditional conflict between Reason and Love appears well on its way to being resolved at this point in the *Roman*.

The *Cleanness*-poet and his readers could find a suggestive resemblance to God's praise of *drwry* in Reason's endorsement of gifts bestowed by the lover, unsolicited by the lady, and unselfishly reciprocated by her (98–99; 4549–56). Just as exchanging adornments of jewelry or apparel can be a way for lovers to pledge themselves without the corrupting motivation of greed, so also Reason envisions here the ideal of bodily pleasures enjoyed without the corrupting urge to grasp: "In this way their hearts join together, they love each other and pledge themselves by their gifts. Don't think that I would separate them; I want them to unite and do whatever they ought that is courteous and well behaved, but I want them to keep themselves from that foolish love which inflames hearts and makes them burn with desire. I want their love to be free of that covetousness that excites false hearts to grasp. Good love should be born of a pure heart; love should not be mastered by gifts any more than by bodily pleasures" (99; 4557–69). The purity of heart, from which such "courteous and well behaved" love is born, resembles the poet's vision of *clannesse* incarnate in lovers who deal honorably with each other and are embodiments of divinely inspired *drwry*. Neither God in the *Cleanness*-poet's representation of lovemaking at its natural best nor Reason in Jean's *Roman* emphasizes marriage, and in this regard both differ from Alain's privileging of the bonds of matrimony guaranteeing the reproduction not only of the generations but of patriarchal society.

The bodily appetites she had earlier reduced to Nature's realm separate from and beneath her own, Reason later dignifies as God's handicraft, a conscious work of art made "with marvelous intention—willingly, not in spite of himself" (133; 6939–40). The incentive of pleasure which earlier she attributed to Nature's strategy for getting people to engage in reproductive sexual union is here affirmed as part of God's own plan.[8] While she does not speak of God as a perfectly wise craftsman who designed these "noble things" (133; 6927) in such a way as to include what Chaucer's Wife of Bath later refers to as "ese of engendrure" (III [D 127–28]), Reason implies precisely that. In refuting the Lover's implication that the genitals and the use to which they are put in intercourse are somehow base and must therefore be veiled by euphemism, Reason affirms both sexual pleasure and the aesthetic value of heterosexual union from both her own and the Creator's viewpoint.[9]

The contrast provided by *Roman*'s teaching about love through Reason's point of view is, however, even more telling than its similarity to *Cleanness*. Reason explicitly addresses, as God does not, the threat of the dangerous love between a man and a woman which "inflames hearts and makes them burn with desire" (99; 4563–64). The means of controlling this greediness, lest it corrupt the lovers' union, is not explicitly included in this passage from Reason's teachings, but from the context her claim is amply clear. The procreative intention, if earnestly pursued, prevents the pleasure principle from mastering love. Unlike God's speech in *Cleanness*, Reason gives no endorsement of sexual delight as itself a form of *drwry*. Pleasure cannot be reasonably legitimated as part of the generous exchange of erotically charged gifts for mutual solace and pleasure that can express and complete love's spiritual bond. Rationally speaking, only the determination to generate progeny in accord with Nature's ends justifies either the pleasures she has built into sexual intercourse or the romantic rituals of *drwry* courtly lovers have constructed around that instinctive drive for intimacy. From Reason's viewpoint, the Creator's praise of the *play of paramorez* in *Cleanness* would be exceedingly dangerous rhetoric, unqualified as his lesson in love is by any mandate to be fruitful and multiply.

The question of the proper place of erotic delight in rational life has evoked a range of answers in these works. Juxtaposing Reason's view of natural love to Nature's teachings in Alain's *Complaint* and to Thomas's account of sexual pleasure in his treatment of temperance, we can see a continuum of ethical generosity toward the sensual and passionate aspects of human existence.

Reason's assessment of sexual pleasure is obviously more generous than Nature's ever was in Alain. Rather than warning against the threat to rationality of a fire blazing too hotly or a torrent overflowing its banks, as Nature typically does in the *Complaint*,[10] Reason's teaching displays at points an optimism about Nature's provision of pleasure that reminds one of Thomas's Aristotelian ethic.[11] When focused upon procreation as justification, the delight of lovemaking is justified. Reason would agree with Thomas that momentarily suspending rational capacities does not obliterate the shaping motivation of the well-ordered sex act, namely to procreate.

In contrast with Thomas, however, Reason denies any positive moral value to the correct pursuit of love's procreative aim for which Nature equips and motivates humankind as well as beasts. Reason has this to say: "However much good it does, this love carries neither praise nor blame nor merit. . . . Nature makes creatures give themselves to it; in truth, they are forced to it. Nor does this love bring any victory over vice. But, without fail, if men do not perform this duty, they should be blamed. When a man eats, what praise is due him? But if he foreswears food, he should certainly be shamed" (116; 5747–58). From Reason's viewpoint, not to will progeny is as unnatural as not to want to eat; the kind of love she calls *par amors* unnaturally eradicates this instinct for survival. Conversely, to want to reproduce children is as natural as to be hungry for food, and it is for this very reason that Reason does not consider the drive Nature instills for sexual union as potentially virtuous (116; 5750–51). Reason in the *Roman* does not recognize that, as Thomas argues, for a human being, self-preservation is the basis of living reasonably and therefore never neutral. For Thomas, moreover, since sex and eating necessarily involve pleasure, they are not only potentially degrading but also potentially beautiful, for the appetites play an essential role in a life that is as well-crafted and shapely as an elegantly fitted garment, suffused with ethical intelligence so that it is as brilliant as the most luminous jewels.

Having diagnosed the Lover as sick because he has no interest in progeny, Reason in the *Roman* does not appeal to his natural desire for fulfilling Nature's reproductive aims nor to his sense of potential freedom over compulsions of bodily appetite by directing them to a rational end. Instead, Reason offers Socrates as the exemplar of the love she wants the Lover to have for her, for by loving Reason a man can liberate himself from being Fortune's hostage: "Whatever might come to pass, he was neither joyous nor heavy because of things" (117; 5818–24).[12] Such transcendence over pleasure and pain radically qualifies Reason's earlier affirmation of the place of delight in a rationally ordered sexual union and does nothing to persuade the Lover to make her his lady. The Rose retains her appeal for the Lover: he snaps that he gives not "three chick-peas for Socrates" (132; 6879–80), and adamantly reaffirms his covenant to Love, thus resuming his romantic quest for the consummate pleasure of bodily intimacy with his beloved Rose.

Nature's and Genius's Legitimation of Pleasure in Love Par Amors

Reason interprets the Lover's service to Love as diametrically opposed to meeting his duty to Nature. In this dichotomizing of courtly versus natural sexual behavior, Reason in Jean echoes Nature in Alain. While clearly alluding to the *Complaint of Nature*, however, Jean radically revises Alain's sexual ethics by characterizing Reason and Nature as two separate allegorical personalities; thus the Lover in Jean's *Roman* is presented with two sharply conflicting points of view on the place of pleasure in natural love. In Jean's text, Reason never encounters Nature, and so the two allegorically personified concepts do not occasion a clarification or reconciliation of differences they represent. Readers of Jean's *Roman*, however, are confronted by the contrasts between the delights of love made naturally in conformity to Reason's principles, on the one hand, and to Nature's, on the other.

To bring Nature on stage, Jean shifts the scene from a battleground (where Venus and Love have just sworn their vows to make all living men and women take part in the game of love) to a forge. Here Nature is putting "all her attention on forging individual creatures to continue the species" (270; 15866–68), an obvious allusion to her counterpart in the *Complaint* who oversaw hammers and anvils in the work of reproducing the species. Thus Jean introduces his portrayal of Nature as deriving from Alain's influential characterization of the cosmic procreatrix, responsible for maintaining the succession of life forms that are constantly threatened by death, and hence responsible as well for maintaining the heterosexual, reproductive norm. Nature in the *Roman* suffers, like her predecessor in the *Complaint*, from humankind's failure to conform to her reproductive sexual norm. Like Alain's Nature, Jean's is a spokeswoman for parenthood. She celebrates the other forms of animal life which "produce their young in their different ways and do honor to their ancestry" (314; 18964–65), and she laments that "man alone, for whom [she] had made all the benefits that [she] knew how" wars against her (314; 18991–92). And like Alain's Nature, she sees irrationality as the root of this evil, as well as of the others she laments in her account of man's waywardness.

However, in shocking contradiction to her predecessor in the *Complaint*, as well as in direct conflict with Reason in Jean's text, Nature does not indict the desire of courtly lovers for the nonreproductive delights of bodily union as the root of all evil. Jean allows Nature to overhear from her forge Venus and Love jointly declare war upon chastity. Nature is elated by their sworn determination that all living men and women shall be made to play their parts in love's game. That she was cheered by hearing Cupid's and Venus's vows (to engage every human being in the game of love) reveals that Nature in the *Roman* will legitimate the worship of sexual desire in the courtly ethos; from her point of view, love *par amors* is seen as salvific rather than corrupting. What Reason denounces as deadly, Nature sees no danger in, nor does she see any difficulty at all in lovers conforming their conduct simultaneously to the God of Love's rules and to her own reproductive principles. Contrary to Reason's teachings, by serving in Love's army, the Lover would seem from Nature's viewpoint not to be avoiding her sovereignty, but instead, along with Love's barons, rendering the tribute all men owe her for the sexual organs she has given them.

Nature has complete confidence, contrary to Reason's teachings, that men and women drawn to each other by the burning sexual attraction intensified in their service to Venus and Love will inevitably find pleasure in putting their reproductive tools vigorously, and hence procreatively, to work. Certain that the God of Love loves her so much that he wants to draw close to her works, "more than iron does to a magnet" (319; 19310–11), she sends Genius, her priest, to assist the forces of Venus and Love by indicting and excommunicating from Nature's religion all who fail to put these organs to use in heterosexual intercourse and, conversely, by offering her blessing and pardon to all who strive to reproduce their lineage.

Alain's plot, culminating in the mystical reunion of Genius and Nature and the somber anathema he pronounces as her priest against those guilty of violating Nature's rules, is thus radically, and comically, revised by Jean. The plot of the *Roman* cleverly links Genius's excommunication of all who deviate from Nature's path with the happy ending of the Lover's courtship. Nature's and Genius's alliance with Venus and Cupid helps fuel the flames of desire which ensure the defeat of the forces of Reason who have defended the Rose.

Specifically, when Genius excommunicates all who fail to render Nature their due tribute for the sexual capacities she bestows, he ignites a conflagration which leaves the Rose unprotected. He marks the anathema by throwing down a candle that sets female desire on fire: "its smoky flame spread among everyone. There is no lady who might protect herself from it, so well does Venus know how to spread it, and the wind caught it up so high that all living women have their bodies, their hearts, and their thoughts permeated with that odor" (338; 20640–48). The Rose is transformed into a surrealistic anatomical representation of female sexuality which Jean plays with throughout the Lover's bawdy account of completing his conquest. Venus shoots her fiery arrow into the tower through the narrow aperture "in front, where Nature, by her great cunning, had placed it between two pillars" (340; 20764–66). Demonstrating the erotic volatility of her sex, the Rose's capacity for Fair Welcoming makes her a victim of the Lover's blandishments. As Venus sends fleeing those who should protect woman's chastity—Shame, Resistance, and Fear— the Rose's whetted appetite for sexual pleasure is left unrestrained. Venus thus makes good her threat to defeat Reason's opposition to Love's game (340; 10748–52). "From that moment no one wanted to put to the test what Reason had taught them" (347; 21245–46). The Castle of Jealousy goes up in flames, Reason's allies desert the Rose, and she is the ultimately defenseless target of unbridled phallic aggression that is represented in terms all too suggestive of rape, despite the narrator's claim that Venus's fire ignites the Rose and every other female's sexual fuse.

Jean's plot attains its unseemly erotic climax by means of Nature's and Genius's complicity with Venus and Love, in opposition to Reason. Have Nature and Genius been foolishly duped into assisting Venus and Love to unleash desires in the beloved Rose that make her as irrational and shameless as the Lover has been ever since he first embarked on his quest? Apparently inflamed by passion ignited by Genius's candle, the Rose parts with her maidenhead. This union between the Lover and his Rose, though potentially fruitful, is nonetheless pathological from the point of view of Reason, who diagnoses such insatiable desire as a symptom of enjoying physical intimacy for its own sake, with no intention of producing offspring. Venus's alliance with Nature and Genius is morally disastrous for all lovers, for it furthers their greedy appetite for sexual pleasure which is the root of all evil. Reason early warned the Lover: "Hearts drunk with love are too much given over to misguided acts. You will know this at the end when you have lost your time and wasted your youth in this sorry pleasure. If you can live long enough to see yourself delivered from love, you will bewail the time you have lost, but you will never be able to recover it, if indeed you escape that far, for, in that love where you are caught, many, I dare say, lose their sense, their time, possessions, bodies, souls, and reputations" (99; 4585–98). As the work concludes, the Lover boasts, in the midst of describing his triumphant possession of the Rose: "I didn't remember Reason, who gave me a lot of trouble for nothing" (354; 21730–31).

When the Lover and the Rose conjoin, they do so with no conscious aim of begetting offspring. Albeit unintentionally, the Lover finally renders Nature her tribute, satisfying the essential terms of her reproductive sexual norm. Jean stages this culmination of the Lover's purely hedonistic determination to possess the Rose as a seminal moment in the genre of romance, for we are told that despite himself, the Lover "so mixed the seeds that they could hardly be separated." Thus he "made the whole tender rosebush widen and lengthen" (353; 21697–700). We might read this alteration in the Rose's size and shape as foreshadowing the changes this mixing of seeds will bring to the female anatomy of "the first pregnant heroine in European literature" (Arden 57). It could also be read as an allusion to the two-seed theory of conception, representing the female orgasm that accompanies her ejaculation.[13]

If so, however, the involuntary nature of the Rose's reluctant complicity in the unintentional act of procreation is portrayed not as an orgasmic moment of ecstasy for her, but as an unpleasing indignity. By Fair Welcoming's firm rebuke of the Lover for breaking the terms of the gift of the Rose, Jean reveals the ambiguity of her ostensible pleasure: "He reminded me of the agreement and said that I was doing him a great wrong, that I was too unbridled" (353; 21707–09). What matters to the Lover is simply that he is nevertheless allowed to take what he has so long wanted to possess: "but he did not forbid me to take, to reveal and pluck the rosebud and branches, the flower and the leaf" (353; 21710–12). Beginning with the flaming arrow shot by Venus into the tiny aperture of the genitalia, the aroused female is portrayed as a victim of a painful assault on her physical and psychic integrity. The penetration of her anatomy is symbolized finally by the bush on which the Rose grew being stripped of leaves and blossoms. If the unintentional mixing of seeds in this union does promise fruitful issue, such potential fecundity is represented negatively at best — simply a regrettable accident on the Lover's part.

Unlike Alain's celebration of the noble joy of marriage, where there is a clear mandate for fatherhood in order to reproduce patriarchal succession of the species, in the *Roman,* the Lover leaves the Rose (if she is impregnated) to bear the enlarging consequences of heterosexual union unmarried. Although Genius stresses the importance of thinking about one's lineage in the act of intercourse, the Lover does not spur himself along the rugged road to victory with any such anticipations of begetting and raising his offspring. Rather, he pursues his sexual adventures down life's endlessly various byways, lifting the lids to taste what is cooking in all the different pots, and as the mating season recurs, adding more roses to his ever expanding collection. While the Lover recommends the superior pleasures to be enjoyed with young virgins like the Rose, he also legitimates the inclination he assumes some readers will have for older women and personally attests to the comfort and delight, as well as the riches, that can be found with them. In his celebration of male entitlement to experience everything, the challenge of stripping the bud is just one example of the range of variation the young lords he addresses may find when they "go gathering roses, either opened or closed" (353; 21649–50). Perhaps this is Jean's commentary on how Nature, despite the conscious aims of her human creatures, gets her reproductive work done, appealing multifariously to their different tastes. The Lover's rhetoric of desire displays a dazzling variety of ways of looking at enjoyment, both remembering past pleasures and anticipating his taking possession of the Rose. Within his narrated experience of one climactic sexual act, he recalls and savors the different, seemingly incompatible, dimensions of his long history of sexual conquest.

Jean's metaphors are playfully witty as he shifts from a devotee's pilgrimage to a rogue's journey, then to a hunt for prey, trapping old and young quail, and later to gathering roses, cutting those that are full blown and those that are yet buds. The ideal of connoisseurship through sampling the entirety of life's banquet comes to feel like a serious mandate as the Lover urges his listeners to pursue a variety of sexual partners in order to become a reliable judge of what is most pleasing: "Indeed I tell you the truth, believe me who will, that it is good to try everything in order to take greater pleasure in one's good fortune, just as does the good lover of luxury who is a connoisseur of tidbits and tastes of several foods — simmered, roasted, with dressing, in a pasty, fried, or in a galantine — when he can go into a kitchen; he knows how to praise and to blame, to say which are sweet, which bitter, for he has tasted several" (351; 21519–31). Faced with judging which of these "tidbits and tastes . . . are sweet, which bitter" (351; 21524–25, 21530), diverse readers will diversely decide.

As his discourse shifts semantic registers from the culinary to the moral and epistemological, the Lover's belief in learning by experiencing everything suggests a potential hermeneutic key for the *Roman:* "In this way know, and do not doubt, that he who has not tried evil will hardly ever know anything of the good, any more than will he who does not know the value of honor know how to recognize shame. . . . Thus things go by contraries; one is the gloss of the other. If one wants to define one of the pair, he must remember the other, or he will never, by any intention, assign a definition to it; for he who has no understanding of the two will never understand the difference between them

(351; 21532–36, 21543–46). As readers we are implicitly challenged to compare and contrast all of the "wise and foolish" (188; 10567–68) speeches Jean has set down, as the God of Love prophesied he would, in continuing Guillaume's unfinished narrative right up to this point where the Lover takes possession of the Rose. Using such an approach to the *Roman,* however, no single definition will be found for the rightful place of sexual pleasure in a well-ordered life. The many conflicting perspectives on love Jean has built into his text can never be simply paired as contraries. Instead they provide an unending series of ever more surreal images, surrounding us with distortions reflecting still more distorted planes, as in a carnival's wall of mirrors.

Modern critics, like their medieval predecessors, exhibit a variety of responses to the *Roman* and especially differ in their attitudes toward the Lover's account of his success. Fleming, for whom Reason's diagnosis of the malady of lovemaking divorced from procreative intent is the true standard of value in the *Roman*'s sexual ethic, stresses how inadvertently conception takes place, arguing that from the Lover's perspective, the mixing of seeds is "the single trespass in an otherwise satisfactory sex act" (*Reason and the Lover* 19). For Wetherbee, that the *Roman* concludes with an involuntary act of semination signals the "inexhaustible vitality" of nature. The fecund union with the Rose strikes him as profoundly suggestive of human potential for generativity, not simply in a procreative sense but in the realm of creativity generally. The Lover, "responding to a creative impulse," is implicitly praised by Wetherbee as blindly assuming "responsibility for the future of mankind" (*Platonism and Poetry* 265). In this interpretation, Jean has replayed the hopeful conclusion of cosmic harmony, marred but potentially restored, that Wetherbee traced at the end of Alain's *Complaint*. In the *Roman,* however, the resolution is less romantic than Rabelaisian, a comic rendering of the earlier dignified reunion of Genius with Nature. As the poem comes at last to its ending, after so many deferments of the long-awaited representation of the Lover's sexual climax, Jean's humorous resolution points to "the almost miraculous fertility of that human nature which, hidden beneath the proliferation of conflicting desires and false visions, is the rock and loam from which all such impulses must necessarily and perpetually spring" (*Platonism and Poetry* 266).

What the Lover's celebration of phallic pleasure suggests when viewed from a feminist hermeneutic is a topic for another study. Here I shall note simply that the Lover, in an apparent fixation on breaking through the barriers to penetration and possession, repeatedly imagines the female genitalia as an enemy fortress. This is at least as baldly unenticing a declaration of the primacy of the male's role in heterosexual coupling as the *Complaint*'s imagery of hammer and anvil or pen and parchment. Despite the various speakers' assurances that Nature's reproductive work is fundamentally pleasing to both male and female, the *Roman* concludes in a frenzy of phallic exertion that impresses me with the combination of brute force, heroic perseverance, and counterintuitive artifice required of the Lover if he is to succeed at a task depicted as so horribly taxing that it feels anything but natural. The Lover's account of coitus problematizes both the male and the female role in the heterosexual process of achieving genital conjunction, but (depending on one's point of view perhaps) especially for the virginal female, it is intolerably painful and degrading. The Lover's graphically detailed instructions to his male readers in the *Roman* has no more to say about the aroused female's desire than Nature in the *Complaint* had to say to Venus about the potential for mutual erotic excitement in the procreative process.

The Lover's account of his frustration, and eventually his delight, calls to mind (perhaps more than any other part of Jean's text) the *Cleanness*-poet's frank legitimation of the burning delight of intercourse, but illuminates it by contrast rather than similarity. The ecstatic intimacy of the *play of paramorez* as God describes it could not be more dramatically different from the Lover's strenuous engagement if the Creator's account of lovemaking in this *maner myriest of* [any] *oþer* had been constructed in deliberate opposition to Jean's reductive burlesque. Quite possibly, the *Cleanness*-poet did just that. Read against the backdrop of the *Roman*, the lyrical idealization of intercourse makes *kynde crafte* appear to be effortlessly passionate play on the part of the man and woman; indeed, it is because of the Creator's consummate skill and teachings that they can enjoy this *doole alþer-swettest*. Thus the *Cleanness*-poet may be "making good" the romance ethos of mutuality and refinement Jean so coarsely parodied not only in the conclusion to the *Roman*, but in the Ovidian satire throughout his text.

Three Constructions of Deviance

Whereas Nature in Alain's vision imposes sober utilitarian constraints on the dangerous urge for playful variations from reproductive, and hence true, standards for sexual intercourse and discourse, Jean plays with the idea of nature from so many perspectives that it is impossible to decide what is the true standard and what value the natural has in a vision of the Good. Reason's teachings about natural sexual relations overlap with, but also conflict with, other voices in the *Roman*, including Nature's own briefly stated points about deviance and desire and Genius's glossing of her excommunication and pardon.

Near the outset of her discourse in Jean's section of the *Roman*, Reason introduces the category of "wrongs against Nature" (95; 4315) as an unusual form of pathology which differs from the Lover's obsession for pleasure. Reason does not, however, pause in her diatribe against his delight-fueled love for the Rose to define these other unnatural offenses concretely; instead, she simply directs Genius to excommunicate such exceptional offenders, thus implying that they are even more grievous to Nature than those who, like the Lover, seek sexual gratification with no procreative aim.[14] It is striking that same-sex deviation is never explicitly designated as the meaning of wrongs against Nature in this discourse of Reason or, in fact, in any other part of Jean's *Roman*.[15]

We would expect that in the *Roman*, Reason (who otherwise so closely resembles Alain's Nature in the *Complaint*) would logically connect the irrationality of the Lover (whose devotion to the game of love *par amors* typifies the folly of Love's servants as a whole) to the peculiar failure of those whom Genius will judge for their still more gravely offensive "wrongs against Nature" (95; 4315). Yet unlike Nature in the *Complaint,* Reason in Jean's *Roman* differentiates sharply between the evils of heterosexual desire when ungoverned by rational concentration upon Nature's procreative purpose and this oddly unspecified mode of acting against Nature which only Genius can properly judge. Until Genius pronounces the judgment, some 15,000 lines later, excommunicating those who violate Nature's laws, Jean leaves the reader guessing precisely what the specific sexual offenses against Nature are. (And even Genius's condemnation of these failures to render tribute to Nature leaves a certain amount of ambiguity about whether they refer to celibates' commitment to avoid all sexual relations or to the propensity of some lovers to avoid "roses" in preference for same-sex relations with males.) Reason's attack on harms against Nature becomes more ambiguous still when what seems to be their comparatively heavier gravity as vice is juxtaposed to her later claim about the "root of all evil" (96; 4389). This radical evil is, she asserts, the greedy desire for sexual pleasure for its own sake, a heterosexual tendency exemplified by the male Lover's quest to possess the female Rose.

Jean's contrast with the *Complaint*'s obsessive emphasis on homosexual deviation becomes even more striking when we listen to Nature speaking in her own voice in the *Roman;* her norm then sounds different from Reason's version of it, even though (like Alain) Jean represents Nature constructing her sexual ethic in terms of reproduction. She bestows her pardon on those men who "work with good heart to follow strictly the rules that are written in my book, those stalwarts who strive mightily to multiply their lines and who think about loving well" (319; 19352–57). In the context of both Nature's pardon and her excommunication in the *Roman,* it seems that failure for any reason at all to use the sexual organs in procreative intercourse constitutes wanting to work against the natural norm. At the end of her long list of vices, Nature indicts man for being "a lazy sodomite" (317; 19204).[16] Arguably, this is an explicit reference to homosexual relations; if so, it is the only one in Jean's portion of the *Roman*. Yet even if *sodomite* is to be interpreted as specifically referring to men guilty of homosexual acts, the context for this accusation is Nature's ambiguous confession of mankind's vice. Just two lines later she defines departure from her sexual norm not primarily as practicing same-sex relations but more generally as denying her "the tribute all men" owe "as long as they receive [her] tools" (319; 19302–4). Of course, the authority of Nature to define a rational norm is questionable, since she joins in the war waged by Venus and Love against chastity and sees any refusal to engage in heterosexual pursuits as a fundamental threat to her order. It becomes still more dubious that Nature is to be believed when we hear Genius railing against celibacy on her behalf.

Genius develops the rationale for compulsive heterosexuality by denying any valid place for virginity. Genius's preaching is often overtly parodic, and never more so than when he claims that men who claim to exempt themselves from Nature's norm based on their religious commitment to celibacy in fact epitomize the failure to inseminate.[17] Such traitors who refuse to strike a blow with their hammers or to thrust their plowshares into the fallow fields "might as well be buried alive when they dare to flee from the tools that God shaped with his hand when he gave them to my lady [Nature]" (323; 19545–48). Jean thus puts celibacy (which Alain ignored in the *Complaint*) back into the moral landscape, but he does so by condemning it ironically as the point farthest removed from Nature's reproductive forge. As Genius pronounces Nature's excommunication on abstinence as the greatest of sexual evils, a medieval reader of the *Roman* would be likely to recall orthodox teaching about celibacy as superior to the goods of marriage. In comic contrast to the conventional elevation of the ideal of sexual purity through the grace conferred upon those who take the religious vow of celibacy, Genius's exaggeration of the goods of hard thrusting and profound penetrating is the more obviously unreliable. His exuberant mandate to the barons of Love that they plow deeply in order to continue their lineage and thus obtain Nature's pardon is rendered problematic by his heretical, and obscenely violent, denunciation of males who fail to make their reproductive contribution to the species.

Celibates are conflated with homosexual offenders, as Genius briefly equates such a refusal of heterosexual intercourse with a preference for false artifice. We are reminded of Alain's rhetoric as Genius accuses deviants (those guilty of celibacy and of homosexual practices) of using the perverting hermeneutics Orpheus taught his followers when he read Nature's rules backwards: "those who are so blinded by their sins, by the pride that takes them off their road, so that they despise the straight furrow of the beautiful, fecund field and like unhappy creatures go off to plow in desert land where their seeding goes to waste; those who will never keep to the straight track, but instead go overturning the plow, who confirm their evil rules by abnormal exceptions when they want to follow Orpheus (he did not know how to plow or write or forge in the true forge — may he be hanged by the throat! — when he showed himself so evil toward Nature by contriving such rules for them)" (323–24; 19610–26). Jean alludes here to Ovid's characterization of Orpheus as a pederast and thus ironically extends Alain's use of this image.[18] Whereas in the *Complaint* it is directed explicitly against gender reversals and homosexual deviance, with no mention of celibacy, in the *Roman* Genius condemns all who fail to use their sexual organs according to Nature, including celibates, to the most sadistic of temporal punishments along with direst eternal consequences: "May they, in addition to the excommunication that sends them all to damnation, suffer, before their death, the loss of their purse and testicles, the signs that they are male! May they lose the pendants on which their purse hangs! May they have the hammers that are attached within torn out! May their styluses be taken away from them when they have not wished to write within the precious tablets that were suitable for them" (324; 19633–46)! Men who prefer homosexual relations are doubtless included in those offenders whom Genius here condemns to castration, but neither here nor elsewhere in Jean's *Roman* is this form of deviation from Nature's reproductive task specifically targeted. Unlike the homophobic rhetoric so prominent in the *Complaint*, Jean replays Alain's theme of wrongs against Nature with little attention to the evils of gender inversion.[19]

The pleasure principle and feminine unruliness are not conflated in Jean's *Roman* as they are in the *Complaint*'s representation of Venus's rebellion; nor does the *Roman* associate homosexual deviation with the pleasure-seeking of the sort Venus exemplifies in her subversive passion with Antigamus. It is Reason rather than Nature who associates the Lover's pleasure-driven erotic quest with a failure to inseminate, and as we have seen, Reason distinguishes this heterosexual pathology from exceptional deviation from Nature's standard. Genius confirms this by pronouncing Nature's judgment on deviants from her order who refuse to sow their seed in "the straight furrow of the beautiful fecund field and ... go off to plow in desert land where their seeding goes to waste" (324; 19612–16). Whereas in Alain's *Complaint* homosexual relations are synecdochally constructed to epitomize men's failure to return Nature's tribute and to suggest allegorically the failure of human nature to maintain a loving union with its divinely creative source, in the *Roman* same-sex desire is relatively unimportant to any of the several definitions of natural virtue.

Alain, Jean, and the *Cleanness*-poet all measure sexual activity against a normal pattern which they associate with the natural order, and all attack deviance from this norm. But the norm and natural order, and therefore the deviance, are understood differently by each. Placing *Cleanness* in the literary tradition of nature as sexual norm illuminates how the fourteenth-century poet constructs homosexual deviance as a scorning of the Creator's art in nature that poses a uniquely complex threat. *Cleanness* differs from both Alain's and Jean's versions of the tradition by claiming that same-sex union harms the natural order in a way that no other vice does insofar as *fylþe of þe flesch* disrupts the Creator's normally generous relation to his creatures in the order of nature. This stress on the cosmically defiling force of homosexual deviance may well have been influenced by Alain's apocalyptic drama, but in the *Complaint,* Genius anathematizes not simply men who fail to maintain the reproductive norms of marital intercourse Nature taught to Venus, but vice of all sorts. Although in *Cleanness,* God's anger against *fylþe of þe flesch* is similarly part of a larger demonstration of his opposition to defilement of any sort, the claim is made, astonishingly, that no form of evil so enrages him as this specific sexual deviation from the heterosexual pattern which he holds uniquely valuable.

If we imagine a continuum with regard to the irresistibility of homosexual deviance, Alain would belong at the extreme end, for he represents male same-sex coupling as a nearly inevitable tendency to deviate from Nature's marital and procreative norm, a feminizing attribute inherent in males that mythologically originates in Venus's fallen weakness for passionate play in an extramarital bond. At the other end of the continuum, Jean constructs homosexual deviance as a not terribly significant blot on Nature's order. Throughout the *Roman,* the attractiveness of the masculine conjoining with the feminine is taken for granted; it is, in fact, Nature's gift, where in the *Complaint,* the heterosexually correct form of intercourse is instead represented as a difficult achievement. There Nature teaches it as an art form, and one whose stylistic purity is from the outset threatened by almost inevitable errors on the part of the male instrument. From Reason's viewpoint in the *Roman,* heterosexual love *par amors* is harmfully deviant from the reproductive aims of natural love, and thus her main concern is that such erotic attraction may be pursued irrationally, for its own sake rather than for progeny. While Reason mentions exceptional offenders against Nature, she is not concerned as Alain's Nature is that such offenders constitute a trend which could endanger the reproduction of the species as a whole. She assigns them to Genius to judge, and from his viewpoint, celibacy looms at least as threateningly as same-sex desire. Venus may refer to male homosexual pursuits in her sly comment that some men will unaccountably "pass up the roses to follow a worse course" (340; 20738), but this unusual preference for something besides the female rose is not explicitly equated by Venus with same-sex desire. It could just as well refer to abstinence. Puzzling to Venus, repellent to Genius, sexual anomalies do exist in Jean's *Roman,* but they are epitomized by celibacy as much as by homosexual coupling. In any case, deviance from the heterosexual norm does not attract the graphic descriptions and satirical wit Jean applies to other topical issues.

The *Roman*'s relative lack of concern with same-sex relations distances it, on a continuum of homophobic intensity, from the *Complaint* and *Cleanness* where nature's heterosexual norm is inseparable from the attack on same-sex desire. Although homosexual desire does not seem virtually irresistible in *Cleanness,* as it does in the *Complaint,* both of these works depict such inclinations as vile and threateningly pervasive. The representation of the Sodomites' determination to teach others their way of making love reads as if the poet lives in a world still polluted by their subversive alternative to the pleasures God designs and teaches within the attractive norm of *kynde crafte.* Despite the representation of its absolute repulsiveness to any man of refined taste, homosexual desire is also figured in *Cleanness* as a danger to be feared; at one point, it is warned against as a deeply private inclination that, however foolishly one might try to hide it, it is ever apparent to the Creator who scrutinizes the loins from which passion springs.

What makes the *Cleanness*-poet's attack on sexual deviance so distinctive in contrast both to Alain's frontal assault and to Jean's rather desultory swipe is intrinsically bound up with the fact that his norm, against which deviance is defined, differs completely from theirs. *Cleanness* frankly celebrates the heterosexual norm as socially refined and sensually fulfilling, and in a tone of unqualified reverence for lovers' joys that differs from any of the affirmations of love as honorable in the *Complaint* and the *Roman.* Sacralizing and eroticizing nature as a heterosexual norm are what is primarily at stake in *Cleanness* in its attack on *fylþe of þe flesch.* Homosexual deviance, constructed as the gravest possible defilement of divine order, provides a foil against which to legitimate the courtly and romance ethos which informs this poem's vision of God's *clannesse* and his *clene* relations to the world. The aristocratic ethos in *Cleanness* privileges refined sensuality and, in particular, gratuitous sexual pleasure, valued for its intrinsic and subjective qualities, not for its subsequent procreative effects. Such erotic fulfillment the poet daringly represents as natural, assigning the *play of paramorez* a place of singular value in the Creator's ordinance. The desire for intercourse which celibate clerics condemned as a ravenous and potentially enslaving appetite *Cleanness* represents as intrinsically sacred, a capacity for a fittingly passionate response to divinely created order.

The creation of a dualistic psychology of praise and hatred is a concomitant backlash of such an affirmative ethical innovation. Homosexual deviance, precisely because it is usually represented as gratuitous and artificed — like the poem's heterosexual norm of *kynde crafte* — provides the logical target onto which the church's usual aversion to pleasure in its own right can be attached. How else can the poet safeguard the idea of an absolute boundary between heterosexual pleasures, licit although unbounded by procreative intent, and illicit homosexual practices that are similarly unconcerned with reproductive consequences? Asserting to the full the immanence of God's aesthetic involvement in the material universe, and privileging the erotic artifice which was conventionally stigmatized as particularly congenial to men with a predilection for same-sex eroticism, the poet's startling affirmations about the *play of paramorez* as God's *kynde crafte* are perhaps only thinkable as the logical premise of so extreme an attack upon the Sodomites' way of making love. These men, who allegedly find in their flesh the worst of faults the Creator denounces as not only scorning nature, but misreading the meaning of sexual bliss as he has conceived it and personally tried to teach it to them (694, 709). In this redefinition of the intrinsic value of sexual pleasure as natural and godly, the poet strategically locates what threatens nature's norm not in heterosexual loveplay but completely outside it. What he excludes as unnatural he does not categorize along with any other form of sexual vice, as Alain, Thomas, and Jean do, but he constructs same-sex deviance in a categorical opposition to heterosexual desire that is unique, so far as I have discovered, in medieval representations of same-sex desire between males.

6

*Privileging the Feminine:
Courtly Revisions of Masculinity*

The *Cleanness*-poet is concerned with the threat homosexual bonding poses to a distinctive masculine quality of excellence, but his ideals of male virtue differ importantly from Nature's standard in the *Complaint*, as well as from both Reason's and Nature's standards in Jean's ironic revisions of Alain's text in the *Roman*. Similarly, Thomas's emphasis upon the rational, because natural, procreative aim of depositing seed in the fitting vessel contrasts significantly with the poet's vision of what defines a man's sexual conduct as honorably in accord with nature. Cumulatively considered, the three precursor texts reveal the centrality of male dominance to their various definitions of what is natural about heterosexual intercourse.

The difference between the three precursor texts and *Cleanness* is not that the three make nature the heterosexual norm and *Cleanness* does not. On the contrary, by its reference to *kynde crafte*, the passage in *Cleanness* where God praises the mutual pleasure that unites a man and a woman in intercourse celebrates nature as heterosexual norm. But it does so in a way that contradicts the precursor texts' traditional ideals of masculine sexuality and virtue. The poem reconfigures patriarchal gender symbolics as it diverges from the masculinist sexual ethic where the male must relate to a female by dominating, and presumably inseminating, her ideally passive but often either resistant or seductive body. The poem's explanation of what is unnatural about men making love with men is not in fact based upon the familiar claim that homosexual pleasure distorts the proper symbolic gender hierarchy of male governing female. The usual misogynyous connection "between denigration of women and denunciation of sexual pleasure as sinful" (Spearing, *Readings* 183) disappears when the ethical standard for natural acts of intercourse diverges from phallocentric control of problematic female sexuality to a playful and trusting mutuality between the sexes: the two lovers "ayþer oþer welde" (wield power over, control each other 705). God's own words sanctify the pleasure-seeking appetite which clerical discourse identified pejoratively with a gynocentric ethos where masculine spirit is subjected to feminine flesh. So far from posing a threat to the male's rational virtue, such lovemaking denigrates neither the man nor the woman, nor the feminine element of desire. But does God's endorsement of mutuality mean that the poem sympathetically presents women as erotically desiring subjects as well as erotically desirable objects? In this chapter, we shall see another speech on *kynde crafte,* this one by Lot, recommending the natural art of heterosexual lovemaking to his Sodomite neighbors; young women are praised as appealing and adroit in the sexual arts, but with no sensitivity to female subjectivity and no requirement of voluntary reciprocity between the sexes. Unlike God's speech, this discourse on erotic pleasures cannot function logically to legitimate intercourse in the romantic mode of two people committed to each other, a man and his mate, combining mutual respect and passionate enjoyment. Instead of a private tryst between two truly tied to each other, it recommends as natural a form of heterosexual activity that is as promiscuous and predatory as the manner of lovemaking the Sodomite men publicly proposed to enjoy, as a group, with Lot's two attractive visitors. That the conditions of natural sexuality could be joyfully fulfilled if dozens of Sodomites took Lot's two daughters as playmates is not only distressing but absurd. In the process of expanding on the biblical text to make it relate it to his theme, the poet renders an already problematic episode still more incongruous.

In order to explain this elaboration of Lot's speech and the effect of the contradiction it offers to the ethos of sexual equality and mutuality we have discerned in God's celebration of *kynde crafte,* it is necessary to think further about the decorum of aristocratic male bonding, for this homosocial relationship between lord and servant, host and guest, is a primary component of *clannesse.* I shall probe in particular the thematic significance of the contrast the poet depicts between two types of masculinity. One is the softened male image which epitomizes the virtue of *clannesse* as an aristocratic aesthetic ideal; the other is exaggerated masculine aggressiveness which epitomizes *fylþe of þe flesch* as boorish. Once we understand the logical necessity to exclude any taint of unnatural eroticism from the culturally feminized ethos exemplified by the courtly male, we can recognize how God's and Lot's discourses recommending the erotic pleasures of *kynde crafte*, however different they are in tone, share a complex function. Not only do they both contradict the church's repressive sexual ethic of masculine dominance and reproductive rationality; just as significantly although more covertly, they both infuse with eros the homosocial bonds that unite the Creator and men of good taste, and they both also protect those bonds from any taint of desire for homosexual relations. This examination of male ideals will lead to a discussion in chapter 7 of how the feminized ethos of courtly masculinity affects the poet's unconventional representations of the relation of the sacred to the profane both in God's response to men's homosexual desires and in his incarnation of *clannesse* in Christ's perfect flesh.

Redrawing Boundaries of Sex and Gender

The *Cleanness*-poet constructs an unconventional opposition between homosexual vice, which he associates with groups of men given to predatory lust and violence, and homosocial virtue, which he associates with aesthetically refined gentlemen of good taste and breeding. It is by exaggerating the virile traits of dominating will and physical aggression rather than by romantically softening these epic virtues that the men who contrive and indulge in homosexual practices do violence to their humanity and offend God's own nature. In portraying the men guilty of *fylþe of þe flesch* as hypermasculine, *Cleanness* departs tellingly from a familiar medieval caricature of same-sex eroticism that links it to effete connoisseurship of aesthetic effects and consequently to a failure of masculine will and prowess.

The stigma of effeminacy attached to men of homosexual inclination and habit is, as John Boswell reminds us, not a necessary one in the Middle Ages (*Christianity, Social Tolerance, and Homosexuality* 24n43). However, Boswell also points out that "in cultures intolerant of gay people" it is a "universal expectation that males will be erotically affected only by what the culture regards as feminine" and so the anticipation is formed that "males who wish to attract other males will be 'feminine' "(24). Certainly the charge that same-sex relations turn men into women is a prominent topos in the rhetorical tradition of nature as sexual norm, as illustrated already in Alain's *Complaint*; in this chapter I shall offer further examples of the traditional association between sodomy and effeminacy. This stigmatizing of the feminine is strikingly absent from *Cleanness*'s denigrating representation of groups of males distinguished by their homosexual practices. What might explain the poem's unusual depiction of the Sodomites and their antediluvian predecessors not as effeminate but rather as exaggerating to the point of parody the warrior's drive to impose his will through physical coercion?

Given the accusation of effeminacy prevalent in medieval representations of men who deviate from the heterosexual norm, the poet must have been familiar with the stereotype of the sodomite as emasculated and must also have sensed the taint of same-sex eroticism associated with the culturally feminized ethos that is central to his theopoetic vision. His definition of nature as sexual norm leaves him open to suspicion because it drops out the reproductive standard and it privileges artifice and pleasure that were tainted by association with same-sex eroticism. Such a taint is effectively removed by associating homosexual filth with men who are brutalizing opposites of the gentler, more aesthetically appealing males who represent *clannesse*. Moreover, such negative depiction of phallic violence lends added appeal to the gentility of his courtly patriarchs Noah, Abraham, and Lot: their homosocial friendship with God and his angels displays a sense of what is fitting to the softened, courtly ideals of manhood.

Thus the poet constructs contrasting exemplars of these two different masculinities. To trace the logic that tacitly supports, if not explicitly dictates, this move, we must recognize how the poem's drastic departure from the usual patriarchal symbolics of normative Christian male sexuality could open *Cleanness* to the charge of encouraging effeminacy in its male audience. Astonishingly absent from God's paradigmatic lesson for lovers in *Cleanness* are the two fundamental precepts which guaranteed the boundary in medieval Christian ethics between licit and illicit sexual pleasure and differentiated masculine from feminine social roles: the procreative end of marriage that provides a utilitarian justification for pleasure, and the closely related gender symbolism of male governing female in sexual acts performed correctly for the sake of progeny. Together, these ethical precepts reinforced the social hierarchy which cast men into dominant and women into marginal roles. Ideally, the wife should serve as the complicitous recipient of the husband's formative agency, offering her womb as a fitting vessel for his sperm. Yet the fallen appetite for sexual pleasure was blamed on the unruly female aspect of human nature, personified in Eve's disobedience and subsequent temptation of Adam, especially as glossed by allegorizing exegetes. Thus, the husband's pleasure in sexual activity is allegorically symbolized as feminine — the potentially subversive although inferior element in his own nature which must be vigilantly controlled by his masculine reason's procreative purpose. Christian men, whether celibate or married, were taught to identify virility with a superior masculine capacity for reason that enabled and entitled them to take control of the feminine. As mind should prevail over matter, so must the male's rationality bridle his feminine desire, and so also must the husband subjugate his wife. Orthodox sexual ethics admonished males to display their masculinity through mastery over the feminine, both internally over the subversively sensual element of their own fallen nature and externally over their weaker but nevertheless dangerously attractive sexual opposites upon whom the patriarchal voice of the church projected all that it distrusted about the life of the senses.

In celebrating the paradisal mirth God prizes in lovemaking, *Cleanness* erases the pejorative association of the feminine with the fallen, anarchic fleshly impulses for pleasure. Because mutual physical desire between a man and a woman is honored as *honeste,* and its intensification through mutually empowering erotic play is legitimated by God as his gift given equally to both lovers, his speech to Abraham significantly subverts the church's ideological basis for male dominance. Even though he limits the *play of paramorez* to a man and his female *make* (partner—and in context, probably wife),[1] the poet imagines the natural norm of intercourse not in social terms with husband controlling wife, nor in allegorical terms with the soul's "masculine" rationality controlling the body's inferior "feminine" sensuality, but in romantic images of the reciprocity of bliss freely provided by God in enjoyable collaboration with the "naturally" heterosexual couple who *honestly ayper oper welde* (honorably exercise power over each other 705).

By these departures from medieval phallocentric norms for masculine sexuality and virtue, *Cleanness* participates in a romantic redefinition evident in modern Western culture's transformation of manhood. The gradual relocation of male virtue in a sexualized concept of the desiring self began at least as early as the twelfth century, when an elite class of males imagined their urges for erotic pleasure to be an ennobling force for self-transformation. By legitimating heterosexual pleasure without any reference to patriarchal family structure, God's speech associates desire with the divine image in man, shifting the paradigm for masculinity from the father who is both propagator and governor of his family to the erotically desiring male who depends on a female counterpart not as a breeder and nurturer of children but as a pleasing sexual partner adept at giving and receiving pleasure. The traditional patriarchal locus of masculine power in reproductive and familial relations is not rejected by the poet, but it is overshadowed by his extraordinary idealization of the natural heterosexual norm as fueled by passionate desire. Such a symbolic change in the aspects of the heterosexual relationship which shape the masculine ideal leaves the relative positions of dominance and subordination occupied by the sexes fundamentally unaltered, as Joan Cocks observes of the movement from traditional to modern society (214).[2] However, as masculine eroticism eclipsed partriarchal fatherhood in the definition of ideal virility, the symbolic role of the feminine in medieval aristocratic culture did change. This change in gender symbolics released the female from her definition as matter to be controlled by form, the weaker, passive recipient vessel of male's reproductive agency. Potentially, the female body as mapped by romance idealizations of heterosexual courtship presents an equivalently dynamic and desiring self; moreover, the realm of sensuality and its erotic refinements—still marked as feminine—are explicitly legitimated as essential components in the male's self-realization through love.

Lot's speech to the Sodomites illustrates that the romantic privileging of women's imagined desire for men in erotic discourse between males does not valorize female subjectivity or woman as desiring subject, except to posit her existence as enabling the male to imagine mutual heterosexual delight. Nevertheless, in the passage where God speaks of lovemaking, the *Cleanness*-poet does indeed position woman as man's collaborator in a reciprocally enjoyable activity where both partners honorably wield power derived from each other's desires. This legitimation of pleasure-focused mutuality in heterosexual lovemaking fundamentally contradicts the privileging association of masculinity with the rationality that bridles unruly feminine desires, a patriarchal ethical paradigm evident in all three of the precursor texts we have explored. By stressing mutual bliss as the reward for the game and play of love made in accord with nature, this passage on *kynde crafte* constructs as God's design an erotically intimate relationship between man and his mate that dismantles the authority vested in the husband/father by the church's teaching on marriage. At this crucial point in the poem, the normative, because natural, heterosexual union is not family oriented or even conjugally defined.

Because the poem borrows terms from secular romance to revise radically the gender symbolics that underlie the orthodox ethical distinction between licit and forbidden sexual pleasures, we need to look at how this literary tradition redefined masculine ideals. Romance ideology at its most optimistic claims that love confers upon the man and woman blessed by mutual desire a joyful fulfillment of their natures and a realization of their noblest spiritual yearnings. Since the late twelfth century, secular literature had been domesticating the heroic warrior of epic into the gentler, and self-consciously erotic, courtier-knight and fusing chivalric virtue with the arts of love. In an innovative realm of sexual discourse, lyric poets and romance writers had converted male desire for consummate joy in heterosexual lovemaking from a sign of insatiable and degrading lust to a sign of worthiness in love's service.

This blending of erotic ideals with the heroic male ethic was attacked by conservative clerical moralists for its subversion of the tried and true manly virtues essential to combating the temptations posed by the fleshly, and therefore feminine, aspect of fallen human nature. The discursive power of Augustinian orthodox dualism continued to constrain medieval European norms as clergy went on teaching Christians to distrust any urge — or techniques — for erotic intensification of the pleasures of sexual union. Clerical discourse condemned courtly refinements of these natural appetites on the grounds that such artifice catered to the flesh as if its potential gratifications were of some intrinsic value; to seek through the *play of paramorez* to enhance the reciprocal satisfactions potential in sexual activity between a man and his mate would contradict rather than fulfill, they would argue, the social and biological objective of intercourse as the means of reproducing the patriarchal family. Attention paid to desire for its own sake is, by the procreative standards of medieval Christian ethics, an unmistakable symptom — and ongoing cause — of human nature's deviation from rational adherence to an extrinsic good. As we saw in chapter 2, the married couple who chastely avoided indulging themselves in sexual union simply for the pleasure it bestowed could hope, despite their fallen wills' attachment to the lustful gratification attendant upon intercourse, to manifest to some degree their originally splendid likeness to God. Such virtue was daunting, however, and virginity was recommended as the more highly prized state of Christian life because it was more godlike in its aspiration to total freedom from the corrupting influence of inevitably sinful sexual passion.

The church's pessimistic rationalism is radically challenged when the *Cleanness*-poet, instead of denigrating passion as inherently destructive of reason and therefore of human nobility, hallows the bodies of men and women engaged in lovemaking. He daringly imagines the Creator blessing the joys of heterosexual coupling in the very idiom of romantic paradox condemned as irrational by clerical discourse. Creating a poetic space that constructs erotic interchange as a protected but highly volatile field for pleasurable sensation, God takes credit for inventing and communicating to human collaborators the *play of paramorez*. Its consummation is figured in this speech as a paradisal foretaste of joys divine, not by displacing sensual bliss with a higher spiritual reality it signifies allegorically, but in God's providing through heterosexual bodily union a physical experience of pure grace. This is as intimate and gracious a communication of the Creator's *clannesse* as the placing of his own divine body at human disposal in the elements of the Mass; the sacramentality of lovemaking between a man and female thus invests the mutual pleasures of their sexual intercourse with intrinsic value, without regard to the possibility of a procreative outcome.

Cleanness advocates an image of masculinity softened by the courtly ethos idealized in romance, an ethos that Christian moral discourse generally associated with an emasculated captivity to sensual attractions fostered in the seductive realm of the feminine. Writing within — and against — a traditional religious context of masculinist denigration of women and the cultural values associated with them, the poet's self-conscious connoisseurship of aesthetic effects and his generosity toward pleasure and play could logically predispose him to construct the Sodomites not as effeminate, but as the reverse of this stereotype, and hence as a foil against which the gentler masculinity displayed by exemplars of *clannesse* shines all the more brightly.

Courtliness and Feminization: A Historical Perspective

A century before the redefinition of masculine ideals that has been widely assumed to have begun in twelfth-century chivalric fascination with the new secular literature of romance and lyric, a classical standard of conduct that fused the aesthetic and ethical had already crystallized in the lives of eleventh-century German clergy preparing for state service in the imperial court. Stephen Jaeger gives an illuminating account of the formative role played by these clerical authors who revived Ambrose's writings and thereby transmitted to the High Middle Ages a "natural ethic" where external refinements and decorum are validated religiously because they mirror the well-ordered inner life, modeled on nature's perfection.[3] Jaeger also delineates the tension between this ethical code's concern with a refined elegance of appearance and bearing which manifests inner virtue and harmony and the worldly excesses of fashionable conduct that were criticized as indecent. The prejudicing effects of anticourtly propaganda by clerical authors stigmatized courtliness as primarily a matter of material comfort and fashionable self-display and forged a pejorative association between courtliness and the feminine. A familiar topos in this polemical mode of discourse is the misogynistic claim that the warrior society's tried and true values of military honor, strength, and daring are being corrupted by the comfort, pleasure, and sloth characteristic of women's lives in a courtly setting; softened by their relationships with such women and a shared enjoyment of fashionable novelties, men are losing their fighting spirit. The influence of women's styles of dress, coiffure, and conduct on men's sense of decorum is repeatedly satirized as a newfangled reversal of ancient and honorable ideals of manhood.

Even in the optimistic genre of romance, a tension remains between the values of an earlier epic ideal and the ethos of the gentler courtier knight; the "otherness" of culturally feminine values are simultaneously perceived as necessary to true masculine excellence and as threatening to the hero's virility displayed in public contests of military strength.[4] *Sir Gawain and the Green Knight* illustrates well the persistence into the late fourteenth century of a contrast between a feminized world of chivalric romance and the sterner values of an earlier warrior society. Whether the courtly world of Camelot corrupts or exemplifies the ideals of Christian civilization is debatable, but few critics would disagree with Robert Hanning's observation that "in the world over which Arthur and his richly ornamented queen preside, aesthetic norms have attained parity with, if not supremacy over, heroic ones." As Hanning describes the feasting which epitomizes the civilized life of Arthur's court, the splendor of the queen's costume—symbolic of the influence of stereotypically feminine concerns with appearance—underscores the contrast being traced between the older ethos of warring Britons and the new order of Camelot: "Guinevere, at the center of the dais, is so surrounded and decked out with fine fabrics and jewels that she seems transformed from a person into an elegant courtly artifact. . . . Instead of heroes, fighting on through generations of 'turned tyme,' we see at Camelot a new young civilization" (11).[5]

Many chroniclers condemned unequivocally aesthetic innovations they saw threatening the older ideals. Such critics of courtliness as Orderic Vitalis, William of Malmesbury, and John of Salisbury register little of the later ambivalence seen in *Sir Gawain and the Green Knight* about whether tried and true warrior values were corrupted or enhanced by softer, feminine-influenced styles of courtly dress and deportment. In the eleventh century, during a period of peace and prosperity in southern France, the sensual comfort and aesthetic appeal of a luxurious peacetime existence struck Orderic as thoroughly reprehensible. He denounces the effete attire of men in the court of Anjou— fancy shoes, long hair curled with hot irons, tight tunics and shirts. Blaming some aspects of moral decadence on women's fashions, Orderic claims that men who adopted these refinements "gave themselves up to sodomy."[6] Since sodomy is, as we have seen in chapter 2, so ambiguous a term, Orderic may not be diagnosing same-sex attractions as the logical outcome of men coming to a new regard for displaying their bodies to best advantage. Indeed, at one point he specifically associates obsessively stylish self-presentation with the attempt to arouse women's erotic interest: "Our wanton youth is sunk in effeminacy, and courtiers, fawning, seek the favours of women with every kind of lewdness" (Orderic, vol. 4 188–89); however, since homosexual liaisons did not exclude heterosexual ones, this does not settle the question. Nevertheless, in the context of similar diatribes in the twelfth century, it does seem to be reasonable to infer that "sodomy" as Orderic uses it here links a new aesthetic self-awareness on the part of courtly men to their desire to engage erotically with each other's bodies.

In another *locus classicus* for propaganda written by clerics anxious over courtly culture's feminizing effect on gender ideals and sexual norms, the pursuit of fashionable dress and seductive posturing is unambiguously condemned as a deliberate imitation of women. William of Malmesbury attacks such gender reversal specifically because it fosters homoerotic relations among males. The English court of William Rufus aroused William (writing his chronicle in the early twelfth century) to represent in vivid details cross-gender styles of dressing—and undressing. Recalling courtiers "with their flowing hair and extravagant dress," he laments that: "the model for young men was to rival women in delicacy of person, to mince their gait, to walk with loose gestures and half naked. Enervated and effeminate, they remained unwillingly what nature had made them, the assailers of others' chastity, prodigal of their own" (quoted by Dynes, *Encyclopedia* 348). Apparently these young men, trapped in their "natural" masculine identity, had nevertheless imitated women successfully enough to be their rivals, tempting other men to unchastity through homoerotic advances.

A jeremiad written by John of Salisbury just after the middle of the twelfth century inscribes even more luridly this rhetorical topos linking courtliness and effeminacy to homosexual predilections. After portraying in horrified detail a seduction scene where one elaborately coiffed and fashionably arrayed male publicly caresses another, John loosely quotes Romans 1: 26–28, thus making explicit the claim that flirtation between two men is emasculating and unnaturally defiling. "Such abomination should be spat upon rather than held up to view, and I would have been ashamed to insert an account of it in this work had not the apostle, in his epistle to the Romans, written even more explicitly on the theme. 'For their women have changed the natural use into that use which is against nature. In like manner the men, also leaving the natural use of women, have burned in their lusts one toward another, men with men working that which is filthy.'" (200). Emphasizing the attention paid to personal appearance by men who are not ashamed to carry on such homoerotic relations openly, John complains that even if there should happen to be "no one to seduce or violate [them], the training of our youth from their earliest years is so bad that with lascivious glances, expression, bodily movements, the very dress they wear, and enticements scarcely permitted harlots, they themselves solicit seduction" (198–99).[7] Both the male seducer (conventionally active, and therefore stereotypically masculine) and the male recipient of sexual attention are here portrayed as adopting an alluring, and therefore feminine, mode of self-presentation that diminishes their natural manliness. For men to adopt female tastes and to play female sexual roles reveals the inherent decadence of males submitting themselves in any measure to inferior standards of the weaker sex.[8]

The felt tension between aesthetic refinement and decadent emasculation is evidenced in Alain's *Complaint*, where marriage is celebrated and personified as Hymen. He is portrayed as a noble male of aristocratic family on whose face "there showed no signs of feminine softness; rather the authority of manly dignity alone held sway there" (196). The narrator makes a further point of observing how Hymen's well-groomed hair "lay in orderly fashion to prevent it from appearing to degenerate into feminine softness by vagaries of devious arrangements" (197). One senses here Alain's anxiety that softer hair styles for the higher nobility, part of the almost androgynous image for elite males that had become fashionable in the twelfth century, threaten their claim to the sexual dominance the *Complaint* insists is man's natural position, both in society and in bed. Alain sounds a related note in condemning as proud the style-conscious men who "overfeminise themselves with womanish adornments" decorating themselves by coiffures, plucked eyebrows, smooth faces, tight sleeves and long-toed (and hence encumbering) shoes (187). Perhaps he reacts here to the same kind of visibly gay subculture that enjoyed cross-dressing as John of Salisbury criticized.

To put oneself on display in a sexual drama, as a lover must who courts a lady in romance terms, is at some level to jeopardize the very virility whose appeal is being demonstrated.[9] The vulnerability of the feminized male who appears to have crossed the gender line in his attempts to make of himself a sexually appealing artifact — and hence to have made himself, unwittingly, the object of male erotic attention — is evident in Guillaume de Lorris's portion of the *Roman de la Rose*. The God of Love warns against any artificial enhancement of the natural ruddiness of a man's cheeks as he teaches the aspiring young Lover to pay scrupulous attention to standards of cleanliness and elegant grooming; the use of rouge is condemned as a custom that belongs only to ladies or to men of bad repute who have had the misfortune to find a love "contrary to Nature" (lines 2169–74, quoted in McAlpine 11). The careful self-presentation required of the youth who would measure up to his lady's discriminating courtly standards of beauty was potentially tainted by effeminacy; his bodily adornments might make such a young man tantalizing to unnatural erotic appetites of men who defied Nature by loving other men.

A society where masculine excellence was coming to include beauty displayed in manners that "are winning, charming, and tinged with the erotic" (Jaeger 142) fostered styles of dress and self-presentation that could catch the eye and appeal to the desiring gaze of others. Such ambiguity in gender traits may have underscored the necessity for differentiating between what Eve Sedgwick has termed the homosocial, homoerotic, and homosexual continuum of male bonding. I am not arguing, of course, that the terms Sedgwick uses to discuss nineteenth-century masculinity were conceptually anticipated in medieval discourse about effeminacy, for indeed one of the virtues of her analysis of gender dynamics is her insistence on change and development. Rather, I am struck by the possibility that, as court life promoted a new aesthetic dimension in what was seen as a desirable self-image, males' increased consciousness of their physical attractiveness could both expand and jeopardize the opportunities for genital relations among males which had always been part of masculine society. When well-turned-out and hence feminized males elicited — perhaps at first unintentionally — the approving gaze of lovers of the same sex, the previously tacit ambiguities of gender and sexuality were not only put on display but were thereby rendered problematic.[10] What may have been acceptable amorous exchanges between warriors in the all-male military world became destabilizing when such manly homoeroticism was perceived as courtly flirtation that imitated, and hence competed with, the heterosexual rituals that were coming, through the romance narratives, to feminize courtly ideals of masculinity. Perhaps it was such a recognition that courtly ideals of elegance could foster flamboyantly homoerotic behavior that prompted a Dominican professor on the faculty of law at Bologna in the thirteenth century to observe in his discussion of the crime against nature that "in certain unnamed regions, men publicly pollute themselves in this way out of 'courtliness' (*curialitater*), heedless of the evil involved" (Goodich 59–60).

Despite virulent diatribes by conservative clerics against newfangled courtly corruptions of old-fashioned male virtue, many of the higher lay nobility embraced the new social code of elegance, urbanity, and refinement. Observing how "long hair, curly topped shoes, and tight-fitting dress swept like wildfire through the European aristocracy at the end of the eleventh and the beginning of the twelfth century," Jaeger suggests that these men's "rash and impulsive eagerness for fashion is only the materialistic and outward expression of a spiritual penchant endemic to the class: its susceptibility to ideals" (265).[11] From the late twelfth century, romance fiction provided for patrons and listeners of both sexes a layperson's textbook of courtship, reinventing love between the socially elite man and woman as an ennobling ideal rather than as denigrating weakness. Mainly written by clerics who were (theoretically at least) celibate, these narratives constructed woman not as a seductive embodiment of ungovernable sensuality infecting the male will but as an ennobling presence illuminating her lover's mind and inspiring his valor. This is not to suggest that the idealized portrait of the lady in romance fails to communicate the sexual desirability of the female body. The blissful possibility of heterosexual union that motivates the adventures basic to the romance plot includes the dream of winning the heroine's love and with that, consummate pleasure in physical and emotional intimacy.[12] The erotic attraction to the beloved's feminine otherness fueled a heroic commitment to achieve a new kind of integrity through measuring up to the standards implied by this idealized image of humanity. The noble lady's refining influence on the knight's conduct became basic to the aristocratic ideology expressed in courtly romances; we shall see the *Cleanness*-poet drawing on this convention in his praise of Christ as the model of *clannesse* for Christians to imitate in order to attain full human integrity and to thereby enjoy God's love.

The striking difference in romance ideals of masculinity from the epic tradition does not argue for a cult of courtly love literature dominated by female patrons and readers of romance, but it does suggest that a society where women's roles were less marginal than they had been in earlier military and administrative hegemonies supported the production of narratives concerned with the civilizing possibilities of heterosexual courtship, a concern with love not evident in earlier heroic narratives. To what degree feminized fictional ideals of courtship affected the ethos of the actual knights who saw themselves figured in the male subjects of romance is debatable, as is the question of how much influence real women ever wielded over their actual husbands' or lovers' erotic ideals and sexual practices or over the mostly male fabricators of romance. But unquestionably the chivalric community for whom the early romances were written included women of status in influential roles as patrons and as readers. This courtly audience supports a redefinition of male subjectivity, creating a discourse of heterosexual courtship that conforms to standards of civility that are, in the world of romance, typically gendered as feminine from their close association with women's culture. Scrupulousness not only in ethical matters but in the arts of dress, table manners, song and dance, gesture and speech, and, above all, in flirtation and debate over questions of love, became part of the paradigmatic behavior of the male subject of romance. The lover-knight in these narratives measures himself by standards which his lady embodies, although they in fact derive from an entire chivalric community—clearly masculinist in makeup, however inclusive of women— which he represents and to which he is accountable. Thus the scope for individual male identity is simultaneously constrained and enlarged by the romance depiction of heterosexual attraction as a force for the courtier knight's spiritual transformation and exaltation.[13]

Medieval texts, secular and clerical, document a cultural debate over whether it lowered or elevated aristocratic male dignity to pursue women's acceptance when such a passionate attachment to the female object of desire requires renouncing—or pretending to renounce—the social and ethical superiority conferred on men by orthodox Christian sexual ethics, by the tradition of nature as sexual norm, and by the epic ideals of the male-identified hero. I shall discuss an extremely negative view of the humbling effects of this passionate pursuit of female approval in chapter 7 in an account of the passage borrowed by the *Cleanness*-poet from Jean's *Roman,* where the Friend warns the Lover that in imitating his beloved's conduct and praising what she does and likes, he will be lowering himself. Whereas some conservative clerics considered the revised male ideals degradingly sensual and hence emasculating, other clerics found the new definition of manhood morally elevating. The cleric-poets who created the romance tradition fit into this category, for their storytelling not only catered to aristocratic patrons' taste, but (as Jaeger suggests) also functioned to express and sublimate their own erotic vision of the Good as the Beautiful.[14] Andreas Capellanus, a late-twelfth-century clerical contemporary of Alain de Lille, writes with ostensible enthusiasm of the gentler masculinity bestowed by courtship that raises sex to an art. He claims that such a discipline ennobles what was otherwise an aristocratic male predilection for satisfying their sexual appetite by cruder, and sometimes even forced, copulations with socially inferior women.[15] The didactic purposes of *De arte honesti amandi* are as much a matter of scholarly debate as those of Jean's revisions of the *Roman,* but Toril Moi argues convincingly that Andreas's text, for all its ironies, functioned (as did Chretien's romances) to construct what she calls the "effeminization" of aristocratic males as a sign of their "cultural superiority" and that this status-marker was taken seriously enough by enough readers to have helped to legitimize as " 'natural' differences between the rulers and the ruled" (19).

As a genre, the courtly romance itself addresses this question of effeminization, projecting into its plot structure a dynamic tension between, on the one hand, the ancient epic ideal of honor among embattled men in a warrior society where prowess is the primary virtue and, on the other, the innovative erotic ideal of nobility attained through love service to a lady who is honored like a lord. The questionable effects of taking a subordinate role to a female and of giving courtship and marriage equal value to male bonding are themes in some of the most influential masterpieces in this genre. Reason and love personified hold internal debates in many a fictional chivalric knight, anxious about compromising loyalties to other knights and to traditional masculine ideals because his pursuit of a lady's love requires of him a new self-definition, acquired through adventure. Susan Crane traces an overlap between courtship and adventure, arguing that adventure itself is gendered feminine by virtue of the mysterious element inherent in it. She claims both that the adventure plot basic to romance serves to provide the male subjects of this genre with a "productively metonymic experience of the feminine in their encounters with the unknown" (187) and that the romance knight's experience with feminine otherness figured by his adventure seems to require him to behave in some ways like women (168–69). In short, becoming lovers of women, the knights of courtly romance venture forth to take on feminine traits.

A thorough analysis of how and to what degree the male subject of romance is "feminized" when he takes on social roles and manifests traits associated with women lies beyond the scope of this study of *Cleanness*.[16] My reading of romance literature and scholarship on gender symbolics in medieval texts leads me to believe that late medieval courtly culture's association of women with the sphere of aesthetic refinements is generally positive, so that the elite male who — like his fictional exemplars such as Sir Gawain, or Chaucer's young Squire, or his Knight in Black — demonstrates his skillfulness in matters requiring artifice and delicacy and cultivated taste for elegance does not problematize his masculine virtue but rather elevates himself. However, I also sense that because of the force of clerical propaganda and ascetic ideals, the stigma of effeminacy that was early attached to courtly males given to self-display and concern with fashion continued to taint these courtly traits. Indulgence in sensuality and corrupting artifice was frequently enough also associated with homoeroticism, even by the elite where courtliness was a positive ideal, to make it reasonable that the *Cleanness*-poet would want to eliminate any such taints from the ethos he calls *clene*. I see this as a plausible explanation for his otherwise puzzling characterization of the Sodomites and their antediluvian predecessors as deficient in feminine grace. Clearly, it was never the case that only homosexual eroticism was stigmatized as emasculating, or that all males pursuing sexual relations with other males left themselves open to being perceived as effeminate.[17] The stigma of effeminacy is nevertheless conspicuously part of the homophobic rhetorical strategy of the European Middle Ages which constructed nature as a heterosexist norm. The ethos of the *Cleanness*-poet's northwest English readers of the late fourteenth century cannot be simply equated with any of the earlier milieus of the illustrative texts cited in this discussion of feminization and effeminacy. But the poem's audience may safely be assumed to have been well aware of the conventional linkage between self-consciously aesthetic self-presentation, marked by a feminine conformity to up-to-date fashionable standards of dress and erotically charged effeminizing relationships between males. A late-fourteenth-century example of this traditional overlap of anticourtly sentiments and denunciation of males relating sexually to males appears in the prologue to the later version of the Wyclif Bible, which alleges Oxford University to be a hotbed of sodomy. While the university clerics are not explicitly named as effeminate, they are attacked for their predilection for "nyce aray," for their many sins of the flesh, and especially for this "cursid synne aȝens kynde" (51).[18]

By the time the *Cleanness*-poet uses decorous adornment of courtly apparel to symbolize the life of all-encompassing virtue, many elite males regarded adorning oneself in modish coiffures and costumes as a masculine duty. To cultivate an elegant personal appearance was a class-marked sign of virtue not only for the lords and gentry as well as clerics of a comparably high social status, but for those who aspired to the aristocratic model of the *gentil* man. Yet the *General Prologue* to the *Canterbury Tales* also suggests that a man's excessive attention to fashionable apparel could signal dubious sexual preference and practice. In contrast to the *Cleanness*-poet's courtly vision of *clannesse* as a virtue that manifests itself both outwardly and inwardly, Chaucer's most ethically honorable pilgrims (the Knight, Clerk, Parson, and Plowman) show little or no interest in their array. The majority, however, do attempt to display their honorable status through their attire, and their attempt generally succeeds with the narrator who is alert to these markers of social position. For our purposes, the Knight's young son and the Pardoner form an instructive study in contrasts, since among the many fashion-conscious pilgrims, these two stand out as particularly devoted to making a good impression by their appearance. Both men are visibly feminized—one positively and the other negatively. The Squire, hoping to win his lady's grace, decks himself out like a meadow in bloom. Not only is he covered in floral embroidery, but his hair style appears to have required the use of curlers. Yet for this charming lad the narrator—and later the Franklin—express only admiration, while the vanity of the Pardoner invites the usual scornful stereotype of effeminacy. Riding almost bareheaded in accord with fashion's dictates, the Pardoner displays lank and skimpy locks that are indeed no more self-consciously coiffured than the Squire's, but with antithetical social effect. Beneath the Pardoner's careful control of his personal appearance there lurks a sexual ambiguity which invites insult—at first veiled, and then overt at the end of his tale. The narrator notes that this feminized male harmonizes with the Summoner in a suspiciously erotic duet ("Com hider, love, to me"). Clearly this pair of degenerates triggers in the narrator the pejorative cultural association of emasculating gender reversal and homosexual habits with fashion-conscious males; he speculates that the Pardoner is a "geldyng or a mare" (I [A] 672, 691).[19] When the Pardoner takes his turn in the tale-telling contest, the initial suspicion of this pilgrim's possible pursuit of sexual relations with another male comes to highly imaginative expression, with allusions to both the *Complaint of Nature* and Jean's *Roman*. What had been a conjecture on the part of the narrator is dramatized in the *Tale*'s ending as a foregone conclusion, at least on the part of Harry Baillie.

In fourteenth-century England the monarch himself was not above suspicion of deviating from sexual and gender norms. The sodomitic reputation of the court of Edward II (d. 1327), notorious for the king's homosexual relations with his favorites Hugh Despenser and Piers Gaveston, lingered through the fourteenth century; at the end of it, Richard II made an attempt to clear his royal ancestor's memory and even to procure his canonization. But the end of the century was also marked by allegations of homosexual conduct between the English king and his favorite, as Richard II himself was criticized for being inordinately fond of Robert de Vere. The most influential indictments came from the histories of Thomas Walsingham. That a political bias shaped his methodical defamation of Richard II is shown by George B. Stow's analysis of how Walsingham, as he became more alienated from the king's policies, rewrote history to transform the king's character into that of a "youthful, degenerate, and feckless tyrant" (84). Walsingham alters his account of Richard's elevation of Robert de Vere from earl of Oxford to duke of Ireland in order to depict the king's favoritism as indicative of homosexual bonding: "he was so much attached to him, he associated with him and loved him so much, not without indication of indecent familiarity" ("tantum afficiebatur eidem, tantum coluit et amavit eundem, non sine nota, prout fertur, familiaritatis obscoenae," quoted from the Royal manuscript of *Historia Anglicana,* Stow 86; my translation). The slur of corrupting physical intimacy between men is obviously no indication of actual sexual deeds, for homophobic rhetoric was used in medieval political scandalmongering in ways that show continuity with modern associations of sexual deviance with political threat (Dollimore 236–40). However, the credibility of Walsingham's sexual innuendo is not relevant to my point, which is rather that Richard II is criticized by his contemporary as both obscenely familiar and tenderly romantic in his attentions to another male. Thus the unseemly bond of same-sex love is equated with exhibitions of courtly erotic sentiment, epitomized by extravagant gifts — in this case titles and lands as well as costly jewelry. In another revisionist text, Walsingham depicts the king's regard for de Vere's body as immoderate both during his lifetime and after his death. During an elaborate burial of the remains which had been removed to England by royal order, Richard II ordered the cypress box in which the body of Robert lay steeped in balsam to be opened so that he could look on his dead friend's face and fondle his fingers, on which he had placed expensive gold rings. Thus, "he demonstrated publicly his love for the deceased, which he had spent upon him earlier during his life" ("Demonstratque dilectionem defuncto publice, quam impenderat prius vivo," quoted from *Annales Ricardo Secundi,* Stow 91; my translation). Richard II was criticized for lavish domestic expenditures, and his penchant for fashionable attire for himself and his court contributed to political opponents branding him as effeminate (Mathew 139, 143; Tuck 39). In politically biased accounts of the erotic dimensions of the king's friendship with de Vere and of the obsessive regard for aesthetic effects that charactcrized the royal court, I see a continuity between homophobic rhetoric in late-fourteenth-century England and the pejorative associations that we saw in earlier polemics against same-sex love, where sodomy was similarly linked to the emasculating effects of courtliness.

Same-sex desire and aestheticized standards of dress and conduct were sometimes linked together when openly homoerotic bonding between males threatened conventional masculine identity within the gender hierarchy. The need to protect his own eroticized ethos of courtliness from the traditional stigma of "softness" may underlie the poet's choice to construct the original proponents of sodomy as parodies of militant maleness. It is striking that *Cleanness* validates religiously and ethically a highly cultivated aesthetic sensibility decried as emasculating over so many centuries by so many clerics and satirists, and that it simultaneously departs from the aspersions of effeminacy cast conventionally on traits and tastes of men who relate sexually to other men. Instead the poem depicts the Sodomites' militant manhood as the very reverse: brutally insensitive to Lot's culturally feminized values. In effect, *Cleanness* reverses conventional gender symbolics as it illustrates *fylþe of þe flesch* by depicting these fictionalized positive and negative exemplars of masculine desire. The men of Sodom, instead of being a decadent counterfeit of women's culture, not only disdain sexual relations with women but also lack all the gentlemanly graces displayed by Lot and the poem's other refined males whose bonds with one another and God are paragons of homosocial courtliness. This unconventional representation of a homosexually active society as unmannerly and violent may well have offered itself to the poet's imagination in order to remove from the aesthetically sensitive and softened masculinity he considers next to godliness any taint of the negative association with unnatural sexual appetites that the courtly ethos sometimes carried with it.

Antithetical Exemplars of Masculinity

Men who pursue sexual relations with other men are portrayed in *Cleanness* as hypermasculine adherents to a parodically violent heroic ethos. The contrast between their aggressiveness and a gentler ideal is introduced when the poet glorifies Adam's descendants in the days before the Flood as exemplars of an unexcelled beauty, still retaining (despite the Fall, which has earlier been recounted) the physical perfection God gave to their forefather at creation. The romantic attractiveness the poet claims for these paragons of masculine strength and beauty is his own invention based neither on the Vulgate, which credits only Seth with being born in Adam's likeness, nor on the Pseudo-Methodius, which (in one of its two Latin recensions) portrays Seth as a giant (Twomey, "*Cleanness,* Peter Comestor" 210-11). These men before the Flood fulfill both the knightly ideal of prowess and the softer courtly ideal of gracefulness. By juxtaposition to the violent generation who bring on the Flood, the society created by these archetypally brawny and good-looking exemplars is harmonious. Although fallen and condemned to die, humankind after the Fall, contrary to the Augustinian tradition, retained its Adamic physical perfection and "alle þe blysse boute blame þat bodi myȝt haue" (all the bliss without a blame that a body might enjoy 260).[20] Thus, it is not the primal disobedience in Eden but rather a series of unnatural couplings many generations later which interferes with the blissful sexual relations established by the Creator. God is outraged when, from these corrupting unions, a generation of men is born whose virility is a parody of heroic excess. Derring-do and boastfulness that could be considered positively exemplary in an epic narrative are satirically exaggerated by the poet:

> Þose wern men meþelez and maȝty on vrþe,
> Þat for her lodlych laykez alosed þay were;
> He watz famed for fre þat feȝt loued best,
> And ay þe bigest in bale þe best watz halden. (273-76)
> (Those men were immoderate and mighty on earth
> That were renowned for their hateful games;
> He was famed as honorable who loved best to fight
> And always the one who did the most evil was regarded as the best.)

Taking combat as the primary test of excellence, these *maȝty on molde* (great men on earth 279) wreak such havoc that God repents creating a world to be corrupted by such foolish creatures.

Noah, on the other hand, is depicted as a paragon of peaceful self-governance, worthy of preservation because he "rewled hym fayre" (governed himself fittingly) and "ay glydande wyth his God, his grace watz þe more" (going smoothly along with his God, he had the greater grace 294, 296).[21] This contrast between Noah and the rest of his generation foreshadows a still more explicit conflict between courtly exemplars and aggressive villains in the story of Sodom. The homosexually inclined citizens of that ill-fated city conspicuously lack the genteel masculine virtues which distinguish God's allies in this second confrontation with *fylþe of þe flesch*.

In his rendering of the Sodomites' attempted sexual assault on Lot's heavenly guests, the *Cleanness*-poet fictionalizes scripture even more freely in order to emphasize as symbolic a contrast that the biblical text merely hints at. In opposition to the positively appealing portraits of the angels as paragons of boyish virtue, and of Lot as a perfect aristocratic host, the native sons of Sodom exemplify homosexual predilections as thoroughly repellent because they are violently pursued. Asserting their rights in militant speeches, with crude gestures of masculine sovereignty and sexual entitlement, the Sodomites underscore the poet's earlier critique of harmful excess licensed by the heroic ethic of warrior brotherhoods. Like the boasting heroes who bring on the Flood, they confidently pit themselves against Lot in armed warfare, battering his wall with their clubs, roaring their determination to initiate his good-looking young guests into the distinctive sexuality of Sodom.

> "If þou louyez þy lyf, Loth, in þyse wones,
> ȝete vus out þose ȝong men þat ȝore-whyle here entred,
> Þat we may lere hym of lof, as oure lyst biddez,
> As is þe asyse of Sodomas to seggez þat passen." (841-44)
> ("If you value your life, Lot, in these lands,
> Send out to us those young men who recently entered here,
> So that we may teach them of love, as our pleasure urges,
> As the custom of Sodom is to men who pass through.")

This assault on Lot's life and his guests' chastity culminates a conflict that the poet stages with consummate narrative artistry. As Lot first appears, he is alone on his porch, staring out into the street where the "stout men" of Sodom are at "play," and it is clear that their crude sportiveness holds no appeal for him. As Lot holds himself aloof, he is a figure of lonely virtue, but his refined taste is rewarded as his gaze is drawn to "swete men tweyne" (lit., two sweet men 788) entering the city, gentle youths whose companionship is obviously an alternative — and superior — form of male bonding. Through the description given from Lot's admiring perspective, we can sense both his and the poet's own delight with this feminized pair, whose good looks and deportment are clearly modelled on the standards of courtly romance which had softened the epic ideals of heroism. Remarking at first on the young strangers' winsome combination of physical prowess and graceful demeanor, the poet conveys their confidence and camaraderie and then moves to an admiring catalogue of their strikingly androgynous features:

> He syȝe þer swey in asent swete men tweyne;
> Bolde burnez wer þay boþe with berdles chynnez,
> Ryol rollande fax to raw sylk lyke,
> Of ble as þe brere-flour whereso þe bare scheweed.
> Ful clene was þe countenaunce of her cler yȝen;
> Wlonk whit watz her wede and wel hit hem semed. (788–93)

(He saw there walking together two attractive men,
Bold men they were both, with beardless chins,
Royal waving locks, like raw silk,
Of complexion like the briar rose, where the skin showed;
Utterly splendid was the expression of their bright eyes.
Nobly white was their clothing and well suited to them.)

By the flawless appeal of face and form, Lot recognizes the heavenly beings. Seeing the beauty of the angels as the poet's means of suggesting "a spiritual excellence superior to all considerations and distinctions of human sexuality," Monica McAlpine nonetheless argues that in this depiction of male attractiveness he has explained "something left unexplained in the biblical text: how the men of Sodom came to desire homosexual intercourse with the angels. It seems likely that a hermaphroditic or feminoid male would have been suspected of sexual deviance" (12).[22] This hermaphroditic ideal she suggests is "a late and perhaps unconscious reflection" of Hellenistic art's rendering of "the male homosexual's supposed participation in the feminine" (12).

Lot displays the correctly discerning response of the courtly male who is impressed by and homosocially attracted to such boyish beauty. He is both charmed and charming as he virtually woos the angels to dine and spend the night in his palatial home. As model guests, they exemplify an aristocratic ideal of masculine excellence found in both epic and romance, but the stress falls on the latter because of the poet's attention to their attractiveness and courtesy. He emphasizes how much pleasure the youths bring to their host by being so thoroughly affable, fittingly attired, well spoken, *and* supremely good-looking—"gay and ful glad, of glam debonere, / Welawynnely wlonk" (well-dressed and lighthearted, gracious in speech / Delightfully handsome 830–31). Lot's exemplary behavior as host illustrates the thin but crucial line differentiating homoerotic sentiment from illicit homosexual lust.

Although they too are attracted by the newcomers' good looks, the men of Sodom fail to grasp the homosocial ethos exemplified in the host-guest bond that controls the genteel interaction between Lot and these romantically appealing young men. The Sodomites' harsh and predatory virility is exaggerated as the poet stresses their stout adherence to a willfully violent sexual code which talks about teaching strangers new ways to make love but is ready to commit gang rape and murder. The virtues of hospitality are at stake in Lot's response to the threat posed by the violent mob outside his gates. Like the angels who are "bolde burnez" (bold knights 789) as well as beautiful boys, Lot combines epic courage and romantic graciousness; he encounters his foes reasonably, balancing horror and inner turmoil with outward equanimity.

Moving with alacrity but not undignified haste, he meets the outrageous proposal of his marauding neighbors in a courtly display of supreme tact and verbal finesse. By his refined demeanor, he attempts to transform the consciousness of the wretches:

> Þenne he meled to þo men mesurable wordez,
> For harlotez with his hendelayk he hoped to chast:
> "Oo my frendez so fre." (859–61)
> (Then he spoke to those men in moderate words
> For the base fellows with his courtesy he hoped to restrain:
> "O, my friends so noble.")[23]

Lot goes on to describe his daughters' sexually appealing features in an earnest attempt to subvert the sexual appetite the Sodomites so openly display toward the angelically beautiful boys. He sets his loathing of his neighbors' "spitous fylþe" (abominable filth 845) and his duty as host so far above even family loyalty or the norm of virginity until marriage that he offers the ravening boors in the street his own beautiful and treasured girls instead of the handsome guests they crave.

Before we contemplate the poet's problematic elaboration of the already dubious sexual role Lot's daughters occupy in the scriptural source for this story, we need to look further into how this exemplum creates a binary sexual opposition. The narrative polarizes *fylþe* and *clannesse* in terms of the Sodomites' disdain for the forms of love they might learn from women; their preference for the same-sex lovemaking they have devised and want to teach to the boyish visitors marks them as utterly devoid of the social sensitivity associated with the aristocratic refinements God has praised in his speech to Abraham defining *kynde crafte*. Lot appeals to a standard of courtly heterosexual decorum as he tries to circumvent his neighbors' determination to invade his house and to force themselves upon the divine guests who have given him such pleasure. The Sodomites are deaf to such ideals and reject with derision Lot's appetizing offer of two young females to educate them in the superior pleasures of love made in accord with nature:

> "Wost þou not wel þat þou wonez here a wyȝe strange,
> An outcomlyng, a carle? We kylle of þyn heued!
> Who joyned þe be jostyse our japez to blame,
> Þat com a boy to þis borȝ, þaȝ þou be burne ryche?" (875–78)
> "Don't you know well that you dwell here as a stranger,
> An alien, a churl? We will cut off your head!
> Who appointed you as a judge to condemn our games,
> You who came as a boy to this town, though you are [now] a rich man?"

Lot's preference of a more fitting form of lovemaking is thus attributed by the Sodomites to the ignorance of a newcomer who, however rich and however long resident in Sodom, is not entitled to judge the native customs. Ironically, for the morally and socially degraded Sodomites, it is Lot who, though rich in goods, is nothing but a churl, because he is an alien to their city's traditions of same-sex desire.[24]

The contrast the poet portrays here between two types of masculinity — one homosexually active and proud of it and the other appalled by the very mention of such practices which he dismisses as detestable "low-class" filth — bears on current historical questions surrounding the emergence of patterns of behavior and social identity that distinguished groups of men who pursued same-sex relations. Wayne Dynes notes the accumulation of evidence of "homosexual patterns of association" in European cities as early as the late twelfth century.[25] The Sodomites exhibit a commitment to a way of life they see as an established social norm to which they expect newcomers will conform once they are taught the necessary skills. They identify themselves as natives of a city they would characterize by the pleasurable sexual uses its male citizens make of each other, as well as of any outsider who arouses their desire. Unlike the marginalized homosexual networking group described by Dynes, the men of Sodom can hardly be said to display an identity as a subculture that deviates from their society's mainstream. Yet they do express a proud sense of group solidarity, of belonging to one another because of the way in which they have learned to make love homosexually typically and habitually.

David Halperin dates the seventeenth century as the beginning of "social gathering-places for persons of the same sex with the same socially deviant attitudes to sex and gender who wish to socialize and to have sex with one another" (8).[26] Although his essay places the origins of a recognizable subculture long after Dynes's suggestion of a twelfth-century urban gay subculture and three centuries after *Cleanness* was written, Halperin suggests that an anticipation of this later development may have occurred in the medieval identification of sexual acts with "certain specifically sexual types of persons" (*One Hundred Years* 8).[27] The Sodomites in *Cleanness* are not portrayed as pathologically deviant or physically incapable of heterosexual relations, but they are sexual types insofar as they deliberately cultivate and transmit a distinctive and, to the poet, perversely horrifying kind of lovemaking. The poet makes clear that by the Sodomites' *japez* (tricks 864), Lot does not refer simply to a once and for all rite of passage to be inflicted on any newcomer to the city; these men appear to have no desire for women as sexual partners, however conventionally appetizing, but an unquenchable lust for attractive young men, and a way of satisfying that carnal longing which is their tour de force. This sexual knowledge they display proudly as "a culturally sanctioned and elaborated source of identity,"[28] and also as their educational mission; they are committed to teaching others something they would otherwise not know. The implication is that in Sodom, male homosexual activity was a deliberately cultivated form of life, a tradition that was socially constructed as honorable, worthy to be passed on with civic pride. *Cleanness* portrays the men of Sodom as having scorned the Creator's prized heterosexual patterns because they have learned a form of sexual desire (*lyst* 693, 843) they identify as their custom. They denounce Lot's rejection of their way of life, attributing his behavior to his alien origins. They are as insensible to the heterosexual pleasures that Lot's speech sets forth as he and the narrator are to lovemaking in the Sodomite tradition. *Cleanness* thus constructs an antithesis between a cultural preference for homosexual love which the marauding mob of Sodomites defend as superior and God's aristocratic passion for heterosexually correct forms of loveplay. Furthermore, it stigmatizes the predilection for same-sex genital relations as associated with male violence, for it is precisely in order to defend their preference for a distinctive version of making love, as their desire prompts, that the Sodomites are heroically ready to murder Lot (841–44).

Such exaggeratedly aggressive advocates of males having sexual relations with other males had, I would wager, no actual social counterpart in fourteenth-century England, for had sodomy in fact been publicly defended by anyone in the poet's society in anything resembling the threatening manner he attributes to the Sodomites, scholars would have uncovered some trace of it. Although portrayed in *Cleanness* as "sexual types," the Sodomites do not reflect a sexual subculture of the late Middle Ages. The poet has fictionalized the biblical episode and developed these characters out of an inventive impulse that exhibits some logic different fron mimetic realism. His homophobic construction of these openly gay ruffians exhibits a striking similarity to phobic constructions of the Jews, both in the Middle Ages and subsequently. Of anti-Semitic discourse rampant in France in the 1940s, Sartre theorized that if the Jews had not existed, the anti-Semite would have invented them (Elon 94), thus echoing Freud's insight that the anti-Semite projects onto the Jew dangers that the anti-Semite feels threatened by and therefore is driven to deny (Spector, "Anti-Semitism" 329). Chaucer's Prioress was revulsed by Jews she describes as representing qualities of spiritual stain and physical defilement that constitute her own negation (Spector, "Empathy and Enmity" 222).[29] Similarly, I see the poet of *Cleanness* repelled not simply by unnatural lust or even by homosexual deeds per se, but by what he imagines aggressively homoerotic men like the Sodomites typically saying and doing with each other sexually. Even though theirs is the sin of which preachers say it is best not to speak, he produces a quasi-homiletic discourse which focuses a formidable amount of narrative talent and energy upon it. In the process, *fylþe of þe flesch* shifts from a generalized periphrasis to an increasingly specific meaning, exemplified by the figure of the Sodomites who signify a rather more precise danger than homosexual lust.

Modern theoretical models of intolerance, drawing on Freudian concepts of displacement and projection, can illuminate *Cleanness*'s virulent attack on men who desire each other sexually and, in particular, its unusual gender symbolics in representing such villains. The poet's homophobic imagination denies similarity of Self to Other by vilifying the Sodomites's sexual customs as violent, thus hiding the proximity of homosexual desire and erotic coercion to homosocial dynamics in a culture informed by courtly masculine ideals. The boundaries protecting privileged gentle masculinity are secured by the opposition that *Cleanness* enables its author and his implied heterosexually desiring audience to believe really exists between "us" and "them."

Cleanness's peculiar depiction of the Sodomites' dominating masculinity may be an example of what Jonathan Dollimore calls the "perverse dynamic" of sexual dissidence. Their predatory insistence on sexual intercourse with Lot's visitors is represented as a threat to the values of heaven itself, and yet these repellent boasters epitomize — by their cut-off-your-head rhetoric — the exaggerated autonomy and aggressiveness that are traditionally idealized in the Christian warrior. As Dollimore observes, "Whatever a culture designates as alien, utterly other, and incommensurably different is rarely and perhaps never so" (182). Rejecting the insulting denigration of the body presented by orthodox sexual ethics, the poet puts its harsh dynamic of interdiction and patriarchal control to work by reasserting the church's absolute prohibition against men making love with each other, and in the process identifying with genocidal violence compulsively unleashed against such perversity by a perversely angry God. The poet's attachment to these cultural realities he in effect overtly denies by emphasizing gentler romance ideals of masculine friendship, but he reveals his tacit attraction to the earlier epic ideal by displacing its violence onto a vilified Other who is blamed for arousing God's helplessly extreme wrath. While revising the gender and sexual ideals which are the symbolic locus of Christian patriarchal thought, the poet holds their repressive violence in abeyance in part by characterizing male dominance parodically; he demeans the masculine predilection for force by portraying as boorish and brutal the men whose lust for their own sex brought on the Flood and the destruction of Sodom. However, the totalitarian vengeance the Creator unleashes against this villainy would seem to cast him in an equally aggressive, overtly dominating role, manifesting his power in the will and capacity to destroy.

The poet's reversal of the gender symbolics of conventional homophobic discourse conveys his denial that the feminized attributes of courtliness the positive exemplars of *clannesse* all display could logically be predicated of men who make love to each other as the Sodomites did. Instead, men thus drawn to sexual acts with each other must exhibit the very opposite trait, crude masculine aggressiveness. If this logic of converse mirroring is indeed at work, what might the curious phrase "on femmalez wyse" (695) denote about the Sodomite men? The *Cleanness*-poet's condemnation of their habit of male coupling with male portrays the partners as symmetrically placed, so that he views them in the plural when he says that "Vch male matz his mach a man as hymseluen" and that they both "fylter folyly in fere on femmalez wyse" (Each man makes his mate a man like himself; they [both] mingle foolishly/crazily together in women's manner 695–96). The action in this parodic pairing is in its debased way as mutual as that of the heterosexual pair of lovers who "honestly ayþer oþer welde" (handle/use each other honorably 705). He cannot mean that both partners in his Sodomitic pair are "passive" and hence effeminate, since he stresses the fact that all Sodomite males, not just half of them, are distortedly macho and aggressive. Thus, despite the reference to these men as being tangled together confusingly in a womanly way, male homosexual relations are not being constructed here as emasculating in the traditional sense of that term. They are not, that is, being condemned because they involve active males betraying their sex by becoming passive partners in intercourse as was so offensive to polemicists like Alain de Lille. We can infer that the *Cleanness*-poet thinks of the Sodomites behaving in a foolish and womanly way not because they are effeminate, which they are not, but because they find each other's maleness sexually appealing. To register that sexual attraction to a male body is precisely what females do when they play the heterosexual game that God portrays for men and women who take their proper roles as *paramorez*. Rejecting females as sexual partners, the Sodomite men exhibit what the narrator considers to be a definitively female trait; their way of taking each other as sexual partners is defined as tangling together confusedly in a womanly manner because they substitute for the desire for sexual relations with a female (a trait that is seen by the poet as natural for males, since it is crucial to the heterosexist culture's definition of masculinity) a desire for a male partner in lovemaking (a trait that culture identifies as female, and so must represent "womanliness" and "confusion" when displayed by a male).

Misogyny and Male Bonding

In place of the Sodomites' unnatural *japez* (games 864), Lot describes for them other forms of sexual play that can simultaneously fulfill both the course of nature and the impulse toward a playful elaboration beyond mere obedience to an extrinsic law. The poet thus further polarizes the contrast he began to make in God's speech on *kynde crafte,* drawing an absolute social and aesthetic boundary between the appalling strangeness of the pleasures devised by men who enjoy each other as sexual partners and the appealing naturalness of pleasures enjoyed by men and women who play with each other in a mode not less but more artful. By the imaginative expansion of the biblical Lot's offer of his daughters to the Sodomites, the poet stresses the seemliness and elegance of men doing what he believes comes naturally when in the company of attractive young women:

> "Oo, my frendez so fre, your fare is to strange;
> Dotz away your derf dyn, and derez neuer my gestes.
> Avoy! hit is your vylaynye, ȝe vylen yourseluen;
> And ȝe ar jolyf gentlymen, your japez ar ille.
> Bot I schal kenne yow by kynde a crafte þat is better:
> I haf a tresor in my telde of tow my fayre deȝter." (861–66)
> ("O, my friends so noble, your ways are too strange.
> Do away with your fierce noise and never harm my guests.
> Away with you! It is to your disgrace; you defile yourselves.
> If you are worthy gentlemen, your jokes are vile.
> But I shall teach you according to nature a craft that is better;
> I have a treasure in my house, my two fair daughters.")

Lot would teach the Sodomites a better craft by offering them a standard of pleasure that is natural, a form of loveplay that involves deflowering his virgin daughters. As Lot markets his daughters' beauty and courtly manners, he stresses their nubile eagerness to be with men who are prepared to "man" them as sexual partners.[30] Yet the audience Lot addresses and his purpose in doing so must erase any idea of mutual pleasure. So long as rape is not a danger for his attractive male visitors, Lot can rephrase the Sodomites' propensity for predatory sexual exploits as simply amounting to a form of sportiveness and then cheerfully offer his daughters to these thugs as playmates.

Although medieval fathers (real and literary) transferred their daughters as sexual tokens, such patriarchal unfeelingness is conventionally situated in the context of marriage, not rape. The virginity of daughters is normatively valued as part of the natural order of marriage, necessary to ensure the paternal lineage of their future husbands. The fictionalizing imagination of the poet makes Lot view his daughters' virginal status as a marker of the superior appeal of heterosexual loveplay. "Hit arn ronk, hit arn rype, and redy to manne" (they are full-blown, they are ripe, and ready for men — 869) Lot promises. What sorts of sexual advances are excluded, if any, in Lot's encouragement that the Sodomites play as they please with his daughters is not clear. What the poet stresses is Lot's belief that they are sexually adept:

> "To samen wyth þo semly þe solace is better.
> I schal biteche yow þo two þat tayt arn and quoynt,
> And laykez wyth hem as yow lyst, and letez my gestes one."(870–72)
> ("If you consort with those seemly ones, the solace is better.
> I shall deliver to you these two that are lively and dainty,
> And play with them as you please, and leave my guests alone.")

The implication is that by uniting with these lovely ladies the Sodomites will acquire the inherently noble tastes and status that Lot's offer courteously, but contradictorily, attributes to them as gentlemen even as he reproves their villainy. In their failure to find the offer attractive, the Sodomites display a lack of sensitivity to proper aristocratic standards of sexual decorum.

Lot seems to be fully cognizant of the Sodomites' sexual brutality (who could miss it, with their clubs banging on the walls?), and he responds to it in countering the threat they pose to his guests; yet this brutality does not worry him in regard to his daughters. What it would mean to the young women to be loosed to this violent mob of all the males in Sodom capable of wielding a weapon, both weak and strong, matters neither to Lot nor, apparently, to the poet. There is implicit here a curious interplay between insensitivity to women's vulnerability and dignity, on the one hand, and, on the other, unabashed devotion to a courtly standard of male beauty and genteel deportment shaped by values that are culturally identified as feminine.

In its incongruity with God's speech to Abraham, the poet's expansion of Lot's speech to elaborate its salacious aspects is particularly unsettling — and therefore intriguing. I have argued that the courtly ethos of *Cleanness*, epitomized in God's speech about love as *kynde crafte*, privileges the feminine and dignifies woman as a sexual subject with intrinsically valuable desires. Lot's offer as the poet elaborates it raises a question about this ideal of sexual mutuality and even equality that made God's earlier speech on love subversive of traditional phallic dominance. The callous prurience of Lot's attitude to women, which in effect parodies God's phrase about *kynde crafte* by applying it to a potential gang rape whose naturalness consists only in its heterosexuality, must make us wonder how *kynde* is defined by the poet after all.

What this legitimation of male dominance in Lot's offer of his daughters reveals is the problem of extricating a romantic ideal of heterosexual bliss from the constraining ideology of male dominance. The two speeches on love when read together suggestively illustrate how courtly erotic discourse by males with males serves complex ideological ends and can enforce the gender system of patriarchal heterosexism even while revising it drastically. Both speeches overtly legitimate an innovative heterosexual norm that replaces the traditional patriarchal reproductive aim of intercourse with the celebration of its mutual pleasures. This erotically suggestive discourse between men about male-female union can function to differentiate and protect the male-male relationship from any taint of homosexual desire, and thus it strengthens homosocial bonding. How crucial a role female sexual attractiveness and accessibility plays in maintaining these male bonds by defining their boundary is revealed in Lot's offer of his daughters to his neighbors in an effort to encourage more genteel conduct toward the angels. The poet emphasizes the incongruity of the Sodomites' preference for same-sex relations by constructing it as a violation of an all-important code of heterosexist culture which dictates that gentlemen should find women to be compellingly desirable, and that women should desire to be thus desired. Desirable and desiring females are obviously crucial to that norm which the Sodomites' same-sex lovemaking threatens. *Kynde crafte* is revealed in Lot's speech as fundamentally linked to a social code of male aristocratic decency; to satisfy it, the requirements are simply heterosexual desire and a female partner.

The girls' roles in this homosocial economy are similarly accentuated by the poet's revisions of the Vulgate. Whereas the biblical source does not mention the daughters until they are offered by Lot to his neighbors, the poet brings the virgins to the door to greet their father and his guests. The specific sexual dimension of the daughters' identity as "maydenez" is alluded to at the outset in terms that stress female submissiveness, marriageability, and good looks properly enhanced by stylish attire:

> His two dere doȝterez deuoutly hem haylsed,
> Þat wer maydenez ful meke, maryed not ȝet,
> And þay wer semly and swete, and swype wel arayed. (814–16)
> (His two dear daughters devoutly greeted them,
> Who were maidens full meek, not married yet,
> And they were seemly and sweet, and very well arrayed.)

They are part of the largesse that an exemplary host puts on display for other males. The poet's emphasis on how beautiful, well dressed, and courteous Lot's girls are suggests how the decorative appeal of young females contributes to the ritualized aesthetic pleasures which help knit the homosocial bond between aristocratic males (see also 899, 932, 938). As he explicitly says to the Sodomites, these two fair lasses are commodities, part of their father's assets.

> I haf a tresor in my telde of tow my fayre deȝter,
> Þat ar maydenez vnmard for alle men ȝette;
> In Sodomas, þaȝ I hit say, non semloker burdes.(866–68)
> (I have a treasure in my house, my two fair daughters,
> That are as yet virgins, unmarred by any men;
> In Sodom, though I say it myself, there are no ladies more beautiful.)

For Lot, his daughters' superlative good looks combined with their virginity signify his own superior social status. What the father owns, he can legitimately dispose of, and in the process, he will transfer to the Sodomites the social standing his daughters' sexual attractiveness confers on him. He assumes that such "jolyf gentylmen" (864) can be appealed to on these class-specific grounds: "To samen wyth þo semly þe solace is better" (To sleep with those seemly ones, the solace is better 870). Such pleasure is better in Lot's scale of value not just because it is sensually pleasing, but because he assumes it is socially more desirable than making sexual conquests of every attractive male who visits Sodom. His daughters' virginal charms are tokens in an exchange by which Lot aims to protect his guests from the mob of lustfully aroused men; their homosexual predilections horrify him but, as they are his neighbors, he also wishes—gentleman that he is—not to offend them.

At this point, *Cleanness* reverts to a phallocentric sexual ethic, as patriarchy joins forces with homophobia. Yet even here, the reproductive aim that traditionally naturalizes male dominant-female submissive sexual relations is missing from the poet's logic. The girls are represented as the natural focus of male desire, not because they are potential wives and bearers of the paternal line, but because they are sexually appealing and can provide pleasure as partners in intercourse, an act to be enjoyed for its own sake. Given the thin line between the sex appeal Lot is marketing in his daughters and the kind of gratuitous pleasure the Sodomites have been in the habit of purveying to visitors, it is evident why the poet might logically need to produce a sharp and, for the homophobic, reassuring distinction between homosexual and heterosexual pleasure.[31]

These speeches considered together in light of modern theory reveal the sometimes permeable boundary between homosexual and homosocial desire. Lot's offer illuminates the heterosexual as the guarantee for homosocial bonding, a logic which in retrospect we may see is implied in God's speech too. The already warm relations between God and Abraham are eroticized by their intimate talk about the delights of sexual arousal and fulfillment. Yet God's speech does not illustrate, as Lot's so clearly does, the traffic in women transacted to infuse the erotic in male bonding, for in this earlier passage women's desire is legitimated as part of their ethical agency. God describes the man and his female partner as mutually responsible to wield control honorably and to enter truly — and hence voluntarily — into a binding commitment. In that definition of *kynde crafte,* mutuality and equality between the sexes are valorized, and the poet's gentle vision of divine governance is epitomized by a romance ideal of blissful reciprocity in love. In Lot's speech, however, where mutuality and equality would impede using women as tokens in male homosocial exchange, the value of his daughters' integrity and pleasure is eclipsed by the value of preserving male bonds from homosexual taint.

Cleanness could infuse a male reader's desire for a tender reciprocity between himself and his Creator with latent homoerotic elements of the kind I have just noted, elements that would be problematic if allowed to manifest openly. I shall argue that the bonding between God and man portrayed by the poet in the stories that focus on homosexual violations of nature is suggestive of the dynamics where the revolting is itself an object of fascination, and where what is feared is what is also desired. What is feared in the homophobia that I am analyzing in *Cleanness* is not simply the pull toward culturally forbidden erotic intimacy with other males but also the pull toward gender inversion, where culturally disavowed attributes become part of what is feared and denied (Downing 49). The pull in a man toward becoming receptively and seductively feminine was what troubled most medieval authors who attacked homosexual conduct, as well as many critics of courtliness. For the author of *Cleanness,* the conventional fear of diminishment of masculinity is not an apparent source of anxiety. In fact, values that are culturally defined as feminine centrally express his argument of why *clannesse* is a virtuous way of life which presents itself as self-evidently attractive, a matter of *fayre formez* such as ceremonious feasting and courtly lovemaking. Rather, what seems instead to threaten the poet are the low domains of male aggressiveness, where passion is expressed with an urgency and ugliness that erode the homosocial bonds of festive decorum in his aristocratic society. The Sodomites are a virulent image of that disturbing force as they deliberately disrupt God's cherished designs for loveplay between male and female and as they unabashedly intrude upon the courtly rhythms of Lot's banquet with his charming visitors. What is striking, however, is how "the difference of the other becomes a displaced and intensified facet of the same, the object of desire and disgust" (Dollimore 247), as God's revulsion comes to expression in acts of vengeance so uncouth that he is said to have lost his *fre þewes* (noble attributes) and to act like a man gone mad.

7

Homosocial Bondings with God and Christ

Cleanness places its male readers in a present-tense divine-human bonding that is comparable to the intimacy and graciousness of the homosocial intercourse Noah, Abraham, and Lot enjoy with the heavenly court through encounters on earth with God and his emissaries. The possibility of an even more intimate relationship is presented at the conclusion of Sodom's destruction when the subject shifts from God's wrath against *fylþe of þe flesch* to the importance of conforming to Christ's *clannesse* in order to become his dear one. The incarnate life of the God-man displays virtues that must be contemplated lovingly and imitated artfully by the reader who would wish to "dele drwrye with Dryȝtyn þenne, / And lelly louy þy Lorde and his leef worþe" (to exchange love with God, then, / and loyally love your Lord and become his beloved 1065–66). Not only in both the stories dealing with the sexual themes of deviance and desire but also in the depiction of Christ as human exemplar of divine *clannesse* incarnate, the poem presents attractively feminized images of a deity who manifests the aesthetically refined standards of a courtly male.

As male readers are shown how their erotic desires bond them to God, the poem suggests potentially homoerotic dimensions in this relationship, but it does so in ways that reinforce the idea of a difference between the homosocial and the homosexual. There are three places in the accounts the poem gives of *fylþe of þe flesch* where the relationship between a male reader and God

166 Homosocial Bondings

imagined as a courtly male verges on the homoerotic. One I have already identified in the analysis of the double function of the Creator's frankly erotic discourse with Abraham about the intensity of pleasures available in the *play of paramorez* (see chapter 6). Another occurs between the two exempla attacking *fylþe of þe flesch* when the poet addresses any man so foolish as to believe that desiring another man sexually could be kept hidden from the Creator. Here males in the implied audience are invited to share God's homophobic rage against men who harbor such desires in their loins and are assumed, like the poet, to think of themselves as a class apart from men base enough to have elicited such hatred from their maker. In this account of how God ceaselessly examines heart and the loins or kidneys of each man to detect these ostensibly secret homosexual longings, the poem celebrates as divine the capacity to know a man's *clannesse*, or conversely his *fylþe*, more intimately than he knows himself by virtue of penetrating the boundaries of his body.

> For he is þe gropande God, þe grounde of alle dedez,
> Rypande of vche a ring þe reyneyz and hert.
> And þere he fyndez al fayre a freke wythinne,
> With hert honest and hol, þat haþel he honourez,
> Sendez hym a sad syȝt: to se his auen face. (591–595)
> (For he is the probing God, the ground of all deeds,
> Examining the loins and heart of every man.
> And where he finds a man completely fair within,
> With a heart that is honorable and undivided, that noble man he honors,
> And sends him a solemn sight: to see his own face.)

To be pronounced free from any shameful inclinations by such a *gropande* (591 searching, handling) God is a heavenly consummation devoutly to be longed for; it is, also, to have been touched intimately in the self's secret places where medieval psychology understood earthly affections to be rooted.

The third aspect of the poem's characterization of God which might arouse a homoerotic identification on the part of courtly male readers is in the graphic account of the wound *fylþe of þe flesch* inflicts on God's inner parts. Whether in the inchoate stirrings of emotional and sexual longings or in the outward behaviors that visibly corrupt a society's mores, the harm done to the natural order by this defilement reverberates in the Creator's very being:

> Bot of þe dome of þe douþe for dedez of schame —
> He is so skoymos of þat skaþe, he scarrez bylyue;
> He may not drye to draw allyt, bot drepez in hast. (597–99)
> (But as to the judgment of mankind for deeds of shame —
> He has such repugnance of that sin, he is provoked immediately;
> He cannot bear to hold back, but destroys in haste.)

God is subjected to grief, pain, and a revulsion that he describes to Noah in terms of an involuntary physical response:

> With her unworþelych werk me wlatez withinne;
> Þe gore þerof me hatz greued and þe glette nwyed.
> I schal strenkle my distresse, and strye al togeder. (305–7)
> (Their unworthy actions disgust me inwardly;
> The filth of it has grieved me and the slime injured me.
> I shall expel my distress and destroy all together.)

In the throes of his disgust, God reacts rather like someone who has been sexually defiled, overpowered both physically and psychically by what revolts him. This profanation is portrayed as penetrating his defenses and invading his very self, and the resulting totalitarian anger, instead of being an expression of heroic fortitude, seems to leave his virtues overcome: "Þat he chysly hade cherisched he chastysed ful hardee, / In devoydynge þe vylanye þat venk-quyst his þewes" (That which he had dearly cherished he punished very severely, / In demolishing the evil that overcame his virtues 543–44). The military metaphor implicit in the image of God's *þewes* being vanquished, as if trampled by an enemy army, emphasizes his initial powerlessness in the face of the *vylanye* which his wrath ultimately obliterates.[1] The experience he undergoes when assaulted by evil of this sort is so intense that he forgets all courtesy and reacts in apparent disregard of his own nobility. This schism in the divine nature between God's vision of order and an anomalous penchant for totalitarian destruction produces unmitigated disaster in the Flood. His outburst of passion, the regret that follows, and the repetition of the same loss of control in attacking the same evil when it recurs in Sodom — all constitute evidence of how close is his affective involvement with the roots of desire in the sexualized male body. Part of the tender reciprocity that the poem invites between the reader and God is empathy with this vulnerability, legitimating a masculine ideal that consists not in reason detached from passion but in a self-image that embodies violability. Because the narrator feelingly delineates God's passion for heterosexual bliss and his correlative horror of homosexual desire and practices, the poem can risk placing the male reader imaginatively so close to God's heart as to feel personally his dependence on men's fitting sexual responses. By overtly reviling the longing for homoerotic intimacy as the most dangerous of human failings, the poem effectively protects from any homosexual taint the male reader's intimate identification with his all-powerful Lord who is nevertheless abjectly vulnerable to the power of the homoerotic in men's lives.

Homosocial identification with God precludes sexual desire for males, but when Christ is presented as model of *clannesse* to be emulated by all who want to be acceptable in the heavenly court, this requirement of a profound separation between identification and desire is problematized. He appears in an overtly feminine guise that seems to legitimate the convergence of identification and desire, of not only desiring to be like Christ but desiring Christ as a lover desires his beloved. Traditionally, when Christian male readers are invited to exchange love with God, they are implicitly placed in the female role, for such metaphors of human-divine erotic union normally assign to the Church or the soul the role of the beloved, wooed as Christ's bride, and to Christ the more active masculine role as lover and bridegroom. But the gender symbolism of the erotic tie between Christ and the Christian is rendered more ambiguous in *Cleanness* by the literary analogy the poem draws between the heroine of romance, specifically Jean's "clene Rose" (1057), and Christ. He is referred to as "that Seemly [one]" whose sweet face the reader longs to see (1055). Thus Christ is metaphorically represented as the beautiful and flawlessly well-mannered female paragon of courtly perfection, a beloved lady whose excellent deportment her lover adores as the mirror of his future perfection. By conformity to Christ's polished sensibility, the implication here is the reader will achieve the integrity of a pearl, the burnished perfection of a beryl — in short, a transformation comparable to that of a courtly male lover who contemplates his beloved's virtues and, by modeling his life on hers, becomes her dear one. But the poem stops short of the physical possession that is the goal of secular courtship and also, in conventionally eroticized religious discourse, the symbol of mystical union.

This framing of the imitation of Christ invites a blending of the homosocial bond of feminized courtly culture with the game and play of heterosexual love, and so for the male reader verges on the homoerotic — but not dangerously so. The contemplation of Christ's beauty is urged while avoiding awakening thereby any longings for sexually charged intimacy with the body of God made man. Strikingly missing from this depiction is the emphasis on an embodied love that had, since the twelfth century, characterized piety focused on the imitation of Christ. There, as Jeffrey Schnapp points out, the "so-called 'feminine' side of Jesus" became foremost in Christian imagination, including "his passivity and suffering, his approachability and affectivity" (146), valorizing the flesh as feminine in a positive sense. Instead of physicality representing the opposite of divine transcendence, the most limiting aspects of the body — pain and death — came to symbolize the ultimate mystery of incarnate immanence. God takes his flesh from a woman who exhibits human nature in its unfallen perfection, and he is born as a creature whose own perfect flesh is ultimately subjected to total degradation; he endures meekly a shameful and painful death, giving himself lovingly to this profanation in order to redeem humankind. *Cleanness* depicts far less of the carnal immediacy of either Jesus or his mother than do most late medieval accounts of the Incarnation. By excluding the aspects of incarnation piety that cast the God-man into maternal roles of suffering and nurturance, of breeding and feeding, the poet meditates on a different sort of gender hybrid.

When we juxtapose the portrait of God that emerges from the fictionalized Old Testament exempla to the culminating description of Christ as courtly exemplar, we can see how the poem's complex gender symbolics bear on the originality of its overall theopoetic vision. There is no trace in the portrait of Christ of the divine passion and vulnerability displayed in the earlier images of God's abject physical horror of *fylþe of þe flesch*. It is not within the wounded body of the incarnate God-man that the sacred and profane interpenetrate, as we would expect in a typical late medieval poem depicting Christ's exemplary life, but in the sexual bodies of human lovers through the Creator's identification of his own well-being with their longings and pleasures. In effect, the stories of God's wrath, fueled to a merciless pitch by his uncontrollable revulsion, enshrine the anomalous element of divine vulnerability in displays of sacred artistry in tension with vengeance at its most destructive extreme. Insofar as *Cleanness* provides no image of the Crucifixion, the poem elides the most intimate penetration of the sacred by the profane. Its unbloodied depiction of God made flesh is unusual, viewed against the horizon of expectations created by late medieval visual and verbal representations of Christ's life. The omission of his Passion and death from *Cleanness*'s imagery of the Incarnation is particularly intriguing, given the erotic metaphor of the imitation of Christ compared to the service of the lady which frames this passage and the sexual focus of the two exempla which precede it. Excising the Crucifixion from his readers' consciousness, the poet thereby avoids the nexus of sexuality that threads through late medieval contemplation of the naked physicality of Christ's vulnerable and pain-wracked body; this unconventional representation of *clannesse* incarnate protects the implicitly homoerotic bond between Christian male readers and their sweet-faced Lord from inciting desire for physical intimacy and union. It also erases the most potent metaphoric site for human transformation through imaginative identification with God's love displayed in history. The elision of divine passion at its ultimate extremity defines the poem's theopoetic logic in ways that deserve further analysis.

The Feminized Christ and Jean's "Clene Rose"

The poem's thematic equations of *clene layk* (noble practices, proper play 1054), required for seeing God, with a culturally feminine set of ideal traits, required for men who want to be seen as courtly, is stunningly clear in the passage celebrating Christ's incarnate *clannesse*. With the poem's privileging of a gentler, feminized ideal of masculinity, it is predictable that the prince of noble peerage should exemplify not epic virility, mightily victorious over the devil, but a more courtly manhood displayed in peaceful settings. As we shall see, Christ exercises his authority with perfect manners, maintaining sovereignty with no apparent effort; born as the king of nature in a bower fit for royalty, his adult lordship is manifest in images of craft and courtesy that epitomize the aristocratic male refinement the poem legitimates as *clene*. He combines the courtier's suave authority with the different, but nonetheless powerful, authority of the female beloved, whose beautiful conduct provides a salvific ethical model for her adoring lover. While it is logical for *Cleanness* to show that God incarnate exemplifies the courtly ethos manifested by Old Testament visitors to Noah, Abraham, and Lot, it is most unusual to cast the God-man into a courtly lady's role and to draw an analogy between Christ and the female beloved whose virtues are the catalyst for her lover's transformation.

Meditation on Christ as an icon of divine perfection in human form is introduced in terms that clearly allude to the conventional idealization of the romance heroine. When the poet begins his account of the Nativity by telling readers to "loke" (look 1069), the implication is that by gazing upon Christ as God's self-representation in human flesh, readers can mirror in their own lives this image of perfection. Readers of Chretien de Troyes will recall the courtier-knight Yvain telling himself that Laudine was made by God, with his own unaided hand (313). The analogy between the lover's admiration of the heavenly traits of his earthly beloved and the poet's marveling at God's *clannesse* incarnate is even more striking when we consider that just as Christ as beloved presents a model of loveliness by which his lovers must judge themselves, so in another of Chretien's romances, Erec gazed at Enide's beauty as in a mirror where he might see himself reflected (42).[2]

Cleanness explicitly draws not on Chretien's romances, however, but on Jean de Meun in this analogy between imitating a woman's sensibility and imitating Christ's *clannesse*:

> And if he louyes clene layk þat is oure Lorde ryche,
> And to be couþe in his courte þou coueytes þenne,
> To se þat Semly in sete and his swete face,
> Clerrer counseyl con I non, bot þat þou clene worþe.
> For Clopyngnel in þe compas of his clene Rose,
> Þer he expounez a speche to hym þat spede wolde

Of a lady to be loued: "Loke to hir sone
Of wich beryng þat ho be, and wych ho best louyes,
And be ryȝt such in vch a borȝe of body and of dedes,
And folȝ þe fet of þat fere þat þou fre haldes." (1053–62)
(And if he who is our splendid Lord loves noble behavior
And you desire then to be known in his court,
To see that seemly One on his throne and his sweet face,
Clearer counsel I do not know than that you become clean.
For Clopyngnel, within the compass of his clean *Rose*,
There expounds a speech to him who would succeed
In being loved by a lady: "Look to her straightway,
What behavior is hers and what she loves best,
And be thus everywhere in your body and deeds,
And follow the footsteps of the companion whom you hold to be noble.")

The authority the courtly lady has over her adoring lover is comparable to the standard which a courtly lord's taste provides to all who would partake in a seemly way of the bounty offered at his feasts. Just as the guest's discerning response to the requirements of festive decorum provides joyful mutuality, so the service rendered to the desirable lady provides new forms of aesthetic connoisseurship for the feminized lover. Modeling himself on his beloved, a man can bring himself into accord with her beauty as it manifests her nobility, thereby achieving in his own life what he admires in hers. To enjoy her presence, he must be cleanly arrayed as she is, both literally and figuratively. Clothing, demeanor, conversation, table manners—all aspects of his behavior must self-consciously reflect the stylized criteria of the courtly feminine culture. Thus Christ's lover can "folȝ þe fet of þat fere" (follow the [literally, footsteps] actions of that companion 1062) and reflect his *clannesse,* just as the romantic lover is transformed through sensitivity to the ideals his lady embodies. Such a sensibility clearly privileges the ladylike traits in the aristocratic femininized male. Moreover, by drawing an explicit analogy between Christ and the female beloved in the role of romance heroine, the poem legitimates in still another vein the game and play of love which generated so many artfully refined erotic performances in the literary world of late medieval aristocracy.

As we have seen in chapter 5, however, in stark contrast to the romantic idealism of God's praise of the *play of paramorez* in *Cleanness,* the *Roman* offers thoroughly cynical advice regarding serving in the court of love. What then are we to make of the deference to Jean de Meun, whose attitude toward the *Rose*'s power to arouse the Lover's lustful appetite makes her a troubling metaphor for Christ's appealing humanity? Is Jean's *Roman,* referred to here as the "clene rose" of "Clopyngnel," being endorsed uncritically? It is, after all, the only text besides the Bible cited by title and author in the entire poem—indeed, in any of the poems in MS Cotton Nero A.x, Art. 3. To readers aware of Jean's cynical stance toward the romantic Lover, who proves to be wholly uneducable by Reason and entirely too compliant to the advice he receives from his unreliable Friend, the recommendation of the *Roman* as an authoritative guide to the courtly discipline of self-transformation through love becomes a downright conundrum. The distance between tenor and vehicle in the metaphorical comparison of earthly and heavenly love deserves further critical consideration.

The passage the poet draws on in *Cleanness* 1053–64 occurs in the *Roman* just after the Lover has rejected his Friend's callous advice simply to "cut the rose by force and show that you are a man" (144–45; 7660–61). The Friend then urges the Lover to manipulate the Rose by flattery to achieve the same end as the rape he is unwilling to carry out, but warns that thus imitating her standards will diminish the Lover's true manhood. In order to copy the manners of the Rose and conform to her values, the Lover must hide his masculine superiority.[3] Readers sympathetic to aristocratic codes of conduct would be more likely to perceive this misogynous satire as a counter-authority than as a positive support to the feminized ethos of romance that informs the poet's praise of the Incarnation, just as it did God's praise of *kynde crafte*. The Friend argues that only the most servile and indiscriminate imitation will succeed in winning the Rose's acceptance, personified here as a male agency called Fair Welcoming: "Pay attention to the way Fair Welcoming looks at you. No matter how he may be nor what appearance he may have, adapt yourself to his manner. If he is old and serious, put all your attention on conducting yourself in a serious way; and if he acts stupidly, you act stupidly. . . . Love what he loves, blame what he wants to blame, and give praise to whatever he does. He will then have much more confidence in you" (145; 7689–96, 7703–6).[4] What could account for *Cleanness* referring to this passage, where Jean ironically relishes the polished deceptions of love service, as the best analogy for what it means to craft human conduct in conformity to the refined standards of the heavenly court?

As so often in medieval literature, it is the tone that defeats us. What Jean makes fun of in his *clene Rose,* the poet redeems in *Cleanness.* We have seen this correcting at work in chapter 5 where the praise of heterosexual consummation in *Cleanness* was compared to Jean's burlesque depiction of the Lover's conquest of the Rose. *Cleanness* obviously alters the significance of the Friend's misogynistic advice by placing it in a context where readers must view through the rose-colored lens of romance the process of pleasing Christ as one would please a deserving and truly discerning woman. That Jean's *Roman* is cited here, and specifically referred to as the "clene Rose," underscores the ironic contrast between the jaded advice given by this ostensible guide and the virtual sacramentality of heterosexual erotic attraction in *Cleanness*.

It is in contrast to the mind-body dualism of the *Roman* that we can best see how the *clannesse* that Christ exemplifies does not denigrate embodiedness but retains the splendor of the desiring self the poet celebrated in God's speech on *kynde crafte*. Whereas Reason in Jean's *Roman* instructed the Lover to model himself on Socrates the philosopher in abstract contemplation of eternal truths, the poet's counsel to imitate Christ teaches a mode of courtly intelligence that is neither noticeably rational nor detached from the pleasures of life.[5] Celestial flesh glows with a romantic aura in the poet's religious imagination as he directs a loving gaze upon the conception and birth of Christ, physical events in the life of a woman collaborating with heaven's courtesy and craft. The world of nature is not simply transcended in God's *comly kest* (comely contrivance 1070) of uniting heaven to earth in the pregnant virgin, but it is perfected as Christ's human flesh displays the aesthetic integrity and social harmony that *clannesse* creates on earth.

Rather than evoking a mystical consummation between the heavenly Beloved and his earthly lovers, *Cleanness* celebrates the erotically charged distance created by rituals of aristocratic courtship. The *Cleanness*-poet's praise of paradisal pleasure sacralizes the joys bestowed by God on the lovers in their heterosexual union. Heavenly exchange of love with Christ is kept distinct from the sexual communion God earlier praises as "drwry . . . doole alþer-swettest" (love . . . sharing sweetest of all 698). Thus, earthly lovemaking is not conflated with the Christian's desire to see the sweet face of the Lord of heaven where that seemly One is seated on his heavenly throne (1055) and to exchange love with him (1065).[6] Instead of a voluptuous union in mystical darkness, comparable to the allegorical reading of the Song of Songs in the Christian contemplative tradition, the images of what it is like to "dele drwrye wyth Dryʒtyn" and to become "his leef" (to exchange love with God and to become his dear one 1065–66) situate the reader in the well-lighted social space of court life. *Cleanness* encourages a joyful anticipation of serving acceptably in the sight of Christ the Beloved and gazing forever upon his sweet features, but remarkably, nowhere does this text counsel renunciation of erotic attachments or other worldly goods. To see that seemly One and to progress toward the eternal enjoyment of dwelling in his heavenly court, the Christian has only to reflect the *clannesse* seen in the *kynde crafte* that is God's design in creation and, above all, displayed in the God-man who is king of nature.

Gender Symbolics in God's Homophobic Wrath

In the warring world of epic, conflict is prized for the sake of glory, and so the dominant heroic trait is courageous action. In the more peaceful world of romance, while the hero remains a warrior, his honor is redefined by gentler virtues. Although obviously modeled on earthly sovereigns, the Lord of heaven is not motivated in *Cleanness* by the aims of epic heroism where greatness is defined by political stature displayed in feats of military conquest. Rather than legitimating delight in mayhem and embodying power grasped through violent means, God is identified with more peaceful values, even in his wrath against *fylþe of þe flesh*. In the first two Old Testament narratives, as in the parable of the wedding feast, the poet characterizes the *Kyng þat al weldez* (King who governs all 17) as a sensitive artist and gentle courtly male—a patriarchal leader of men who is sometimes militantly aggressive but still exemplary of the chivalric ideal where warrior valor was harmonized with courtliness, prowess with restraint.

According to the narrator's interpretation of the mercy shown in the judgments first on the rebellious Satan and then on disobedient Adam and Eve, temperate control of personal aggression is a quality God characteristically exhibits in his gentle governance of the world, even while punishing wrongdoers.[7] This masterful self-restraint fits more within the peaceful paradigm of romance masculinity than in the warring world of epic. As Bonnie Wheeler aptly observes, "If life is war, courageous action is the dominant value; if life is peace, then control and temperance, usually gendered as feminine, are the dominant virtues" (9). God's homophobic wrath is presented as exceptional—a contrast to his usual exemplary moderation and ability to bear abuse patiently. Even in in the midst of terrifying displays of power, the Creator is not compared to a conquering hero on a military rampage.[8] The third Old Testament exemplum does depict such epic conquests between earthly rulers, some allied with God and some who are the objects of his wrath, but until that view of history as ongoing political struggle emerges later in the poem, divine sovereignty is primarily characterized by the metaphorical dimensions of *clannesse* that we have called aesthetic. These values emphasize the Creator's artistic relationship to nature as an order he makes and prizes for its pleasing grace.

The stories of the Flood and Sodom are told with an emphasis on this more vulnerable ideal of masculine virtue. That his wrath is fueled by an experience of helplessness separates God's recklessness in homophobic vengeance from the punishing displays of heroic power celebrated in epic paradigms of virility. Despite the violence of his apocalyptic acts of judgment in the Flood and the destruction of Sodom and Gomorrah, these events are constructed by the poet not as a glorification of an avenging warlord, but as a scenario to display God's *clannesse*—his aristocratic aversion to what is ignoble. This is the negative expression of his positive yearning for all that is honorable, including friendly relationships to his creation and close bonds of affection and compassion with other similarly genteel males. The poet rewrites his scriptural sources to make God exemplify these softer elements of the courtly ethos.

That the *Cleanness*-poet should have even momentarily idealized the sharing of erotic power between a man and a woman as part of God's plan for love made in accord with nature makes this poem a romantic landmark in religious discourse. But despite the poet's privileging of the feminine in his revision of the symbolic locus of male dominance, it is obvious that an ethos of sexual equality is not fundamental to his theopoetic uses of the romanticized ideals of courtly masculinity to exemplify *clannesse*. Misogyny is evident not only with regard to Lot's daughters, but also in the absence of women in the elaboration of the wedding banquet in the parable and in the stress on Sarah's subordination and Lot's wife's insubordination as they feed their guests under their husbands' authority but do not otherwise participate in the feasts where the men are homosocially bonding. In the third Old Testament exemplum, women exhibit a more ambiguous but still dubious status, as Belshazzar's gorgeously arrayed concubines exemplify the narcissism of their foolish lover, in contrast to his wise queen whose role begins only after the feasting has come to its abrupt conclusion with the handwriting on the wall.

Nor is the *Cleanness*-poet inherently uncomfortable with social hierarchy that subordinates one class of males to another. Homosocial bonding is not any more egalitarian with regard to class than it is with regard to gender. Rather, what is central and striking is the emphasis placed on reciprocal aesthetic enjoyment as an essential feature in what the poet depicts as the potentially blissful relationship between Creator and creature. God's order is paradigmatically presented as a beautiful design aimed at mutual enjoyment and harmony, whether that is imagined as a public display of honor at a feast or a private exchange in a lovers' tryst. As the inventor of the *play of paramorez* and, by implication, all other cultural forms where natural human appetites for pleasure and beauty attain artful fulfillment, God is vulnerably involved with the order he imagines; he cannot simply impose it, just as the lord of the feast is hostage to his guests' attraction to his designs and their fitting collaborative response. As in the parable, so in the encounters between God and his earthly servants, successful lordship is measured against an aesthetically refined standard of pleasure generously bestowed, fittingly pursued, and mutually enjoyed.

176   Homosocial Bondings

By his empathetic account of divine wrath against those who reject this mutuality, the poet weaves a friendship between himself, his audience, and the sovereign to whom he refers frequently as *oure Lorde*. By implication, this present tense divine-human bonding is comparable to the intimacy and graciousness of the homosocial intercourse depicted in the earthly encounters of three men—Noah, Abraham, and Lot—with the heavenly court. In scenes where the mutuality of lord and vassal coalesces with that of earthly host and divine guest, each patriarch exemplifies the ideals of honorable service to a superior expressed in aristocratically refined hospitality. God's dependence on such good men to recognize his claims to sovereignty and to accomplish his ends reinforces the elite tradition of aesthetically sensitive males promoting each other's honor and interests through ritualized conviviality. While the social exchanges are hierarchical, they are also depicted as mutually pleasing and based on a shared standard of what brings satisfaction to both parties.

As Lot does when he entertains the two angelic visitors, so Abraham greets his three guests with discerning reverence because they are fine, gracious, and of great beauty.[9] The hospitality he offers is worthy, like Lot's, of the aesthetic standards embodied in his guests' refined personal appearance and conduct. Although it takes the form of a simple picnic on the grass, the meal he serves perfectly accommodates his visitors' sense of decorum. Thus they in turn amiably compliment their host: "And God as a glad gest mad god chere / Þat watz fayn of his frende, and his fest praysed" (And God, like a glad guest, made merry / As one who was pleased to meet his friend, made merry and praised his feast 641–42). Afterwards, God opens his heart freely to Abraham, explaining what so infuriates him about the way the men of Sodom mate with each other and in the process waxes lyrical in a courtly mode, freely detailing the *drwry* he has located in the pleasures of heterosexual loveplay.

God has already been depicted as enjoying similarly close communication with Noah, even though the Flood narrative does not permit the poet to dramatize the host-guest relationship in a literal meal. When Noah offers animal sacrifices in a ritual of thanksgiving after the Flood, the smoke ascends to heaven like a breath whose savor attracts the Creator's courteous response, and God is drawn into what feels like not just a visit, but tabletalk between a guest and his host. Here the poet freely changes the Vulgate narrative, where God speaks his heart first to himself and then publicly converses with Noah, addressing his sons as well. Instead, the Creator is brimming with tenderness as he opens his heart intimately to the man on whom he has depended to save the creatures, both human and wild, who will begin life anew in a reordered world. Responding fittingly to the good aromas coming from Noah's "comly and clene" (lovely and clean 508) burnt offerings, God communicates "comly comfort [in] ful clos and cortays wordez" (lovely comfort in very intimate and courteous words 512), promising never again so cruelly to curse the earth. This private and affectionate male tie (evident as well in their conversations before the Flood but developed even more obviously here) suggests that it is because of his passion for the gracious civility embodied in Noah's exemplary conduct that God grows so immoderately furious at the other antediluvian males who war upon each other perpetually and boorishly disregard his heterosexual designs for bodily bliss.

Although telling stories that illustrate God's wrath against such men, the poet's pervasive tone is positive; by implication, neither he nor his male listeners could be attracted by this obviously low-class filth or foolishly think that their sexual desires were hidden from the Creator's scrutiny. Instead, like the good men of old who were God's confidants, they can share fully in the divine sensibility which is revulsed by homosexual deviance. As insiders, the poet and his implied audience can watch what unfolds from God's point of view, located safely within the boundary which the Creator draws to protect himself from *fylþe of þe flesch*.

Yet there is not complete safety, for to be this close to God is to experience his loss of boundaries when confronted with the *fylþe of þe flesch* he abhors. Inherent in the poet's conception of the deity as creator and connoisseur of *fayre formez* is not only the privileging of sensual delight as a godlike experience, but also an endorsement and even glorification of its shadow, God's abject physical horror at any tampering with what he perceives to be an already perfect heterosexual order. Displaying an acute sensitivity to the plight of the Creator who must suffer such intense inner conflict, the poet appeals to his listeners' empathy with these divine passions and at the same time heightens their sense of the sacred by enshrining the anomalous elements of vulnerability and boundary-breaking violence in God's sovereign artistry.

The thing God most abominates he is also drawn to, for he attends to it ceaselessly; in order to maintain the boundary between himself and *fylþe of þe flesch*, he must dissolve the differences that distinguish the incipient roots of desire in the human body from its conscious expression in thought or deed. Such defiling visceral urges, however inchoate they may be, not only harm the man who experiences them but injure God in the inner reaches of his own being, which the poet has earlier described graphically as wounded by *fylþe of þe flesch*: "With her vnworþelych werk me wlatez withinne; / Þe gore þerof me hatz greued and þe glette nwyed" (I inwardly loath their unworthy work; / The filth of it has grieved me and the slime injured me 305–6). To expel this distress he is compelled to mar what he has made.[10]

This notion of being subjected to compulsion from a rift in his own nature is not only an unorthodox image of God, but also an unusually vulnerable image of earthly lordship. At the outset of the Flood narrative, we hear the poet unapologetically compare God to a man gone mad with revenge (204). First invaded by the pitiless hatred of his creatures (393–96), after God purges this passion through vengeance, he then suffers equally intense feeling of "swemande sorȝe" (grievous sorrow 563) at the consequences of the waters he called upon to wash his world. God talks to himself by analogy with a man who is "sorrowful within" once his heart is wounded by *felle temptande tene* (cruel afflicting anger 283). While the suffering the Flood causes the various species is noted in detail, the story is not told predominantly from these victims' perspectives; the narrator identifies with the Creator who is portrayed not only as the powerful agent of destruction, but also as powerless in his subjection to grief, rage, and revulsion. In short, he is an image of pathos who invites the poet's and his implied audience's compassion.

God's incapacity to defend himself from passionate and immoderate rage — and hence primitive aggression against the *fylþe of þe flesch* — while exceptional to his characteristic moderation, also is paradigmatic for understanding the divine nature. Even if God is temporarily robbed of his *fre þewez* (noble qualities 203), this heartfelt anger arises out of fastidiousness and thus discloses the nobility of God's standards and his passionate commitment to them. The aggressive, dominating role of a traditionally powerful male whose will is manifest in his power to destroy is ameliorated by the poet's depiction of the fragile boundary that separates this Creator from what he abominates. The marring of the natural landscape that results from the brute power of divine vengeance reflects the violence unleashed within God's very nature, an unorthodox inner conflict the poet develops in explicitly anthropomorphic terms to which he assumes his readers will sympathetically respond.

Reconfiguring Relations between the Sacred and the Profane

The comfortable sense afforded to the reader of being placed, along with the narrator, securely within the boundary of *clannesse* is endangered, it would seem, by the permeability of that protective line when dissolved by homosexual desire. The poem presents the staggering anomaly of a God who is perfectly *clene* and yet can be invaded by such fury that his normally noble and creative nature is obscured by violent vengeance on a cosmic scale. A. C. Spearing notes how terrifying are the elemental forces that defilement unleashes, dangerous forces which do not seem to strengthen the boundaries between purity and pollution so much as they obliterate distinctions and create even more disorder, or filth in a literal sense. The stories of the Flood and

Sodom show how violations of God's sexual designs elicit hatred that leaves in one instance a mud- and carcass-strewn wasteland and in another a travesty of nature where the fundamental categories of creation seem permanently confused (*Readings* 189–90). Admittedly, there is the "re-establishment of the order of things on the firm basis of the rainbow covenant" at the conclusion of the Deluge; this story ends in a display of God's and the poet's passion for clean separations and clear divisions, but as Spearing rightly observes, "from another point of view, very powerfully expressed in the poetry, the Flood is a manifestation of *fylþe*, not *clannes*" (189).[11]

By looking at these cosmic transgressions of boundaries from Mary Douglas's anthropological viewpoint on the ambiguity in the general relation of disorder to pattern, Spearing justifies the imaginative energy invested by the poet in violence and mayhem as energies which empowered his ritualistic harnessing of the forces of disorder for good. Douglas explains why renewal rites in tribal societies often require contacts with "those attacking forces which threaten to destroy good order"; it is precisely these dangerous forces which represent in primitive myth and ritual the chaotic powers inhering in the cosmos (Douglas 161, quoted by Spearing 190). For Spearing, the "purity" of *clannesse* is less a moral standard than a cosmological connectedness, an ordering of reality at every level: "In his treatment of *clannes* and *fylþe* in the sexual sphere, as in other spheres, he is concerned less with morality and sin than with system and the pollution that endangers it" (183). While this "writer prophet" (188) would appear from his announced topic to be producing discourse in a moralizing vein, he in fact functions, for Spearing, more like a priest who organizes experience through symbolism and ritual in order to construct a mythic vehicle for cosmogonic renewal (178, 190–91). Seen in this light, *clannesse* embraces the cosmic energies of both order and disorder, and thus the poetic meditation on this concept of the divine provides a systematic ordering of "symbolic oppositions that were part of the experience of [its] time and that may indeed be part of universal human experience" (188).

The poetic force of *clannesse* and its opposite derives for Spearing from the author's grasp of the power and danger which are inseparable from God's holiness. It is precisely by including them within what the poet means by God that *Cleanness* renders ambiguous the Creator's relationship to the powers of disorder inherent in the cosmos of his making and thus provides a "secular equivalent to a ritual which harnesses the forces of disorder for good" (191). *Cleanness* sanctifies a system of categories that depend on separation and fittingness; at the same time, it paradoxically enshrines the inappropriate elements that threaten this "systematic ordering and classification of experience, an ordering and classification that are conceived as divinely ordained" (181).

This anthropological approach maintains that ritual celebration of sacred order or purity must include the power of disorder or defilement and illuminates why, while stressing how *clannesse* depends on clear boundaries and clean separations, a poem devoted to its commendation invests so much energy in displays of what Spearing aptly terms "boundary-wrecking violence and destruction" (188). He usefully applies Douglas's concepts to explain how, on the one hand, "the exemplary punishments of human *fylþe* by God can be seen as 'not a negative movement, but a positive effort to organize the environment,' and thereby as a demonstration of God's own *clannes*" (188) and yet, on the other hand, how much of the poem's dynamic derives from the anomalous overriding of cosmological and theological categories. Readers are thereby invited to contemplate divine perfection not just as a still life or an icon, nor yet as simply thrown into clearer relief by its polar opposite, but as a manifestation of how the forces of disorder and profanation contribute to the attraction and terror evoked by the idea of the holy. As Mary Douglas points out, "The danger which is risked by boundary transgression is power" (161; see Spearing 190).

Spearing's insight into how anthropological concepts illuminate the way *Cleanness* "celebrates God by meditating on the power and the danger which are inseparable from God's purity" (190) can be extended by using Sara Beckwith's analysis of the changing dynamic of the sacred and profane in late medieval symbolic uses of Christ's body. Her study documents the increasing production of narratives of Christ's life, written or translated in the fourteenth and fifteenth centuries for a lay audience, enabling them to use his Passion as a model for their lives. In examples from this vernacular genre, she shows how crucifixion imagery generates a language for interiorizing Christ, thereby transforming the self's relation to itself. It also transmutes the daily, and ostensibly profane, aspects of a layperson's life into matter to be formed into God's human image. Beckwith argues that the "simultaneous strategies of profanation and sacralization" evident in devotional texts and mystery plays that fetishize "Christ's torn and bleeding body as the object, indeed subject, of compassion and passion" (53) could reshape an individual's sense of the self. Such crucifixion images furnish a "metaphoric site of conversion and transference" precisely because Christ's vulnerable body thematizes "the interpenetration of the sacred and the profane" (56).

Using a revisionist reading of Douglas's *Purity and Danger,* Beckwith shows how this symbolic interpenetration could — by rendering ambiguous the differences between within and without, above and below, male and female, with and against — subvert the prevailing classifications of society which depend on such distinctions (61). Ecclesiastical authorities stressed their control by ritualistic manipulation of the division between the sacred and profane, and hence the preeminence of this boundary between secular and religious realms. No longer essential to Christian devotion at its most intense was the monastic regimen that had defined the religious life and guarded the boundaries of the sacred from what could defile or dissipate it. Since the profane was potentially salvific, the secular could be used in the service of the sacred.[12] Devout lay Christians, leading mixed lives, became audience for and participants in an intensely personal and communal imaginative enterprise which reconfigured the profane world of human pain and suffering as inseparable from the sacred and accessible to its service.

Inasmuch as *Cleanness* represents the Creator as personally implicated with and vulnerable to the embodied and sexual desires of his human creatures, the poet seems to be in his own way renegotiating differences between the secular and the sacred and subverting the distinctions between the two realms that clerical ritual and discourse manipulated. *Cleanness* provides images of the interpenetration of sacred and profane—not within the incarnate God-man, as we would expect, but within the human sexual body with which, in its longings and pleasures, the Creator is astonishingly implicated. As an artist whose divinely conceived idea is expressed in the intensely collaborative medium of erotic play which he portrays and teaches to lovers in secret, the Creator is immanently involved in human sexual arousal. The territory of greatest symbolic potential for defilement and profanation in the economy of the sacred and profane, the very territory represented in most clerical discourse as fraught with danger and especially in need of vigilant and unceasing control, the poet remaps as paradisal space, a physical medium where God loves and expects to be loved. The closeness of the Creator to the material world he prizes as his artifact involves as a corollary the danger posed when homosexually desiring men desecrate the masterpiece of nature, heterosexual loveplay.

As illuminating as Spearing's anthropological approach to *Cleanness* is, his idea that "the powers inhering in the cosmos" are what the poet means by God obscures the degree to which the divine is anthropomorphized to permit an empathy with a homophobic Creator. God's subjectivity is dramatized with extraordinary confidence in the resemblance between his divine interiority and the affective and personal expressions of a sensitive courtly male. Since Spearing sees the poem as a whole integrated by an anthropological pattern of meaning, he defines the disparate examples of *fylþe* and disorder as essentially all the same; this obscures the poem's emphatic distinction between defilement or disorder per se, exemplified in the ill-clad guest angrily cast out by the lord concerned to preserve the splendor of life in his household, and what the poet describes as the abject physical revulsion caused by *fylþe of þe flesch,* which evokes uniquely immoderate vengeance. It is true that in the final exemplum, the defilement of the sacred vessels affects God in ways very similar to his revulsion against homosexual practices.[13] I am arguing, however, that while God is portrayed as revulsed by Belshazzar's defilement and the sins that it symbolizes, this encounter with evil does not subject the deity to the dissolving of boundaries within himself; thus the connection between the final exemplum and the previous two does not revoke the poet's claim that *fylþe of þe flesch* is more infuriating than any other offense. In summary, "the dangerous energies" that Spearing sees the poet ritualistically celebrating as "inherent in the very substance of the world as God created it," I see as the shock penetrating God's being when confronted by homosexual deviation, a profanation of the holy that creates within himself the very loss of definition that he hates. The consequent extremities of suffering and wrath he endures are, I believe, both uniquely threatening and uniquely effective in communicating the power and danger that attacks boundaries.

Out of such dissolution, fresh orderings can arise. In the imaginative attention *Cleanness* pays to the rituals by which the cosmos is reordered out of the chaos of the Flood and its ugly aftermath, there is compelling evidence of what Spearing calls the poet's notorious "passion for pattern" and "rage for order" (*Readings* 191). The poet communicates delight in God's supreme artistry in separating and ordering parts of the cleansed creation into a renewed plenitude and harmony. The courtly sense of a serious game being played joyfully and in strict accord with the rules controls the depiction of the inhabitants of the ark awaiting merrily and eagerly their exit and return to land. Their rediscovery of the world outside of the ark bonds all of the "sely bestez" (harmless beasts 490) who inhabited it—and by this phrase, the poet designates human survivors as well as all of the other species. Together, they are bonded to the Creator by whose bounty they were preserved and by whose wise separations ("skylly skyualde" 529) they harmoniously divide themselves to inherit their different niches in nature.[14]

God's artistry in accomplishing these new beginnings is emphasized in order to resolve a terrifying account of disorder, not only in the material world but in the Creator himself. In the context of this ritualistic restoration of nature's order, the source of both life and death promises his good friend Noah never again to act with such indiscriminate and hasty violence. The poet dramatizes the intimate conversation of God and Noah and (many lines later) returns to comment that the covenant God made there came out of intensely felt regret—for having wished that he had never created humankind and for having on their account destroyed what he had formed. Acknowledging that the mind of human creatures collectively considered is inclined to evil, from their very birth, is an admission of the limits of divine control. This restores God to his normal measured mode of response; he "knyt a couenaunde cortaysly" (knit a covenant courteously 564) never again to kill off all of life because of any evil men commit.[15] The promise to control his wrath has been kept, observes the narrator, insofar as that particular form of judgment never again escaped the limits the Creator there imposed on himself (569). While the vengeance against Sodom and the other cities of the plain issues from the same extremity of divine anger, only one region of the world is targeted for destruction. Moreover, God expresses a willingness, because of Abraham's negotiating skills, to delay punishing the sinful majority for the sake of a virtuous minority. If there were to be found fifty, or even ten, men who have kept themselves clean from the *fylþe of þe flesch* of their fellow citizens (729–30), the sinful could have been given a chance to repent and Sodom might have been saved.

Yet Lot alone was virtuous (women do not count in this tallying up), and thus the poet claims that the very same fault which precipitated the Deluge did in fact again produce vengeance of the same merciless intensity. In this second mythic account of elemental disruption, the poet again describes in admiring detail the Creator's power and artistry displayed in another genocidal storm.[16] This one rains fire and brimstone, followed by an earthquake that sinks five cities and their surroundings into hell and leaves behind an infernal landscape where natural properties and functions are reversed.

The poem's violent description of the destruction the judgment of Sodom unleashes upon its once Edenic landscape is followed, in sharp contrast, by the description of the first Christmas. This juxtaposition echoes the earlier account of God's wise separations and orderings that renewed the creation after the Flood, a ritual of reordering which the poet situates on New Year's Day. By revising the Vulgate's chronology, he has situated the covenant with Noah at the turning in the year's cycle when Christian societies engage in ritual festivities providing cosmogonic renewal in the midst of nature's dormancy. By ending the Sodom narrative with the coming of Christ and the celebration of the first Christmas, the poet reinforces the ritual significance of the year's turning as the anniversary of God's covenant with humanity and his blessing on all his creatures after the Flood. In both conclusions, the poet draws the readers' attention away from the volatility and vulnerability of the aesthetically sensitive maker and toward his generosity and skill. In recurring moments of ceremonial joyfulness, the poem itself provides a ritualistic experience of festive decorum. Indeed, it is not difficult to imagine it being recited in the household of a provincial magnate who aspired to the Christmas solemnity and gaiety comparable to the joyful rituals in *Sir Gawain and the Green Knight*'s account of the holy season.

Christ's Clannesse *as Courtly Exemplar*

In his portrayal of the Christ event, the poet conceives the sacred as invulnerable to the profane elements in creation, which pose no threat to it. The dynamic of the sacred and profane in *Cleanness* shifts as the transformation of nature in and by the God-man provides, in effect, a coda and surprisingly happy ending to the horrific account of Sodom's continuing significance for witnesses of the permanently hideous transformation of the Dead Sea and its surroundings. Close to the center of *Cleanness,* in a verbal triptych of forty lines (1069–1108), the poet composes a panoply of positively splendid sensual details of incarnate *clannesse*. The perfection of nature delineated in Christ's conception and birth (1069–88), healing ministry (1089–1100), and breaking of bread (1101–8) seem as accessible to contemporary sight as the deformation that travelers to the Dead Sea can still view. Christians can, it appears from the analogy to the devoted lover's mirroring his lady's virtues, embody through loving imitation the splendid order of heaven manifest in the Incarnation.

To appreciate such *clannesse,* the reader is asked to look and to marvel at the ceremonial magnificence of the Christ child's arrival, for in this royal reception his divine and human dignity is displayed. When the poet asserts "non so clene of such a clos com neuer er þenne" (none so clean from such an enclosure had come before then 1088), he is praising not only the purity of Mary's body and the luminous flesh of the newborn king of nature, but the elegance and integrity of the whole occasion. Christ enters the world surrounded with appropriate refinement, comparable to the ceremonial splendor a lord manifests in the festive decorum of his household and his guests.

> For, loke, fro fyrst þat he lyȝt withinne þe lel mayden,
> By how comly a kest he watz clos þere,
> When venkkyst watz no vergynyté, no vyolence maked,
> Bot much clener watz hir corse, God kynned þerinne.
> And efte when he borne watz in Beþelen þe ryche,
> In wych puryté þay departed; þaȝ þay pouer were,
> Watz neuer so blysful a bour as watz a bos þenne,
> Ne no schroude hous so schene as a schepon þare,
> Ne non so glad vnder God as ho þat grone schulde.
> For þer watz seknesse al sounde þat sarrest is halden

And þer watz rose reflayr where rote hatz ben euer,
And þer watz solace and songe wher sorȝ hatz ay cryed;
For aungelles with instrumentes of organes and pypes,
And rial ryngande rotes and þe reken fyþel,
And alle hende þat honestly moȝt an hert glade,
Aboutte my lady watz lent quen ho delyuer were.
Þenne watz her blyþe barne burnyst so clene
Þat boþe þe ox and þe asse hym hered at ones;
Þay knewe hym by his clannes for Kyng of nature,
For non so clene of such a clos com neuer er þenne. (1069–88)
(For, look, from the time he first alighted within the faithful maiden,
By how comely a contrivance he was enclosed there
Though no virginity was vanquished, no violence done,
But much more clean was her body — God [having been] conceived therein.
And after, when he was born in Bethlehem the splendid,
In what purity they became separate; though they were poor,
There was never so blissful a chamber as a byre was then,
Nor a sacristy so shining as a cow shed there,
And none so glad under God as she who should groan.
For there was sickness all sound, that is held to be most grievous,
And there was the fragrance as of roses where rot has always been,
And there was solace and song where sorrow has always cried;
For angels with instruments — organs and pipes,
And royal, ringing rebecks and just the right fiddle —
And all gracious things that could with dignity gladden a heart
Were abiding about my lady when she had been delivered.
Then was her blithe babe burnished so clean
That both the ox and the ass worshipped him at once;
They knew him by his cleanness as the King of nature,
For none so clean from such an enclosure had ever come before then.)

The pearl-like perfection of divine *clannesse* that is mirror and model to the Christian reader is manifest as much in the regal surroundings as in the Virgin and child whose birth is thus adorned and dignified.

The aesthetic integrity and joyfulness of the first Christmas the poem credits to God's consummate artistry; implicitly, the splendor evoked by the passage attests as well to the craft by which the poet himself constructs *fayre formez* that commend divine *clannesse*. The humble structures seem raw materials out of which he fashions, as did so many other artists meditating on this subject, a tour de force of courtly elegance.[17] The poverty into which Christ was born the poet notes only in order to emphasize the opulent beauty of the Nativity scene. Not only is Bethlehem described as splendid (1073), but, with no suggestion of irony, he refers to the cowshed as a "blysful . . . bour" (blissful bower 1075) and to the cattleshed as a "schroude hous so schene" (sacristy so shining 1076). The latter is at first a puzzling image; but it calls to mind the gleaming lustre of vestments and altar hangings, liturgical *gere* which are earthly reflections of heaven's courtly splendor. These were made of such opulent materials and with such decorative craftsmanship that even the place where they were stored becomes sacred.[18] When conjoined with the domestic space of a "bour," the sacristy image perhaps suggests the rituals of birth in families affluent enough to have their own chapels as well as elegantly furnished bedchambers and dressing rooms.[19]

Mary's body is imagined as a monument of natural integrity, a shrine that is all the more radiant when she encloses, and then releases, the jewel-like perfection of Christ's flesh.[20] The ox and ass lend an air of pastoral simplicity which does not dispel the aura of festive decorum, but instead confirms the significance of the unprecedented brightness of the newborn infant's body: because none had ever before then come so cleanly from such an enclosure, the very animals recognize the blithe baby as their sovereign and, indeed, as king over all nature.

The impression is one of nature renewed, perfected by heavenly artistry. The air is redolent with the scent of roses and resounds with music played by angels on organ, pipe, and stringed instruments. Even without a description of how these envoys from the heavenly court look, we can—recalling Lot's guests—readily visualize the angels as paragons of masculine beauty and charm. Bringing gracious mirth and merriment, these musicians contribute to the poet's creation of an atmosphere akin to courtly celebrations of the high and holy day of Christmas, where it is fitting to enjoy "alle hende þat honestly moȝt an hert glade" (all the gracious things that could properly gladden the heart 1083). Just as the host in the parable of the wedding feast served his guests to the brim with "menske and with mete and mynstrasy noble / And alle þe laykez þat a lorde aȝt in londe schewe" (honor, and food, and noble minstrelsy / And all the play that a lord of the land ought to display 121–22), so the poet imagines the festive decorum displayed at Christ's coming.

The second panel (1089–1100) of this verbal triptych portrays Christ, born as king of nature, cleansing its defilement through his healing ministry. The miraculous *clannesse* God exhibited in the conception and birth of celestial flesh through a woman is communicated to suffering humanity through Christ's courtesy extended to the sick and dying. A tension between bodily existence in nature corrupted by the Fall and nature restored by grace was implied in the contrast between the normal painfulness of labor and Mary's joyfully easy birthing of Christ. Now this tension becomes more dynamic as

Homosocial Bondings 187

Christ's courtesy is exemplified by his despising everything that pertained to evil. Having been so nobly born, and then nobly nurtured as well, he must not touch anything base.

> And ȝif clanly he þenne com, ful cortays þerafter,
> Þat alle þat longed to luþer ful lodly he hated,
> By nobleye of his norture he nolde neuer towche
> ȝt þat watz vngoderly oþer ordure watz inne. (1089–92)
> (And if cleanly he came thence, [he was] most courteous thereafter,
> So that all that belonged to evil with loathing he hated;
> By the nobility of his nurture he would never touch
> Anything that was vile or that ordure was in.)

Imagery of pollution and loathing reinforce the opposition between the gentle ethos of aristocratic life embraced by Christ and the realm of things that partake of vileness or villainy and hence can threaten courtesy's sacred value. This suggestively parallels God's hatred and revulsion when *fylþe of þe flesch* threatens his integrity, and the detail of *ordure,* or excremental filth (1089), strengthens the possible allusion to anal products and hence to sodomy. No matter how fastidious Christ was, however, he did not shun contact with a range of people of the wrong sort, a bundle of suffering humanity that the poet reviles as altogether loathsome (1093). For all their repellent unlikeness to Christ's perfect humanity, these people do not pose the same kind of threat that the profane posed to the sacred in the previous two exempla or, for that matter, in the introductory images of divine *clannesse.* There God was said to be unable to abide the shock of *fylþe* approaching his body when a priest who is inwardly impure celebrates Mass (31–32); here, on the other hand, while Christ refuses to touch anything unclean, he graciously transforms the loathsome into conformity with his own nature.

Courtesy is personified in this imaginative account of the magnetic attraction Christ held for precisely the evils he despised. His courtly graciousness becomes a model even for such lowly people, and they therefore approach him with touching dignity and fitting respect. Even as the beggars, lepers, lame, and others that the poet suggests are equally vile lay claim to Christ's grace, they mirror his nobility by their respect for his aristocratic refusal to defile himself through contact with their despicable ills. Christ extends a healing hand, but in fact heals them initially simply with his "hynde" (noble 1098) speech.

> ȝet comen lodly to þat Lede, as lazares monye,
> Summe lepre, summe lome, and lomerande blynde,
> Poysened, and parlatyk, and pyned in fyres,

> Drye folk and ydropike, and dede at þe laste,
> Alle called on þat Cortayse and claymed his grace.
> He heled hem wyth hynde speche of þat þay ask after
> For whatso he towched also tyd tourned to hele,
> Wel clanner þen any crafte cowþe devyse. (1093–1100)
> (Yet loathly ones came to that Lord — many diseased beggars,
> Some leprous, some lame, and the stumbling blind,
> Poisoned and paralytic, and injured by fires,
> The desiccated and dropsied, and the dead at the last,
> All called on that courteous one and claimed his grace.
> He healed them with noble speech according to what they ask for,
> For whatever he touched at once turned to healing,
> Far cleaner than any craft could devise.)

In this imaginative coalescing of a wide variety of episodes from the biblical accounts of the people Christ cured physically, the dilemma the poet poses is how divine lordship could have been exercised amidst such unpromising — nay, repulsive and even dead — human subjects.

Divine masculinity is depicted here as supremely tactful and therapeutic, both by nature and through nurture. Christ's courtly graciousness betokens the lofty peerage of his heavenly descent, but it also suggests an earthly education that developed his native courtesy. He is depicted as having mastered the arts of social decorum that enable the truly gracious to interact with the unclean — those with whom Chaucer's Friar refused to associate, because "it is not honest; it may not avaunce" (I [A] 246). Yet this courteous one does not come into any closer physical contact with those he helps than does the Friar — not until Christ has already cleansed their diseased flesh does he actually display the healing touch associated with royalty.[21] This part of the meditation on Christ concludes by the poet marveling that the health transmitted by this *Cortayse* to a diseased humanity is "wel clanner þen any crafte cowþe devyse" (far cleaner than any craft could devise 1100).

The third vignette accentuates the now familiar ideals of courtesy and craft and emphasizes above all Christ's affinity for the aesthetic values by which *clannesse* is being defined. Since the first two vignettes stress the elegant displays of decorum in divine *clannesse* incarnate, it is logical that the third one concludes the meditation by envisioning Christ's impeccable deportment at table, where his avoidance of filth and his miraculous touch displayed in the healing ministry are connected to the remarkable dexterity by which he divides a loaf of bread.

> So hende watz his hondelyng vche ordure hit schonied,
> And þe gropyng so goud of God and man boþe,

Þat for fetys of his fyngeres fonded he neuer
Nauþer to cout ne to kerue with knyf ne wyth egge;
Forþy brek he þe bred blades wythouten,
For hit ferde freloker in fete in his fayre honde,
Displayed more pryuyly when he hit part schulde,
Þenne alle þe toles of Tolowse moȝt tyȝt hit to kerue. (1101–8)
(So fastidious was his handling that all ordure it shunned,
And [his] handling so adept [who was] God and man both,
That because of his fingers' skill he never bothered
To cut or to carve with knife or with edge;
Therefore, he broke bread without using blades,
For it fared more perfectly in fact, in his fair hand,
Revealed itself more mysteriously when he would part it
Than all the tools of Tolouse could manage to carve it.)

Breaking, rather than cutting, bread (as Christ does both at the Last Supper and in the story of how the disciples recognized him by the way he breaks bread during supper at Emmaus, an episode from Luke's gospel often dramatized in the mystery plays) violates aristocratic fourteenth-century etiquette which dictates that the loaf be cut rather than torn. For a poet so apparently committed to social proprieties, such a breach of courtly manners on the part of the paragon of courtesy must have been troubling, but he has resolved it in this symbolic apprehension of Christ's mastery of the physical world through "fetys of his fyngeres" (elegance/skill of his fingers 1103). With his bare, and very beautiful, hands, Christ achieves a more clean-cut division than the sharpest of blades could have. Despite the apparent low status marker of his failure to use a knife, Christ's manners display his nobility. The king of nature can surpass, without minimizing, the aesthetic ideal aimed at in the social norms of etiquette. This beloved model is unfailingly "hende," in the circumstances of his birth, attended by "alle hende þat honestly moȝt an hert glade" (all the gracious things that could properly gladden the heart 1083); in the manner by which he heals the sick, by his "hynde speche" (gracious speech 1098); and in the way he prepares his food—"so hende watz his hondelyng" (so fair was his handling 1101).[22]

This concluding vignette of Christ at table thus functions not as a literal model to impersonate, since not using a knife profanes the code of aristocratic decorum which makes celestial *clannesse* clear and appealing, but as a symbol of ideal courtesy, an eloquent gesture effortlessly realized under difficult circumstances. Given the embodiment of *clannesse* in courtly forms in the preceding vignettes, the image of bread behaving perfectly when parted by the Lord's lovely hands is both extraordinarily oblique and suggestive.[23] The avoidance of ragged edges by an utterly natural finesse, incorporating artifice within natural courtesy, evokes what Baldasarre Castiglione would later describe as the ideal of "grazia." Christ displays a courtliness akin to the Renaissance courtier's light touch of "sprezzatura," a grace not reducible to particular properties or skills to be taught explicitly, but the expression of a natural endowment brought to fulfillment through intelligent observation of the best models.[24]

Yet how can such a divinely nurtured model be followed as an ethical paradigm? Perhaps the king of nature is portrayed here as a human paragon of the sort Thomas Aquinas had in mind when he wrote "External motions are signs of interior disposition" (2a2ae. 168, 1) and counseled "Let nature be our model, and her likeness the pattern for learning and the form of gracefulness" (2a2ae. 168, 1). The notion that virtue confers gracefulness made the skills of the handcraftsman a metaphor for the construction of a life of aesthetic splendor. Late medieval manuals of courtesy show how children of the elite class (as well as of families who sought such status) were "programmed from an early age to see the content of their 'curriculum' as a continuum and not to separate, or to be surprised at the conjunction of, religious and practical educational matter." This "implicitly wholistic view of elementary education" cited by Marie Denley (226) helps explain how courtesy, craft, and *clannesse* all represent "the Christ-like nature to be imitated by man" (225).[25] The nobly born, and those for whom courtly ideals had an aesthetic as well as an ethical appeal, could find in the poem's images of Christ's decorous life a curriculum for nurturing their conformity to a standard of decorum that was simultaneously social and sacred.[26]

Incarnation without the Crucifixion

Because the poem begins by contemplating the vulnerability of divine *clannesse* in the hands of the priest who handles in transubstantiated wafer and wine the very body of God, the neatly divided bread in Christ's hands may reasonably allude to the eucharistic wafer, elevated and broken at the climactic moment of the Mass. However, if the Mass is thus recalled, it is so in a way that excludes consciousness of Christ's self-representation of giving his body and blood to the faithful in the literal offering he made of his Passion and death. The passage theopoetically relocates the meaning of divine immanence, pointing away from the symbolic register of redemptive suffering toward God's perfect realization of the human condition by making embodied existence a beautiful expression of celestial artistry. This meditation on Christ's salvific excellence identifies his humanity with the divine artist's transformation and fulfillment of the flesh, rather than with its vulnerability.[27] A physically realistic depiction of Christ's torn and bleeding body would be at odds with the courtly refinement and optimism of *Cleanness*. However, it is not just the gruesome details of the Crucifixion which are bypassed by this meditation on Christ's perfection; it does not represent his dying at all.

As the culminating image of the Creator's proximity to the creatures, the portrait of Christ seems discontinuous with the preceding series of exempla which demonstrated God's violability, first in irascible fastidiousness as the offended host at the feast, and then in uncontrollable rage over *fylþe of þe flesch*. Because *Cleanness* lacks any image of the Crucifixion, its account of the Incarnation leaves unaddressed the conflict between the dangerous energies of defilement and those of divine *clannesse*. Where we would expect to find the climactic instance of God's art, the revulsion of his boundary-wrecking violence associated with *fylþe of þe flesch* drops out of sight. The genteel portrait of the Beloved, for all its blend of gracious charm and scrupulous refinement, seems a pale imitation of God's *clannesse* dramatized as a passion for order.

Late medieval meditations on a dying Christ typically represent "divinity as systematically debased, humiliated, and degraded, where the sacred, by lending itself to humanity that degrades it, traduces its own nature in profanation" (Beckwith 56). They offer the crucified Christ as a vivid model for imitation, where his symbolically exemplary Passion could be individually interiorized by each reader. Beckwith illuminates how this theopoetic strategy renegotiates the sacred and the profane in such a way as to enable in the lay Christian a self-transforming love comparable to the devotion aimed at in monastic piety.[28]

Cleanness may point to a similar renegotiation of the boundary of the sacred and the secular, as table manners become a revelation of Christ's perfection. How different, though, this expression of incarnational piety is from that generally found in meditations that focus on Christ's exemplary love. Although certainly gracious to those degraded specimens of humanity that the poem pronounces "loathsome," Christ as the epitome of courtliness retains an objectified distance. Rather than playing the active role of the physician whose own suffering provides the transforming dynamic that makes sinful humanity whole, Christ seems to be trapped in the more or less passive role assigned in early troubador lyrics to the courtly lady. Like the female mirror of perfection, Christ personifies courtesy as a virtue that excludes vulnerability. Seen under the aspect of the beloved whose beauty and graceful demeanor move her lover to imitate her, God incarnate resembles more the unmoved mover than the embodiment of passionate and compassionate divine love. Omitting the traditional centrality of the Passion of Christ, the poet's story of *clannesse* incarnate celebrates the flesh in a curiously sensuous yet abstract way.

For a poem that asks its male reader to admire the good looks of Lot's youthful guests but to abominate the very thought that such masculine beauty could arouse erotic longing for homosexual intimacy, the contemplation of Christ's embodied Passion could be problematic for two reasons. First, the Passion might obliterate or at least render threateningly ambiguous the difference between male and female identity in the deity, so that Christ's fetishized wounds could be experienced as a connection to the mother, and hence as an erotically pleasing source of comfort.

Cleanness logically avoids, therefore, the well-established image of Christ's motherhood in which the Crucifixion becomes a scene of childbirth, as the church is born from the Savior's bloodied side. By association with such images of birth and nurture, Christ's symbolically exemplary Passion was individually interiorized by many writers of devotional prose. Beckwith uses one such text, *The Prickynge of Love,* to illustrate how the sacred and profane interpenetrate in late medieval imaginative devotion to the cross, where Christ's wounds are mapped as both the most defiled and the most life-giving locations on his tortured body. Commenting on the densely elaborated maternal imagery, she notes "As well as functioning as a breast to be sucked, the wound at the side is also a womb in the act of perpetual parturition" (58). Linking the Nativity to the Crucifixion, James of Milan writes: "& him þat i eer fonde in his modres wombe I fele now how he voucheth-saf to bere my soule as his child with-inne his blessid sides. Bot I dred ouer soon to be spreid ouȝt fro þe delites þat I now fele. Certeynli ȝif he caste me ouȝt he shal neuerþeles as my modir ȝef me sowke of his pappis" (quoted Beckwith 58). In the same writer's *Stimulus amoris,* the equation between feminine openings and wounds in the body of Christ becomes still more overt, as he equates *vulnus* (wound) with *vulva* (female genitalia) (Beckwith 59).

The second reason the Passion could arouse homoerotic desire in a male reader is through the sensual fantasies of same-sex conjoining stimulated by the vulnerable and attractive naked body of Christ as suffering victim. When in devotional meditation the torn and bleeding body of the Savior is the object not only of pious empathy but of an erotic fixation as well, sensations of pain and pleasure merged into erotic intensity. Margery Kempe desired that the figure on the crucifix "should loosen His hands from the Cross and embrace her in token of love" (34). Her retrospective critique of this naive and direct response to Christ's love shows that she thought at the time that to enjoy bodily intimacy with God was a normal Christian entitlement. For males meditating on the Passion, this kind of sensual intensity could exert a homoerotic appeal that would have threatened the *Cleanness*-poet's sensibility.

While he is attracted to the idea of celestial beauty manifest in Christ's and Mary's human flesh and at the outset of his celebration of heavenly cleanness affirms the bodily presence of God at the disposal of the priest who handles the eucharistic elements, the poet's vision of the Incarnation does not evoke the kind of sexualized piety typically featured in devotional writings about Christ's sacrificial suffering. *Cleanness* does not associate Christ's aesthetically appealing life with his death or with an experience of the Eucharist as the sacrament that makes this offering of love a recurrent physical event in the life of the Christian. A vivid example of the consciousness of the Crucifixion which I am arguing the *Cleanness*-poet must logically exclude from his meditations comes from the pen of a contemporary — Nicholas Love — writing at the beginning of the fifteenth century. In translating an earlier meditation on the life of Christ, Love pauses in the narrative of the Passion to recount that a person he knew had, in meditating on the Crucifixion during the Eucharist, both seen inwardly the body of Christ hanging on the cross and in his own body felt "sensiblye þe bodily presence of oure lorde Jesus . . . with so grete joy and likyng þat þere can no tonge telle it fully, nor herte vndurstande it, bot onely he þat feliþ it" (155). To be thus tangibly and viscerally aware of the crucified Christ's physical presence in the Eucharist was an occasion of the most erotically charged intensity, filling the man's body with such joy and pleasure that all its members "bene enflaumed of so deletable and joyful a hete þat him þenkeþ sensibly alle þe body as it were meltyng for joy" (154). Rather than being reserved for the heavenly nuptials of Christ and the Church, or for only the most saintly of mystics in this lifetime, this kind of sensual intimacy with God is described by Love as a paradise on earth that is possible for all who come to the Eucharist disposed to experience the true body and blood of Christ in the bread and wine. "A lorde Jesu in what delectable paradise is he for þat tyme þat þus feleþ þat blessede bodily presence of þe, in þat precious sacrament, þorh þe which he feleþhim sensibly with unspekeable joy as he were joynede body to body?" (154)[29] Such an erotically charged bodily joining between the poet and his beloved exemplar would, I believe, radically disrupt the theopoetic logic of *Cleanness*, for while the poem celebrates the homosocial bonding between God and his devoted servants, it must protect courtly male ideals from the threat of homoerotic desire. It does so by erasing the bruises and brokenness that made Christ's flesh an object not only of compassion but of sexual longing. Avoiding the vulnerable body of God graphically represented by the wounds in Christ's hands, feet, and side, *Cleanness* fixes its readers' attention on the fastidious skill of Christ's fingers. A male reader of *Cleanness* is thus allowed to imagine himself physically attracted to Christ, but only at the most desexualized perimeter of his body.

While missing from *Cleanness,* meditations on how lovably vulnerable God appears in his bodily entrance into human history are not inherently at odds with the courtly poetic sensibility, as is obvious from two of the poem's manuscript companions.[30] In *Pearl* the paradoxical vision of God's pain and joy in uniting with human flesh is central to the Dreamer's courtly vision of heaven. The Pearl-Maiden describes the wounded Lamb's bloody sacrifice for humanity's redemption, noting that her lover was slain and torn on the cross by bold ruffians and his face that was once so fair to behold was torn by buffets (805–16). As the Dreamer's delighted gaze moves across the civic rituals of celebration in heaven's streets—hundreds of thousands in elegantly matching garments—it comes to rest on the figure at the center of the winding procession, and he is taken with a great desire to join the courtly company in the praise of the Lamb (1095–1130). Instead of envisioning Christ's physical form as emblematic of sacred wholeness and clean-cut boundaries of divine order, as it is in *Cleanness,* the poet shows us a Dreamer moved by the fact that in the center of the jeweled city where all seems so ceremonial and well-formed, the best and blithest of beings, clad in such spotlessly white array, is actually a torn and bleeding body (1131–39). As limited as his vision is in absolute terms, the still sinful Dreamer can see more feelingly than the Pearl-Maiden the meaning of the fact that the sacred form of Christ, at the center of heaven's perfection, is as fully a site of suffering as his own finite and limited humanness. While Christ is thus revealed as forever wounded, bloody, and torn, he is gloriously happy, so that his semblance is one of delight rather than grief (1141–44).

In the equally courtly milieu of *Sir Gawain,* there is a similarly paradoxical grasp of Christ's suffering which suggests a richer penitential subjectivity than the ostensibly homiletic enterprise of *Cleanness.* The divine sacrifice upon which the celebration of the feast of the Nativity depends is recalled both in the Mass Gawain longs to attend on Christmas Eve and in the good times at Sir Bercelayk's Christmas festivities (750–52, 995–97). Here the images of the Nativity point quite explicitly to the Crucifixion—Christ's reason for being born and the ultimate cost he pays in suffering alongside and on behalf of sinful humanity. In *Cleanness,* although Mary's unique motherhood is forecast in the account of the Fall, Christmas is divorced from any consciousness of Christ's death or the conflict he dies to resolve. Rather, the Nativity scene is an idyllic portrait of the harmonious splendor of the heavenly court in nature's midst. Significantly absent are the sorrows which traditionally paralleled Mary's joys. Instead of alluding to the paradoxical connection of her painless birthing of Christ with the grief she will have later to endure in compassion for her dying son, the *Cleanness*-poet celebrates the Nativity simply as the joyful beginning of a fresh manifestation of heaven's power to restore nature's wholeness.

Deficient Images of Sin and Penance

An upward spiral in history in which nature is restored augurs both communal and personal fulfillment in the first two-thirds of the poem. The Creator acts and is acted upon in ways that may be momentarily destructive and terrifying but in the long run bring about changes that are self-evidently desirable — at least to the narrator and his implied audience. Despite the illustrations of the horrific consequences of sin, the poem is pervaded with a promise of something "glorious, splendid, clean and joyous" for which one is intended.[31] This promised something is of course explicitly named from the outset as the vision of God, every Christian reader's destiny, to be obtained by living in loving anticipation of it. What is required is simply to participate wholeheartedly in God's *crafte* and to want to conform perfectly to its exemplary manifestation in Christ. Throughout *Cleanness*, an impossible standard is set alongside a serene assumption that such perfection is naturally fitting to human nature and destiny.

Although *Cleanness* is neither a theological treatise nor a devotional meditation, the ethical, the religious, and the aesthetic are so fused in this poem that it cannot be satisfactorily evaluated in purely literary terms. The poem's assimilation of the idioms and metaphors of courtly romance into the language of homily and biblical paraphrase suggests at certain points the creative potential of a revisionary mythopoesis to recover muted truths at the core of dominant values; at other points, it displays the limits of an uncritical embrace of a class-specific secular ethos. *Cleanness* fails to present us with what we might reasonably expect from a celebration of heavenly perfection embodied in earthly forms — namely, an exploration of the connection between human finitude and an all-encompassing ideal of the Good as the Beautiful. The ladylike control of boundaries manifest in Christ's beautiful handcrafting neatly broken bread into clean-cut portions avoids any intensely personal or communal identification with a world of human evil and so skirts the reconfiguration of the sacred and profane that could ensue from imagining the Crucifixion. Because no image of transformation is provided by the Incarnation that is comparable in impact and development to what we have seen in the encounters of God with the sinful world that arouses his wrath, penance feels perfunctory;

the crucial topic of the discrepancy between the actual and the ideal is given short *schryfte*. The omission of the Crucifixion from the poem's incarnational aesthetic becomes most theopoetically problematic when considered in the context of this deficient representation of penance, for lacking the suffering of Christ, this sacrament lacks the dynamic for transformation associated with contemplating God's incarnate (and hence shockingly costly) grace. What is omitted from the Incarnation is the empowering of the sacred by conceptualizing, and experiencing, the interpenetration with the profane where its symbolic force is most acute. Avoiding the Crucifixion, the poem locates no other metaphorical site for transformation and so generates no imaginative energy for the subjective process of modeling oneself as a lover of Christ in response to his love.[32]

That a human life, by analogy to the beryl or pearl, can flawlessly reflect the glory of heavenly order expresses the poet's basically aesthetic grasp of the reward promised to the clean in the Beatitude and his assurance that God's *clannesse* corresponds perfectly to human desires. Secure in an aristocratic sense of entitlement, the poet encourages his implied audience to believe that they, like him, will naturally present themselves in impeccably good form to their Creator's court.[33] At the conclusion of the passage on the Incarnation, however, the narrator's confidence flags momentarily, and he acknowledges personally the need for transformation. Having shown how fastidious and pure Christ is, the narrator concludes that we (here the first person plural tactfully identifies the speaker with his implied sinful listeners) are not prepared to conform to this dear one, but are instead sore, sinful, and soiled.

> Þus is he kyryous and clene þat þou his cort askes;
> Hov schulde þou com to his kyth bot if þou clene were?
> Nov ar we sore and synful and sovly vchone;
> How schulde we se, þen may we say, þat Syre upon throne? (1109–12)
> (Thus he whose court you aspire to is fastidious and flawless;
> How should you enter his kingdom unless you were flawless?
> Now we are afflicted and sinful and spoiled, each of us;
> How then might we say that we were to see that lord upon his throne?)

It is as if the account of Christ's healing grace transforming the infirm has turned the speaker's attention to the parallel between the suffering of those *lodly* (loathsome ones) and the malaise of sinful humanity. Even the poet himself might not be fit as yet for the bliss he anticipates with such confidence that it seems an already experienced reality. The need for cleansing becomes, albeit briefly, a matter of existential importance.

To be like Christ, "euer . . . polyced als playn as þe perle seluen" (polished as fully as the pearl itself 1068), purifying sacramental grace must come into play. And *play* is the right verb here, for the poet is disengaged from any heavy-handed moralization, or indeed from any recognition of the problem to which penance is the solution. In place of any analysis of the persistent human inclination to prefer evil, or at least to choose lesser goods than God, the poem offers an extended metaphor, comparing the cleansed soul to a pearl restored to brightness. Sin is like the accidental neglect of a beautiful treasure, a mere oversight easy enough to commit by someone who owns more jewels than could be regularly worn. With no image of personal responsibility or shame, the reader's consciousness is focused on a class-specific domestic mishap — a beautiful gem tarnished by disuse. The remedy? — simply retrieve it from oblivion and dip it in wine. The soul's healing is thus a natural process, analogous to the restoration of a pearl left unworn instead of being displayed publicly as it deserves:

> ȝet þe perle payres not whyle ho in pryse lasttes;
> And if hit cheue þe chaunce vncheryst ho worþe,
> Þat ho blyndes of ble in bour þer ho lygges,
> Nobot wasch hir wyth wourchyp in wyn as ho askes,
> Ho by kynde schal become clerer þen are.
> So if folk be defowled by vnfre chaunce,
> Þat he be sulped in sawle, seche to schryfte. (1124–30)
> (Yet the pearl does not deteriorate so long as she is prized;
> And if by chance it happens that she is neglected,
> So that she becomes dim of color in the bedroom where she lies,
> Simply wash her with reverence in wine as she requires,
> And by nature she shall become brighter than before.
> So if someone were stained by [some] ignoble chance
> So that he were soiled in soul, [let him] hie [himself] to confession.)

The tidy prescription for brightening up one's soul tactfully reinforces the optimistic vision of human nature's intrinsic congruity to God's design and hence its capacity for being restored to its perfect state.[34] The pearl is central to a constellation of images that evoke imaginatively a feeling for divine order as congruent with the rhythms of life in a courtly household. It is hard to imagine anyone who does not share the narrator's serenity, his cheerful sense of entitlement to the good life, feeling at home with the confident tone in which he appraises their naturally gemlike *clannesse* and the ease with which it can be restored through penance.

The implied aristocratic readers' perception of their unlikeness to Christ's nobility is made tolerable by the immediate assurance that they share his pearl-like qualities and can instantaneously attain the beauty needed to enter his kingdom once they get themselves to a priest and "take penance." Among the sacraments, penance is unique insofar as it requires the layperson's subjective involvement through the steps of contrition, confession, and a willing submission to the works imposed as satisfaction. What is to be accomplished by the sacramental act is not just absolution, but a reordering of the ingrained habits of the sin-distorted human nature. The easy removal of a superficial layer of soil from an essentially unflawed object is almost necessarily misleading as an analogy for the metamorphosis required for a Christian to conform flawlessly to Christ's own perfect *clannesse*. Neither the polishing advocated at the conclusion of the pearl analogy (1131), nor the other two images offered of penance—washing with the water of "schryfte" (penance) and shaving the parchment—adequately suggest the effort and costliness of spiritual transformation afforded by the sacramental grace of penance.

An essential distance between God and humanity, briefly faced in the confession of the poet's own and his listeners' sinfulness, is overcome in what amounts to a metaphorical finesse, for the image of the tarnished pearl restored to brightness deals with sin apart from any exploration of how sacramental grace operates as a transforming force in Christian subjectivity. If the remedy of dipping the soiled gem in wine alludes to the eucharistic chalice and wafer (the latter round and white like the pearl), this image of the Mass nevertheless elides the sacrificial love manifest in Christ's Passion, the historical event upon which sacramental grace depends.[35] To judge by the poet's depiction of penance, the Incarnation imagined as a display of divine craft and courtesy does not precipitate the kind of intense desire and affect that transforms Christian self-understanding. *Cleanness* jettisons any identification with the Creator's most intimate sharing of human flesh and so any understanding of what is salvific about the Eucharist or penance.

Cleanness is neither a homiletic nor a penitential poem.[36] Its idea of sinfulness is as strangely distanced as its idea of penance is superficial. The inadequate representation of evil and suffering in the context of Incarnation and penance fails to provide the symbolic resources needed to model the subjectivity that it claims is required for the vision of God. This is all the more curious, considering that it is "in connection with the doctrine of penance, and particularly in the penitential literature of the later Middle Ages that the idea of cleanness/uncleanness is most fully discussed by theologians and homilists, usually with reference to the sixth beatitude" (Anderson 5). This Beatitude, promising the vision of God to the pure of heart, is the text on which the poet initially bases his praise of this virtue (27–28).

In place of penitential identification with God's suffering, the *Cleanness*-poet celebrates Christ's mercy as a magical force at the priest's disposal, transmitting the lucid perfection for which human nature is created. The pearl imagery allows a reader to feel that once absolved by the priest, a soul is easily preserved in Christ-like perfection. But how easily can this brightness, thus gracefully restored, be retained? In *Cleanness* penance is described as a once and for all purification, almost as baptism was for early Christians.[37]

However appealing the poet's gentle spiritual pedagogy may be in the conclusion to the first two-thirds of the poem, divine perfection incarnate in Christ cannot engage the resistant complexity of the human psyche when the Crucifixion is missing. Traditionally, Christ's death reconciles opposing claims of divine justice and mercy, demonstrating God's compassionate identification with sinful humanity through the Father's offering his Son and the Son's willingness to die in order to reconcile humanity and God, thereby bringing together the divine passion for order with the capacity for forgiving a perpetually sinful creation. In the Atonement, the Creator takes on ultimate responsibility for the evil he cannot overcome apart from becoming mortal, where he must suffer to the fullest its damaging force. With the omission of the ultimate danger and anomaly of God's death, the power of the sacred appears diminished.

The poet avoids dealing with Christ's death as the definitive exposure of the vulnerability of God's designs and dignity. Traditional meditations on the Passion invite the Christian to identify with Christ as victim but also to recognize complicity with those who inflicted pain; even if the human agents of the Crucifixion are cast into the role of Other (whether as Jews or uncouth ruffians, or both, as in *Pearl* 799–816), the penitent sinners must own the resemblance between themselves and the villains. In *Cleanness*, however, there is no image of human failure to recognize God's sovereignty when it is paradoxically displayed in suffering. Instead, the poet scapegoats male same-sex lovemaking as the most damaging affront to the divine order. By thus demonizing what his society had already constructed as intolerable difference, he maintains a homosocial bonding between God and man that rests upon their mutual loathing of — and obsession with — homosexual deviance.

After presenting Christ as incarnate *clannesse*, the poet returns to God's wrath. On a dire note, the brief discourse on penance is followed by a warning about the consequences befalling anyone who fails to live a life of total perfection after they are sacramentally cleansed (1133–38). Here the poem echoes suggestively a passage in 2 Peter: "For if, after they have escaped the defilements of the world . . . , they are again entangled in them and overpowered, the last state has become worse for them than the first. For it would have been better for them never to have known the way of righteousness than after knowing it to turn back from the holy commandment delivered to them" (2 Peter 2:20–21). These chilling verses conclude a chapter which bears other resemblances to *Cleanness*, for both deal with a similar sequence of Old Testament events—the fall of the angels, the Flood, the destruction of Sodom and Gomorrah, the sparing of Lot.[38]

While the poet was probably influenced in his choice of stories by this biblical passage and was very likely afraid that those who turn back from a life of *clannesse* offend God more than if they had never accepted his standards, a reasonably thoughtful medieval reader could not be expected to take literally the notion that yearly administrations of penance would not cleanse mortal sins repeated after the sinner had been shriven. After all, the annual confession of sins mandated in 1215 remained a requirement for all Christians. Yet the narrator claims that any sin committed after penance evokes God's anger at its extremity, just as Belshazzar's defilement of the sacred vessels did. Soiling the soul once it has regained all its baptismal purity by the sacramental grace of penance is represented here as virtually an unforgivable evil. Clearly the poet is not giving pastoral guidance here but insisting on the extreme gravity of any sin after penance in order to defer the conclusion of his theopoetic enterprise by introducing yet another story of God's wrath, this one presenting a different view of the relation between the sacred and the profane.

Following the admonition to seek penitential cleansing in order to be perfectly conformed to Christ, *Cleanness* presents a third and final exemplum which depicts divine vengeance as a constant factor, aroused to an extreme no longer by sexual sin specifically but by any sin at all after penance, and reconceives the locus of God's activity within history, constructed as a cycle of political reversals. The result is that God's *clannesse* loses its cosmic power to resolve and reorder the sinful state of humankind.

8

Theopoetic Coherence: Cleanness *among Its Manuscript Companions*

From Numinous Beauty to Historical Contingency: Theopoetic Disjunctions in the Final Exemplum

Concluding *Cleanness* after a third historical demonstration of divine wrath, the poet continues to imagine himself and his readers as splendidly part of the divine order. His final claims echo the aesthetic idealism of the opening contrast between the *fayre formez* that present themselves when praising *clannesse* and the difficulties that ensue in doing the opposite. Linking the three major exempla together as three demonstrations of how pleased God is by *clannesse* and how pained by its opposite, the last lines sound a final note of confidence in the solace to be enjoyed while serving so fastidious a Lord:

> Þus vpon þrynne wyses I haf yow þro schewed
> Þat vnclannes tocleues in corage dere
> Of þat wynnelych Lorde þat wonyes in heuen,
> Entyses hym to be tene, teldes vp his wrake;
> Ande clannes is his comfort, and coyntyse he louyes,
> And þose þat seme arn and swete schyn se his face.
> Þat we gon gay in oure gere þat grace he vus sende,
> Þat we may serue in his syȝt, þer solace neuer blynnez. Amen. (1805–12)
> (Thus in three ways I have shown you thoroughly
> That uncleanness cleaves/rankles the noble heart

Of that gracious Lord who dwells in heaven,
Provokes him to be angry, builds up his vengeance;
And cleanness is his comfort, and elegance/wisdom he praises,
And those that are seemly and sweet will see his face.
May he send us the grace to go gaily in our attire
That we may serve in his sight where solace never ceases. Amen.)

By the time the cheerful "amen" is pronounced after this jaunty benediction, it rings a bit off-key, for a hiatus has been glimpsed between the numinous beauty of divine order celebrated in the first two-thirds of the poem and the ambiguous course of history narrated in the final exemplum.

Courtliness as a theopoetic metaphor, so evident in the final image of the poet and his listeners gaily proceeding in elegant array to take and give pleasure in God's company, is problematized in the final third of the poem because the felt mutuality of the human-divine attraction to beauty diminishes as the poet unfolds the complex history of the vessels defiled at Belshazzar's feast. God's punishment of those who dishonor him by their treatment of the liturgical objects made for his service is recounted, ostensibly to show how closely identified he is with what belongs to him and, by analogy, how extreme his anger is when a soul consecrated to him through penance is defiled by sin. The conflation of several sources (one secular and several biblical texts) and the narrator's commentary produces an uncertain thematic blend. On the one hand, there are familiar images of God's impeccable splendor and of the aesthetically attractive standards fueling his anger; on the other hand, there is a surprisingly fatalistic perspective which underscores the certainty of death and dissolution. Kings are defeated or, if victorious, come at last to the grave, and their kingdoms fall; the commentary traces a pattern resembling the bliss and blunder depicted by chroniclers, so that the *clene* lines of the Creator's order are overwritten with the transciency of earthly goods.[1]

The final exemplum dramatizes the fate of the treasures Solomon made for the temple in Jerusalem and of the people responsible for them. When in the reign of the idolatrous King Zedekiah the Jews become faithless, God's wrath is raised to so high a pitch that he devises the downfall of the people he had consecrated as his own. This echoes the Flood narrative, where he severely punishes what he had once cherished so dearly; however, the merciless punishment of the Jews in the latter episode does not express God's rage directly but issues from the human will of their political enemy, the Chaldeans, bent on the epic conquest of the kingdom of Judea. Nor is God's will immediately accomplished, for it is only after two years of warfare that the king of the Chaldeans takes the king of the Jews prisoner, starved into a reckless escape attempt from the beseiged Jerusalem. Nebuchadnezzar savors this hard-won moment, cruelly forcing his royal captive to witness the slaughter of his sons and his best warriors before digging out his eyes and casting him into a dungeon. As a final gesture of power, the Chaldean army is sent to raze the now defenseless city and ravage the surrounding countryside.

The poem provides characteristically vivid elaboration of violence merely suggested in the biblical sources, but the effect is distinctly different from the elemental vengeance manifest in the Flood and the destruction of Sodom. The epic siege and conquest of Jerusalem culminate in the massacre of civilians by Nabuzaradan, a "gentyle duc" (gentle duke 1235) whose determination to punish the city is described as fueled by heartfelt rage. This belligerence and zest for mayhem is much greater than in the biblical sources. Although such bloodthirstiness might seem a fittingly destructive instrument of God's own wrathful vengeance, the lapse from the chivalric ideals of moderation and fairplay evokes from the narrator a slur on the honor of this captain. Nebuchadnezzar is initially introduced as "mayster of his men and myȝty himseluen, / Þe chef of his cheualrye his chekkes to make" (master of his men and mighty himself, / The foremost of his chivalry in making assaults 1237–38). But with King Zedekiah and his best warriors already captured and the remaining Jewish men so weak from starvation that the four strongest had the negligible force of one woman, the successful invasion is hardly a sign of military virtue. Instead of praising it, the narrator exclaims, "What! þe maysterry watz mene" (Well! this was a poor victory 1241) and then portrays in a tone of horror the unrelenting butchery of women and children.

The effects of God's vengeance were traced with some empathy for the victims in previous exempla, but not with such graphic depiction of physical suffering. Here Jewish babies are bathed in their own blood as their brains are spilled; women and girls have their bellies carved open so that the bowels burst out; priests are pulled by their hair to their beheading — to name only three categories of defenseless victims. The issues involved in debate over what constitutes a just war are inescapably, albeit implicitly, raised. With the final causal agency for the destruction of the Jews explicitly assigned to God rather than to the human powers of military leaders like Nebuchadnezzar, these added atrocities problematize the alliance between heaven and earthly kingdoms. The meticulous account of the techniques of military operations and the implied critique of Nabuzaradan's savagery emphasize the secondary causality of warfare. Moreover, the previous two exempla portrayed the conflict between divine power and vulnerability, and between the cleansing and destructive effects of divine rage, as a dynamic interpenetration of sacred and profane within God; in this final story the suffering is entirely human and results from unbridled aggression. Here what is anomalous in God's nature can hardly be said to be enshrined in any numinous displays of his elemental power in the cosmos. Nor does the boundary-breaking violence of a hate-filled army contribute to a cosmogonic ritual reordering humanity and renewing nature.

At its outset, this exemplum is introduced, as the earlier two were, as a historical demonstration of God's wrath at its extreme. Nevertheless, the claims about just what is being demonstrated differ in this final instance from the previous assertions about unparalleled vengeance aroused by *fylþe of þe flesch*. Rather than God's wrath being defined as superlative and unique, here its degree is articulated in comparative terms: Belshazzar, who defiled God's vessels, suffers a heavier judgment than did Nebuchadnezzar, his erring father, who wrongfully stole these sacred objects from the Jews. Guilty of the lesser of two evils, Nebuchadnezzar is impugned at the outset as well as Belshazzar, but in telling the story, the poet shifts responsibility to the unruly Nabuzaradan and develops an entirely positive role for Nebuchadnezzar as protector of the vessels. Nabuzaradan and his army like wild robbers carry off these treasures before burning the temple to the ground. God is presumably responsible for this as well as the other military endeavors, having allied himself with the Chaldeans to punish the Jews, but in any case, he is completely distanced from the action. While the narrator has assured us at the outset how loath the heavenly proprietor is to lose the most modest of objects from his household, only the careful listing of the various nobly formed ornaments and furnishings Solomon fashioned to his Lord's honor conveys how offended God must be at their being wrenched out of his sanctuary by contemptuous warriors. This is the first of three such descriptions of the treasures, each emphasizing their splendor and their sacred functions in the temple.[2]

Back in Babylon, the religious objects are part of the booty presented to Nebuchadnezzar, along with gold from the treasury, cattle herded from the outlying plains, and many Jewish noblemen and women now destined for lives of hard labor. In describing the transmission of the vessels, going against the grain of his announced point in telling Nebuchadnezzar's story and with no biblical basis, the poet ably dramatizes the salvific impact of God's glory manifest in the material forms Solomon shaped, imbued as they are with divine *clannesse*. The disrespect shown by Nabuzaradan and his men for the treasures they snatched from the holy of holies becomes a foil for Nebuchadnezzar's awe as he discerns their religious significance. Where he was at first simply gleeful over his chieftain's exploits, the king is invaded by a different feeling of joy mixed with wonder when he sees the vessels. Instead of the pride he felt in his army's military accomplishments, he is humbled by the magnificence of the "juelrye so gentyle and ryche" (noble and rich jewels 1309) which he recognizes as honoring the sovereign who is not only Israel's Lord, but the one who reigns gloriously over all. The salvific force of beauty initiates the transformation of this paragon of epic aggression and pride to a gentler ideal of kingship. He is suitably moved by the vessels' beauty, and—as if he were providing hospitality to emissaries from heaven—he takes reverent custody of them and provides for their safety by placing them fittingly in his treasury. At this point, his announced role in the didactic plot forecast in the introduction to the exemplum undergoes drastic change. Instead of a greedy king who seized the vessels by force and robbed the church of all its relics (1155–56), Nebuchadnezzar becomes the antithesis of the proud and idolatrous Zedekiah and thus in effect the spiritual successor to Solomon. Like that wise Jewish king and supremely skilled collaborator with God's artistry, Nebuchadnezzar takes his place in the poem's series of human exemplars of *clannesse,* men who are homosocially bonded with their Creator through ritualized moments of aesthetic connoisseurship.

Before the exemplum ends, Nebuchadnezzar is humbled more than once, by the vessels, by the teaching of the prophet Daniel, and, most dramatically, by God's direct punishment. But the death of Nebuchadnezzar closes the first half of the exemplum by bringing a glorious and apparently pious reign to a strikingly simple end with the proverbial observation that "Bi a haþel neuer so hyȝe, he heldes to grounde" (However great a man is, he falls to the ground 1331). The imagery of a downward force that exerts itself on every mortal and every human achievement, no matter how noble, links the king's demise to other reversals in such a way as to undercut the moral significance of his lessons in humility and of the dissolution his forces inflicted on Jewish grandeur. While the plot is clearly intended to illustrate divine control of earthly events, God's allies' victories and his enemies' losses seem to be blurred by commentary and imagery that emphasize the universal force of mutability. Who wins and who loses matters only temporarily, for everything earthly is precarious and ultimately must fall down. This fatalistic note is sounded throughout the exemplum: the Jewish gentry and their rich city are drawn downward to earth (1159–60); Zedekiah is subjected to his fate in a dungeon (1224); the city of Jerusalem is brought to the ground (1234); its noble citizens are demoted to churls by enslavement in exile (1258–60). The motif extends to the vessels themselves; what took Solomon so many years of excellent work to make is despoiled in a matter of minutes, a dissolution the narrator both demonstrates and comments upon. Although they do not lose their power to communicate God's glory when they are seized by pillagers, their new protector dies as all men must. In the hands of his idolatrous son, Belshazzar, the sacred vessels are destined for still more serious profanation and apparently permanent separation from the realm of the holy.

Although God does not protect these material embodiments of his splendor, he is instantaneously and directly responsive when his precious vessels are profaned by Belshazzar. Mysterious runes inscribed by a great hand on the palace wall bring a sudden end to the Babylonian orgy where sacred cups and bowls have been brought out of safekeeping in the treasury to be used in toasts drunk in homage to concubines and, still more disgusting, idols. The extremity of God's anger is expressed in the physical brutality which brings death to Belshazzar. Murdered in his bed, his bloody corpse is dragged by the heels out of a palace of pride into a ditch where it is left to decompose with no more dignity than a dead dog. This violent overthrow of a thoroughly evil king the very morning after his climactic display of vice reveals providential justice in history. Heaven's vengeance against the villain permits yet another greedy conquest; the political motives and military means of the Persians are narrated in enough detail to make their overthrow of Babylon feel like part of an endless cycle of earthly violence, controlled by the reversals of fate. The representation of God's *clannesse* as divinely ordering nature in the vengeance accomplished by the genocidal cataclysms in the previous two exempla is here qualified as the Creator's control of history appears to depend on recurring conflicts between earthly kingdoms.

The poet concludes the final exemplum by a movement out of that ever-changing realm of history, the realm which by its nature seems to obscure the intelligibility and attractiveness of divine order. The last word on Belshazzar's downfall is spoken from the supra-historical perspective of the Last Judgment, asserting the congruence of the order of earthly justice with that of heaven, the realm above the mutable:

> He watz corsed for his vnclannes, and cached þerinne,
> Done doun of his dyngneté for dedez vnfayre,
> And of þyse worldes worchyp wrast out for euer,
> And ȝet of lykynges on lofte letted, I trowe:
> To loke on oure lofly Lorde late bitydes. (1800–1804)
> (He was cursed for his uncleanness, and caught therein,
> Cast down from his dignity for unfair deeds,
> And from this world's worship thrust out forever,
> And even deprived from the pleasures above, I believe;
> To look on our lovely Lord happens late to him.)

For the first time the poet condemns an Old Testament evildoer in terms that allude to eternal punishment. Doing so by reference to heavenly pleasures that Belshazzar will never enjoy modulates the tone, however, and thus provides a graceful transition to the cheerful concluding prayer.[3]

Yet the effect is not unequivocally cheering, because the exemplum shows that all alike must die—good and bad rulers, heroes and villains, God-fearing fathers and foolish sons, men and dogs. The depressing succession of a good to an evil king in Chaldea echoes a similarly depressing succession in Judah from the wise Solomon to the wicked Zedekiah. So also the image of one royal corpse invites the recollection of another. Nebuchadnezzar is clearly worthier than his son, yet the death of this good king has been recounted as if it simply exemplifies the rule of necessity that determines the fate of princes. For all his empire so high, King Nebuchadnezzar was buried in the earth (1329–32). Thus the theopoetic strategy of celebrating the continuity between earthly and heavenly order is obscured, and in fact overwritten, by a recurring sense of the near futility of all human achievements. This part of the poem is reminiscent of the mood in Reason's discourses in the *Roman* on the overthrow of powerful kings by Fortune and may owe something to that portion of Jean's text. The fatalistic assumptions of the *de casibus* genre that pervade the third Old Testament exemplum dilute its demonstration of the gravity of Belshazzar's defilement and distract as well from the poet's allegorical warning against sin after penance.[4]

Problematizing the Courtly Aesthetic as a Model for the Relationship of Divine and Human

In the latter third of *Cleanness*, what angers God is no longer the specific sin of homosexual *fylþe of þe flesch* but general *unclannesse*, as in the story of the wedding feast. Like the introductory parable, the poem's closing exemplum is allegorically interpreted by the narrator. Just as the ill-clad guest signifies any failure to achieve the all-encompassing perfection required for the vision of God, so the defilement of the vessels represents any failure to maintain the pearl-like integrity graciously conferred in the sacrament of penance. God's artistry and anger are significantly altered from the previous two Old Testament exempla by being relocated in the narrative context of historical contingency. Divine artistry is now evident indirectly in the manmade objects furnishing the temple rather than revealed directly in the divinely ordered *play of paramorez*. Anger, now focused on *unclannesse* in general, is expressed distantly through the secondary causality of human warfare, rather than directed at homosexual *fylþe* and expressed personally with an all-consuming obsession displayed in natural catastrophes. By thus altering God's character in the different context afforded by the history of the vessels, the poet alters the representation of the homosocial bond to be enjoyed with God.

Although no longer concerned with homosexual deviance from God's heterosexual design for paradisal pleasure, the final exemplum bears significantly on our study of the poem's sexual themes because the vessel is a traditional image used figuratively to equate human virtue with clean perfection and vice with defilement and sacrilege. Moreover, sexual integrity is conventionally figured in terms of vessels consecrated to divine purpose, and sins of lust are conventionally equated metaphorically with theft of holy vessels or other sacrilegious use of them. Still more specifically, forms of lust which violate nature are frequently figured allegorically as idolatry, and idolatry is what the poet places in the foreground in the final exemplum.[5] The history of the temple's treasures, including the vessels, begins with the Jews departing from the true faith in the reign of Zedekiah who practiced "abominaciones of idolatrye" (abominations of idolatry 1173), and it ends with Belshazzar defiling the sacred cups he lifts in homage to false gods. Idolatry's conventional association with sodomy in exegetical commentaries was based in part on Paul's argument (in Romans 1:18–27) that same-sex intercourse practiced by the Romans was the consequence of men and women having rejected God as he is revealed in creation in preference for the worship of graven images. What Paul regarded as unnatural and perverse sexual behavior he diagnoses as symptomatic of the Romans' religious perversity. Because of their inexplicable refusal to recognize in the beauty of the world the signs of God's own immortal splendor, and their choice to worship instead idols resembling earthly creatures, "God gave them up in the lusts of their hearts to impurity, to the dishonoring of their bodies among themselves" (Romans 1:24).[6] Paul's condemnation of homosexual practice may have influenced the poet's depiction of divine wrath against the Sodomites, where the Creator views their way of making love as a misreading of his meaning and a scorning of nature. The poet's description of the vessels in the final exemplum extends his earlier celebrations of nature as God's *clannesse* embodied for human aesthetic appreciation and collaboration, for the sacred artifacts bear cascades of enamelled blossoms and jeweled fruits with sculptured birds fluttering amidst the foliage. The courtly aesthetic of *clannesse* thus continues in this final exemplum, which depicts idolatry as worshipping the unnatural, symbolized by gods crudely carved from wood and stone, in foolish disrespect to the glory of the Creator embodied in the elegant vessels Solomon fashioned from precious metal and gems as a visible expression of divine order.

The poet portrays the moral failure epitomized by Belshazzar's folly in aesthetic terms as a lack of proportion; the evil king's mind is fixated on "misschapen þinges" (misshaped, i.e., wicked, things 1355). This misshaped mentality is exemplified in many different violations of festive decorum, framed by an initial account of Belshazzar's love-hate relationship to false gods and climaxed by his final expression of idolatry. The lifeless statues to which the king turns with his petition (and against which he turns, wielding a club, when his wishes are not granted) are obviously counterfeits, powerless to act or speak. As such, superficially gilded artifacts of wood and stone stand in striking contrast to the sacred artifice of the golden basins, ewers, cups, and candelabra, adorned with the beauty of natural forms that eloquently testify to the splendor of both the creation and its Creator.

The traditional association between sodomy and idolatry may be deliberately alluded to in the imagery of filth as a substance that like yeast energetically overflows boundaries, used first in the poet's invective against the Sodomites and then in Daniel's prophetic indictment of Belshazzar. The Sodomites' utterance, when they offer to teach their ways of making love to Lot's attractive guests, is described as frothing filth ("ȝestande sorȝe" 846), and Daniel similarly describes as a physically revolting frothiness Belshazzar's sacrilegious use of the treasures from God's temple.[7]

In spite of the more obscure delineation of divine order in the third exemplum's shift from nature to history as the medium of God's vengeance, some of the poem's earlier celebratory tone is evident in the description of the vessels and candlesticks. They are playful and gratuitous artistry, reproduced in playful and gratuitous verbal detail, and so illustrate excess as good in contrast to the yeasty bad excess which overflows boundaries. These fanciful representations of Late Gothic taste for the decorative represent nature refined by artifice; they echo and reinforce the gratuitous excess of pleasure legitimated in the Creator's account of his own compassing and portraying of the *play of paramorez*. I see in this extraordinary passage not an accumulation of "somewhat naive technical detail" suggesting that "the astonished gaze of the drunken revellers" perceives the treasures "simply as ornate and costly objects of art" (Andrew and Waldron 24), but nature's transient beauty raised to near permanence by a combination of human and divine artifice. Just as God's craftsmanship combines with the lovers he teaches to transmute their desire into a blaze brilliantly impervious to earthly troubles, so Solomon collaborates with the Creator to fix forever the flower's momentary loveliness in the enduring brightness of pearls and to form from flaming gems ripe fruit that never falls.

The vessels are subjected to earthly change when their sanctity is dramatically profaned first by Zedekiah's idolatry, then by Nabuzaradan's pillaging of the temple, and most appallingly, by Belshazzar's idolatrous sacrilege that climaxes a reign of sheer evil. Belshazzar's entire way of being is portrayed as a violation of the decorum of aristocratic life that the poem holds sacred. He ascends stone steps to sit on his massive throne in a palace of pride, but he has obviously none of his father's military talents nor the exemplary meekness Nebuchadnezzar learned. The feast is a showcase for his connoisseurship of new foods and foolish fashions, with every lavish gesture of hospitality displayed only to impress guests with their host's unexcelled greatness.[8] In confirmation of this illusory good, he intends to hold court in such magnificence that the king of every land will "reche hym reuerens, and his reuel herkken, / To loke on his lemanes and ladis hem calle" (do reverence to him and listen to his revelry, / and look at his mistresses and call them ladies 1369–70; see also 1352). The rhetoric used to caricature the effete king of Babylon resembles clerical anticourtly satires denouncing the emasculating effects of sumptuous food and fashion. As an extension of Belshazzar's glory, his dukes and lords must also subordinate themselves to the royal harem, addressing as ladies the dubious women who are seated above them on the dais and thus share more of the king's honor than they do. Belshazzar manifests his evil nature by this reversal of the honorable display the poet celebrated in the ordered seating of guests at the wedding feast as well as in the image of angels arrayed "in alle þat is clene" in the heavenly court. The city of God and the city of man are thus opposed, and the banquet of pride presents a dramatic antithesis to the feast to be enjoyed by Christians with the heavenly bridegroom in the new Jerusalem.

Even with its typological significance and its echoes of anticourtly satire, this exemplum's emphasis on the courtly aesthetic confirms a discriminating audience in its aspiration to earthly ideals of honorable elegance. By emphasizing "þe clernes of his concubines and curious wedez / . . . notyng of nwe metes and of nice gettes" (the comeliness of his concubines and exquisite apparel / . . . indulging in newfangled foods and foolish fashions 1353–54), the poet condemns modishness prized for its own sake, distinguishing it from *clene* conformity to aesthetic standards based on a reasonable sense of what honor requires. The warmth and dignity, the mannerly graciousness of the Lord's concern for his guests' joy elaborated in the poet's retelling of the parable of the wedding banquet is the standard for earthly *clannesse* to which Belshazzar's caricature of courtliness is implicitly contrasted. Isolated from his guests and concerned only with displays of "vayneglorie" (1358), the merriment of concubines, and the drinking of still more wine, he is "a boster on benche" and "dotes þer he syttes" (boaster on bench; dotes where he sits 1499–1500). His drunkenness invites contrast to the convivial use of wine to further the ordered communal ends of the wedding feast (123–24). The impulsive call for servants to display the sacred vessels is followed by the proposal of using them in a drinking game: "Weȝe wyn in þis won! Wassayl!" (Bring wine in this house! Wassail! 1508). With his mandate, implicit in the term wassail, that wine be quaffed in one gulp, this king fashions a knavish counterfeit of truly festive decorum.

Theopoetic Coherence 211

When the urges for display and for imaginative refinements of natural functions like sex, food, and clothing are not shaped by a sense of what is honorable, self-indulgent deformities and cacophony result. Judged in strictly aesthetic terms, the poet's description of the ritualistic features of a fabulous banquet seems to appeal to the imaginative impulse for artifice he legitimates throughout the poem. Meats adorned by elaborate paper sculptures of birds, beasts, and fearsome grotesques, expensively enamelled in azure and indigo, arranged carefully on silver platters and carried into the hall on horseback — such a procession is, on the right occasion, fit for a king. But given Belshazzar's purpose for this gathering, the copiousness of food and the lavishness of the ornamentation symbolize a failure of the sense of proportion required for *clannesse*; thus the image of "broþe baboynes abof, besttes anvnder" (fierce baboons above, animals underneath 1409) seems negatively emblematic of the decadence of this household. The opening notes of the musical accompaniment to the procession are violent rather than pleasing, resounding so forcibly against the palace walls that the sounds seem to be trying to escape the disorder they herald (1413–16).

We have seen why in his portrayal of the Incarnation, the poet excludes the dangerous proximity of the profane to the sacred. In the decadence of Belshazzar's feast precisely this proximity or blurring of boundaries resurfaces as God is evoked as a Creator who is personally identified with the jeweled vessels made in his honor. Continuing to imagine the relationship between God and the world in aesthetic terms, the poet again invites his listeners to imagine the Creator's revulsion when his beautiful order is thus desecrated:

> Leue þou wel þat þe Lorde þat the lyfte ȝemes
> Displesed much at þat play in þat plyt stronge,
> Þat his jueles so gent wyth jaueles wer fouled,
> Þat presyous in his presens wer proued sumwhyle.
> . . . .
> So þe Worcher of þis worlde wlates þerwyth
> Þat in þe poynt of her play he poruayes a mynde. (1493–96, 1501–1502)
> (You may well believe that the lord who rules the sky
> Was much displeased with that sport under those unnatural conditions,
> That his jewels that were so noble were defiled by coarse men
> That were previously shown to be precious in his presence.
> . . . .
> The maker of this world was so sickened at it
> That in that climax of their play he determines on a purpose.)

The vivid rendering of God's anthropomorphic aversion to this defilement and his consequent intervention in human history connects the didactic strategy in the final exemplum to the emphasis on God's vulnerability in the previous two.[9]

212 *Theopoetic Coherence*

Nevertheless, in the overall impact of the final exemplum, the continuity the poem has traced between heavenly order and human experiences of festive decorum is problematized. The intimacy and mutual delight of lord and servant, which is the basis of the social stability celebrated in courtly ritual, is significantly diminished. The comforting aura of reciprocity between host and guest, lord and servant fades as God's motives are revealed to be after all closely akin to the epic warrior's. The gentler images offered earlier—of God as eager host at the wedding feast and as collaborative Creator in friendship with Noah, Abraham, and Lot—are obscured by military displays of power aimed at enforcing humility and meek compliance to his will. Though not himself portrayed as pursuing glory through battle, God is cast into a role more akin to epic than romance ideals, for his honor depends on forcibly humbling others, enemies and allies alike. The loving description of the treasures, in its evocation of natural beauty and courtly artistry, symbolizes the attractiveness of God's order, but when correctly interpreted by Nebuchadnezzar, these objects reveal to him the inferiority of his and any other earthly sovereign's claims to glory. Rather than exemplifying the romantic paradigm of reciprocity in shared pursuits of courtly pleasures, God's character models the patriarchal authority that established the hierarchies of the medieval church and its normative construction of gender.

In part this difference between the first two and the third Old Testament exempla reflects the poet's turning from the Genesis narrative to different books in the Hebrew Bible, written after patriarchal clan leaders had been replaced by kings governing a divided Israel amidst other states. A specialized ecclesiastical institution had emerged to manage the relations between God and his people, with privileged roles for prophet and priest, who alone had access to the temple's inner sanctuary (1492). Daniel is such a specialist, uncovering God's secret intentions to the Chaldean rulers (1600, 1628). This prophet is described as arriving along with the other survivors of the conquest of Jerusalem, and hence suffering the consequences of the faithless Jews; while Daniel is clearly a virtuous exception to Jewish idolatry, the poet focuses neither on this nor on how the prophet retains his religious integrity in the corrupt society of Babylon during Belshazzar's reign.[10] Daniel plays a role in the final exemplum similar to that of Noah, Abraham, and Lot in the Genesis narratives, but unlike those exemplars of righteousness who enjoyed warm homosocial intercourse with God and his angelic emissaries, the prophet is not characterized in dialogue with an externalized and gracious divine presence; instead he is described as one who has God's ghost or spirit within him (1598, 1607). In the final exemplum, God does not appear on amicable speaking terms with anyone. His message does sound once, delivered directly into

Nebuchadnezzar's ears, but it is not clear if the voice is God's own, and in any case, this stern sentencing of a proud opponent is the antithesis of the friendly encounters between God and man dramatized in the earlier exempla. What Nebuchadnezzar learns from his punishment at God's hands reinforces the vessels' witness to the superiority of divine sovereignty to any earthly king's pretensions to power and glory.

Not only does the final exemplum move away from the courtly models of God graciously enjoying the company of his human allies and informing them of his schemes for their safety in the coming storms of vengeance, but it lacks any expression of divine affectivity. When angered by the faithless Jews or the proud Nebuchadnezzar, God's distress is not articulated; even when the poet asks his listeners to empathize with how revolted God must have been with the defilement of jewels that had once proved precious in his presence, the motives and effects of divine revulsion are not elaborated as they were in the exempla illustrating *fylþe of þe flesch*.[11] Hence there is no longer at work in the depiction of vengeance the same ritualizing dynamic of God's power and powerlessness; the deity is not subjected to the dangerous forces of the creation and of his own nature. And without this energizing penetration of the sacred by the profane, there is no cosmogonic renewal, no equivalent to the recreation of order marked by God's covenant after the Deluge or the restoration of fallen humanity in the Incarnation after the story of Sodom.

Despite the assurance given in the various biblical sources that the Babylonian exile of the Jews lasted only until the establishment of the kingdom of Persia, when they were sent back with the charge to rebuild the temple in Jerusalem, the poet tells a story in which the vessels seem to have no future once they have been defiled at Belshazzar's feast. This omission of their return to their properly sacred use in God's service may be viewed as logical, given the allegorical interpretation at the outset of the exemplum.[12] However, the cumulative effect of Zedekiah, Nebuchadnezzar, and Belshazzar being judged and found wanting is to emphasize the inevitability that earthly kings will fall out of conformity with divine order. Although Darius makes peace with the Babylonian nobles after he overthrows Belshazzar, their fate along with their new sovereign's seems merely a matter of time; obviously earthly kingdoms are plagued by pride, and so another army will have to reduce yet another set of boasters to a humiliating, and doubtless bloody, end. In contrast to the biblical account, where the coming of the Persians is the beginning of God's long-intended return of the Jewish remnant and the temple's treasures to Jerusalem, here the vessels are not again mentioned after they are raised in homage to idols. As their gracefully carved lids clatter across the palace floor, their disappearance from the narrative adds to its grim theme of mutability and its gloomy picture of God's order endlessly contradicted by the vicissitudes of history in a fallen world. The vessels' evocation of natural beauty and courtly artistry does not epitomize this exemplum's mood but rather highlights by contrast the dark tone that pervades it.

Human Fallibility and Moral Realism

While these changes in the representation of divine sovereignty weaken the poem's theopoetic coherence by problematizing the courtly aesthetic as a model for the relation between God and humanity, they open up the possibility of greater moral realism. As the narrative shifts from specifically sexual themes to more general ones, and from mythic to chronicle narrative sources, new options emerge for exploring the threats to God's order posed by the human sinfulness of specific individuals, rather than of groups of nameless men denounced for their homosexual habits. Because of the individualization of several clearly differentiated evildoers in the third Old Testament exemplum, the threats to God's order are revealed as more pervasive, more various, and more ominous than in the monolithic portrayal of ruffians who inexplicably scorn all heterosexual pleasure and (in the single other instance of rebellion) of Lot's wife who fails to respect her husband's guests' dietary requirements. Zedekiah's, Nebuchadnezzar's, and Belshazzar's evils are shown in sufficient detail to dramatize the energy which subverts God's designs, so that evil becomes more recognizably human. Taken sequentially, these antagonists in the final exemplum are cumulatively diagnostic of evil not as unwitting defilement but as the human will engaged in a power struggle against God's.

This effect is especially clear in the story of Nebuchadnezzar's fall from the height of his glory. After telling Belshazzar of the "gentyle wyse" (noble manner 1432) in which his father received the vessels taken from the temple in the conquest of Jerusalem, Daniel goes on to recall how Nebuchadnezzar later grew so boastful that the Almighty took vengeance upon him directly. (The queen, in recommending Daniel's services to Belshazzar as an interpreter of God's secrets, had already noted that the prophet's holy speech had many times allayed Nebuchadnezzar's anger.) The once humble king becomes convinced of his unmatched mastery in building Babylon. By the strength of his own arm, he has virtually established each stone in a city he views as the richest of all time. The boast of his might as equivalent to God's is scarcely out of Nebuchadnezzar's mouth when he hears divine words of judgment. A sudden metamorphosis leaves him no longer king of the Chaldeans and builder of Babylon, but a beast grazing on all fours and fully aware of his degradation. After seven years living in the field like a bull, an ox, a cow, or a horse, his humanity returns as he finally realizes who it is that neatly carves up the countries of the earth. Restored to true reason by apparent insanity, a chastened Nebuchadnezzar lives with dignity thereafter, happily restored by his barons to the throne from which he had been so ignominiously exiled.

The power relations between lord and servant are incisively studied in this episode, whereas they were previously masked by the emphasis on reciprocity and mutual delight. Nebuchadnezzar's story offers a more pessimistic account of the differential in God's authority and that of his human allies than was modeled in the stories of the Deluge and the destruction of Sodom and the other cities. Even when God ultimately dooms all of the Sodomites except Lot's family, Abraham has been able to negotiate for his kinsman's safety. The poet rewrites the biblical narrative to give Abraham this special plea for Lot, a point that exemplifies the value of homosocial bonding both between the two men and between Abraham and his Lord. God's sovereignty does not preclude bargaining, which necessarily implies that a creature is worthy to challenge the Creator. The final exemplum is thus more realistic in portraying a human subjectivity that, although bonded with God through many encounters, is capable of significant opposition and, although judged and found wanting, can come to fulfillment through suffering humiliation. Nebuchadnezzar exemplifies the recurrent need for humility when one is privileged to enjoy earthly success, for his belief concerning the power that came directly from God (1653–54) could not withstand the pride of lordship that comes with a rich life and far-reaching control. Under the chastening effects of God's sovereignty, this Old Testament ruler models the possibility of a new self-understanding achieved through a penitential process of suffering.

This shift is also a shift in gender dynamics. To portray fallibility and redemptive suffering of this kind in a heroic conqueror offers a model of masculinity that is unique in the poem's sequence of gentle exemplars. Up through the passage celebrating the Incarnation as a model for its readers, *Cleanness* supports an all-or-nothing perfectionist ethos, with no room for a speck or spot that would diminish baptismal perfection. The treatment of penance after the passage on the Incarnation is—compared to the attention given in this account of Nebuchadnezzar's repentance—perfunctory. Implicit in the story of Nebuchadnezzar's suffering is the human need for more than earthly beauty in order to understand that God is the source of all good. Only the painful medicine of his long mental illness and the marring of his human form finally cure the king of his pride, a fact that seems to contradict the earlier image of penance as instantaneous and without cost, the equivalent of dipping a pearl in wine.

The story Daniel relates of Nebuchadnezzar's lesson in humility provides the closest to a penitential homily that *Cleanness* offers. Yet it is told in the course of warning an already doomed villain of his imminent, and irreversible, downfall.[13] Admittedly, the prophet's narrative implicitly warns the audience of *Cleanness* to heed well the lesson Belshazzar could have learned from his father's life but so obviously did not. This pagan ally of God thus serves as the poem's single exemplar of a good man who is less than perfectly righteous and its single instance of a sinner permitted to learn from his mistakes. The diminishment of his stature from king on a throne to beast of the field is not simply retributive justice but a means of restoring Nebuchadnezzar's lost balance. Yet of this renewal of earthly order we hear only two lines, and nothing about the celebrations or positive outcome recounted in scripture. Thus, neither the story of Nebuchadnezzar's metamorphosis nor *Cleanness* as a whole invites fallible human beings to feel what it is actually like to try to live a life congruous with the splendor of order communicated in the courtly imagery of the pearl.

Courtly Ethos and Spiritual Journeys: The Other Cotton Nero A.x, Art. 3 Poems

The disintegrative effect of the final third of *Cleanness* dissolves its theopoetic coherence, but the questions regarding God's immanence in history to which this structural failure points are precisely those addressed in the other three poems of the Cotton Nero A.x, Art. 3 manuscript. The connections and contrasts between *Cleanness* and its more impressive manuscript companions do not require an assumption of common authorship.[14] They do, however, depend on seeing the four as deliberately juxtaposed in the single extant manuscript and on seeing the collection as an important context for exploring what is distinctive in each of the poems. This book, focused on the violent dichotomies I see the poet of *Cleanness* projecting upon the Creator, posits a contrast between *Cleanness*'s psychological dualism and the nondualistic explorations of the tension between ideal and actual that characterize the manuscript's other, more theologically mature, poems. The quasihomiletic framework, with its neatly symmetrical oppositions between cleanness and filth, and the exempla's repeated display of God's anger and his vengeance in response to the disruption of his order by evildoers do not give an adequately dramatic image either of being human in redemption history or of God's being as he makes this history happen through the paradoxes of mercy and righteousness. Compared to its manuscript companions and other contemporary texts similarly concerned with stories of religious significance, *Cleanness* does not reach deeply into what it means to live as a Christian. The poem's ethical vision posits a totalizing aspiration for an all-encompassing order as the trait in the human creature in which its likeness to God consists; this aspiration links life at its best on earth with the transcendent fulfillment the poet imagines the heavenly court to afford. Life in harmony with God's *clannesse* is envisaged in terms inseparable from the class-specific ethos that emphasizes aesthetic criteria for behavior. Nor do the artistic juxtapositions of *Cleanness* finally create a satisfying whole; they provide no formal correlative to the poet's vision of God's orderly perfection. This text achieves no structural equivalent of the overarching order it celebrates as arising from the rich potential of disorder and anomaly. In contrast, developing an adequate dramatic image of human redemption and God's nature, portraying an image of human fallibility and spiritual transformation that is not entirely bound by class consciousness even though implying a courtly milieu, and creating an artistic whole of form and content — these are the achievements that make the other three poems in the Cotton Nero A.x, Art. 3 so similar to each other theopoetically and so artistically outstanding.

With its extended paraphrase of Old Testament narrative dealing with God's power to avenge evil, *Patience* obviously needs to be read in conjunction with *Cleanness*. Both are instructive landmarks in the fictionalizing of scripture in order to create ethical paradigms. Both explore and recreate the meaning of God's dealings with men and women in the Hebrew scriptures without the usual Christian emphasis on allegorical exegesis. In each retelling of biblical history, a Christian poet identifies with the lives of his Jewish forebearers, meditating upon the Old Testament narratives not in order to distinguish the old from the new revelation, but to acquaint his readers with the nature of God's responses to and expectations for human creatures.

The two poems are often referred to as homilies, for both begin with a scriptural text, and since each is based on a Beatitude, they may well have been written as companion pieces, whether by one or more authors. The homiletic prologue of *Patience* presents not just one Beatitude, as does *Cleanness*, but all eight of them. While the *Cleanness*-poet implicitly personifies his theme as a woman who demands by right the commendation that the poem goes on to provide, in *Patience* the feminine qualities of the eight virtues are praised in the Beatitudes by a narrator who personifies them explicitly as a bevy of courtly ladies whose good manners deserve loving imitation (*Cleanness* 1–2; *Patience* 31–34). Although this resembles the simultaneously aesthetic and ethical appeal of the passage on the imitation of Christ in *Cleanness*, *Patience*'s narrator is at odds with that romantic ideal of modeling life according to the tastes and habits of the female beloved. In his catalog of feminine personifications, "miry Clannesse" appears in good company, between "dame Mercy," on the one hand, and "dame Pes, and Pacyence" on the other; in an obviously ironic tone, he expresses the idea that whereas a man might be happy to have one, to enjoy all of these ladies would be better. For him, two are quite enough; however, he is involved with "dame Pouert" and "Pacyence" by constraint rather than by choice, having learned that to be associated with Poverty without being equally a friend of Patience is impossible. That they are playmates by necessity ("nedes playferes" 45) is almost a contradiction in terms. The narrator's association of himself with two such imperious ladies as Poverty and Patience suggests less of the high playfulness of Francis of Assisi's idealization of Poverty as his beloved than a practical stoicism born of personal experience: it is simply futile to try to avoid suffering if you are poor.[15] Only paradoxically does the narrator of *Patience* point to the sphere of aesthetic refinement and gratuitous order so fundamental to *Cleanness*. Despite the ritualized courtesy connoted by identifying the virtues as "Dame This" or "Dame That," the power relations are ungraciously overt. While he acknowledges the importance of imitating the *þewes* (30) and of praising the *lotes* (47) of the eight virtues he dresses up as ladies, the narrator of *Patience* does not claim to be engaged in a loving identification with any of them.

Even more than *Patience*, *Sir Gawain* and *Pearl* are infused by aristocratic aesthetic sensibility and so illuminate how the *Cleanness*-poet's inextricable confusion (sometimes creative, sometimes disastrous) of social and religious values points to questions about the transcendence of God and the relation of divine order and human idealism. In a way that *Patience* clearly does not, both of these longer poems depend on the courtly ethos as a vehicle for religious imagination. *Sir Gawain* takes a sympathetic but critical approach to the chivalric aspiration toward a state of all-encompassing perfection uncritically celebrated by the poet of *Cleanness*. The blissful fulfillment such idealism leads him to imagine turns out, under the keener scrutiny of *Sir Gawain*, to be more complicated than the courtly ethos supposes.[16] Its shortcomings are comically exposed in the outcome of that hero's quest; yet they are also celebrated, for the replacement of the hero's pentangle with the green sash that led to his shame is seen from the point of view of Christmas, the feast that celebrates God's acceptance of human finitude and forgiveness of human fallenness. The idea of *felix culpa* is integral to the meaning of Christmas as it is depicted in the poem as a whole. The holiday atmosphere of Camelot as it is first presented is a dramatic image of the ideal courtly order the poet praises in *Cleanness*; by the conclusion of *Sir Gawain*, however, the vision of the mutability of nature and history, and of human fallenness and redemption, has been included in the celebrative consciousness manifest in the narrator's own perspective, altering the theopoetic image of perfection from a static to a more dynamic whole.

From Gawain's perspective, the court's celebration of the completion of his quest is painful; his shame may be viewed as excessive, a denial of the joy appropriate to sins forgiven, but the court's response is equally ambiguous in its meaning for the poet's presentation of Christmas. To take the knowledge of human fallibility into the atmosphere of an aristocratic holiday would seem to require a revision of consciousness more drastic than that exhibited in the immediate courtesy of the court's offer to make the emblem of Camelot the green sash that Gawain wears penitentially as the reminder of his moral frailty. By this gesture, do they include the awareness of spiritual poverty in their ceremonies of earthly honor, or do they wholly avoid the shameful consciousness of the gap between the ideal and humanity's noblest efforts to embody it? The latter complex awareness is, of course, close to the ideal of patient poverty, and a *noble poynt* it is, if we are to believe the final lines of *Patience*; such a sensibility does not at all exclude such joy as is befitting to Christmas feasting. Perhaps the final image of *Sir Gawain* is a reminder of just this point, for Christ is viewed there as the king, thorn-crowned, who brings men to bliss precisely because of his willingness to suffer. Christmas cannot ultimately be celebrated without complementing it with the reminder of an Easter from which Good Friday is not elided since the wounds are still present in Christ's resurrected body.

Although *Sir Gawain* finishes with this hopeful vision, heaven's bliss does not pervade that poem's thematics as it does *Cleanness*; in this respect, *Pearl* and *Cleanness* resemble each other more. Yet despite the common fascination with how life must feel in the heavenly court, *Pearl* is no closer to the naive optimism of *Cleanness* than is *Sir Gawain*. *Cleanness* depicts no essential difference between heaven and the idealized order of earthly courts. Heavenly bliss is comparable to earthly joy of festive decorum and is attainable apart from any fundamental alteration to natural human desires and values. To be *coupe in his courte*, we need only look at Christ's perfection and model our lives according to this *fayr forme*, availing ourselves of the grace of penance but thereafter living a perfectly virtuous life. The poet's presentation of Christ's *clannesse* obscures the need for redemptive suffering, so that even though the final image of God's dear heart rankling with the persistence of "vnclannes" (1806) reminds readers of the divine obsession for order, nothing in this spiritual courtliness reveals the woundedness of God's heart in suffering love for humankind.

In *Pearl*, in contrast, the image of the Atonement is as central as the image of heavenly splendor, and the paradoxical juxtaposition of the two is subjectively realized in the narrator's struggle to accept the discontinuities between his ideal of good and God's order as it manifests itself to him in earthly experience. The Crucifixion and eucharistic imagery in *Pearl* shed light on what is missing from the incarnational aesthetic in *Cleanness*. Both by comparison and by contrast, it suggestively illustrates the theopoetic limits of the courtly in this poem, which cannot admit the reality of fallibility and suffering as an ingredient in the Christian life.

Pearl focuses on both fallibility and suffering, for the narrator is a bereaved father who inconsolably mourns his lost little girl.[17] After recounting a dream in which she appears to him, fully grown and spiritually far more of an authority on the divine order than he can easily believe or intellectually comprehend, the still grieving Dreamer concludes his poem with several wide-awake responses to his visionary experience. He ultimately takes comfort not so much from the memory of seeing his Pearl as a beautiful maiden, reigning as queen with the court of heaven; although he is able finally to begin to be pleased that she is blissful and that the Prince of Heaven finds her pleasing, more important to him is his own bond to Christ. He says that for a good Christian it is easy to come into harmony with him, an idea that suggests the optimism that pervades *Cleanness*; both poems share the paradigm of the life to which the Christian is entitled by birthright of baptism as one of festive decorum and aristocratic ease. For both poems, the central metaphor is life in the household of a courtly lord whose relations are warm and harmonious with his guests and servants. Hierarchy is celebrated as a means of mutuality, imposing no stressful or laborious requirements but providing pleasure and beauty for all.

Yet in *Pearl*, the Dreamer says that for the good Christian it is pleasant to please the Prince of Heaven or (and this difference, though not stressed in the poet's language, makes a difference) to be reconciled. This definition of the good life as one that is not necessarily one without tension is followed with a personal statement that sounds like the fruit of his struggle to reconcile himself to the painful loss at the end of the dream when he spontaneously tried to cross the stream to join the Pearl-Maiden in heaven and failed. Tacitly, he admits that he is not yet himself conformed as she is to the heavenly household's standards, which he can only imperfectly grasp. In the dream, the breach of decorum displayed by plunging into the stream shows that, despite progress, he is still unable to accept separation and to yearn for no more than what is allowed. In waking, however, he is penitent for this violation of the restraints placed on him in the dream. Finally, with his blessing and invoking Christ's, he commits his "little queen" to God, and thus continues the process of reconciling himself to the difference between divine order and his sorrowful attachment to the perfection he enjoyed while loving this pearl of a girl.

The tension between the best earth has to offer and what heaven requires locates *Pearl* in a different realm of theopoetic discourse from *Cleanness*, where divine order and its rewards are not essentially different from courtly ideals. Such restoration as our sinful souls might require is easily available in penance, which operates objectively like an external remedy removing an accidental and superficial flaw. Hence the Incarnation is celebrated without any reference to the need for and costliness of sacrificial suffering.

In *Pearl*, the image of the crucified Christ is as important as the image of courtly splendor. The paradoxical juxtaposition of the two is subjectively realized in the narrator's struggles to accept discontinuity between his ideal of good and the astonishing truths he saw and heard in his dream of the Pearl-maiden. His closing description of his waking state of mind attests to having found the Prince of Heaven to be "a God, a Lorde, a frende" (1204) and suggests a process of increasing confidence and trust in the divine artistry he has witnessed. This has not been easy, for even the most appealing features of the dream shattered his expectations. The Pearl-Maiden, although decked out in courtly splendor and transformed physically into the beautiful lady she did not have a chance to become on earth, has turned out to be less like the lovable sweetheart he has been missing so painfully than like a stern schoolmaster determined to teach him a lesson.

Gazing devotedly upon the bread and wine which the priest elevates at the moment of consecration, the Dreamer in his waking life perceives Christ in these eucharistic elements. Although it is not specified how he envisions Christ's presence revealed in the elements of bread and wine in the Mass, it is obvious that for the poet of *Pearl*, the Prince of Heaven who is God, Lord, and a fine friend must exemplify both courtly perfection and human suffering. Blessing the Pearl-maiden as he gives her over to God, the Dreamer invokes Christ's blessing on her as well. The benediction pronounces the narrator's blessing on himself and his audience, expressing the aspiration to be both a pearl pleasing to the heavenly prince (a jeweler in his own right who is an unequalled connoisseur of gems) and to serve simply in his household, as one of the "homly hyne" (1211) — unsophisticated, familiar servants who are not of the courtly class but are nevertheless identified as part of the lord's household.

The phrase resists translation for, as usual, the modern cognate would mislead; "homely" for most speakers of English no longer means something simultaneously appealing and commonplace. The humble connotations of both *homly* and *hyne* that precede the more aristocratic and aesthetically attractive image of the pearl in the closing line suggest the contrast between the poet's notions of earthly service in the heavenly household in *Cleanness* and *Pearl*. In the former, to be God's servant is to pre-enact one's place in heaven by living a life that manifests externally in deeds a wholehearted identification with God's designs; like the angelic servants, Christian go gaily arrayed (1811), already resplendent with the beauty of God's order. In the latter, the Christian life is one of bearing up with great loss and unfulfilled longing; it cannot be called pleasing and yet there comes a point when, after a long and not always pleasant educative process, such a life does seem easy because through suffering the soul has found Christ to be not only God and Lord, but a friend, one who also suffers and does so happily. In the center of heavenly perfection there is the visual oxymoron of an always bleeding and wounded, always joyful and gracious Lamb.

Looking at *Cleanness* against this backdrop of the centrality of issues of anger and forgiveness in the other poems, I see it falling short of their theopoetic suggestiveness. Primarily this is because, of all the four poems, *Cleanness* adduces the greatest interest in divine artistry and anger and the least in the aspects of God's relationship to his creatures that traditionally are articulated in reflections on Christ's Passion, where the Creator suffers willingly on behalf of the very creatures who do harm to his designs.

An assessment of common authorship and probable order of composition lies outside of the theopoetic focus of this study, but the contrasts I have noted suggest that *Cleanness* was written by someone less artistically and theologically accomplished than the author(s) of the other poems, whether that person was the same poet at an earlier stage, someone else, or more than one other person. The other three poems do not jettison the unifying elements evident in *Cleanness,* but they each supplement structural juxtapositions and thematic echoes and contrasts with the cumulative development of a single protagonist and plot. All three show the poet managing the presentation of themes and stories with sophisticated perspectival irony, an artistic balance of comic detachment and sympathetic identification to achieve a narrative whole which is appropriate, both in structure and tone, to an essentially ironic and comic vision of what it is to be human in God's order.

Most important, the three poems I see as wonderfully more complex than *Cleanness* all include a consciousness of the tension between infinite and finite, the inevitable conflict between creature and Creator, the costliness to both parties of the resolution afforded in redemption, and the paradoxes of the heavenly order experienced in people's earthly lives. *Patience* seems to me the first fruits of a change in this direction; besides its intrinsic merits as a work of art, it heightens our appreciation of the achievement of *Sir Gawain* and *Pearl* and enables us to define retrospectively the limits as well as the achievements of *Cleanness* in contrast to the more mature works of this poet.

The order that God creates in nature and the order human creatures display in culture merge inextricably in the *Cleanness*-poet's vision of sexual and ethical norms. The poet's view of both nature and culture is inescapably aristocratic, and his imaginative engagement with the theme of *clannesse* as a virtue cultivated by the leisure class takes the coalescence of divine grace and class-specific graciousness to an extreme. The Incarnation comes close to being reduced to a function of numinous courtesy and sensuous elegance.

The readers of this book may find, as I have, that *Cleanness* is initially seductive and enchanting in its positive vision but claustrophobic and repellent almost in proportion to its initial appeal. *Cleanness* anticipates a theological celebration of erotic pleasure that the church has only in this century begun to articulate (see, for example, Carter Heyward's *Touching Our Strength*, a work that affirms the erotic without privileging hetero- or homosexual lovemaking). The legitimation *Cleanness* offers of heterosexual love, without mention of its reproductive consequences, and the emphasis on mutually pleasing play of passion combine to subvert the usual patriarchal repression of sensual desire, part of the self which the clergy had for so long taught was the feminine and therefore inferior. By affirming pleasure rather than reproduction as the most fundamental aim of God's designs for sexual communion between lovers, this text opens up the possibility of valorizing nonprocreative, pleasure-focused Creation sexuality per se, and hence of dismantling the most significant traditional theological argument against same-sex love. The poem's celebration of pleasure and mutuality would seem logically to apply potentially to homosexual lovemaking as well. Yet this and other affirmative dimensions of this poem's ethic are so intrinsically tied up with its elitism and with privileging the male point of view that its myopic optimism about the Good as the Beautiful produces ultimately a mixture of attraction and revulsion.

Although appreciative of Spearing's probing into the unifying pattern of thought in *Cleanness* and particularly indebted to his later essay taking into account Douglas's anthropological insights, my reading departs from his claims for the imaginative coherence of *Cleanness*. In the final third of the poem, its vision of cosmic separations and violated classifications functions more as a downward spiral than as the rich potential out of which the poet draws "material for the creation of further order" (*Readings* 190). Charlotte Morse begins her book on the poem by acknowledging that "*Cleanness* has exasperated some readers with its seeming incoherence and the poet's puzzling insistence that filth of the flesh makes God angry as other sins do not" (2). I argue that it repays closer study in its own right and in the context of other medieval writings documenting attitudes toward sexual desire and deviance, but not because the poet's ideas in this strange work were influential, popular, widely known, or — as Morse and Spearing and other critics have claimed — coherent. Quite the contrary. Rather, the ethical difficulties and theological inadequacies the poet creates in articulating his unique views are what make *Cleanness* so fascinating and frustrating to read, so difficult to interpret, and such a telling witness to astonishing originality and self-incurred restriction in late fourteenth-century theological insight, spiritual vision, and literary creativity.

Notes

Introduction

1. The five cities destroyed because of the sin named after the Sodomites are emblems of paradise lost, as the original Edenic beauty and fruitfulness of the landscape is destroyed by fire and earthquake and replaced by the sterile waste of the Dead Sea. On its banks grow beautiful apples, but inside where there should be fruit and seeds there are only ashes.

2. Two of these essays were published after my revised manuscript had been accepted. In order to minimize further revisions, the main arguments of Calabrese and Eliason and of Frantzen are summarized here rather than in the survey in chap. 2 of commentary on the poem's sexual themes.

3. I, too, question the "innocent" idealism which accepts uncritically the romantic myth of paradisal heterosexual union and agree that we should be wary of the high flying hyperbole in God's praise of pleasure, echoed as it is in the poet's shocking amplification of Lot's later description of his daughters' feminine charms as the means to supreme erotic gratification. My study takes seriously the disgust evoked in a modern reader "sensitive to the commodification of women" (248–49), feelings that, like Calabrese and Eliason, I find "difficult to suppress" (271) in reading Lot's offer of his daughters to rapists. The troubling resemblance between the two passages praising heterosexual love for its gratuitous delights is addressed in chap. 6.

4. Frantzen sees this black hole of the Dead Sea as an emblem of the back of the male homosexual's body, and reads it as the poet's "perfect analogy for the Sodomites' foul and infertile nature" (461).

5. See the conclusion to chap. 5.

6. Dinshaw outlines the sexual themes of *Cleanness* as a context for showing how homosexual relations are produced as a possibility in the plot of *Sir Gawain and the Green Knight* only to be contained by the discourse of normative heterosexuality that constitutes Christian courtliness ("A Kiss" 216–20). Analyzing *Cleanness*'s structure in terms of a sociological theory of deviance, where the deviant ends up performing a defining function, she points out that God's threat against the Sodomites (711–12) shows quite precisely how the "norms of heterosexuality produce the deviant—Sodom and Gomorrah—as negative example." She goes on to analyze how the poem subtly reconfigures the norms of heterosexuality which produce and contain deviance, adjusting the traditional Christian categories based on procreation by "shifting priority from an opposition between natural and unnatural to an opposition between pleasurable and unpleasurable, and even between physically attractive and physically repulsive" (217). Her view of the "strongly homosocial cast which provided the general social setting of" *Sir Gawain* is very close to my reading of *Cleanness*, where I see the poet as a spokesman for a courtly "society . . . bonded by homosocial desire, even as it strove to suppress homosexual enactment of such desire" (222). While I am not as confident as she is in the link Michael J. Bennett (and more recently John M. Bowers) propose between the poems in the Cotton Nero A.x, Art. 3 manuscript and the royal household of Richard II, I share Dinshaw's sense that what some would dismiss as the "old canard" of the king's alleged homosexual intimacy with his associate Robert de Vere has possible relevance for interpreting the peculiar constructions of sexuality and gender in *Sir Gawain* (222–23). For my view of how the unusual representation of the Sodomites in *Cleanness* might have been useful in deflecting the connection between emasculating aesthetic refinements of courtliness and homoeroticism, twin stigmas that are evident in the politically motivated slander of Richard II as effeminate and as guilty of excessive intimacy with his close male friend, see chap. 6.

7. In the Middle Ages, all such sexual relations between people of the same sex were constructed as vicious acts against nature because the reproduction of the species was conceived to be the sole natural aim of sexual appetite. Even though "the sin against nature" was widely used to designate forbidden same-sex relations, we cannot simply refer to them by this term since it often designates as well other activities which were defined as unnatural by their nonreproductive character rather than by the sex of the persons (or the person, in the case of the solitary sin of masturbation).

8. Historians who are revising the modern understanding of same-sex relationships in the past have clarified how the categories we use must themselves be scrutinized historically. Eve Sedgwick has aptly reminded me of how many dimensions of sexuality "aren't well described in terms of the gender of object choice at all" (35). She has also shown how "homosexuality as we conceive of it today" comprises not "a coherent definitional field," but "a space of overlapping, contradictory, and conflictual definitional forces" (45).

9. Complete translations have been provided by Derek Brewer, John Gardner, Brian Stone, William Vantuono, and Margaret Williams. Many editors have usefully translated whole passages in their notes.

Chapter 1. The Narrative Theology of Cleanness

1. Unless noted to the contrary, all quotations from *Cleanness* or its manuscript companions (*Sir Gawain and the Green Knight, Pearl, Patience*) follow the edition of Malcolm Andrew and Ronald Waldron, *The Poems of the Pearl Manuscript*, with line numbers identified in the text. I have not followed their practice of capitalizing pronouns referring to God.

2. This study of *Cleanness* does not locate the poem in one or another of the specific social stratum that scholars have proposed for the works of the *Gawain*-poet. Dissenting from Pearsall's interpretation of the poem's treatment of love as "a divinely sanctioned biological imperative," I see *Cleanness* as an exception to the distinction his essay suggests between alliterative poems and those written for "courtly society in which women played a prominent part" and hence in which love is depicted as "the principle motive and preoccupation of life" ("Alliterative Revival" 47). He may be correct that the absence of interest in the theme of love in the alliterative poems in general stamps them as part of "a provincial household culture, inheriting the conservative and old-fashioned tastes of provincial Anglo-Norman society and closely associated with the local religious houses" (47). *Cleanness*, however, seems to me to exhibit not only a distinct interest in erotic refinements associated with the romantic literature of courtly society, but also a self-conscious taste for courtly artifice that conforms to Elizabeth Salter's account of ritualized life in households of magnates in the northwest Midlands dialect region (the area reflected in the language of the MS Cotton Nero A.x, Art. 3 poems). Salter's impression of the *Gawain*-poet's desire to "cater to tastes no less subtle than those for which Chaucer provided" (Salter 233) is not modified by her later acceptance of Turville-Petre's conclusion that "the milieu of the poetry of the revival was not the higher nobility, but a wide-ranging group of gentry, knights, franklins, and clergy" (Pearsall 35, 48). Michael Bennett (1979 and 1983), associating the *Gawain*-poet with a power base that was independent of baronial control because directly allied to Richard II's court, shows that the aristocratic lifestyle of the magnates described by Salter was imitated by opulent Chester careerists in the 1390s.

Finally, we must heed Pearsall's warning, in his excellent account of the scholarship on the Alliterative Revival that "the diagnosis of the prospective audience of a poem on the basis of the perceived level of sophistication in that poem is a very subjective business indeed" (50). "The audience implied may not be the audience addressed; the circumstances of manuscript survival may be no guide at all to the circumstances of production; and sophistication is a difficult thing to quantify" (49).

3. To say that such description is gratuitous does not imply that it has no didactic purpose. Rather, *Cleanness* displays the "personalization of the lives of scriptural characters and ... of their situations" which Janet Coleman finds remarkable in many Middle English metrical versions of biblical narrative designed to teach a "practical message about moral standards to be observed by Christians in the world" (187). It also exemplifies the way "secular vocabulary bore a close relation to spiritual and moral attitudes" (197). Still, although our reading of *Cleanness* is illuminated by Coleman's account of how biblical paraphrases function didactically by "educating men and women

into the standards obtaining in their world" and providing "a moral guide to the making of political, social, and religious choices" (124), I argue that the poet uses what Coleman terms *personalization* to focus on God's own aesthetic sensitivity and this dimension of *clannesse* required in divine-human interaction.

4. This is not to deny, however, as Pearsall himself asserts (in "Alliterative Revival") that the poet "was a cleric of some depth of training" (51).

5. See Dorothee Metlitski Finkelstein on the *Pearl*-poet's sense of himself as a "divinely inspired artist setting his theme to perfection in a masterpiece of literary art" and the possibility that he associated himself with Bezalel, the jeweler-craftsman of the Book of Exodus, as did the author of *The Cloud of Unknowing,* a Middle English treatise contemporary with the poet (422).

6. For a consideration of feast, ritual, and aesthetic order as these pertain to the idea of play, see Johan Huizinga, *Homo Ludens*.

7. See Thomas (2a2ae. 134, 1) for an analysis of magnificence as a virtue that empowers the lavish outlay of resources on great works of art for the common good and God's honor. All citations to the *Summa Theologiae* will be to the translations in the Blackfriars edition; magnificence is discussed under the virtue of *Courage*, vol. 42. An English contemporary of the *Cleanness*-poet, Roger Dymmok, uses Aristotle's *Ethics* (Thomas's authority for the *Summa*'s approach to the cardinal virtues) to advocate the ideal of magnificence as a necessity for the social elite. Writing against the Lollards who criticized costly works of art and architecture indulged in by both secular and religious patrons, Dymmok defends the right of Richard II and his nobility to live amidst aesthetic splendor: "It is appropriate for kings, princes, and others installed in solemnity to be adorned magnificently in grand buildings, just as Aristotle recommends in Book IV of his *Ethics;* certainly it is necessary for them to have residences that are vast, sumptuous, beautiful, and well decorated by a variety of artisans, such as painters, sculptors, glassworkers, artists, goldsmiths, and other craftsmen too numerous to mention" (quoted in and translated by Bowers 120).

8. Charlotte Morse, for whom the image of the vessel is the controlling metaphor of the poem, ignores the protracted description of surface detail, as do many other critics who read *Cleanness* as homily or penitential treatise; others, like Spearing, see the description as "mere catalogue" (*Gawain-Poet* 64), while still others, like Davenport, argue that, although beautifully executed, its romantic indulgence attests to the poet's failure of didactic control (76). However as Sarah Stanbury aptly notes, the poet's protracted description of the objects emphasizes their "signatory value, although that value eludes the idolaters at Babylon." I agree that it is precisely "through the visual rhetoric of the description in which they are presented" that these "holy vessels reveal their sanctity" (60–61).

9. That the temple and its ornaments were adorned together (1290) suggests a fourteenth-century aesthetic concern to make sacred architecture and liturgical furnishings congruent in the latest style. To my knowledge, the *Cleanness*-poet's description of the covered cup does not conform in precise decorative detail or shape to any of the splendid vessels from the Middle Ages that remain extant. It is worth noting, however, that in this late medieval period opulent chalices produced for the eucharistic altar and similarly luxurious cups produced for the secular banquet table were increasingly ornate;

typically, they were adorned with sculpted, enameled, jeweled, and engraved images framed by miniaturized architectural elements in the elongated Late Gothic style. A stunning example of medieval decorative art applied to secular rituals of cleanness and festive decorum is a Franco-Burgundian table fountain. With its elaborately battlemented parapet accented with finials, the fountain is a late-fourteenth-century "masterpiece of fanciful architecture in miniature" (*International Style* 124–25). It resembles the covered cups described in *Cleanness* insofar as both objects are influenced by Late Gothic architectural playfulness; what they reproduce in miniature is not the fancifully attenuated spires of churches in the late-decorated style, however, but the turrets and outworks of fortifications adorning domestic buildings constructed to look like castles even though they no longer served any military purpose.

"Couered cowpes foul clene, as casteles arayed, / Enbaned vnder batelment with bantelles quoynt, / And fyled out of fygures of ferlylé schappes. / Þe coperounes of þe c[ou]acles þat on þe cuppe reres / Wer fetysely formed out in fylyoles longe; / Pinacles py3t þer apert þat profert bitwene" (Very clean cups with covers, decorated like castles, / Embellished under their battlements with skillfully made stepped corbels, / And fashioned out of figures of marvelous shapes. / The tops of the covers which arise from the cups / Were elegantly formed into tall columns, / Pinnacles plainly placed there that jutted out between them 1458–63). These miniature versions of mock battlements, themselves designed primarily for elegance and ornamentality, exemplify well the chivalric aspiration toward the elevation of all of life, including conflict, into gamelike forms.

The towers of Belshazzar's own castle are described as "troched," (adorned with small pointed pinnacles 1383) and on his table the food is covered by canopies having the same kind of turrets, "on lofte corven / Pared out of paper and poynted of golde" (carved on top / Cut out of paper and tipped with gold 1407–8). This typically late-decorated mode of architecture is even more elaborately described in *Sir Gawain and the Green Knight;* Sir Bercilak's castle is provided with *bantelles* ("enbaned vnder þe abataylment in þe best lawe" [embellished under the battlements in the best style 790]), with towers that are "trochet ful þik" (crocketed thickly 795), and with marvelously ornate pinnacles and chimneys, so delicate and bright that they seem not carved from stone and painted but "pared out of papure" (cut out of paper 802), thus resembling the structure adorning Belshazzar's table and completely undercutting any implication of functional solidity. The stepped corbels, or *bantelles,* adorning the roofline of castles had by the time *Cleanness* was written become fancifully elaborate remnants of what was originally a crenellated wall designed for maximum fortification.

10. See *Middle English Dictionary* s.v. *clene,* adj., sense 4(a), "clear, fair, unclouded," and sense 5(a), "splendid, elegant; shapely, comely; excellent" and s.v. *clene,* adv., sense 2(a), "brightly, splendidly, excellently; handsomely, neatly, properly." (Subsequent citations to this dictionary will use the standard scholarly abbreviation *MED.*)

11. In some contexts of *Cleanness, usen* has an overtly sexual meaning (see 202, 251, 267). See *Oxford English Dictionary* s.v. *use,* v., senses 20, "to employ (a person, animal, etc.) in some function or capacity, especially for an advantageous end," and 10(b), "to have sexual intercourse with." In line 11, *usen* specifically refers to the act of eating the eucharistic wafer. See *MED* s.v. *use* v., sense 11(b), "to partake of (the sacrament); to take or receive (the Eucharist)." Still the latent sexual force of the term allows us to feel the

sheer physical vulnerability of God's body given to human hands to use. Also see lines 31–32, which further emphasize the physicality of the shock God feels when his body is approached by anyone not clothed in *clannesse*: "For he þat flemus vch fylþe fer fro his hert / May not byde þat burre þat hit his body neȝe." Andrew and Waldron translate (and here I retain their capitalization of the pronouns to emphasize the references to God): "for He who banishes all filth far from His heart cannot endure the shock of its approaching Him (*lit.* that it should approach His body)." (Subsequent citations to the *Oxford English Dictionary* will use the standard abbreviation *OED*.)

12. This is also epitomized in the rightly ordered sexuality which, as we will see, God describes to Abraham as "kynde crafte" (natural craft 697).

13. While I will dispute this latter assertion (and will show in chap. 7 how this critic's subsequent essay on anthropological concepts of danger and purity puts *fylþe* in a more positive light), Spearing's initial account of the poet's definition of his theme by synthesis rather than analysis, by contexts rather than by concepts, is a crucial insight into *Cleanness* which provides a valuable starting point for any further clarification of the poet's didactic method.

14. Gervase Mathew describes membership of an affinity, in which "a man commended himself to his lord for maintenance or perquisite, salary or preferment," as being derived from "the temporary fealty that a guest owed a host" (143). Regardless of whether the poet himself experienced such an affinity to an earthly "lord," he imaginatively represents man's relationship to God in terms of this kind of loyalty.

15. See *MED* s.v. *honeste,* adj. As applied to the members of an earthly or heavenly household, sense 1(a), "of persons, their reputation, desires: honorable, respectable, noble; also fig."; 2(a), "of persons, their attributes, countenance: proper, seemly, becoming, ?also competent, qualified"; 2(c), "befitting one's social status or office; socially or customarily proper or correct; decorous"; and 4(a), "of persons, or their hearts: virtuous, upright, good."

16. By not describing in specific detail the heavenly raiment in *Cleanness,* the poet allows the reader to imagine these garments in terms of contemporary visual representations such as the Wilton Diptych, where King Richard is depicted being greeted by eleven angelic emissaries of the heavenly court, all splendidly arrayed in jeweled livery. Perhaps for some of its early readers, the poem's reiterated praise of the well-dressed servant of God might have brought to mind the actual ceremonial finery of Richard II and his court. The king had commissioned for himself a "tunic of pearls and other precious stones worth 30,000 marks" in 1385 along with "special robes with White Harts embroidered with pearls for the Feast of the Purification of the Virgin" (Bowers 138). Readers familiar with *Pearl* might recall how the Maiden's elegantly cut and richly bejeweled garment epitomizes for the Dreamer, a jeweler, the refined aesthetic appeal of the heavenly court, where Christ himself is described as a jeweler and hence an appreciative connoisseur of the Pearl-Maiden's costume. She wears, under a loose, flowing surcoat with fashionably long sleeves, a matching gown with its sleeves fitting close at the wrist. Both sets of sleeves are embroidered with pearls, and the portions of the underdress visible through the side openings of the surcoat are also trimmed with pearls, as is the hem of the overgarment (see *Pearl* 194–207). This fashionable silk or linen gown gleaming with adornment both inside and out makes it understandable how someone could be literally radiant both "withinne and withouten" (as in *Cleanness* 20).

17. Knowles's account of the way the metaphysic of Platonism was embodied in Thomas's work is particularly suggestive in the light of the later nominalist attack on platonic forms and universals. A more substantial treatment of the movement, though still condensed, is Oberman's "Some Notes on the Theology of Nominalism."

18. The Dominicans were active preachers in England, and their priories included a large center for theological studies in Northampton. Philip O'Mara speculates that the *Gawain*-poet probably studied there under Robert Holcot (1300–1349), who spent his last years teaching or serving as the superior of this large Dominican priory (103–4). The argument that the works of this Dominican philosopher and theologian provide some parallels to *Sir Gawain and the Green Knight* is less convincing than O'Mara's demonstration of common concerns about grace and natural goodness of the created order. In any case, whether at this or another Dominican priory (see Hinnebusch), or in the many other libraries in England where the works of Thomas Aquinas were available, the poet could easily have had access to the discussion on temperance, but my comparative analysis of Thomas's aesthetic ethic with *Cleanness* is not intended to demonstrate the direct influence of the *Summa*.

19. Gollancz sees this passage as one piece of evidence among many to support his claim that the *Cleanness*-poet was "intimately acquainted" with the *Book of the Knight of The Tower* in its original French, a text he dates 1371–72, and he gives an excerpt from it in his note on *erigaut*, a word for a cloak or upper garment used by the poet in line 148. In the fifteenth-century English translation, the vignette is titled "How thauncyent were wonte to lerne the yonge" and emphasizes the value of shaming as a corrective to breaches of honor. The offender against social decorum dresses in a "coote hardye after the maner of almayne," a costume fitting for a minstrel but not for a young man of noble breeding. The lord's reproof takes the form of humorous jibe, but as the wearer seems unconscious of his fault, the joke is lost on him (*Book of the Knight of the Tower* 152–53).

20. The overlap between social and sacred decorum, between the secular and the heavenly households, that informs the poet's sensibility is illustrated by another episode from the *Book of the Knight of the Tower*. The knight counsels his daughters to wear their best clothes to Mass, and to support this advice, he recounts a cautionary tale about a lady who reserved her good gown for secular occasions since there were no men of estate to see her at Mass: "a ha said the damoysell / god and his moder ben more grete than ony other / And they ought to be honoured more than ony worldly thing. . . . / and on theyr hooly dayes we ought to arraye vs the better" (45). The poet's and Thomas's emphasis upon how a person's dress should express a standard of due measure is echoed here in the knight's approval of the maidservant's acute sensitivity to the importance of attiring her mistress appropriately for church. Since the celebration of the Eucharist was conceived as a pre-enactment of the heavenly banquet, to attend worthily such an exalted moment dictated appearing at one's most honorable, both inwardly and outwardly.

21. Andrew and Waldron translate *lyued* in line 172 as "given life to" (see *OED live*, v.2).

22. See *MED* s.v. *queint*, adj., sense 1(a), "wise, clever, prudent," where this use of *quoynt* is cited as an example; it could have more aptly been cited as an example of an aesthetic register which is clearly applicable in this instance, as defined by the *MED* in sense 1(e), "gracious, courteous," or even more specifically in sense 1(f), "well-dressed, fashionable, elegant," where the description of Lot's daughters in *Cleanness* 871 is given

as an example. The lord's invitation to the feast specifies that the guests should come in "comly quoyntis" (54), which the *MED* cites as an example — see *MED* s.v. *queintis(e)*, n., sense 3(b) — of "elaborate clothing or ornament, finery." Throughout the poem, the elasticity of these terms is exploited to explore the overlap of wisdom and sensitivity to social and aesthetic standards.

23. Andrew and Waldron discuss but do not resolve this disturbing effect in their footnote to 139ff: "The lord has specifically requested that people should wear their best clothes to his feast (53f) and therefore considers that the ill-dressed man is treating him with disdain. Modern readers may find the lord's reaction extreme or not entirely just; but it does not appear to have caused anxiety to medieval commentators, perhaps because the wedding garment could so readily be allegorized as good works — as indeed it is in 169ff — the lack of which was self-evidently reprehensible. It is also possible that at the literal level there was the understanding that wedding garments were available to all who chose to ask for them (cf. 4 Kgs. [AV 2 Kgs.] 10:22)" (117).

Chapter 2. Homophobic Wrath and Paradisal Pleasure

1. Following Robert L. Menner's editorial observations on line 204, most explications of *Cleanness* take note of the contrast between the mercy that constrained divine judgment in response to the rebellion of Satan and the disobedience of Adam and Eve, on the one hand, and the unmitigated wrath illustrated in the Flood and the destruction of Sodom and Gomorrah, on the other. Typically, however, although these accounts stress the structural importance of the distinction between two kinds of divine vengeance, they still do not probe what form of evil evokes God's merciless punishment but instead interpret simply by paraphrase (e.g., Menner and Sir Israel Gollancz who refer to fleshly impurity or defilement of the flesh). Edward Wilson, while less abstractly positing lust as the meaning, still leaves the form of sexual sin unexplicated: "In other contexts, 'filth of the flesh' might be argued to have some general sense (as 'the sinful state of man'), but since the poet is here concerned to distinguish it from all other vices (199), it must be highly restricted in sense and should, most reasonably, be taken as = 'sexual sin'" (87).

2. While she strongly implies that God's wrath is aroused both in the Flood and in the destruction of Sodom by same-sex relations between males, in keeping with her view that the stories progress toward greater specificity, Morse does not use the terms *sodomy* or *homosexual* until she discusses the Sodomites (159, 167–69). She sees Nicholas of Lyra as a possible influence on the poet's interpretation in 265–68 of corruption in Genesis 6:11 as the sin against nature (*Pattern of Judgment* 154). Morse does not discuss how *Cleanness* legitimates heterosexual desire by vilifying homosexual deviance; rather, she sees marriage as inferior to celibacy in the poet's hierarchy of values and hence takes the poem's praise of heterosexual loveplay as mainly signifying allegorically the Christian's spiritual marriage to God (42; 173–74).

3. Twomey credits Ferdinand Holthausen's note, "which has been ignored or dismissed since it appeared in 1901," for proposing as a source for *Cleanness* 265–68 Peter Comestor's image from the *Historia*, "'exarserunt homines in alterutrum coeuntes' ('coming together, men caught fire in one another') from Ch. 31 on Gen. 6" ("*Cleanness*, Peter Comestor" 204). While probably alluding to Romans 1:27, this image of men

conjoining homosexually in Peter Comestor's *Historia* derives (Twomey argues) not from scripture directly but from the following passage from the first Latin recension (eighth century) of Pseudo-Methodius's *Revelationes*, a late seventh-century work: "In the 500th year of the second millennium, all men in the abodes of the Cainites burned even more greatly in obscene fornication than the previous generation, and coming together, they went into each other after the fashion of animals" (Twomey's translation 207–8). Another writer influenced by this aspect of Pseudo-Methodius's history, William of Auvergne in his *Summa*, is cited by Michael Goodich as blaming "sodomy as one of the causes of the Deluge; sodomites are marked as destroyers of humanity and imitators and worshippers of nature" (62). Twomey points out the popularity enjoyed by *Revelationes* by Pseudo-Methodius, while noting that the passage blaming the Flood on homosexual relations occurs not in the Syriac original but in the Latin recension, and only in the first of these (eighth century). The *Cleanness*-poet is thought by Twomey to be gathering materials not only out of Peter Comestor, who depends on the first Latin recension, but also from several other texts in the same tradition (207–8).

Contrary to Twomey's claim that "only in this source and in its successors do we find the apocryphal story of pre-diluvian homosexuality" (206), I note that one manuscript of 2 Enoch, an apocryphal-pseudepigraphic text, twice blames the Flood specifically on anal intercourse. (I do not think this was known by the poet. All of the twenty known manuscripts of 2 Enoch are in Old Slavonic, and none are older than the fourteenth century; the date of the one manuscript that links the Flood and sodomy is unknown. The book itself may have been produced anywhere from pre-Christian times to the late Middle Ages, probably in Greek.) In 2 Enoch 34, God predicts that "all the world will be reduced to confusion by iniquities and wickednesses and [abominable] fornications [that is, friend with friend in the anus, and every other kind of wicked uncleanness which it is disgusting to report], and the worship of (the) evil (one). And that is why I shall bring down the flood onto the earth" (2 ([Slavonic Apocalypse of] Enoch). F. I. Anderson, the editor and translator of this text, brackets phrases he considers to be interpolated because found in only one manuscript of 2 Enoch; it focuses on sodomitic vice in one other passage where Enoch is shown a place of punishment "prepared for those who do not glorify God, who practice on the earth the sin which is against nature, [which is child corruption in the anus in the manner of Sodom]" (2 Enoch 10). This age-specific, anatomically explicit description of Sodom's customary form of homosexual intercourse is interpolated in a list of many other vices, ranging from fraud to failure to care for the physical welfare of the poor.

4. Some critics view the poet's emphatic contrast as less significant structurally than what they see as a more fundamental continuity between all of the episodes of God's judgment in this section of *Cleanness*, or indeed in its entirety (e.g., Vantuono, "Review of C. Morse" 180, Glenn 79, Potkay 104). While they all downplay the poem's contrast between *fylþe of þe flesch* and Satan's and Adam's and Eve's sins, and all deny literal importance to sexual relations between men, their views differ concerning the meaning of *fylþe of þe flesch*. Earl Schreiber exemplifies a theologically informed critic reading *fylþe of þe flesch* in general terms, with no reference to sexual sins. The poet's indictments of Noah's neighbors and Sodom and Gomorrah (listed without any differentiation from other sins in a long sequence which begins with Lucifer and ends with Belshazzar) all

illustrate for Schreiber how "societies fall through pride, which leads them to break the laws of God and nature and to commit more specific sins" (141). He erases any distinction between filth in particular and uncleanness in general: "thus *fylþe* and *unclannesse* are not merely sins of the flesh; rather they are any offense against God's law, and these offenses come primarily from pride, as the poet has specifically argued at the conclusion of the prologue [177–92]" (142). Michael Twomey's source study points out that it is homosexual lust which the poet judges as responsible for both the Flood and the destruction of Sodom and the other cities on the plain, but his later article obscures any distinction between God's wrath recorded in these exempla and his punishment of disobedience generally. Both stories illustrate, along with every other instance of divine judgment in the poem, how "sinners are judged according to the covenant of faith and obedience — *trawþe* — and then destroyed by a Deity whose demand for purity is absolute and inflexible" ("Sin of *Untrawþe*" 117). Stephen Coote similarly denies the literal importance of homosexual deeds: "the exegetes were less interested in Sodom as a place or with sodomy as an act of lust than with homosexuality as the expression of a more general concern with the perversion of God's law. Homosexual deeds themselves were subsumed by Aquinas under *luxuria*, the seventh Deadly Sin, and are seen partly as such by the *Gawain*-poet" (Coote 254); he goes on to read the various exempla as instances of one fundamental sin (255).

5. Cf. William of St. Thierry's use of Latin terms which convey the same contempt for heterosexual desire as a defiling love of the flesh. Cited by Pamela Gradon (251), this passage explicitly links "filthy love of flesh" to love pursued under the influence of Ovid: "For formerly the filthy love of the flesh [Nam et fedus amor carnalis feditatis] also had masters of its filthiness; they professed corruption and so acutely and so effectively did they corrupt, that the master of the erotic art was compelled, by the very lovers and companions of filthiness, to recant that which he had more intemperately sung and to write of the remedy of love, he who had written of the fire of love" (quoted from *De natura et dignitate amoris*, ed. M.-M.Davy, Paris: 1953, 72).

6. Indeed, in most homiletic contexts, to say *fylþe of þe flesch* would be redundant; bodily appetites, from the point of view of medieval orthodoxy, are defiled and defiling, and flesh conventionally refers in theological discourse to this rampant sensuality which is humankind's legacy from the Fall of Adam and Eve, though Eve is usually blamed since the weakness of the flesh is associated specifically with femininity in most moralizing discourse. This is the way Sir Gawain uses the terms when, in an intensely penitential (and misogynistic) frame of mind, he agrees to keep the green girdle; looking at it, he will be reminded how susceptible he is, because of the "fayntyse of þe flesche crabbed," to catch the blemishes of sin "to entyse teches of fylþe" (frailty of the crabbed flesh . . . to entice stains [*Sir Gawain* 2434–35]). What he conceives his sins to be, and how his linking of vulnerability to filth is related to his assessment of himself as a victim of female guile, are debatable (e.g., Benson, *Art and Tradition*, 239, and Dinshaw, "A Kiss" 218–20).

7. For *usen*, see chap. 1.

8. The term *sodomy* is extraordinarily ambiguous in medieval (and later) moral discourse and was perhaps avoided by the poet in order to prevent his readers from defining *fylþe of þe flesch* either too narrowly or too broadly. At its most narrowly specific meaning, it could designate one particular form of male homosexual activity. Payer (based on his study of penitentials from 550 to 1150) sees specific mention of "sod-

omites" (Latin) or "the use of a derivative linguistic form" as probably referring to male anal intercourse (*Sex* 40–41, 136). When "covering ecclesiastical persons, the intention of the reference to 'what the Sodomites did' is probably a general reference to any form of homosexual relation" (136).

In contrast, sodomy (like the sin against nature) could cover sins committed in heterosexual as well as homosexual relations. Technically it is often defined as the deposit of sperm into an unfitting vessel; thus, although it is epitomized by males using each other sexually, it can refer to masturbation, heterosexual intercourse in positions deemed unnatural, and intercourse with animals. Boswell, working with a much larger range of documents and spanning a broader time period than Payer's analysis, attempts to exclude the term *sodomy* (*sodomia* in Latin) from his study, "since it is so vague and ambiguous as to be virtually useless." He notes that it has "referred almost exclusively to male homosexuality" at some points, and "at others almost exclusively to heterosexual excess" (*Christianity, Social Tolerance* 93n2).

9. Homosexual intercourse was ranked by Thomas Aquinas (following a traditional hierarchy of unnatural sins, starting with masturbation as the least grave and descending to intercourse with beasts) as the second most gravely offensive form of lust. Alain de Lille, in *Sermones de peccatis capitalibus*, introduces in the late twelfth century the view that "the two most serious crimes of all are sodomy and homicide, both of which are described in Scripture" as creating a loud disturbance that calls forth God's eternal wrath (Goodich 34). William of Peraldus (c. 1274) likens sodomy to homicide, since it violates the injunction to multiply, and notes that for this reason even the innocent perished in Sodom (Goodich 63). William of Auvergne notes that confessors should urge the sodomite in particular to repent because he has only barely escaped eternal punishment; following the standard gloss, William "links androgyny and by implication homosexuality with the errors of pagans and idolators" (Goodich 62).

10. On Wisdom of Solomon 10:1–7 and 2 Peter 2:4–10 see Margaret Williams 35. Also cf. Wilson 96–97; Anderson 6; Johnson 107–8.

11. One of the standard glosses on the story of Sodom (the interlinear commentary attributed to Walafrid Strabo, d. 849) explicitly contrasts the unnatural sin responsible for the city's destruction with the natural sin of concupiscence responsible for the Flood; because the Sodomites violated nature, the deluge of sulphur and fire is a graver punishment than the waters of the Deluge (Goodich 36).

12. Accusations of sexual perversity and effeminacy were part of political rhetoric in poems and songs of the period, as in "Dispute between the Englishman and the Frenchman" (Wright ed. I, 91ff).

13. Pope Leo IX, to whom Peter Damian addresses the *Book of Gomorrah*, mildly rebuked the diatribe, distinguishing between various modes of homosexual offenses, thus allowing some guilty priests to be readmitted after penance to ecclesiastical rank (Boswell, *Christianity, Social Tolerance* 18).

14. The image, derived from Josephus, recurs throughout medieval commentaries and encylopediac writing (see note by Andrew and Waldron on 1043–48). Gollancz (xxvi) suggests Wisdom of Solomon's closing verses (19:18ff) as a source, calling attention to the poet's special emphasis in 1024 on how Sodom's unnatural sins changed the qualities of nature.

15. Oxford University as a whole is accused of sodomy in the prologue to the later

version of the Wyclif Bible (1395–96); for quotation see chap. 6 n18. Heyworth observes that the Lollards "had no monopoly when it came to accusations of depravity" (192n45); he also refers to an anti-Lollard poem "Gens Lollardorum gens est vilis Sodomorum" (in Wright ed. II, 128).

16. "He sende toward Sodomas þe syʒt of his yʒen, / Þat euer hade ben an erde of erþe þe swettest, / As aparaunt to paradis, þat plantted þe Dryʒtyn; / Nov is hit plunged in a pit like of pich fylled" (He sent toward Sodom the sight of his eyes; / It had ever been the area on earth that was sweetest / Like a colony of Paradise that the Lord planted; / Now is it plunged into a pit as if filled with pitch (1005–8). The "now" in Abraham's perception of Sodom's devastation is continuous, by implication, with the "now" of the poet, and also with the "now" of anyone reading/hearing this recounting of the transformation of the Dead Sea landscape seen as evidence of God's vengeance against *fylþe of þe flesch*. The "dedez of deþe" (deeds of death) that "duren þere ʒet" (endure there yet) are offered as continuing testimony to the corruption of nature caused by men making love with men.

17. As Andrew and Waldron note, in the explanation God gives of why he is going to punish the Sodomites (697–708), the "poet is at some pains to exempt heterosexual behavior from the stigma of *fylþe*" (23).

18. Admittedly, unnatural lust was more broadly specified in the church's moral discourse to include, in addition to homosexual intercourse, any practice that obstructed the generative purpose of marriage. Yet *the* sin against nature seems to have been most commonly understood, at least in Thomas Aquinas's milieu, as referring to males having intercourse with males (Boswell, *Christianity, Social Tolerance* 328; cf. my discussion in chap. 4; also see Frantzen, "Disclosure of Sodomy" on Robert of Flamborough's use of the phrase "generalities that everyone knows are sins" to avoid naming what is meant by "a particular way" in which one commits the sin against nature [455]).

19. The prevalent medieval reluctance to name sexual relations between males as the vice against nature derives from Ephesians 5:3–12, which lists "the unspeakable vice" among things that bring the wrath of God upon the children of disobedience, a text that was frequently linked with the story of Sodom, Gomorrah, and the cities of the plain. While not naming the Flood or Sodom specifically, the warning against divine wrath in this passage was linked to both events by two influential commentators, Augustine and Nicholas of Lyra. Nicholas of Lyra glossed Ephesians 5:6 as referring to "the corrupt generation that perished before the Flood," and "Augustine seems to have become the source for the perennial identification of these lines with sodomy" (Goodich 38; on the unspeakable vice and Ephesians 5:6–12 cf. Heyworth 186).

20. Compare John Myrc's *Instructions for Parish Priests,* written before 1450: "Also written well I find / That of sin against kynde / Thou shalt to thy parish no thing teach, / Nor of that sin no thing preach" (quoted in Bullough 66). It is clear from what follows that Myrc is referring to men turning from relations with their wives to partners of the same sex. See also McAlpine's interpretation of Chaucer's Pardoner's conventional reticence when preaching about "synne horrible." She concludes, "the shame that attends the naming of the sin even in the confessional seems a clear allusion to homosexuality" (15).

21. This Lollard article clearly equates sodomy with the compensatory homosexual outlets sought by clergy who are bound by celibacy; the ascetic ideal itself is blamed on

misogyny of the very priesthood whose pleasures it seeks to regulate. This ostensible connection between celibacy mandated for priests and their predilection for unnatural sexual relations resembles David Greenberg's argument that "closing off heterosexual relationships for the medieval clergy" had important "emotional consequences" both in the "homophile clerical discourse of the twelfth century" and in the "fear and loathing of homosexuality developed . . . as a psychological defense mechanism against the inner conflict created by imposition of clerical celibacy and the rigid repression of all sexual expression" (288–90).

Conversely, St. Bernard lists a great many sins of lust, natural and unnatural (including but not limited to homosexual intimacy), that he predicts as consequences of the devaluation of marriage being preached by heretical sects of the twelfth century: "If you deprive the church of honorable marriage . . . you will fill her with concubinage, incest, seminal emissions, masturbation, homosexuality, and every other kind of filthiness" (Goodich 7).

22. See also Jane Dempsey Douglas: "Geiler's concern that the people be warned about sin in any form aroused protests on other occasions as well; for example, he also justifies his exceedingly frank sermons on the ethics of marriage on grounds that the laity must be taught how to avoid sin" (81).

23. The same logic appears in William of Auvergne's explanation of why "preachers dare not mention" sodomy, for as Gregory notes (in commenting on Ezekiel 16:27), "the air itself is corrupted" when the word is spoken (Goodich 62).

24. Andrew and Waldron gloss *Cleanness* 847ff as describing the foul smelling vomit of the Sodomites' venomous words, noting that sin is often associated with foul smells. The idea of a fart is more likely, given the anal association of *brech*, a pun for *brych*. *MED* cites 848 s.v. *bruche*, n., sense 2(a) "A transgression against moral law; an offence, sin." Here, as in several other *MED* and *OED* translations, the editors' preference for the ethical sense of words that can be also taken more literally obscures the *Cleanness*-poet's metaphorical method; the pun in 848 draws on *MED* s.v. *brech*, n., sense 3(a) "The buttocks, rump." Frantzen discusses this and several other similar puns in lines 842–48 ("Disclosure of Sodomy" 458) as important evidence for the poet's surprising narrowing of the sin of sodomy to anal intercourse between males (451).

25. Celibacy itself is often imagined in terms of a spiritual marriage, and in this metaphorical context, desire is granted greater dignity; still gendered as feminine, erotic longing is located in the soul rather than the flesh, as the Christian, like a bride, yearns for union with God, figured in the active role as loving bridegroom. While the negative aspect of continence is transformed by this promise of spiritual nuptials, every trace of impure desire must be expelled. For the secular Christian who aspires to communion with the heavenly bridegroom, there must be the same process of self-knowledge that Michel Foucault describes as "an indispensable and permanent condition" of the chastity-oriented asceticism which developed in the church's mystique of virginity after the thirteenth century. Even for those married Christians living outside the monastic sexual mores of celibacy, the church insisted on the standard of chastity, requiring an "endless self-questioning to flush out any secret fornication lurking in the inmost recesses of the mind" ("Battle for Chastity" 24–25). The daunting goal for men and women in the married estate was to achieve, despite their sexual activities, a detachment from and mastery over the transgressive urges of physical appetites and as well control of the

subjective sources of sexual passion which could catch the mind up in an internal play of pleasure-driven thoughts.

26. Owst does observe that "now and then a kindlier, fairer attitude is expressed, as for example in the typical marriage sermon of the day" (384). However, d'Avray's account of marriage preaching in France traces in both thirteenth- and seventeenth-century discourse on married love an emphasis on "a moral obligation" which "does not imply sexual attraction (while not necessarily excluding it)" and which, because it "belongs to the domain of free will and choice," is antithetical to the sentiments of love found in courtly literature (215–16). Despite a positive note sounded on behalf of marital affection between spouses, the texts surveyed by d'Avray say nothing favorable about sexual pleasure per se. Instead, the sexual ethics in the sermons preached to the married are predictably concerned with the sins this union occasions rather than those it prevents. (For examples of the limits preachers placed on the time and nature of sexual intercourse between husband and wives, see D. L. d'Avray and M. Tausche 96ff). While sermons that provide written models of this genre were not reproduced in full in living speech, it is still evident that preachers referred to sexual relations in degrading metaphors such as Jacobus de Vitriaco's warning against entering "into marriages in such a way that they exclude God from themselves and their mind, and give themselves over to their lust, like the horse and mule, who lack the faculty of reason" (quoted in d'Avray and Tausche 98).

27. Admitting these uncertainties, Tentler nevertheless concludes: "The morality of the conjugal act was only one subject for inquiry in the confessional, and we cannot even be sure how detailed it was. Yet, one can hardly imagine a more sensitive subject or one more likely to arouse scruples. Only a very selective and scholarly reading of the literature on the forgiveness of sins could give a confessor a consoling view of conjugal morality" (231). In a revisionist reading of the church's attempt to "enforce and consolidate standards that differed from behavior," Jean-Louis Flandrin interprets "the exhortations of moralists and theologians" as evidence for "the conjugal eroticism that the Church wished to discourage" (cited by Edwards and Spector 2). Edwards and Spector cite another revisionist historian, Philippe Ariès, who "concedes that it is hard to penetrate the silence concerning love and sexuality in medieval married life: '. . . more than unspoken, it is unutterable. . . . So conjugal love could be one of the secret places of the old society'" (Ariès and Béjin, 136–37, quoted in Edwards and Spector, 2–3). Unless the evil was to be compounded by being shrouded in sinful secrecy, however, the pursuit of sexual pleasure—even in the marriage bed—was subject to the church's control in the practice of confession which was required of Christians at least annually.

28. While Noonan and Tentler both show that most sexual moralists taught that conscious seeking for pleasure with no intention of procreating offspring or of paying the marital debt is mortally sinful, doubts are raised on this point when we read d'Avray and Tausche quoting from a marriage sermon of Jacobus de Vitriaco (Jacques de Vitry, d. 1240): "We do not however say that a man sins mortally whenever he exceeds the proper limit (*modum*) in having intercourse with his wife, so long as the marriage act takes place at a proper time and place and in a proper manner (*modo*)." Their footnote observes: "It is not quite certain what this venial 'exceeding of the limit' means in concrete terms. In the light of medieval marriage doctrine one possibility is a situation in which a man performs the marriage act purely for sensual pleasure (not to avoid incontinence) but without being

in such a state of mind that he would do it even if she were not his wife" (99). Also, Pierre Payer notes an early Parisian school of moralists at the beginning of the thirteenth century, exemplified by Robert of Courson, who recognized that simple men could not attend to the intricacies of the morality governing intercourse but were not therefore to be condemned "because they have a great love to hold their wives or because they approach them frequently" (quoted in *Bridling of Desire,* 129). In the later thirteenth century, the theoretical concerns produce greater moral stringency. Payer knows of only one author, Durandus of St. Pourcain, who even "questions the possibility that sexual relations for pleasure between a husband and wife are a mortal sin" (127–28).

29. See Payer's fascinating history of this text, from its origins in the *Sentences* of Sextus the Pythagorean, through its appearance in Jerome's literary pastiche using a lost work by Seneca on marriage, and its medieval usage by Gratian and his legal and theological successors (*Bridling of Desire* 120–22). "With such authoritative sources using this epigram, it is not surprising to find a huge variety of medieval literature condemning 'too ardent love' as adulterous" (Tentler 174).

30. Payer's comprehensive history of the teaching about sexual desire in thirteenth-century accounts of marital relations appeared after this chapter was completed. He further documents how the general morality of sexual relations was "a matter of conforming behavior to the natural finality of reproduction in the proper institutional setting" of marriage (*Bridling of Desire* 130) but takes a more positive view than either Tentler or Noonan do of the clerical discussion which he believes shows that "the first sophisticated reflection in the West since Augustine could boast some achievements.... The radical goodness of gender differences, coitus, and marriage was clearly affirmed." In a similar vein, what Payer sees at stake in the discussion of the immorality of the man who loves his wife as if she were not his wife is "the desire to make the point that the marriage requires a type of interior psychological orientation between spouses. In our contemporary language, marriage does not permit one to use one's spouse purely as a sex object" (128).

31. Cadden finds "very little medical disapprobation of contraception or homosexual behavior" even though the "rhetoric for the enforcement of sex definitions and gender constructs ... sometimes draws upon the language of nature"; in short, "natural philosophy and medicine did not produce a program for the control of sexuality the way theology did" (219).

32. For discussion of *on femallez wyse,* see chap. 6.

33. Kelly and Irwin observe that "fader" is used as a synonym for God nine times, as well as nine other times to refer to natural human fathers (242n12). Their emphasis on patriarchal authority obscures how the poet appeals to reciprocity by privileging romantic ideals of festive decorum and love service. Similarly, I differ from Twomey's view that the poet uses legal metaphors in God's praise of love to emphasize the "contractual obligation" the couple has to the procreative law. Where for Twomey the "feudal, covenantal nature of man's relationship to God" issues in a deontological ethic based on legal authority ("Sin of *untrawþe*" 119), I maintain that obedience to a heteronomous standard is a less prominent motif in the ethos of *Cleanness* than fidelity to a standard that is mutually valued by Creator and his naturally obedient creatures; God and his positively human exemplars, including the narrator and his implied audience, share a scrupulous

but joyful regard for the aesthetically grasped details of conduct by which life attains the perfection of art. The point here is that rather than representing natural law as commandment, a mandate to procreate, the poet traces sexual joy back to the nature of things, a structure of order which God creates in loving relationship to his creatures; the legal associations of some of the vocabulary in God's denunciation of the Sodomites should be read within the context of his delight in the pleasure afforded in *play of paramorez* by the *ordenaunce* which he claims is peculiarly dear to him.

34. For Schmidt, it is crucial that this is "marital union" (104) and that the poet's positive vision of love as paradisal joy is "unimpeachably orthodox" (the phrase J. A. W. Bennett uses of *Cleanness,* quoted in Schmidt 121).

While it is true that the erotic is fundamental to much of medieval mystical experience and discourse, the image of desire is attributed to the "male" spirit rather than the "female" flesh when the longing is for blissful union with God. The doctrine of sacramental marriage does not bring with it a re-evaluation of desire as appropriately directed to bodily union except as a means to procreation. Since Christian conjugality is so unlikely an ethical context for the sensual pleasures celebrated in a spiritual sense when the Song of Songs was read allegorically, it is not accidental that *Cleanness*'s celebration of passion does not explicitly evoke nuptial bonds between the couple. The celebration of the embodied passions that Schmidt rightly sees the poet providing as he evokes a paradisal darkness of sexual union moves desire into the sphere of the bodily appetites, and in the process brings God into play as part of the refinement of eros through cultural artifice or romance language and ideology.

35. Critics differ concerning "unstered wyth sy3t" (706). As noted in the introduction, Frantzen reads this as placing the acceptable heterosexual mode of intercourse "in the dark," thus guaranteeing protection from surveillance (presumably priestly rather than divine), and at the same time protecting the couple from the temptation of lust aroused by sight. Dinshaw does not refer to darkness but nevertheless senses a similar taint of "fallen love" in this line which recalls Augustine's repressive view of sexuality in *De civitate Dei* 14.18; there he argues that intercourse, even when it is conjugal and aimed at procreation, is shameful, because it naturally requires "a private room and the absence of witnesses" ("A Kiss" 217). Schmidt interprets *unstered* as meaning both that the lovers are "unsteered"—unguided by sight as they exercise *kynde crafte* by touch—and that they are "unstirred"—not aroused to lust by the sight of each other's body (118). Schmidt stresses the darkness as crucial to the supernatural quality the poet gives to the lovemaking: "deed of darkness as it is, its *luf-lowe* (707), a finely synaesthetic image for orgasm, is enkindled in an enigmatic encounter where the darkness is the darkness of God. More specifically, the darkness is that of the love-garden in the Song of Songs" (117–18). To say that such passion is part of the Godhead makes sense, given the erotic model St. Bernard develops for the relations between the Father, Son, and Holy Ghost, but the image of love blazing "vnstered wyth sy3t" (706) seems quite different to me in tone from the mystical "blynd steryng of loue" Schmidt compares it to, quoting from *The Cloud of Unknowing.*

36. The doctrinal parallels which Schmidt sees as underlying the poet's treatment of love are "the love of Christ for his Church (and, by extension, of God for his beloved, the Soul)" but neither of these suggest the immanence of God in the sexual activities of human lovers. It is this heterodox suggestiveness, however, that we see in the close

identification God makes between himself and the play of paramours he portrays, a phrasing that constructs the male and his mate as partners in a tryst which in some sense emulates the divine nature. In fact, the spirituality of heterosexual love in this passage from *Cleanness* may resemble Jewish more closely than Christian mystical traditions (see chap. 3 for discussion of Tetragrammaton).

37. Schmidt stresses as crucial the poet's opposition between, on the one hand, human artifice, which man "learns for himself, by exploring his own flesh in an amoral and as it were instrumental fashion," and on the other hand, "what God 'teaches' (... through the Natural Law accessible through man's reason or *skyl*)" (123). By this emphasis on the reasonableness of nature's patterns, Schmidt merges the ethics of *Cleanness* with Thomas Aquinas's procreative justification of sexual pleasure, thereby missing the poet's distinctive departure from this naturalistic tradition.

38. For Frantzen, the *Cleanness*-poet alludes to a tradition which blames the invention of unnatural sexual practices on Sodomite women who were so dissatisfied with the pleasures of heterosexual intercourse that they devised new and perverse processes to satisfy their lust ("Disclosure of Sodomy" 456). According to Frantzen's source, "men ... had been all too ready to take up these womanly perversities, and thus unnatural vice spread through the world" (Brundage 534). Brundage states in his account of the period 1348–1517 that late medieval "legal theorists contended that sodomy had begun historically with the practice of the women of Sodom and Gomorrah." Yet the dates of the two jurists he cites make their contributions to such a misogynistic pseudo-history irrelevant to *Cleanness*—Egidio Bossi (1487–1546) and Paulus Grilandus (sixteenth century). Jean Gerson (1363–1429) is noted as the other authority for this legal theory; yet the relevance to the poem of the portion of the text cited by Brundage (Glorieux 8.72) is puzzling. It refers to the graver level of sodomy that one descends to when masturbation is committed with a companion, and it also warns against the false notion that a man who does not think of a woman carnally does not commit a sin by touching himself sexually. Nothing suggests that male sodomy originated in the Sodomite women's lustful pursuits of same-sex pleasures. Even if there were to be found evidence that such a theory was extant in late-fourteenth-century England, the *Cleanness*-poet seems to me to refute it by drawing a clear parallel between the homosexual practices of Sodomite men and those which brought on the Flood when an earlier generation of similarly violent men committed the very same sin against nature. There is, in summary, no evidence that the *Cleanness*-poet anticipates the legal theory, articulated in the early sixteenth century, that it was the women of Sodom who ventured first across the boundary between licit heterosexual and illicit homosexual pleasures, thus earning themselves the title of "the mothers of lust" (Bossi's phrase, quoted by Brundage 533 and then by Frantzen 465).

39. See chap. 3 and chap. 6.

40. See chap. 4.

41. Can this text justifiably be said to give "the reader the sense of the positive value of the rule of Nature, of the paradisal bliss of love in an ordered, honest, and modest human society" (Davenport 61)? See also Spearing, whose earliest commentary on the poem concludes that the loveplay that "God himself is made responsible for" is "a kind of *clannesse* that is open to all, and this is the firmly stated positive that lies behind the poem's fierce negatives" (*Gawain-Poet* 73). Who is included and who excluded by

Davenport's reference to "the reader" and Spearing's reference to "all"? As Calabrese and Eliason put it, "At one time, one could simply appreciate the poet's praise of heterosexual love. But once we understand that that praise both springs out of and leads into a desire to condemn the Sodomites, we need to reevaluate our admiration" (275). While I do not agree that the poet's break with the repressive morality of the church's distrust of heterosexual pleasure can logically be accounted for simply as a desire to condemn the Sodomites, Calabrese's and Eliason's conclusion about the opportunity the poem gives us "to initiate our own critical reformations" (275) rings true to my experience. Rereading in 1990 my own essay, written in 1975 and published in 1983, I found that my admiration of God's praise of love understated the poem's homophobic aspect.

Chapter 3. Educating Love

1. For the philosophical tradition of Nature as a cosmic force, see George D. Economou, *Goddess Natura*. Nature's literary career as a goddess begins with Bernard Silvestris's allegory, *De mundi universatate,* mid-twelfth century; she unites body and soul of humankind and in each generation "skillfully forms the seminal fluid so that ancestors are revived in their children" (Economou 71). Although she is thus "procreatrix," not until Alain's elaboration of Bernard's figure was Nature portrayed as the teacher of the heterosexual norm, lamenting over humankind's deviance from her laws.

2. John Gower also alludes to Nature's complaint, referring no doubt not only to Jean de Meun's representation of her in the *Roman,* but also to the *Roman*'s source in Alain's *Complaint*: "whereof that sche full ofte hath pleyned" (*Confessio Amantis* 2341). See H. A. Kelly 154, and Economou, "Two Venuses" 31–32.

3. With the exception of Jean de Meun in *Cleanness,* a puzzling citation (discussed in chaps. 5 and 7), nowhere in the MS Cotton Nero A.x, Art. 3 poems are literary, as opposed to scriptural, sources or influences cited by name.

4. Jeanne Krochalis's dissertation reveals that while the *Complaint* was frequently assigned in schools and universities as an example of elegant literary style, it was also widely interpreted as an attack against sodomy. A colophon "Explicit Alanus pereat sodomita prophanus" and a heading indicating that it is directed "contra sodomitam" are common features. Glosses and even brief prefaces praised it as a moral treatise against sodomy in particular. Although vice in general is condemned by Nature in her excommunication, scribes and other commentators usually focus on her attack against unnatural sexual conduct. One scribe "solemnly prefixed a brief treatise on natural coition, since the *De planctu* spent so much time discussing unnatural coition" (540). Walter de Burgh (an Englishman who died in 1346) added three extra verses about sodomy and a particular sodomite abbot against whom he prays for protection to his transcript of *Vix nodusum,* a poem attributed to Alain; this topically relevant epilogue (in Oxford, Bodleian Library, Digby 166), although it does not appear in a manuscript of the *Complaint,* clearly is linked to it by an explicit: "Epilogum fratris Walteri de Brugo super Alanum in opere suo de planctu nature contra prelatum sodomitam" (557).

5. Häring judges that the *Complaint* was "rather slow in winning publicity." He notes that the first citation may be by an author who died early in the fourteenth century; "not

much later, the Dominican Robert Holcot (d. 1349) extolls the *Planctus* of 'Alan the great' as an effective campaign against sodomy" and by far the "greatest number of extant manuscripts was actually written in the 14th and 15th centuries" (802). Based on an exhaustive study of the manuscripts, Krochalis contests the idea that Alain's *Complaint* was any less widely read than the later *Anticlaudianus*, a poem which every well-stocked late medieval library would probably contain (535). She describes thirty manuscripts of the *Complaint* of English provenance.

6. All English quotations from the *Complaint* follow Sheridan's translation except where Moffat is indicated; in addition to page numbers cited from these English texts, the prose and metric numbers are cited when Häring's edition of the Latin text is quoted.

7. Economou (*Goddess Natura* 194n52) points out that Alain does not identify Nature with the sublunary world but instead views her as its queen and ruler. This is evident in the praise Largitas, or Generosity, renders to her: "O first principle of all things born, O special preserver of all things, O queen of the earthly regions" (Sheridan 214). As Sheridan points out (33–34 and 147n44), no adequate motivation is given for Nature's lack of interest in the work God gave her to do and no cause is suggested for a fatally poor choice of Venus as deputy.

8. See R. H. Green for an allegorical reading which focuses exclusively on the figurative interpretation of sodomy. Jan Ziolkowski, in contrast, addresses Alain's concern with sodomy in a literal sense along with the rhetorical use of this vice to symbolize fallen humanity's alienation from God. At points, he see Alain's emphasis on the disruption of cosmic order by moral disease overriding any interest in the literal meaning of same-sex deviations: "Alain does not seem to have been concerned with homosexuality any more than with any other activity he considered sinful; consequently he aims the censure . . . not so much at the individual failing of what he considered wrongful sexual preference as at the general rupture of the bond of divine love" (42). On the whole, however, Ziolkowski's focus on grammatical metaphors to draw attention to the practice of sodomy does justice to the *Complaint*'s representation of homosexual offenses as literally monstrous, unconscionable, and outlandish; see the comparisons to Walter of Chatillon (67) and *Prisciani regula* (74), where Ziolkowski makes it clear that Alain was not alone in his castigation of contemporaries for their homosexual misconduct.

9. On Alain's confusing analyses of grammatical analogies, see Ziolkowski 37 and 158; Boswell 259n60; Sheridan 157–58n12.

10. What is missing in Alain's portrayal was not lost on Jean de Meun (see chap. 5); in Genius's sermon, Jean makes clear how enjoyable such work can be, at least for the male (like so much of Jean's revision of Alain, that sermon is clearly ironic), and in the consummation at the end of the *Roman*, Jean dramatizes penetration and ejaculation in a tone that remains controversial. In many ways the infantile brutality of Alain's text that seems designed for schoolboys (Ziolkowski 142) is less prurient than Jean's more self-consciously salacious evoking of male sexual prowess.

11. The family relationship between Venus or Love, Hymen or Marriage, and their offspring Cupid or Desire, could be a figure for the fruitfulness of erotic pleasure in a rightly ordered heterosexual union. In Bernard Silvestris's imaginative iconography, Venus, "the power that excites man's desire for pleasure ('voluptas') holds the infant

Cupid at her left breast" (Economou, *Goddess* 71). Yet the *Complaint*'s mythology overall suggests no positive role of this sort for eros. Venus seems unattached to both her offspring, Cupid, and his bastard brother.

12. I construe "And þe play of paramorez I portrayed myseluen" to assert a resemblance between the loveplay of earthly *paramorez* and the loveplay of God's nature. (See chap. 2 n36.) Although the first meaning to occur to a modern reader may be "to portray" in the sense of "to act out" as in portraying a character in a dramatic performance, the earliest example given in the *OED* of the word meaning "impersonate" or "enact" is in the eighteenth century — sense 3b: "to represent (e.g., dramatically) . . . 1798 Mrs Inchbald *Lovers' Vows*, Introd., The actor . . . forms his notion of the passion he is to portray . . . from the following lines." A preferable translation is "to draw a picture of" either by sketching or describing in words (as the Squire in Chaucer's *Canterbury Tales* is said to "purtreye well" I. 96). This suggests that God himself makes a picture of the loveplay he teaches (as in the notion of love within the Trinity, or in the notion of God making man and woman in his image) and that God himself depicts in the lovers' own beings the design of their loveplay.

13. That such an idea of the heterosexual significance of the Tetragrammaton could have been known by the poet is my conjecture, based on accounts of medieval Christian scholars' interest in the rabbinical learning of their time and on Metlitski Finkelstein's argument for the *Pearl*-poet's possible use of Jewish mystical ideas of the name of God (428–32).

14. "Antigenius" receives support from its presence in what scholars consider the best manuscripts and is logically better since it emphasizes his opposition to Genius, underscoring how Venus's task of reproduction is subverted by this misalliance (Sheridan 163n27; cf. Maureen Quilligan 214n12).

15. The pejorative contrast of *mechanicum* (craft) to *liberale opus* (a noble work) suggests the Greek estimation of handicrafts as low and vulgar, for which Sheridan cites Aristotle (163n28). It is curious that Nature uses this hierarchy here when she did not invoke it in her account of educating Venus to exercise proficiency in the use of hammer and anvil, of pen and parchment, and as well in the trivium, three of the liberal arts.

16. See Ziolkowski, who says Alain may be writing not only about but for the schools; sensitive to the decorum required by pedagogy, he can use the metaphors of grammar to "skirt outright discussion of topics such as sexual orientation which he deemed too risqué for open discussion" (142). Putting aside the question of whether sexual orientation per se could have been a topic in the twelfth century, I question this interpretation since Alain's metaphors do not skirt risqué topics with decency as often as they pique voyeuristic curiosity about what clothing conceals.

17. "Why do so many kisses lie fallow on maidens' lips, while no one wishes to harvest a crop from them? If these kisses were but once planted on me, they would grow honeysweet with moisture and . . . they would form a honeycomb in my mouth. My lifebreath . . . would go out to meet the kisses and would disport itself entirely on my lips so that I might thus expire and that, when dead myself, my other self might enjoy in her a fruitful life" (70–71).

18. Sheridan glosses *felici* as having "its basic meaning of 'fertile' or 'fruitful.' In the background is the idea of a man continuing to live in his offspring" (71n18). Wetherbee,

in contrast, sees the reference to *felix vita* as "both a conventional hyperbole for sexual fulfillment and an allusion to the primal state in which rhetoric and experience were harmonious" (*Platonism and Poetry* 190).

19. For a pertinent example of how this kind of verbal glossing had become a conventional feature of the "play of paramorez" and "drwry" and could be played upon as such, see the dialogues of Gawain and the Lady in *Sir Gawain and the Green Knight,* part 3. Cf. Dinshaw ("A Kiss" 218).

20. See John Baldwin on the "ubiquitous" but varied metaphor of love's fire in discourses of desire (804–13). As a negative figure, it involves the "raging blaze" that torments unsatisfied loves; as a positive figure, it is usually seen as a "warming, comforting sensation," like a fire on the domestic hearth.

21. Alain's view thus has some affinities with Greek and Roman views of homosexuality which saw the *erastes* and the *eromenos* as completely distinct in the nature of their sexual roles, either of which, along with heterosexual activity, any man might perform at different stages of his life, or even at the same stage; see Halperin, *One Hundred Years* 29–39.

22. Oddly missing from the list, which otherwise suggests the Augustinian triad of the goods of marriage, is any mention of progeny. The ideal of marital affection seems to underlie the narrator's first two points, and the ideal of "one flesh" underlies the third and fourth.

23. The masculinist elements in this resolution deserve some attention. The reunion of Nature and Genius accomplish at a cosmic level the restored hierarchy of male agency and female passivity fundamental to the heterosexist idealism of the *Complaint*. The right relations between male and female are perhaps more winsomely imaged in the kiss by which Truth issues from the union of Genius and Nature than in the thinly, and even grotesquely, veiled accounts of intercourse presented by the metaphors of hammer and anvil, pen and page, and the various grammatical constructions. All these gendered images, however, display the dualistic paradigm evident in Alain's allegorical deployments of form controlling matter, the fundamental motif of Platonic cosmology. Although Nature is endowed with divine authority, as a female figure, she, too, is conceived as needing male direction. At first, she arrives in a chariot driven by a man who "kept a position above the head of the maiden and . . . supplying what is wanting to the female sex, by a series of moderate suggestions guided the car on its course" (Sheridan 108–9). And she is finally reunited to a consort who, even though he is addressed as her alter-ego and comes in response to her call of love, displays the superior standing of patriarchal husband over wife.

24. Alain's revision of the classical myth of the two Venuses conflates the positive and negative into a single figure, whose creative agency is transformed into a cosmically destructive force by her defection from marriage and Nature. Before her fall, Venus lacks any association with physical passion; yet Economou claims that in her "appointment as Natura's subvicar in procreation," the cosmic function of the heavenly Venus is represented, from which we can infer that "physical passion under Natura serves God, is holy, natural, and responsible to God's law through its submission to Natura's law" ("Two Venuses" 24). It is hard to find basis for such an inference; in the contrast between the courtly Hymen and Cupid, on the one hand, and the buffoons Antigenius and Jocus, on

the other, Nature defines the pleasures of marriage strictly in terms of socially correct aesthetic standards, opposing urbane courtesy to provincial boorishness.

Chapter Four. The Sexual Ethics of Cleanness

1. "Especially in Augustinian theology, human *sensualitis* can be considered to harbour moral evil; cf. 1a2ae. 74, 3 & 4. For Thomas, however, *sensualis* is not an ugly epithet" (vol. 44, 12, editor's note b). See also vol. 42 for editorial comments by Anthony Ross on Thomas's unusual generosity to the senses: "His teaching was condemned in his lifetime and attacked vigorously after his death. It was accepted as a guide by no more than a minority at any time. . . . Some [of his opponents] disliked his attitude to feelings as an essential element in human personality which should be developed, not merely crushed. On his deathbed he expressed a longing for fresh herrings; it was characteristic of a saint and mystic who never despised the ordinary things of life, but it could appear frivolous and shocking if one held the grim views of some more puritanical ascetics" (vol. 42, xxi).

2. See Noonan on how inescapable Augustine's sexual doctrines were, even for Thomas, "the most independent of medieval theologians" (*Contraception* 308).

3. Cf. 1a2ae. 94, 2: "The order in which commands of the law of nature are arranged corresponds to that of our natural tendencies."

4. "The 'fit way' was with the woman beneath the man. Theologians following Aquinas attacked deviation from this position as unnatural and as mortal sin" (*On the Sentences* 4.31, "Exposition of text" and *Summa Theologica* 2-2.154.11; cited by Noonan, *Contraception* 290).

5. John McNeill calls attention to another perspective on homosexual activity offered by Thomas, when he discusses it among other examples of pleasures that are "according to nature," even though they appear to be unnatural. "In a particular individual there can be a breakdown of some natural principle of the species and thus what is contrary to the nature of the species can become by accident natural to this individual" (98; as Boswell points out, the citation to the *Summa* is inaccurate in McNeill's note, and should be 1a2ae. 31, 7—see *Homosexuality* 323n68). Such acknowledgement of some men as "naturally" inclined to same-sex relations with men may underlie advice given in *Speculum Sacerdotale*, a manual for confessors. Too heavy a penance could be bad medicine for a man who commits sodomy because he "feleþ him buxom and lusty to that synne" — i.e., feels strongly and pleasurably drawn to sexual relations with other men. The confessor is advised to treat such an offender as fairly and with as light a penance as if he had committed fornication or adultery, lest he be driven to despair and "contynue forþ by the clowde of desperacion" (77–78).

In contrast, naturalizing same-sex desire comes at a price, for Thomas links same-sex intercourse with the socially and morally repugnant practices of cannibalism and bestiality; such cravings for food or sex, while appalling, are represented as necessitated by the physical or mental circumstances which have skewed the normal human disposition. They are thus symptomatic of pathological compulsion for pleasures which "are unnatural, absolutely speaking, but may be called natural from a particular point of view" (1a2ae. 31, 7). Boswell notes that medieval literature "abounds in suggestions that there is something special about homosexuality, that it is not simply an ordinary sin" ("Revolutions, Universals, and Sexual Categories" 28). He goes on to discuss medieval counterparts to the modern tendency to associate "homosexual preference with certain occupations or social positions, clearly indicating that it is linked in some way to personality or experience" (28–29). Albertus Magnus saw homosexual practices as contagious, especially among the rich, but on the other hand also diagnosed the appetite for same-sex erotic relations as innate (*Homosexuality* 316).

6. 1a2ae. 94, 2: "Secondly, there is in man a bent towards things which accord with his nature considered more specifically, that is in terms of what he has in common with other animals; correspondingly those matters are said to be of natural law which nature teaches all animals, for instance the coupling of male and female, the bringing up of the young, and so forth."

7. Boswell notes that in this matter, as perhaps in other aspects of his ideas of nature, Thomas "bows to the speech patterns and the zoological notions of his contemporaries" (*Homosexuality* 328–29).

8. Peter Damian ranked sodomy as even more vicious a sin against nature than intercourse with beasts (42). Thomas does not go into detail as Peter Damian does (and confessors' manuals had to) about the various ways men can commit sins of homosexual lust. In general, Thomas's ranking agrees with other medieval moral authorities on the relative gravity of the types of unnatural lust, which are usually differentiated by the broad categories in this portion of the *Summa*.

9. Albertus Magnus had pronounced "the woman beneath the man" (on her back, of course) to be the "fit way instituted by nature" and had defined four other positions in intercourse as (in varying degrees) unnatural. Thomas condemns all such variations in the aggregate as "rather beastly and monstrous techniques" (2a2ae. 154, 11). Cf. Tentler 189–90 for Albertus's contribution to the casuistry of the unusual positions considered unnatural because intercourse was carried on in an improper manner. Noonan believes that "not the usual concept of nature but mere precedent" accounts for this teaching and its acceptance; he goes on, however, to observe that it "also reflected a belief in the natural superiority of man to woman," and that there was also "some connection with the primary insistence on insemination" based on the law of nature as a generative sexual norm. Medical opinion since Avicenna taught that male seed was poorly retained by a woman when she was above the man in coition (*Contraception* 290).

Although deviation from the natural manner of intercourse is classified on Thomas's scale as less offensive morally than the other category of improper mode where the seed is deposited outside of its natural vessel, he unequivocally condemns as a sin against nature marital intercourse in a wrong position. By this logic, intercourse in a relationship of adultery, fornication, or incest that violates the order of reason but conforms to nature's procreative norm is outweighed on a scale of moral viciousness by the evil of unnatural marital relations in which the couple adopts a posture designated as unusual.

Whether all such deviations from the most natural of positions are mortally sinful is unclear in Thomas's account of the "unnatural sins of lust." Medieval theologians differ on this point, with the less rigorous following Albertus's in allowing that there were sometimes extenuating circumstances justifying the use of unusual positions. Pregnancy, for example, might prohibit the natural way because it was potentially harmful to the fetus. Tentler's account of unnatural sins within marriage shows that, based on Thomas and Albertus, confessors taught husbands and wives that illness could justify their adoption of something other than the missionary position, so long as this variation was not adopted in order to intensify sexual pleasure or prevent conception.

10. Sedgwick, noting that "it remains ambiguous whether every denizen of the obliterated Sodom was a sodomite," identifies the "inveterate topos of associating gay acts or persons with fatalities vastly broader than their own extent. . . . Bloodletting on a scale more massive by orders of magnitude than any gay minority presence in the culture is the 'cure,' if cure there be, to the mortal illness of decadence" (128).

11. Masturbation is delineated by Thomas as the least grave of the various sins of unnatural lust. Yet he does not take lightly the violation to nature committed "outside of intercourse where an orgasm is procured for the sake of venereal pleasure" (2a2ae. 154, 11). The "solitary sin" is not as serious as loveplay between a man and woman that does not lead to insemination (or even worse, caresses between two men or two women) but it is nonetheless condemned as more gravely offensive than any sexual act from which procreation might result. Again, Thomas's classifications of relative gravity of various sexual offenses defy modern common moral sense.

12. Cf. 2a2ae. 153, 3: "A man who inordinately uses his body for lechery wrongs the Lord who is its principal owner. Thus Augustine, 'The lord who governs his servants for their benefit, not his own, made this command, lest by illicit pleasures you ruin his temple which is what you are beginning to be.'"

13. To refute the idea that for a man to lack anger is not a vice, Thomas begins by acknowledging that it might seem that "by being devoid of anger" such a man "becomes like God, *who judges with tranquility*" (2a2ae. 154, 12; italics added). The same point about God's passionlessness is made in the claim that wrath's opposite extreme is not virtue but vice, the vice displayed by a man who lacks the passion of anger: he "bears a resemblance to God with respect to the point of passionlessness, not of vindicating justice by judgment" (2a2ae. 158, 8).

14. Thomas argues that the "sensory feelings of anger cannot be wholly absent except the will's motion of anger be withdrawn or weak. As a consequence the lack of high tempered feeling will be wrong, as also the lack of the will to vindicate according to the judgment of right reason" (2a2ae. 158, 8).

15. Thomas commends those who are called to a life of chastity in the specific sense of doing without the sexual "pleasures rightly enjoyed by those called to physical labor and raising a family" only with the proviso that they should "enjoy bodily activities to the extent that reasonable activity needs bodily activity." Since the senses are fundamental to knowing truth in Thomas's Aristotelian epistemology, they must be sustained in order for the mind to be usable. Therefore, even for someone called to a predominately intellectual or contemplative life, they have an essential place: "Pleasurable activities keep the body going; if he cuts them out he destroys the basis of that good which consists in living reasonably" (2a2ae. 142, 1).

16. Whereas a lion in pursuit of a meal takes pleasure at the sight and sound of a deer simply for the sake of feeding upon it, a man "enjoys these sensations, not just because they promise a prey, but also because they are pleasing to sense" (2a2ae. 141, 4). By analogy, humans are capable of enjoying a beautiful body in a way that transcends the

predatory gaze of a beast whose only appetite is for the tangible sensations of sexual intercourse.

Josef Pieper argues (166–67) that Thomas has in mind here the tendency of lust "to relate the whole complex of the sensual world, and particularly of sensual beauty, to sexual pleasure exclusively. Therefore only a chaste sensuality can realize the specifically human faculty of perceiving sensual beauty, such as that of the human body, as beauty, and to enjoy it for its own sake, for its 'sensual appropriateness,' undeterred and unsullied by the self-centered will to pleasure." Such a view, however, gives insufficient force to Thomas's defense of sexual pleasure as achieving the mean of virtue even in pleasure so great as to temporarily suspend reason. Yet, because the pleasure which accompanies intercourse should be thought of as purely instrumental to that necessary end which the human species shares with other animals, the more directly visceral and hence animal-like the pleasure is, the more innocently natural it is.

17. See Keiser, "Festive Decorum" 72–73 and n38. As disordered excess, Belshazzar's "mischapen" design contrasts to the magnificence Thomas considers appropriate to a feast celebrating an appropriate occasion, such as the marriage of nobility or the installation of a bishop (2a2ae. 134, 1).

18. Not however, "to pretend to a loveliness one doesn't have, but to hide some ugliness arising from disease or the like." Although Thomas acknowledges women having sexual relations with women as an example of unnatural lust, his androcentric perspective gives no consideration to the possibility that women who adorn themselves may do so to attract other women.

19. Thomas relates this Aristotelian precept to the pleasure of sexual intercourse specifically: "The delight which occurs in the matrimonial act, although it is most intense in quantity, does not exceed the limits fixed by reason before its commencement, although during this delight reason cannot set the limits" (*On the Sentences* 4.31.2.1, reply to objection 3). Hence, "the pleasure experienced in coitus in Paradise would have been still greater than that known by fallen man" (Noonan, *Contraception* 354).

20. In contrast to a literal view of this sexual norm Thomas conceived by analogy with a static world order, in terms which emphasized the givenness of biological imperatives, John Noonan gives a suggestive account of natural law in a modern redefinition. In a "personalist" reconception, natural law "appeals to the authentic choice of man, who from his very being as a person, must fashion a concrete universal image of man, more in the manner of a creator than a conformist. . . . [It possesses] a dynamic functional character because of its active orientation toward the ideal personal community" (*Contraception* 573; Noonan cites M. G. Plattel, "Personal Response and the Natural Law," *Natural Law Forum* 7 [1962] 36–37).

Chapter 5. Revising the Complaint

1. All quotations from the *Roman* are from Dahlberg's translation; both his page numbers and Lecoy's line numbers will be cited.

2. Note that Guillaume de Lorris is still identified by the God of Love as the Lover (187; 10496) even though the God of Love states (187; 10535) Jean's writing of the *Roman* begins when Guillaume's ceases after his last prison speech to Fair Welcoming

(88; 4029—some 6,506 lines earlier than this announcement of the dual authorship of the text). Guillaume is replaced not only as author but eventually also as protagonist; Jean depicts himself (257; 15073) as the Lover and also the Dreamer/Author (258; 15117–20) of the text which narrates in the first person the successful end of the Lover's long quest to enjoy possession of the Rose.

3. For the vexing issues of textual delineation of units and authorial attribution, see David Hult: few medieval readers of the *Roman* make any mention of the authors and those who do focus their praise upon Jean de Meun, who subsumed the poem under his own doctrinal program" (56). Yet there is also a certain amount of evidence "for a different reading of the *Rose,* one that could separate the authorial attributions in the face of an overwhelming cult that had developed around the author-figure of Jean de Meun" (59).

4. See Baird and Kane. For an introduction to this debate on the merits of the *Roman,* known as the *querelle de la Rose,* or simply as "the Quarrel," see Luria 63–67. He prints part of Pierre Col's letter of June 1402 to Christine de Pisan (the heart of the defense) and her response (183–202).

5. This is John Fleming's assessment: "The English alliterative poet who wrote *Cleanness* and other fine pieces of unchallenged orthodoxy makes an overt reference to Jean de Meun and his 'clene Rose' much to the confusion of the poem's editor [Gollancz] who can explain the citation only by suggesting that the poet 'ignored certain aspects of its teaching'" ("Moral Reputation of the *Roman*" 434).

6. Scholars who have engaged with these elements of the *Roman* arrive at such different results that there is no consensus to which we may turn on such questions as whether Reason's views alone are normative, whether the poem in the aggregate is religiously orthodox, whether the poem's multiple ironies cancel each other out, and whether the poem is as cynical, prurient, and dangerous to its readers as Christine de Pisan and Jean Gerson thought it was. I am most indebted to the conflicting analyses of Arden, Badel, Brownlee, Dahlberg, Economou, Fleming, Huot, Luria, Nichols, Spearing, and Wetherbee.

7. The adjective will be retained in discussing loving "par amors," a frequent usage in the *Roman,* whereas in discussing the "play of paramorez" in *Cleanness* (700), the Middle English is retained or translated by the modern English noun *paramours.*

8. To thus celebrate God's agency in the natural force of sexuality is unusual. Peter Dronke provides a fascinating account of a fable in a Florentine manuscript of notes on Martianus Capella, influenced by the thought of William of Conches, where the conviction is revealed that a divine power manifests itself in sexual love. Here "Hymenaeus is both the hymen that is penetrated on the wedding-night and the god of weddings" (105). Moreover, "the God Hymenaeus . . . is both the natural sexual creative force, and the glory of mutual love" (105), sent down by "the Christian God whose Spirit is present in the elemental harmony, in the sexual act, and in the ardour of charity. The love experienced in the human soul *is* divine love, it has been generated by the Christian Hymenaeus. The theophanies of this Spirit are not exclusively 'spiritual': they can be experienced not only through the theological virtue charity, but by couples through their sexual love and joy in procreation—as well as by the scientist contemplating the cosmic harmonies" (106).

9. She claims that the male sexual organs are "noble works," made by her Father;

moreover, having given her the task of naming them, God "who is wise and sure, considers whatever [she has] made well done" (135; 7091–92). Both the words she chose and the things they name are worthy in her eyes as well as the Creator's: "'Testicles' is a good name and I like it, and so, in faith, are 'testes' and 'penis.' I have hardly ever seen any more beautiful. I made the words and I am certain that I never made anything base" (135; 7086–90). This identification of God's good work in making the male sexual organs and Reason's good work in naming them suggests she sees the world exhibiting the prelapsarian harmony of the signifier with the signified. Alienated from that lost paradise, the prudish Lover plays pruriently (albeit unwittingly perhaps) with the double entendre of the "testicles" as not only disgraceful parts of speech but ungraceful parts of the body, objecting that "they are not well thought of in the mouth of a courteous girl" (133; 6900–01). In contrast, Reason optimistically implies the possible restoration of that harmony between word and thing; when women find pleasure in lovemaking, their perception of, and hence their language about, the male organ is reformed. Such misnomers as "purses, harness, things, or prickles, as if they were thorns" are not used by women once they have experienced intercourse as pleasurable: "when they are well joined to them and feel them, they do not consider them piercing; then they name them as they are accustomed to do" (136; 7111–16).

10. Nature's most generous appraisal of desire is nevertheless ambivalent at best: "I bring no charge of dishonourable conduct against the basic nature of Desire, if it restrains itself with the bridle of moderation, . . . but only if its tiny flame turns into a conflagration, if its little fountain grows into a torrent" (154–55).

11. Although Reason laments that "everyone who gives himself over to the work of love turns only to Delight" (98; 4527–28), such folly is not inevitable for men and women who take their fair share of pleasure while earnestly intending the reproductive consequences of their activity. Reason's reliability on this point is debatable. Fleming sees her as explicitly addressing the moral presuppositions undergirding Christian teaching, namely, the connection between sexual love and procreation, and the dangers of pleasure seeking. Her authorization of pleasure in the pursuit of offspring seems to him to fit within the Augustinian mainstream of moral theology. Others, like Thomas Hill, argue that Reason's discourse lacks the theological awareness of the Fall, and so her understanding of sexual ethics is deficient; for example, she does not acquaint the lover with marriage or celibacy as the two reasonable alternatives for defining his sexual nature. See Fleming's *Reason and the Lover* and Hill's review of it.

12. The Socrates Reason portrays as intended to represent the desirable life exemplifies neither friendship nor universal human love. His devotion to Reason herself, while referred to in terms that suggest a love affair, seems entirely abstract. Hence the connection between Socrates' transcendence of all emotion and the "right mean" Reason earlier told the Lover "one must find" (116; 5730) is not clarified by the one thousand lines on Fortune which develop her idea about the philosopher's excellence as a lover of Wisdom. For a comparison to *Cleanness*'s admonition to take Christ as the beloved exemplar, see chap. 7 n5.

13. The two-seed theory and its relation to the promotion of female pleasure (briefly described by Brundage 450n174) is dealt with thoroughly in Cadden's analysis of sex differences in the medical theories of pleasure. The relation of the female seed to

reproduction was sufficiently obscure that women's arousal and orgasm was not scrutinized or promoted as man's sexual satisfaction was. Cadden observes that medieval exchanges and disagreements concerning female seed "do not represent a debate between feminists and misogynists" (122).

14. Reason may well be suggesting that men who pursue homosexual pleasures are even more degraded than the Lover who, though foolishly lacking any interest in progeny, nevertheless more nearly conforms to Nature's heterosexual norm. Recalling that Jean's contemporary Thomas Aquinas noted that common parlance in the late thirteenth century equated "the" sin against nature with sexual relations between men, we might assume that the category of offenses Reason reserved for Genius's condemnation is distinguished from the Lover's more commonplace wrongdoing precisely because in these exceptional cases, there is not only an absence of procreative intention but no possibility at all of procreative outcome.

15. See chap. 6 for a passage from Guillaume de Lorris's portion of the *Roman* that illustrates the connections between effeminacy and men suspected of homosexual deviation from natural practice.

16. For ambiguity of the meaning of *sodomite* see chap. 2 n8.

17. For an account of Genius's discourse as "a fine example of a *sermon joyeux*," a genre which "inverts the spirit of medieval orthodoxy, but neither its structure nor content," see Patterson, "'For the Wyves love of Bathe'" 674 n34.

18. In the *Complaint*, Nature laments: "Man alone turns with scorn from the modulated strains of my cithern and runs deranged to the notes of mad Orpheus's lyre. For the human race ... adopts a highly irregular (grammatical) change when it inverts the rules of Venus by introducing barbarisms in its arrangement of genders" (Sheridan 133). Dahlberg, commenting on 19651 of the *Roman,* notes the influence of the "Boethian image of Orpheus as one who desires to turn his thought to the clarity of the Sovereign Good but instead fixes his eyes on the gulf of hell 'that is, who turns his thought toward earthly things' and loses all the celestial good that he had" (418). Clearly Genius has another point in mind, as he makes Orpheus responsible for those who follow a life of celibacy.

19. Ironically, later in his sermon Genius laments the injury done when men are castrated, depriving them not only of the power of engendering and of heterosexual attachments to wife or sweetheart but of their masculine boldness. Yet his own mandate to castrate all celibate males would render them eunuchs and hence dangerously effeminate, "perverse and malicious cowards because they have the ways of women" (329; 20029–30).

Chapter 6. Privileging the Feminine

1. *Make* means "partner, mate" because the word implies considerable, if not complete, equality, as is evident from line 248, which uses the word for a pun, common in lyrics, praising the Virgin Mary as *makeless,* meaning both "without a mate," i.e., unmarried and virginal *and* "without an equal," i.e., peerless.

2. For Cocks, the primary ground of male power in sexual relation changes in modernity from the reproductive and familial alliance to the desirous body. I see the late medieval redefinition of masculinity as a predecessor to this shift in the symbolic locus of male

dominance away from the structure of patriarchal family relations; the medieval shift—like the modern one—did not alter the institutional power base which defines sexual difference hierarchically to the disadvantage of women's status in society.

A shift in gender symbolics is evident in the poet's feminized version of aristocratic male sensibility he calls *clene*, but to see this shift as ethically significant is not to claim that he envisions an ethos of sexual equality as part of heaven's order.

3. Jaeger notes that this ethical-social sensibility does not originate in Christian life as its "native context" but is a classical model transmitted through Ambrose's use of Cicero's ethics (15). Jaeger acknowledges that the aristocratic ethos is not simply European, and that its exact beginnings in earlier medieval Europe are impossible to specify, but he maintains that it was evident in Germany in the late eleventh century (141) where it spread through imperially appointed bishops to local clergy, and through cathedral schools as well in their role of preparing men for state service (259). For men of lesser nobility, courtly ideals of masculinity made themselves felt later, most visibly in the fictional chivalric knight of courtly romance, a character and a genre invented by poet-clerics who amalgamated "ideals . . . of court clergy with those of the warrior class" (266).

4. What I am pointing to here as feminine "otherness" is the aesthetic dimension that is associated with women's culture and offers alternative criteria for male excellence that revise the epic ideals of heroism. On the different element of sexual mystery in the otherness of the feminine, see Jean-Charles Huchet's comment on woman in romance as the "metaphor of alterity" (Crane 171) and Freud's statement that masculine fear of feminine sexuality as based on "the fact that woman is different from man, for ever incomprehensible and mysterious, strange and therefore apparently hostile" (Crane 187). The sexually mysterious dimension of the feminine is not present in *Cleanness* for this mysterious element depends upon a romance plot of adventure and courtship, both missing from the poem. While Christ is portrayed analogous to the courtly lady, in that passage the eroticized mystery of feminine otherness is downplayed in favor of lady-like displays of courtly decorum.

5. Hanning focuses, by attention to the decorative aesthetic embodied in these and other similar details, on the poem's "resistance to straightforward positive or negative evaluation" (9) of its courtly elements. "Whether this Arthurian modification of traditional British values constitutes the triumph or failure of civilization is a question the text prompts us to ask but prevents us from answering" (12). For Stephen Knight, the ethos at Camelot is discredited by juxtaposition to that of Bercilak's castle with its "vigor and natural activities . . . hard hunting, true hospitality, and clear-eyed non-traditional assessments" (115–16). Yet the architectural elegance of that castle, and the interest its inhabitants express in Gawain's reputation as Camelot's most courteous representative, makes Bercilak's court aesthetically equivalent to Arthur's. The festive decorum of the holiday season in the provincial setting does not suffer by comparison to Camelot.

6. "At that time effeminates set the fashion in many parts of the world: foul catamites, doomed to eternal fire, unrestrainedly pursued their revels and shamelessly gave themselves up to the filth of sodomy. They rejected the traditions of honest men, ridiculed the counsel of priests, and persisted in their barbarous way of life and style of dress. They parted their hair from the crown of the head to the forehead, grew long and luxurious

locks like women, and loved to deck themselves in long, over-tight shirts and tunics" (Orderic, vol.4 188–89).

7. Sodomy was frequently understood to be a relationship between one active and one passive partner, often with an adult in the former and a boy in the latter role, but in John of Salisbury's pejorative construction, the same-sex relationship seems fluid in terms of age.

8. Homoerotic affection and even covert homosexual relations seem to have been widely tolerated in the High Middle Ages among men living in an all-male society—as for instance, in the domestic intimacy of the medieval monastery or the intensely communal world of military comradeship. (Regarding the latter, Georges Duby implies that amorous exchanges united the *juvenes*, younger sons excluded from inheritance who sought their fortunes together in roving bands of fellow knights. See note 11 below and Crane 42). These passionate friendships and flirtations between males doubtless contributed to the power dynamics and ritualized forms of courtly dalliance between men and women. However, when such homoerotic bonding was carried on openly in social settings where heterosexual courtship was becoming a norm for establishing masculine identity, amorous exchanges between men might be perceived as imitations of male-female couples, with one of the two males taking on the role that twelfth-century romances and lyrics were scripting for women of the elite class. For a male to play a female part on the social stage of courtly life seems to have been singularly objectionable, for it elicits at least as much polemic intensity as the inversion of gender associated with the man who allowed himself to be rendered effeminate by submitting to anal penetration. While greed and ambition might have been regretted but tolerated in homoerotic relations between young men and their social superiors in an all-male society, when these relationships are staged in the courtly milieu, the display of such mercenary motives might unmask the ostensible humility and devotion of a knight excluded from inheritance who courts a lady of superior financial and social status. Males prostituting themselves to males seem to be particularly outrageous to the twelfth-century critics. Alain's Nature complains of unnatural lust fueled by greed when the male who fails to conform to her heterosexual norm exposes himself "for a professional male prostitute" (131); she indicts the young men who "clothed . . . in grace and beauty, intoxicated with thirst for money, converted Venus's hammers to the functions of anvils" (136). In the romance *Eneas,* contemporary with Alain's *Complaint,* Lavine bitterly resents what she believes is Eneas's rejection of her love in preference for the seductive appearance of young men in "hose breeches and tightly tied thongs;" these male whores are "at his service, and their breeches often lowered: thus they earn their wages" (9147–64, Yunck ed. 238).

9. See Crane 187.

10. George Duby speculates that there was between the twelfth-century knight William Marshal and his close friends, besides the camaraderie of combat, a more explicitly homoerotic attachment, discernible "if, reading between the lines, we suspect that there is also involved, scrupulously muffled, that love which men bear each other in the knightly companies" (*William Marshal* 142–43). Commenting on how few are the references to feminine figures in William's biography, Duby notes that the "word love, throughout the entire *chanson,* never intervenes except between men" (48). Such an emphasis on the "love of men among themselves" is not surprising, he claims, for "we are beginning

to discover that love *à la courtoise*, the love celebrated, after the troubadors, by the *trouvères*, the love that the knights devoted to the chosen lady, may have masked the essential — or rather, projected into the realm of sport the inverted image of the essential: amorous exchanges between warriors" (*William Marshal* 47).

11. Why the innovative ethos diffused among knights and barons is a complex question, as Jaeger concedes, and lies beyond the scope of this study as well as of his. But it seems likely that the courtly ideals were indeed appealing to the imaginations not only of aristocratic readers, but of those who wrote for that audience. Jaeger speculates that the poet-clerics whose secular narratives fostered new chivalric standards of male excellence not only felt responsible to create an "educational model for knights and laymen to imitate," but were also "indulging in their own wish-dreams of a form of life that combines the freedom, heroism, and amorous license of the knight with the civilized ideals of the courtly cleric" (267).

12. Even in the most optimistic romances, however, the idealized image of woman and the possibilities of the hero's and heroine's enduring happiness in marriage are offset by a view of woman's historical status that problematizes gender relationships and sexual fulfillment in the heterosexual mystique. Analyzing the irreconcilability of the roles of the Lady and woman in the troubador lyric, Jane Burns argues that beneath the disguise of love service lies a rhetoric of coercion: "Service is but a thinly veiled form of seduction leading ultimately to subjugation" of the beloved by her ostensibly submissive lover. (266).

13. Against the often stressed view of man in romance as the "essential, transhistorical individual," Crane claims "identity in romance partakes of the collectivity" (34). Qualifying Foucault's observation "that self-surveillance follows from institutional regulation," she argues that "resistance to social forces gives way to self-regulation not as a concession to power . . . , but as an enlightened recognition of the interdependence of subject and society" (33, 34).

14. Recalling the cleric-lover in Andreas's *De Amore* chafing at the restraints on his role, Jaeger speculates on the envy the clerics must have felt, recognizing that despite their "superiority . . . of learning and manners . . . their form of life denied to them the heroism of the knight's," as well as his "amorous license" (226–67).

15. Sexual liaisons across class boundaries are not ruled out by Andreas; females of the *vileyn* class, while incapable of verbal artifice and other erotic refinements, can nevertheless yield the different but apparently not degrading satisfaction of rape, which is what Andreas advises in case a man of respectable birth should be attracted to a peasant girl. In short, he should not attempt to communicate his desires in ways only a lady of his own class could understand (Benson, "Courtly Love" 243–44).

16. Generally speaking, gender ideology in romance seems to me to authorize the inclusion of feminine traits as a positive expansion of the knight's humanity, without the stigma of effeminacy attached by clerical discourse to traits associated with women. Precisely what these traits are, and the degree to which male and female divisions in human traits are generally heightened, blurred, or erased by the male romance writer's tendency to project aspects of an idealized masculine self-image onto the lady of romance are questions much debated in contemporary analysis of medieval gender symbolics. Drawing on Frederic Goldin, Jane Burns argues that the "troubador's Lady" is "a travesty

of male identity used mainly to confirm the lover's worth as a courtly man," and that the traits the poet typically admires in the lady are male-identified — "a set of idealized public virtues which mark one as noble and courtly" (258–59). These ideals do not so much elevate feminine traits as they deny the otherness of female sexuality. Femininity in this literary dynamic is in fact a male poet-lover's ideal of the man he "wants to become" but "never can be" (Goldin, *The Mirror of Narcissus in the Courtly Love Lyric* 74, quoted in Burns 259). Elaine Hansen argues that in Chaucer's works, masculine dominance is so endangered by the social inferiority of the feminine position the male must occupy in courtship that the successful courtier-knight lover must be unfaithful to the terms on which he enters the heterosexual union. To demonstrate his manhood, he must reestablish the difference and power difference between male and female and so must not gratify for very long the heroine's unconscious desire to bond with her own sex. The similarity to women he displays in courtship but ultimately disowns includes such feminized traits as "irrationality, self sacrifice, submission, service . . . passivity, coyness, vulnerability, dependence, and even looks" (61). (Hansen's problematizing of heterosexual union as "a necessary yet perilous part of . . . homosocial bonds among men" draws on Eve Sedgwick). Jill Mann denies that taking on women's traits poses in Chaucer's work any fundamental threat to masculinity, arguing on the contrary that woman's experience becomes for this poet "the exemplar for male heroism" and that he integrates "activity and passivity into a fully human ideal that erases male/female role-divisions" (*Geoffrey Chaucer* 182, 185). Susan Crane persuasively asserts, however, that the "fully human ideal" Mann sees as transcending gender distinctions is in fact (in Chaucer as in romance generally) "finally masculine" since the "complications of masculine behavior that femininity figures contribute to enlarging and universalizing rather than feminizing the masculine experience" (21).

17. See Dante's *Inferno,* where the sodomites include a range of characters, some of them (the soldiers in Canto XVI) decidedly more masculine in appearance and conduct than others (the clerks in Canto XVI).

18. Oxford University as a whole is accused of sodomy in the prologue to the later version of the Wyclif Bible (1395–96): "Loke now wher Oxunford is in thre orrible synnes . . . the ij. [second] orrible synne is sodomye and strong mayntenaunce thereof, as it is knowen to many persones of the reume, and at the laste parlement. Alas! dyuynys, that schulden passe othere men in clennesse and hoolynesse, as aungels of heuene passen freel men in vertues, ben moost sclaundrid of this cursid synne aʒens kynde" (51). The sin of sodomy (allowed despite the publicity given to it in the Articles posted at Westminster during the last parliament) seems here to be attributed specifically to "cyuylians and canonistris" who once took little interest in resting in bed but now are said to be "ful of pride and nyce aray, enuye, and coueitise, with leccherie, glotonie, and ydilnesse" (51). Thus the passage links attention to style ("nyce aray") and sins of the flesh, especially sodomy.

19. My discussion of the Pardoner, although indebted to McAlpine's points about effeminacy, does not assume that *homosexual* is the best gloss for the terms *geldyng* and *mare* (11–12) since this may imply a modern essentialist notion of sexuality that clarifies what Chaucer leaves ambiguous in the prologue's description. Steven Kruger aptly says that the Pardoner "is consistently associated with the physical, and with a particularly

feminized physicality; his concern with fashion, his high voice, his long smooth, yellow hair, his beardlessness—all lead to the conclusion that he is at least devoid of the properly masculine ('a geldyng') and perhaps [is] fully feminine ('a mare,' I. 691)" (132). He concludes, "Chaucer wants us to see, as part of the Pardoner's sexual 'queerness,' the possibility of homosexuality" (125). In the context of Alain's *Complaint*, Kruger speaks of the Pardoner as "this feminized man, deeply involved in body and grotesquely distorting the proper uses of language," and hence as dramatizing "a fear of that loss of meaningful signification so often affiliated, in the Middle Ages, with heterosexual fecundity" (135). Two other recent essays on the Pardoner have similar relevance to reading *Cleanness* as part of a literary tradition of nature as heterosexual norm. Gregory Gross convincingly glosses the Pardoner's claim to be "a ful vicious man" (VI. 459) as an allusion to Alain's *Complaint,* and both he and Calabrese illuminate Chaucer's uses of Jean de Meun in constructing the Pardoner's sexuality.

20. The poet's vision of this idyllic situation before the Deluge resembles the legendary stories Jews told of the conditions of life the antediluvians enjoyed, knowing "neither toil nor care," but unlike *Cleanness,* the Jewish narrative blames the vices of that generation on "their carefree life that gave them space and leisure for their infamies" (Ginzberg 70–71).

21. Translating "Noah was a righteous man, blameless in his generation; Noah walked with God" (Genesis 6:9), the poet alludes also to the frequent biblical injunction that a man should walk humbly with God. The phrasing "ay glydande wyth his God" is a striking instance of the poet's recasting of the relationship between man and God into a courtly mode valorizing a homosocial bond where relations between superior and inferior are seen as effortlessly harmonious.

22. Cf. Spearing, *Gawain Poet* 61–62, cited by McAlpine. Jonathan Glenn also quotes from Spearing's reading of the description ("the passage . . . makes us understand why the Sodomites found them so attractive") in order to underscore the contrast between these "perverted creatures' inability to see accurately" and Lot's understanding that the young men's beauty is angelic (86, 91).

23. By Lot's approach to the Sodomites as his friends and social equals, the poet appeals to his implied audience's standards of decorum. Lot's poise in addressing the coarse aggressors, although it seems facetious in the modern sense of insincere, may also reflect the poet's appreciation of the courtly ideal of *facetia,* the polite use of irony and wit, and even a biting eloquence, by social superiors in order to skewer their opponents tactfully (Jaeger 146, 161–65).

24. This sense of the protagonist's lonely virtue is reinforced in the angels' later explanation of why his family is to be spared from God's vengeance against the city: "For þou art oddely þyn one out of þis fylþe" (For you are uniquely your self apart from this filth 923). See Lynn Staley Johnson for an opposing reading, likening Lot, who is blinded by riches and luxury, to the Sodomites who are blinded by lust (122).

25. Dynes offers a clarifying distinction between the "subjective sense of belonging to a particular group, set apart from the rest of society" and "the objective pattern of same-sex networking." Along with Warren Johannson, Dynes presents in this article the "earliest unambiguous proof . . . of such a phenomenon in Europe"—an 1192 chronicler's account of a "kind of homosexual networking possessing affinities with the marginalized,

even criminal underworld" of London, "rather than with intellectual or artistic circles" (5). This occurs during the reign of Richard Coeur de Lion, who was linked homoerotically, before he became king, with King Philip Augustus of France (5). The evidence presented is four terms "with a certain or at least probably homosexual reference" (7) in a description of "some eighteen types of denizens" of the "London underworld" (6). Of these four terms, two of them associate effeminacy with male youths, who are, by implication, hustlers: *glabriones* ("smooth cheeked, pretty, effeminate boy[s]") and *molles* ("effeminates," from I Corinthians 6:9).

26. See also Randolph Trumbach's argument that "by the early eighteenth century, ... an adult effeminate male was likely to be taken to be an exclusive sodomite" or, in the language of his day, "a *molly*, and later as a *queen*" (134).

27. "Homosexuality and heterosexuality, as we currently understand them, are modern, Western, bourgeois productions. Nothing resembling them can be found in classical antiquity. A certain identification of the self with the sexual self began in late antiquity; it was strengthened by the Christian confessional. Only in the high middle ages did certain kinds of sexual acts start to get identified with certain specifically sexual types of person: a 'sodomite' begins to name not merely the person who commits an act of sodomy but one distinguished by a certain type of specifically sexual subjectivity which inclines such a person to commit such acts; nonetheless, sodomy remains a sinful act which any person, given sufficient temptation, may be induced to commit" (Halperin, *One Hundred Years* 8). Since the *Cleanness*-poet is so concerned with the innermost thoughts and sensibilities of his characters (including God), the capacity for fitting or filthy responses is necessarily constructed as a subjectivity that is as intuitive as it is cognitive or voluntary. However, the poet's characterization of the Sodomites stresses their deliberate misreading of God's meaning in nature and their willful assertion of their rights to disseminate to anyone they find attractive their discovery of a superior form of pleasure in making love to men like themselves.

28. The phrase is Crane's, when she speaks of heterosexuality glorified in *Eneas* and similar romances as a "culturally sanctioned and elaborated source of identity," constructed in contrast to "sodomy's illicit irregularity" (45). While she sees competition, she does not see any evidence in romance for a social construction of sodomy as an alternative orientation which opposes the heterosexual identity of romance knights. Masculine intimacy and homoeroticism threaten the romance plot of adventure and courtship, but they are not constructed as its "exclusive opposite" threat (41). In *Cleanness*, in contrast, I see same-sex coupling being constructed by the poet as a habit that does indeed challenge the very existence of heterosexual *crafte*. God attacks male homosexual pairing as if it could erase the lineaments of the play of heterosexual *paramorez* he has inscribed as his *kynde crafte*, and the poet extends that impression by his subsequent characterization of the Sodomites' refusal of Lot's offer. In *Cleanness*, the sense of an oppositional identity based on homosexual desire and activity is clearer than in the passage from *Eneas* quoted in note 8 of this chapter where Lavine perceives a group identity among the young boys who all dress similarly to attract Eneas's sexual interest and who all engage in homosexual relations with him in exchange for money.

29. Stephen Spector traces a similar enemy formation psychology at work in the late medieval mystery plays' depictions of Jews as representatives of precisely those evils

"most threatening to the goals of the plays" ("Anti-Semitism" 330) and in Chaucer's *Prioress's Tale:* "By creating the Prioress and matching her so precisely with the tale, Chaucer introduced a detailed self-referentiality between teller and tale. In consequence, the Jews in the tale are not generalized bogeymen, as they may appear to be in the analogues, or in the tale considered in isolation" ("Empathy and Enmity" 222).

30. In the biblical narrative, as Robert Alter notes, "Lot clearly imagines he is offering the rapists a special treat in proclaiming [the girls'] virginity" (151). Their virginity is construed by the poet's expansion of the Vulgate as a marker of this superiority, suggesting their aptness for giving males sexual pleasure rather than their unfamiliarity with it. That both girls are betrothed is not revealed until line 934. This makes Lot (as an accomplice in the rape of his daughters) guilty both of a crime against himself, as their father, but also against their prospective husbands. As the story unfolds in the Vulgate, an "implicit judgment against Lot is then confirmed in the incest at the end of the chapter" (Alter 152) when the daughters trick their father into deflowering them, an episode of heterosexual but taboo copulation the poet's exemplum logically excludes.

31. Janet Halley's exploration of the dynamics of production and reception of Donne's love poems in his homosocial context illuminates the connection between God's lyrical talking about love to Abraham and Lot's eloquent recommendation of heterosexual pleasure. "Textual Intercourse" shows how Eve Sedgwick's concepts of nineteenth-century homosocial relations between men can apply to an earlier century; these bonds exist on a continuum with explicitly homosexual relations but must deny the permeability of the boundary that distinguishes these forms of male bonding. Using the theories of Luce Irigaray and Gayle Rubin, Sedgwick explains how male power relations transverse female bodies. In *Cleanness* the ostensible desirability of Lot's daughters is the territory upon which a conflict over the primacy of homosexual and heterosexual pleasure is played out (25–26).

Chapter 7. Homosocial Bondings with God and Christ

1. See Anderson's translation, as opposed to that of Andrew and Waldron who interpret *þewes* as the virtues God had established as norms for human beings.

2. The comparison of a person's beauty to a mirror is current in the Latin poetry of Chretien's day; the idea that the Beloved's beauty is made by God and Nature to be used this way is adapted by Chretien from Alain's *Anticlaudianus,* where Nature proposes to create a perfect man so that the Virtues can observe in him, as in a mirror, what their qualities should be (Luttrell 13–14). See *Pearl* 745–54.

3. "And if a man wise in the ways of love speaks to a foolish girl . . . let him make his manners like hers; otherwise he would be shamed" (145–46; 7719–20, 7725–26). Not only does the Friend's counsel rob the Rose's feminine standards of conduct of any ethical value, but "foolish girl" that she is, she is portrayed as scorning whatever manly virtues her suitors would display, behaving like the she-wolf who "always takes the worst of the wolves" (146; 7736).

4. After detailed instructions in self-serving subservience, the Friend concludes: "In short, on any occasion, do whatever you think may please him [i.e., Fair Welcoming]. If you do so, never fear, for you will never be repulsed. In this way, you will come to your

goal just as I propose it" (146; 7760–79, 7783–94). This devious strategy Jean adapts from Ovid, *Ars Amatoria;* for citations, see Dahlberg's note to *Roman* 7307–94.

5. Reason's offer of herself as divine mistress to the Lover in place of the Rose in Jean's *Roman* will similarly illuminate, by comparison but even more by contrast, the poet's analogy from earthly to heavenly love. Read in this context, the depiction of Christ as the object of the Christian's desire raises the question of whether, like Reason's advice to the Lover, the *Cleanness*-poet counsels his readers to supersede the physical delight of earthly eros with the spiritual joy conferred by a higher love.

First, let us pay attention to the transcendental dimension of Reason evoked when she offers herself to the Lover as both mirror and model for him to gaze upon. Like Christ portrayed as the shining exemplar of God's courtesy and craftsmanship, Reason may be seen here as the radiant mirror of divine Wisdom, immanent as creative and ordering power in human nature and the entire creation. Inviting the Lover's intimate gaze, Reason makes her bright countenance a source of self-knowledge: "Look at my form and at yourself in my clear face. No girl of such descent ever had such power of loving as have I, for I have leave of my father to take a friend and be loved" (117; 5783–93). In spite of her offer of herself to the Lover as more desirable than the Rose, Reason as a mirror is not developed by Jean in terms of the feminine object of desire. Rather, she reinforces the importance to the Lover's true nature of his masculine rationality, exemplified by Socrates whose heroic detachment from all the transitory pleasures and pains of earthly life the Lover must imitate in order to stand up to Fortune and the God of Love as a man should (132; 6853–64 and 117; 5817–23, 5830–33). While according to Fleming, Reason is evidence that the "image of God is not obliterated inalienably," Jean's theopoetic rendering of her as the "continuity between creature and Creator" employs the classical and Christian mind-body dualism (*Reason and the Lover* 32–33). Fleming sees Jean alluding to Augustine's choice of the higher love offered to him by *Continentia* who offers herself as a replacement of his old friends; he is enabled to follow Paul's counsel to make no provisions for the flesh but to put on Christ Jesus. This resembles the dualism between bodily appetite and spiritual love in the *Roman,* for God's image within humanity is, from Reason's perspective, a purely mental capacity for rational contemplation, which at best renders a man utterly insensible to the joys and sorrows of embodied human existence.

6. Critics looking at the poem through the lenses of exegetical commentaries see the analogy from earthly courtship to the imitation of Christ as conforming to a familiar topos of Christian contemplative writing, where spiritual marriage between the soul and God is foreshadowed in earthly nuptials, a tradition that depends upon allegorizations of the Song of Songs (see Morse, *Pattern of Judgment* 173–74, citing Origen, *Commentaries in Cantica Canticorum* as a gloss for the poet's use of this analogy). While this approach may recognize the poem as validating earthly love by analogy to divine love, the dualistic anthropology of body subordinated to soul that pervades Christian orthodox marital ethics reduces the earthly delights of sexual intercourse to at best "an imitation and shadow of the divine marriage" (174). Morse interprets God's speech on love (697–712) as teaching that: "Natural human marriage is the way back to paradise under natural law, or to be more precise, that it offers a way, under the law of nature, to approach paradise. Human marriage is the foundation for the concept of divine marriage between Christ and man, the marriage that ends in paradise regained, the celestial wedding feast, and the *visio dei*" (166). The value of earthly love at its best in the age of nature is thus, by implication,

superseded in the age of grace by the Christian's nuptials with Christ as husband; the sexual consummation celebrated in God's speech is not seen by Morse as intrinsically valuable but instead as praised by the poet simply in order to reveal later that the *visio dei* is more blissful than any earthly joy. "The *Cleanness*-poet implies the spiritual consummation is more playful, more delightful, more joyful than its nearest equivalent in physical, bodily experience, the consummation of sexual marriage. The sexual sinner ought to give up his transient pleasure for much greater spiritual reward" (202). The last sentence carries with it the implication that not only is earthly pleasure inferior to heavenly but is somewhat sinful because transient.

7. Even the assertion that God moderates his anger with mercy is problematic for Thomas; since God is passionless, he always "judges with tranquility" (2a2I3. 154, 12). See chap. 4 n13.

8. For God in the warrior role, see Moses' song in Deuteronomy 32; there God speaks against the idolatrous: "'See now that I, even I, am he, and there is no god beside me.... As I live for ever, if I whet my glittering sword, and my hand takes hold on judgment, I will take vengeance on my adversaries, and will requite those who hate me. I will make my arrows drunk with blood, and my sword shall devour flesh—with the blood of the slain and the captives, from the long-haired heads of the enemy'" Deut. 32:39–42.

9. Where Lot is visited by two angels, Abraham receives God in the form of three men, although the poet alternates between singular and plural forms, as does the biblical narrative: "Þenne watz he war on þe waye of wlonk Wyȝez þrynne; / If þay wer farande and fre and fayre to beholde / Hit is eþe to leue by þe last ende" (Then he was aware on the way of three splendid men; / If they were handsome and noble and fair to behold, / It is easy to believe, given the final outcome 606–8).

10. This embodied quality of divine hostility is evident in God's fiery breath, breathing down the back of anyone who would flee his fierce hatred; the flames that destroy Sodom are imagined by Lot as emanating from this fierce respiration. Not yet aware that the angels' prophecy of Sodom's imminent destruction carries with it a guarantee of his own safety, Lot asks: "If I me fele vpon fote þat I fle moȝt, / Hov schulde I huyde me fro hym þat hatz his hate kynned / In þe brath of his breth þat brennez alle þinkez" (If I were to conceal myself as far as I could flee on foot / How should I hide myself from him who has engendered his hatred / In the ferocity of his breath, which burns all things 914–16)?

11. Although the poet enhances the ritualistic elements in the narrative of the Flood's ending and thus creates a strong image of renewal, he in fact omits the Vulgate's rainbow. Perhaps this is because the bow foreshadowed the cross by typological association emphasized in the mystery plays' dramatization of the Flood narrative. As we shall see, the poet omits the Crucifixion when he celebrates in the Incarnation a restoration of nature that echoes the renewal of the created beauty of the earth after the Flood.

12. Specifically with regard to this dynamic between sacred and profane, Beckwith explains how late medieval mystery plays and Franciscan texts that made such a fetish of Christ's torn and bleeding body involve simultaneous strategies of profanation and sacralization that reconfigure the division between the sacred and the profane. She distinguishes the piety that was nurtured by crucifixion images, which displays interpenetration of the sacred by the profane, from the ritualized images, which were manipulated by the clergy to monitor and strengthen the division between sacred and profane realms.

Beckwith argues that the borders and boundaries of Christ's body, rather than a unitary and unifying image of the host, become the object of obsessive interest in crucifixion piety. The urgency with which so many late medieval writers and readers were exploring the wounds and the blood of Christ has to do with the fluidity of economic and political structures and the need for symbolic redefinitions of the secular self and society. These devotional practices by the laity enabled Christians, drawing on an incarnational aesthetic created by over two centuries of meditation on God sharing human flesh, to create a positive reciprocity between two apparently distinct realms of being.

13. Daniel applies the same imagery of a pollution which froths like yeast to Belshazzar's vices as the narrator uses in his invective against the vices of the Sodomite men. Spearing notes these passages and aptly observes that the antithesis of the ideal of a seamless and perfect enclosure God prizes is like a "nauseatingly uncontrollable expansion of a substance that resists and attacks enclosures, overwhelms and obscures boundaries" (148).

14. Expanding the Vulgate's brief account of how animals and people were relocated in their earthly habitats, the poet creates an enhanced and lovingly detailed image of social cohesion. Just as he concretely named different animals who fled the Flood and traced their various searches for safety, here in ten leisurely lines he displays thirteen kinds of wild creatures returning to their homes in poetically ritualized procession (531–40). In contrast to the hopelessness and confusion evoked earlier, now each beast goes where he likes best, thus concluding the confusion of the Flood with an image of the animal kingdom as an orderly part of a benevolent nature. Wisely separated by their maker into different domains, the wild creatures in *Cleanness* are not divided from each other through enmity any more than they are put in dread of humans.

15. Davenport notes that although "in God's own acts there is 'malys mercyles,'" so that "the distinction between man and God becomes a distinction between weakness and strength, rather than between evil and good," nevertheless God "learns, softens, forgives, recognizing that the descendants of the man he has preserved will repeat the sins of the men he has destroyed" (58).

16. Cf. chap. 4 n10.

17. In a fourteenth-century meditation written by an aristocratic layman (a chamber knight of both Edward III and Richard II) occurs an image of the Nativity that contrasts significantly with the courtliness of *Cleanness*. John Clanvowe, in *Two Ways*, stresses that Christ was born "in þe cooldeste of þe wynter, and in a poore logge and a coolde" with nothing to keep him warm except a "fewe poore clooþis" and the bodily heat of the ox and ass between whom he had to lie (724–28). In this poor and meek entrance into this world, Christ gives us "ensaumple of meeknesse and of wilful poverte" (720ff). This contrast is all the more striking because it occurs in a devotional treatise that, like *Cleanness,* affirms God's courtesy and is ethically generous toward physical satisfactions of earthly life. Thus, Clanvowe espouses a middle way between "glotonye" and "over muchel abstinence" (304–5), claiming that "God of his greete curteisye wole þat we leete oure flesh have al þat hym nedeth skilfulliche and þat he ordeyneþ for us ynouȝ booþe mete and drynke and clooþing. And he wole þat we taaken so þerof in swyche mesure as best is for vs" (350–54). Yet this nobleman's representation of the Nativity does not consist, as the poet's does, in marveling at how joyfully God unites himself with this flesh toward which he expresses such courtesy, surrounding the mother and infant with all that is needful—which, given the royal birth taking place, means that "all that is needful"

comprises not only the bare necessities of shelter and warmth, but perfume of roses, harmony of heavenly musicians, and "alle hende þat honestly moȝt an hert glade" (And all gracious things that could with dignity gladden a heart 1083).

18. See Anderson's gloss on 1076 *schroude-hous:* "vestry, sacristy," comparing Old English *scrudelhus*.

19. A noble lady would give birth amid a host of friends and acquaintances, and for such occasions the sacred and secular objects over which she had charge could be put on display to enhance the lustre of the family (Duby, *Revelations of the Medieval World* 248). See Christine de Pisan's indignant account of the upward mobility of merchant wives, one of whom arranged her lying-in to take place on a scale fit for a princely household, suggesting a public display in a bedroom, similar to the "blysful . . . bour" (1075) prepared for Mary's birthing of her royal babe: "Not long ago she had a lying-in before the birth of her child. . . . In this chamber was a large, highly ornamented dresser covered with golden dishes. The bed was large and handsome and hung with exquisite curtains. . . . On top of this bedspread of tissue of gold was another large covering of linen as fine as silk, all of one piece and without a seam (made by a method only recently invented) and very expensive. . . . It was so wide and long that it covered all sides of this large, elaborate bed and extended beyond the edge of the bedspread, which trailed on the floor on all sides. In this bed lay the woman who was going to give birth, dressed in crimson silk cloth and propped up on big pillows of the same silk with big pearl buttons, adorned like a young lady. And God knows what money was wasted on amusements, bathing and various social gatherings, according to the customs in Paris for women in childbed (some more than others), at this lying-in" (154)! In an earlier medieval royal prototype of such households, the wife of the king would have supervised the liturgical objects used and vestments worn by the resident clerics. Magnificent artifacts reflected the glory of the heavenly sovereign, but they also were expensive extensions of the dignity of the prince and his family (Duby, *Revelations of the Medieval World* 15, 60, 187–88). Such *objets de luxe* could be most safely stored in the privacy of the bedchamber. Thus the description of Mary giving birth in so "blysful a bour" (1075) might remind an aristocratic listener of a handsomely decorated chamber's many accessories, including not only the bed and its associated intimate items of comfort but the valuable household objects that could be stored in the sideboards that surrounded the bed and put on display when a show of wealth was called for.

20. For incarnating his *clannesse*, God's vehicle is a woman. He connects the heavenly realm to Mary's flesh and in doing so brings himself to a birth that erases aspects of humanity's fallenness. The poet stresses Christ's mother's miraculous freedom from the sickness, groaning, and smells that are normally a repellent part of the labor of childbirth, the curse God laid upon a guilty Eve and all women after her. Although doctrinally and poetically conventional with respect to Mary's joy, the poet's imagery here emphasizes not the immaculate conception of the Virgin which exempted her from the effects of the Fall, but the craft God displays in becoming flesh. He accomplishes his entry and separation from the Virgin's body with no violence to her, no profanation to him. Each aspect of birthing that could mar the integrity of either the sacred or the mundane is sanctified by the ease and cleanliness with which God makes himself into an infant who can be conceived in and born from a Virgin's womb.

21. "The healing touch of Kings had by the thirteenth century become a self

perpetuating miracle, at once drawing on the enchanted atmosphere of kingship and reinforcing it," according to Carrolly Erickson (132).

22. The manuscript reads *clene* in 1101, but *hende* (Gollancz's emendation, adopted by Andrew and Waldron) restores the alliteration.

23. The final stanzas of H.D.'s poem about Christ, "Magician," bear an uncanny resemblance to the remythologizing freedom displayed in this meditation on incarnate *clannesse*. Her portrait of Jesus resembles *Cleanness*'s privileging of the sensuous in depicting the Christ's coming as the graceful fulfillment of earthly possibilities for aesthetic integrity. H.D.'s Christ is a connoisseur of creation's beauty, whether of the scent and flavor of the fish and bread he serves to the disciples, or the sparkling light of gems:

> he named these things simply
> sat down at our table,
> stood,
> named salt,
> called to a friend;
>
> he named herbs and simples
> what garnish?
> a fine taste,
> he called for some ripe wine;
> peeled a plum,
> remembered the brass bowl
> lest he stain our host's towel;
>
> was courteous,
> not over-righteous;
>
> . . . .
> He liked jewels,
> the fine feel of white pearls;
> he would lift a pearl from a tray,
> flatter an Ethiopian merchant
> on his taste;
> lift crystal from Syria,
> to the light.

Both artists discard the standard version of Christ's life that is dominated by his death and provide, rather than guilt-inducing images of a suffering lover, the idea of a transformative presence who is magnetically attractive. H.D. describes her encounter with the crucified Christ of Velasquez's painting in a similarly revisionist mode in "The Walls Do Not Fall." Both H.D. and the *Cleanness*-poet seem to understand the Incarnation as Irenaeas did, not merely as a rescue operation for humanity after the Fall but rather as part of the divine plan from the beginning of creation.

Utterly different from Julian of Norwich, whose vision is centrally concerned with the suffering endured by Christ, the poet's avoidance of guilt psychology is nevertheless comparable to her optimism and emphasis on divine courtesy. In *A Book of Showings to the Anchoress Julian of Norwich*, the Crucifixion is not required to atone for human sinfulness or to propitiate God's wrath, but to express the loving participation of both Father and Son in the human condition.

24. Jaeger employs the term *sprezzatura* to describe the continuity between the tenth-century ideals of courtliness fostered by Latin texts used to educate secular clergy for service in imperial settings in Germany and the ethos taught in Castiglione's textbook for Italian courtiers five centuries later (42, 102). For a brief discussion of "grazia" and "sprezzatura" in Book One of *The Courtier*, see Mazzeo (143–48).

25. This fits well with Andrew's and Waldron's formulation of the continuum between *cortaysye* as a set of social values (among them *clannesse*) and as an attribute of heaven and the Godhead. They point out that where in *Sir Gawain*, "*clannesse* is an element in the hero's *cortaysye*," in *Cleanness*, "the relationship between the two is more difficult to pin down because there is an indeterminate metaphorical factor in almost every use of the two terms. On a purely mundane level cleanness and courtliness go together because aristocratic people are noticeably cleaner than the noncourtly; in *Sir Gawain* they wash before meals, wear clean linen, put white surcoats with brightly embroidered badges over shining armour. In addition, this freshness and fairness is ideally an attribute of conduct and morals. Words like *honest, ha3er(lich), clene, pure, fayre* are equally at home in both the material and the moral world of courtesy" (21–22). To their list, I would add *crafte* and, most theopoetically interesting of all these terms, *coyntyse*, which evokes the sapiential tradition of Wisdom. Of course, "menske" and "hende" and other terms as well belong to this continuum linking heavenly and earthly modes of order. See Brewer's "Courtesy in the *Gawain*-poet" and Wilson's chapter on *Cleanness* for fine overviews of the poet's deliberate use of this constellation of terms blending the aesthetic, the religious, the social, and the ethical.

26. Marie Denley's observation about the sacramentality of life fostered by the spirit of the courtesy books, where manners are the "outward and visible sign of inward and spiritual grace" (as the sacraments have been defined), aptly points to the "indissolubility of the inner and the outer in the *Gawain*-poet's complex concept of *cortayse*" (225). We feel the need to speak of symbol and metaphor as we analyze the connections the poet makes between *clannesse* as the splendor of the cosmic and the Christological order, on the one hand, and of the social, moral, and sexual order, on the other. The connections we labor to understand were for many medieval readers part of what they were educated from their earliest years to feel as natural. For another instance of the intertwining of courtly nurture and Christian self-fashioning, see *Sir Gawain and the Green Knight* 864–70 and 902–27, where Gawain is praised simultaneously as the most beautiful knight ever made by Christ and as an exemplar of high civilization, "the fader of nurture" (father of nurture) who excels in "sle3tez of þewez" (courteous devices) and especially in dalliance or "luf-talkyng." Hanning stresses the poem's ambivalence on the conflation of secular and spiritual ideals: "We have seen Gawain's heroic virtue and lonely isolation in the forest, seen him as well cry for his sins. Does the praise he now receives as an ideal courtier, and the subtler suggestion of Messiah-like qualities about him, constitute a graceful compliment by society, an accurate assessment of his worth from the perspective of a refined civilization, or a confusion of heroic essence and courtly decoration by the courtiers who greet him — or even worse, a trivialization of Christmas solemnity (by applying its attributes to a chance visitor) that skirts close to blasphemy" (21)?

27. Most critics who see a sacramental framework to *Cleanness* trace typological references to the Mass in each of the meals depicted in the poem. But even if the poem is interpreted as alluding literally and typologically at some or all of these points to the

Mass, the absence of the Crucifixion is striking. It is a feature of the poem not generally discussed because Christ's Passion (instead of being missed) is often inscribed into critical commentary as, for example, by Kelly and Irwin: "The idea that Christ's pure flesh redeems man's corrupt flesh through suffering suggests the renewal of that redemptive act in the sacrifice of the Mass. And this in turn recalls lines 1093–1108 of the poem where Christ's manual efficacy in healing diseased bodies by his touch is compared to his skill in breaking bread" (245). See also Anna Baldwin (126, 139). The ideas referred to by these and other critics are certainly central to the tradition of meditations on Christ's incarnation as exemplary for the Christian, a tradition the poet is drawing on when he urges his audience's active participation in visualizing concretely what God embodied looks like. Compare "For, loke," (Therefore, look, 1069) with the various similar verbal clues noted in Sandra McEntire's account of the Franciscan texts urging devotion to the crucified Christ (120). The point is that the poet, looking at the Incarnation in this tradition of "a more human and dramatic visualization of the Christian mysteries" (McEntire 121), does so through the peculiarly limiting metaphor of the courtly heroine.

28. This kind of affective piety among lay Christians in the late Middle Ages has not only spiritual implications, but obvious cultural and political ones as well. In effect, it denies any special place or person control over Christ's presence. The sacred becomes accessible in his crucifixion in a form that is not controlled by the church as an institution, not confined to the church as a building, and not dependent upon the priesthood's sacramental operations.

29. See Beckwith for a useful account of Love's *Mirrour of the Blessed Life of Jesus Christ*. Love asserts the centrality of the sacrament and, in response to Lollardry's attack on the received understanding of transubstantiation, he differentiates between lay readers as receivers and clerical readers as the makers of the Eucharist. While the indispensability of the clergy is reaffirmed, lay piety is given an extraordinary dynamism which subverts clerical authority. The prayer with which the *Mirrour* concludes both merges and divides "the mass where Christ's body is a clerically administered spectacle and as an act of 'inward devocioun'" (Beckwith 69).

30. Even in a courtesy manual, one finds reference to the harsh pains God had to suffer in order that humanity, through self-discipline and good nurture, as well as divine grace, might attain bliss. *The Babees Book* concludes with this prayer, linking God's grace that perfects human manners with the vulnerability shown in Christ's Passion: "And myhtefulle god, that suffred peynes smert / In curtesyse he make yow so experte, / That thurhe your nurture and youre governaunce / In lasting blysse yee mowe your self auance" (Denley 225).

31. The phrase comes from a modern theologian's account of how glory enters human experience with a sense of promised brightness, "the echo of an inner voice, this sense of something glorious, splendid, clean and joyous for which this being and all being is intended" (Niebuhr 80). Resembling the poet's aesthetic sense of *clannesse*, the image of an ideal community in glory is developed by H. Richard Niebuhr as a promise of splendor in existence already realized and yet to be fully enjoyed.

32. See Beckwith, chap. 3, on Christ's crucified body as a medium "in which to love and to be loved" (52) and hence as axiomatic to the language of subjectivity that was forged in the late medieval *imitatio Christi*.

33. The poet's account of the Flood ends with God's own acknowledgment of the universality of evil in the human heart: "For I se wel þat hit is sothe þat alle seggez wyttez / To vnþryfte arn alle þrawen with þo3t of her herttez, / And ay hatz ben, and wyl be 3et; fro her barnage / Al is þe mynde of þe man to malyce enclyned" (For I see well that it is true that all men's wits / Are all turned to wickedness with the thoughts of their hearts, / And always have been, and will be yet; from their childhood / Always the mind of man is inclined to evil 515–18). Note that Andrew and Waldron follow Gollancz's emendation of line 515 to read "seggez" rather than "mannez," as in the MS. For a discussion, the reader is referred to their edition.

Not many lines after this judgment on humanity's unwillingness to conform to the Creator's design, the poet affirms heaven's standard with no concern that he or his listeners need to fear that its exigence will exclude them. Perfection is within his and — by implication — every man's reach: "On spec of a spote may spede to mysse / Of þe sy3te of þe Souerayn þat syttez so hy3e; / For þat schewe me schale in þo schyre howsez, / As þe beryl bornyst byhouez be clene, / Þat is sounde on vche a syde and no sem habes — / Withouten maskle oþer mote, as margerye-perle" (One speck of a spot may cause one to miss / The sight of the Sovereign who sits so high; / For that [which] [any] one is going to display in those shining dwellings, / As the beryl burnished it behooves [it to] be clean, / That is sound on each side and has no seam, / Without a mark or a speck, like a margery-pearl 551–56). "Byhovez" carries the sense of a fittingness, a congruity between what the poet sees as necessary and what is suitable, what properly belongs to man's nature. (See *MED* s.v. *bihoven* v.)

34. The "polishing" he advocates (1131, 1134) does not require the kind of encouragement Richard Rolle stresses in conjunction with the suffering required when God burnishes the heart through penance: "Forþy ne pleyne þe not þo3 God furblisshe þi hert þat hit shyne and be made clene; for in no oþer maner þou may not se god; as sais seynt Matheu: 'Blessid be þo clene of hert: for þai shal se god'" (Therefore do not complain though God burnishes your heart so that it shines and is made bright; for in no other way may you see God; as St. Matthew says, "Blessed are the pure of heart: for they shall see God" Menner 104).

35. Kelly and Irwin (252–53) interpret 1124–32 as contrasting venially and mortally sinful souls. The pearl symbolizes a soul that is only "slightly stained" and so can be cleansed of venial sin by the Eucharist (alluded to by the image of pearl as "margarita," that is the bit of the host broken off and placed in the consecrated wine); in contrast, the soul that is "stained with mortal sin" requires penance in order to be a pearl. However appealing this explanation is of the eucharistic allusion linked to the puzzling symbolism of effortlessly dipping the pearl in a mildly acid solution, their interpretation that this is not intended to illustrate penance is unconvincing. "So" in 1129 cannot logically mean, as their reading must assume, "But, on the other hand"; rather, it signals a conclusion to the theme of penance that is introduced in lines 1111–16. The need for, and the ease of, this sacrament is developed throughout, both in the image of the pearl cleansed by wine as well as in the image of polishing the pearl.

36. One of the most thorough refutations of the frequent claims that *Cleanness* is either a penitential treatise or a homily is D. J. Williams's unpublished dissertation. There he observes: "Its whole tone and range separate it from practical treatises whose concern is

to define and clarify.... We are impressed with the necessity of attaining [purity], but the question 'how' is not answered in terms appropriate to the more practical kind of sermon or penance manual" (19–20). "It would tell the repentant sinner little of how he must look in his soul and confess, for its main role is to fill out further the nature of purity ... and its place in God's sight. The area explored, so to speak, is between God and man, and the resulting picture, to which the highly wrought narratives contribute far more than they would as sermon exempla, is set up for the audience to appreciate at a certain distance" (20–21). Another critic (arguing against Zavadil's interpretation of the poem as a penitential discourse) observes: "The focus is kept on the virtue of purity itself, and there is little more than a passing reminder, necessary though it is, of the way to return to a state of purity" (Means 171). More recently, Calabrese and Eliason contrast the poem's "treatment of the 'filthy' sinners" with the kind of "insight and pastoral sensitivity" found in *Piers Plowman* (265); there Haukyn's filthy clothing signifies humanity's incapacity to maintain the purity achieved through penance, and so the contrast is all the more striking when we consider *Cleanness*'s warning that sin after penance is unforgivable.

37. Perhaps the poet is drawing on the traditional association the pearl had with the mire and the consequent "tendency to regard the pearl as something which emerges with its brightness unimpaired from the *limo profundi* of man's fallen nature" (Kean 151). In P. M. Kean's discussion of the pearl as a regeneration symbol as well as a symbol of perfection, she notes that "by a natural transition, the pearl also denotes the purity brought up from the water of baptism" (152).

38. While the New Testament source does not explicitly name the defilement of the vessels and the subsequent overthrow of Babylon, as Edward Wilson points out, "the poet may have been prompted to his Belshazzar's feast by verse 13's condemnation of riotous feasting" (98).

Chapter 8. Theopoetic Coherence

1. Wilson notes that "the sudden fall from fortune" is "one moral scheme which is used to organize" the poet's thesis about the gravity of defiling the vessels and goes on to observe that the "reversal brought about by death is treated quite differently" in the case of Nebuchadnezzar than in the wrathful punishment of the disloyal Israelites (108): "his fate is that of every man and not only that of an emperor," illustrating the universal necessity of death (109). Davenport argues (against Spearing) that "the sudden reversals of fortune ... seem indirectly to work against any sense of an intelligent power, by cumulatively building up a world of instability and chance in which kings can become cows and imprisoned Jewish prophets princes in the twinkling of an eye.... Within the confines of the tale the poet does not invite us to judge God's actions, however, nor to apply logic to them. What we are invited to do is to accept the arbitrariness of fortune and action as the quality of the world in which unstable, mortal kings exist, and to sit back and watch, with appropriate feelings of wonder and horror, a series of tableaux in which history is seen as a rising and falling of kings" (73–74). He sees the "essentially arbitrary nature of the world" in the final exemplum as another indication of the *Cleanness*-poet's "developing a style appropriate for" the episodes he selects to narrate—in this case, a

"romance-chronicle" rather than telling the story in a manner "appropriate to the illustrative purpose for which it is professedly told" (77).

2. These interpolations (1270–80; 1309–16; 1441–92) draw on a variety of biblical sources in addition to those providing the exemplum's story line. Andrew's and Waldron's notes show how intrigued the poet was by descriptions of ancient Jewish liturgical artifacts, those made by Bezalel for the tabernacle of Moses as well as by Solomon for the temple. (In a similar use of visual detail from biblical sources, the Pearl-Maiden's costume is modeled not only on aristocratic fashions of the period but also on the priestly garment described in Exodus 28; see Metlitski Finkelstein 426–27 and *Pearl* 197–208). For the objects described in greatest detail, the covered cups and candlestick, the poet turned to a secular source, Mandeville's *Travels* (probably from the French version) which also provides details for descriptions of the Flood (448) and the Dead Sea landscape (1025ff).

3. Morse sees judgment as *Cleanness*'s major theme, with the poem as a whole looking "forward to the time of absolute division of the saved from the damned" ("Image of the Vessel" 202). Thus, along with Belshazzar, "the nameless multitudes of Noah's age and of Sodom, as broken, defiled vessels will be cast out to the shapeless chaos of hell" (215). Kelly and Irwin (259) sum up the poem's method as apocalyptically warning that many are called but few are chosen. (Yet this is textually unsupported, since when the poet paraphrases Matt. 22:14 in 163–84, he eliminates that very phrase—"few are chosen"). I see the poet's apocalyptic emphasis as tenuous and claim that far more important to his enterprise than dramatizing the rewards and punishments to be anticipated at the Last Judgment is pre-enacting the delights of the heavenly court in an earthly life lived in conformity to the generous designs of divine order. God is represented not as judge but as maker and courtly lord, and the implied audience's relationship to the divine is modeled on the homosocial bonding of the patriarchs and exemplified in Christ's courtliness. When the splendor of God's nature is not visible in history or nature, as I argue it mostly is not in the final exemplum, the poet's didactic strategy suffers.

4. For a brief account of the *de casibus* tradition and its connection (along with the lines referred to in the *Roman de la Rose* on mutability [5842ff]) to the Monk's presentation of tragedies, see Robert K. Root, "The Monk's Tale" in Bryan and Dempster.

5. In her essay and later book-length study, Morse emphasizes the centrality of vessel imagery to the poetic logic that "grows out of Old Testament association of sexual sin with idolatry" (*Pattern of Judgment* 20). She argues that the chief offense against God changes after the first two Old Testament exempla in *Cleanness* from "sexual sin to idolatry" because of the poet's respect for the three ages of law (151). The first two Old Testament exempla take place in the age of nature, before adultery is prohibited, and so the chief offense of the Flood generation and the Sodomites is their sinning against nature, which she interprets as attesting to "the centrality of procreative obligation under the natural law" (28). My reading of *Cleanness* makes the relation of the first two Old Testament exempla to the third one more problematic than it is for Morse, who speculates that it is because of the difference between the ages of nature and of law that the poet focuses first on sexual sin against nature and then on adultery. While idolatry rather than adultery is the literal sin focused on most in the third exemplum, Belshazzar does devote himself to a bevy of concubines and so exemplifies sexual impurity. Moreover, his defilement of the vessels by sacrilegiously using them to drink toasts not only to his concubines

but to idols makes him an example, allegorically speaking, of adultery, since idolatry is conventionally "a sin understood . . . to be adultery, a desertion of God the husband for other lovers" (151). Thus, the sin against nature in the first two Old Testament exempla is analogous to adultery and idolatry in the third.

6. On the association of idolatry and sodomy, see Morse *(Pattern of Judgment* 22ff and "Image of the Vessel" 211ff). Gross, when interpreting the "vicious" Pardoner in the *Canterbury Tales,* draws attention to the further connections medieval thinkers had drawn between idolatry and sodomy and the corruption of language, citing Alain de Lille's association of sodomy and "uicium" — in its double sense of grammatical and rhetorical fault — in the *Complaint.*

7. "Louande þeron lese goddez þat lyf haden neuer, / Made of stokkes and stonez þat neuer styry moȝt. / And for þat froþande fylþe, þe Fader of heuen / Hatz sende into þis sale þise syȝtes vncowþe, / Þe fyste with þe fyngeres þat flayed þi hert, / Þat rasped renyschly þe woȝe with þe roȝ penne" (Praising in these [vessels] false gods that never had life, / Made of stumps and stones that never could stir. / And for that frothing filth the Father of heaven / Has sent into this hall this strange sights, / The fist with the fingers that terrified your heart, / And scraped the wall strangely with the rough pen 1719-25). This verbal link of yeastiness, suggesting the poet's consciousness of a traditional association between the two evils, is reinforced by a repeated description of the false artifice of the Babylonian gods which echoes the earlier presentation of sodomy as a counterfeit of God's *kynde crafte.*

8. Recall that for Thomas, excess is not defined by the abundance of material, but by the departure from a rational end; whatever is done to fulfill Belshazzar's "misschapen" design for a feast aimed at display of concubines and the increase of an ill-founded reputation must be judged as disordered excess. The particular ingredients of the display, however, may be entirely appropriate for an occasion reasonably demanding such a magnificent outlay, as in a marriage of nobility or the installation of a bishop (see 2a2ae. 134, 1). Belshazzar's failure is fundamentally one of proportion rather than of the attention he pays to the menu and its ornate presentation.

9. God's wrath against Belshazzar and the other louts who defile his noble treasures is depicted as rooted in revulsion, and this use of *wlatez* (1500), previously used by God to describe the physical effects of his anger before the Flood, also helps to connect the two episodes.

10. The poet changes the biblical sources, where Daniel is taken captive when Nebuchadnezzar's forces first besieged Jerusalem in the reign of Jehoiakim, Zedekiah's predecessor (Daniel 1:1-7).

11. Morse notes that besides intensity, "anguish" differentiates God's anger against *fylþe of þe flesch,* and she explains that this is because God recognizes that the sinners who break the natural law deny him only by default, because they have no intellectual understanding of their acts (unlike Adam or Lucifer or, later in the poem, Nebuchadnezzar and Belshazzar): "they seem to have no consciousness of God or of God's law and no awareness that their acts are a refusal of God" *(Pattern of Judgment* 150). Given the poet's dramatization of God, the pity for those who break natural law without understanding the religious significance of doing so seems less credible an interpretation than the self-inflicted pain the Creator suffers when the boundaries of rage overflow in re-

sponse to men finding sexual relations with each other more attractive than heterosexual loveplay he prizes.

12. Johnson suggests that the poet omits the image of renewed love and service to God in the return of the vessels to the temple that is rebuilt in Jerusalem because he intends the absorption of Jerusalem into Babylon to reflect the intermingling in the present world of the two cities of God and man. They will be identified and sorted out only at the Second Coming of Christ (137).

13. For a different reading of penance, see Mary Braswell, who believes that "the king is given his chance to repent" but "does not heed the warning, even when he hears the meaning of God's words; he continues fasting as before" (91). She argues that "the poet intended his audience to judge Belshazzar against the standards of the penitent" spelled out in his passage on the pearl, but I do not sense, as she does, that the "penitential motifs in this poem ring like a tolling bell to which Belshazzar never hearkens" (91) for once Belshazzar's doom is pronounced, it is too late for him to repent.

14. While I read all four poems as probably the works of a single poet, there are no conclusive arguments on behalf of common authorship and some good reasons to hold such a hypothesis very lightly if at all — including *Cleanness*'s theopoetic disjointedness in comparison to the coherence of the other three. Andrew and Waldron refer to many readers who recognize "an unbroken consistency of thought throughout"; I am not in that group, but I do sense "an individual poetic personality" at work, despite the current unpopularity of taking as evidence of an author's consciousness any text, much less a group of four (16). For me to imagine common authorship is to think of *Cleanness* as the earliest work, written at the beginning of a spiritual journey of no less heroic proportions than, and akin to, what he tells of the prophet Jonah in *Patience*.

15. Andrew and Waldron (n37–39) observe that the "quoyntyse" which patience and poverty have in common according to the poet can refer both to the "metaphorical beauty of the 'ladies' and the wisdom of the virtues they represent." By pursuit of their "quoyntyse" on the model of courtship, the narrator expects to earn the reward of "heuen-ryche" (the kingdom of heaven) which Christ, in the first and the last Beatitudes, promises to both the poor and the patient. This links Christ to a figure of courtly female beauty in a way different from, but reminiscent of, the Jean de Meun paraphrase in *Cleanness* (1057–68).

16. See Kirk's "'Well Bycommes Such Craft upon Christmasse'" for further exploration of *Sir Gawain and the Green Knight* from this perspective of the centrality of the courtly to the poem's serious playing with the meaning of the feast of the Nativity.

17. See Kirk's "Anatomy of a Mourning" for a reading of *Pearl* that focuses on the validity of the Dreamer's experience of love.

Selected Bibliography

Editions and Translations of Cleanness *(or* Purity*)*, Patience, Pearl, *and* Sir Gawain and the Green Knight

Anderson, J. J. *Cleanness*. Manchester: Manchester University Press, 1977.

Andrew, Malcolm, and Ronald Waldron, eds. *The Poems of the* Pearl *Manuscript: Pearl, Cleanness, Patience, Sir Gawain and the Green Knight*. Berkeley: University of California Press, 1979.

Borroff, Marie, trans. *Pearl*. New York: W. W. Norton, 1977.

———, trans. *Sir Gawain and the Green Knight*. New York: W. W. Norton, 1967.

Cawley, A. C., and J. J. Anderson, eds. *Pearl, Cleanness, Patience, Sir Gawain and the Green Knight*. London: J. M. Dent; New York: E. P. Dutton, 1976.

Gollancz, Israel, ed. Trans. D. S. Brewer. Cleanness: *An Alliterative Tripartite Poem on the Deluge, the Destruction of Sodom, and the Death of Belshazzar, by the Poet of* Pearl. Cambridge, Eng.: D. S. Brewer; Totowa, N.J.: Rowman and Littlefield, 1974.

Gordon, E. V., ed. *Pearl*. Oxford: Oxford University Press, 1953.

Kottler, Barnet, and Alan M. Markman, *A Concordance to Five Middle English Poems: Cleanness, St. Erkenwald, Sir Gawain and the Green Knight, Patience, Pearl*. Pittsburgh: University of Pittsburgh Press, 1966.

Menner, Robert J., ed. Purity: *A Middle English Poem*. New Haven: Yale University Press, 1920.

Stone, Brian, trans. *The Owl and the Nightingale; Cleanness; St. Erkenwald*. Harmondsworth, Eng.: Penguin Books, 1971.

Vantuono, William, ed. *The* Pearl *Poems: An Omnibus Edition.* New York: Garland, 1984.

Williams, Margaret, R.S.C.J., trans. *The* Pearl-*Poet: His Complete Works.* New York: Random House, 1967.

Editions and Translations of Other Primary Sources

Alain de Lille. *Anticlaudianus or the Good and Perfect Man.* Trans. James J. Sheridan. Toronto: Pontifical Institute of Medieval Studies, 1973.

———. *The Art of Preaching.* Trans. Gillian R. Evans. Cistercian Studies Series 23. Kalamazoo, Mich.: Cistercian Publications, 1981.

———. [Alan of Lille.] *Plaint of Nature.* Trans. James J. Sheridan. Toronto: Pontifical Institute of Medieval Studies, 1980.

———. [Alan of Lille.] *De planctu naturae.* Ed. Nikolaus M. Häring. *Studi medievali* 3d ser., 19 (1978): 797–897.

Baird, Joseph L., and John R. Kane. *La Querelle de la Rose: Letters and Documents.* North Carolina Studies in the Romance Languages and Literature 199. Chapel Hill: University of North Carolina Press, 1978.

Biblia Sacra Iuxta Vulgatum Versionem. Ed. Bonifatio Fischer et al. 2 vols. Stuttgart: Wurttembergische Bibelanstalt, 1969.

The Book of the Knight of the Tower. Trans. William Caxton. Ed. M. Y. Offord. Early English Text Society. London: Oxford University Press, 1971.

Bryan, W. F., and G. Demptster, eds. *The Sources and Analogues of the Canterbury Tales.* London: Routledge & Kegan Paul, 1941.

Chaucer, Geoffrey. *The Riverside Chaucer.* 3d ed. Ed. Larry D. Benson. New York: Houghton Mifflin, 1987.

Chretien de Troyes. *Arthurian Romances.* Trans. William K. Kibler. (*Erec and Enide,* trans. Carleton W. Carroll.) London: Penguin Books, 1991.

Clanvowe, Sir John. *The Works of Sir John Clanvowe.* Ed. V. J. Scattergood. Cambridge, Eng.: D. S. Brewer; Totowa, N.J.: Rowman and Littlefield, 1975.

Damian, Peter. *Book of Gomorrah: An Eleventh-Century Treatise against Clerical Homosexual Practices.* Trans. Pierre J. Payer. Waterloo, Ont.: Wilfrid Laurier University Press, 1982.

Eneas: A Twelfth-Century French Romance. Trans. John A. Yunck. New York: Columbia University Press, 1974.

2 (Slavonic Apocalypse of) Enoch. Ed. and trans. F. I. Andersen. *The Old Testament Pseudepigrapha.* Ed. James H. Charlesworth. Garden City, N.Y.: Doubleday, 1983.

Gerson, Jean. *L'oüvre spirituelle et pastorale.* Vol. 8 of *Oüvres Complètes de Jean Gerson.* Ed. Mgr. Palémon Glorieux. Paris: Desclée, 1960.

Gower, John. *The Major Latin Works of John Gower.* Trans. Eric W. Stockton. Seattle: University of Washington Press, 1962.

Guillaume de Lorris and Jean de Meun. *Le Roman de la Rose.* Ed. Felix Lecoy. 3 vols. Classiques français du Moyen Age 92, 95, 98. Paris: Librairie Honore Champion, 1965–70.

———. *Le Roman de la Rose.* Ed. Daniel Poirion. Paris: Garnier-Flammarion, 1974.

———. *The Romance of the Rose*. Trans. Charles Dahlberg. Hanover, N.H.: University Press of New England, 1986.

H.D. *Collected Poems 1912–1944*. Ed. Louis L. Martz. New York: New Directions, 1983.

Henri de Grosmont. *Le Livre de seyntz médecines*. Ed. E. J. Arnould. Anglo-Norman Text Society. Oxford: Basil Blackwell, 1940.

John of Salisbury. *Frivolities of Courtiers and Footprints of Philosophers, Being a Translation of the First, Second, and Third Books and Selections from the Seventh and Eighth Books of the Policraticus of John of Salisbury*. Ed. and trans. Joseph B. Pike. Minneapolis: University of Minnesota Press, 1938.

Julian of Norwich. *A Book of Showings to the Anchoress Julian of Norwich*. Pt. 2. Ed. Edmund Colledge, O.S.A. and James Walsh, S.J. Toronto: Pontifical Institute of Mediaeval Studies, 1978.

Kempe, Margery. *The Book of Margery Kempe*. Trans. W. Butler-Bowdon. Intro. by R. W. Chambers. London: Jonathan Cape, 1936.

Love, Nicholas. *Nicholas Love's Mirrour of the Blessed Life of Jesus Christ: A Critical Edition Based on Cambridge University Library Additional MSS 6578 and 6686*. Ed. Michael J. Sargent. New York: Garland, 1992.

Le Menagier de Paris. Ed. Georgine E. Brereton and Janet M. Ferrier. Oxford: Clarendon Press, 1981.

Middle English Sermons, Edited from British Museum Ms. Royal 18 B. xxiii. Ed. Woodburn O. Ross. Early English Text Society (209). London: Oxford University Press, 1940 [for 1938].

Orderic Vitalis. *The Ecclesiastical History of Ordericus Vitalis*. Ed. and trans. Marjorie Chibnall. 6 vols. Oxford Medieval Texts. Oxford: Oxford University Press, 1969–80.

Speculum Sacerdotale. Early English Text Society. London: Oxford University Press, 1936.

Thomas Aquinas. *Pleasure (1a2ae. 31–39)*. Ed. Eric D'Arcy. Vol. 20 of *Summa Theologiae*. Gen. ed. Thomas Gilby, O.P. Blackfriars edition. London: Eyre & Spottiswoode; New York: McGraw-Hill, 1975.

———. *Law and Political Theory (1a2ae. 90–97)*. Ed. Thomas Gilby, O.P. Vol. 28 of *Summa Theologiae*. Gen. ed. Thomas Gilby, O.P. Blackfriars edition. London: Eyre & Spottiswoode; New York, McGraw-Hill, 1966.

———. *Courage (2a2ae. 123–40)*. Ed. Anthony Ross, O.P., and P. G. Walsh. Vol. 42 of *Summa Theologiae*. Gen. ed. Thomas Gilby, O.P. Blackfriars edition. London: Eyre & Spottiswoode; New York: McGraw-Hill, 1966.

———. *Temperance (2a2ae. 141–54)*. Ed. Thomas Gilby, O.P. Vol. 43 of *Summa Theologiae*. Gen. ed. Thomas Gilby, O.P. Blackfriars edition. London: Eyre & Spottiswoode; New York: McGraw-Hill, 1968.

———. *Well-Tempered Passion (2a2ae. 155–70)*. Ed. Thomas Gilby, O.P. Vol. 44 of *Summa Theologiae*. Gen. ed. Thomas Gilby, O.P. Blackfriars edition. London: Eyre & Spottiswoode; New York: McGraw-Hill, 1972.

Wright, Thomas, ed. *Political Poems and Songs Relating to English History, Composed during the Period from the Accession of Edw. III. to that of Ric. III*. Vol. 1. London: Longman, Green, Longman, and Roberts, 1859.

Wycliffe, John, trans. *The Holy Bible*. Ed. J. Forshall and F. Madden. Oxford: Oxford University Press, 1850; New York: AMS Press, 1982.

Secondary Sources

Allen, Don Cameron. *The Legend of Noah: Renaissance Rationalism in Art, Science, and Letters*. Urbana: University of Illinois Press, 1949.

Arden, Heather. *Romance of the Rose*. Twayne Series. Boston: G. K. Hall, 1987.

Ariès, Philippe, and André Béjin, eds. Trans. Anthony Forster. *Western Sexuality: Practice and Precept in Past and Present Times*. Oxford: Basil Blackwell, 1985.

Armstrong, Elizabeth. "Purity." *The Explicator* 3, no. 1 (1977): 31.

Badel, Pierre-Yves. "Raison, 'Fille de Dieu' et Rationalisme de Jean de Meun." *Mélanges de langue et de littérature du Moyen Age et de la Renaissance, offerts à Jean Frappier*, Tome I. 41–52. Geneva: Librairie Droz, 1970.

———. *Le Roman de la Rose au XIVe siècle: Étude de la réception de l'oeuvre*. Publications Romanes et Françaises 153. Geneva: Librairie Droz, 1980.

Baldwin, Anna P. "Sacramental Perfection in *Pearl, Patience* and *Cleanness*." In *Genres, Themes and Images in English Literature*, ed. Piero Boitani and Anna Torti, 125–40. Tübingen: Gunter Narr Verlag, 1988.

Baldwin, John W. "Five Discourses on Desire: Sexuality and Gender in Northern France around 1200." *Speculum* 66 (1991): 797–819.

Barber, Richard. *The Knight and Chivalry*. Ipswich, Eng.: Boydell Press, 1974.

Barnie, John. *War in Medieval English Society: Social Values in the Hundred Years War, 1337–99*. Ithaca: Cornell University Press, 1974.

Beckwith, Sarah. *Christ's Body: Identity, Culture and Society in Late Medieval Writings*. London: Routledge, 1993.

Bennett, Jack A. W. The Parlement of Foules: *An Interpretation*. Oxford: Clarendon Press, 1957.

Bennett, Michael. *Community, Class, and Careerism: Cheshire and Lancaster Society in the Age of* Sir Gawain and the Green Knight. Cambridge: Cambridge University Press, 1983.

———. "*Sir Gawain and the Green Knight* and the Literary Achievement of the Northwest Midlands: the Historical Background." *Journal of Medieval History* 5 (1979): 63–88.

Benson, Larry D. *Art and Tradition in Sir Gawain and the Green Knight*. New Brunswick, N.J.: Rutgers University Press, 1965.

———. "Courtly Love and Chivalry in the Later Middle Ages." In *Fifteenth-Century Studies: Recent Essays*, ed. Robert F. Yeager, 237–57. Hamden, Conn.: Archon Books, 1984.

Biddick, Kathleen. "Genders, Bodies, Borders: Technologies of the Visible." *Speculum* 68 (1993): 389–418.

Bloch, R. Howard. *Etymologies and Genealogies: A Literary Anthropology of the French Middle Ages*. Chicago: Chicago University Press, 1983.

———. "Silence and Holes: the *Roman du Silence* and the Art of the Trouvere." *Yale French Studies* 70 (1986): 81–99.

Borroff, Marie. Sir Gawain and the Green Knight: *A Stylistic and Metrical Study*. New Haven: Yale University Press, 1962.

Boswell, John. *Christianity, Social Tolerance, and Homosexuality: Gay People in Western Europe from the Beginning of the Christian Era to the Fourteenth Century*. Chicago: The University of Chicago Press, 1987.

———. "Revolutions, Universals, and Sexual Categories." In *Hidden from History: Reclaiming the Gay and Lesbian Past*, ed. Martin Duberman, Martha Vicinus, and George Chauncey, Jr., 17–36. New York: New American Library, 1989; London: Penguin, 1991.

Bowers, John M. "*Pearl* in Its Royal Setting: Ricardian Poetry Revisited." *Studies in the Age of Chaucer* 17 (1995): 111–55.

Boyd, David Lorenzo. "On Lesbian and Gay/Queer Medieval Studies." *Medieval Feminist Newsletter* 15 (spring 1993): 12–15.

Braswell, Mary Flowers. *The Medieval Sinner: Characterization and Confession in the Literature of the English Middle Ages*. East Brunswick, N.J.: Associated University Presses, 1983.

Brewer, Derek S. "Courtesy and the *Gawain*-Poet." In *Patterns of Love and Courtesy: Essays in Memory of C. S. Lewis*, ed. John Lawlor, 54–85. Evanston, Ill.: Northwestern University Press, 1966.

———. *English Gothic Literature*. London: Macmillan, 1983.

Brownlee, Kevin. "Reflections in the *Miroër aus Amoreus*: The Inscribed Reader in Jean de Meun's *Roman de la Rose*." In *Mimesis: From Mirror to Method, Augustine to Descartes*, ed. John D. Lyons and Stephen G. Nichols, Jr., 60–70. Hanover, N.H.: University Press of New England, 1982.

Brownlee, Kevin, and Sylvia Huot, eds. *Rethinking the* Romance of the Rose: *Text, Image, Reception*. Philadelphia: University of Pennsylvania Press, 1992.

Brucker, Charles. *Sage et sagesse au Moyen Age (XIIe et XIIIe siècles): Étude historique, sémantique, et stylistique*. Geneva: Librairie Droz, 1987.

Brundage, James A. *Law, Sex, and Christian Society in Medieval Europe*. Chicago: University of Chicago Press, 1987.

Bullough, Vern L. "The Sin against Nature and Homosexuality." In *Sexual Practices and the Medieval Church*, ed. Vern L. Bullough and James Brundage, 55–71. Buffalo, N.Y.: Prometheus Books, 1982.

Burns, E. Jane. "The Man behind the Lady in the Troubador Lyric." *Romance Notes* 25 (1958): 254–70.

Bynum, Caroline Walker. "The Body of Christ in the Later Middle Ages: A Reply to Leo Steinberg." *Renaissance Quarterly* 39 (1986): 399–439.

———. "Introduction: The Complexity of Symbols." In *Gender and Religion: On the Complexity of Symbols*, ed. Caroline Walker Bynum, Stevan Harrell, and Paula Richman, 1–20. Boston: Beacon Press, 1986.

———. "'... and Woman His Humanity': Female Imagery in the Religious Writing of the Later Middle Ages." In *Gender and Religion: On the Complexity of Symbols*, ed. Caroline Walker Bynum, Stevan Harrell, and Paula Richman, 257–88. Boston: Beacon Press, 1986.

Cadden, Joan. *Meanings of Sex Difference in the Middle Ages: Medicine, Science, and Culture.* Cambridge: Cambridge University Press: 1993.

Calabrese, Michael A. "'Make a Mark that Shows': Orphean Son, Orphean Sexuality, and the Exile of Chaucer's Pardoner." *Viator* 24 (1993): 269–86.

Calabrese, Michael A., and Eric Eliason. "The Rhetorics of Sexual Pleasure and Intolerance in the Middle English *Cleanness*." *Modern Language Quarterly* 56, no. 3 (1995): 247–75.

Cocks, Joan. *The Oppositional Imagination: Feminism, Critique, and Political Theory.* London: Routledge, 1989.

Coleman, Janet. *Medieval Readers and Writers: Literature and Society, 1350–1400.* New York: Columbia University Press, 1986.

Coletti, Theresa. "Purity and Danger: The Paradox of Mary's Body and the Engendering of the Infancy Narrative in the English Mystery Cycles." In *Feminist Approaches to the Body in Medieval Literature,* ed. Linda Lomperis and Sarah Stanbury, 65–95. Philadelphia: University of Pennsylvania Press, 1993.

Collins, Marie. "Love, Nature and Law in the Poetry of Gower and Chaucer." In *Court and Poet,* ed. Glyn S. Burgess. ARCA 5. Liverpool: Francis Cairns, 1981.

Coote, Stephen. *English Literature of the Middle Ages.* New York: Viking Penguin, 1988.

Cormier, Raymond J. *One Heart One Mind: The Rebirth of Virgil's Hero in Medieval French Romance.* Romance Monographs. University: University of Mississippi Press, 1973.

Cormier, Raymond J., and Harry J. Kuster. "Old Views and New Trends: Observations on the Problem of Homosexuality in the Middle Ages." *Studi medievali* 3d ser., 25.2 (1984): 587–610.

Courtenay, William J. *Schools and Scholars in Fourteenth-Century England.* Princeton: Princeton University Press, 1987.

Crane, Susan. *Gender and Romance in Chaucer's Canterbury Tales.* Princeton: Princeton University Press, 1994.

Davenport, William A. *The Art of the* Gawain-*Poet.* London: Athlone Press; Atlantic Highlands, N.J.: Humanities Press, 1978.

D'Avray, David. "The Gospel of the Marriage Feast of Cana and Marriage Preaching in France." In *The Bible in the Medieval World: Essays in Memory of Beryl Smalley,* ed. Katherine Walsh and Diana Wood, 207–24. Oxford: Basil Blackwell, 1985.

D'Avray, D. L., and M. Tausche. "Marriage Sermons in *Ad Status* Collections of the Central Middle Ages." *Archives d'histoire doctrinale et littéraire du Moyen Age* 46 (1980): 71–119.

Denley, Marie. "Elementary Teaching Techniques and Middle English Religious Didactic Writing." In *Langland, the Mystics and Middle English Religious Tradition: Essays in Honour of S. S. Hussey,* ed. Helen Phillips, 223–41. Cambridge, Eng.: D. S. Brewer, 1990.

Dinshaw, Carolyn. "Chaucer's Queer Touches / A Queer Touches Chaucer." *Exemplaria* 7, no. 1 (1995): 75–92.

———. "A Kiss Is Just a Kiss: Heterosexuality and Its Consolations in *Sir Gawain and the Green Knight*." *Diacritics* 24, nos. 2–3 (1994): 205–26.

Dollimore, Jonathan. *Sexual Dissidence: Augustine to Wilde, Freud to Foucault.* Oxford: Clarendon Press, 1991.

Doob, Penelope B. R. *Nebuchadnezzar's Children: Conventions of Madness in Middle English Literature*. New Haven: Yale University Press, 1974.
Douglas, Jane Dempsey. *Justification in Late Medieval Preaching*. Leiden: E. J. Brill, 1966.
Douglas, Mary. *Purity and Danger: An Analysis of the Concepts of Pollution and Taboo*. London: Routledge & Kegan Paul, 1966.
Downing, Christine. *Myths and Mysteries of Same-Sex Love*. New York: Continuum, 1989.
Dronke, Peter. *Fabula: Explorations into Uses of Myth in Medieval Platonism*. Leiden: E. J. Brill, 1974.
Duby, Georges, ed. *Revelations of the Medieval World*. Vol. 2 of *A History of Private Life*. Trans. Arthur Goldhammer. Cambridge: Harvard University Press, 1988.
———. *William Marshal: The Flower of Chivalry*. Trans. Richard Howard. New York: Pantheon Books, 1985.
Dynes, Wayne, ed. *Encyclopedia of Homosexuality*. New York: Garland, 1990.
Dynes, Wayne, and Warren Johansson. "London's Medieval Sodomites." *Cabirion and Gay Books Bulletin* 10 (winter-spring 1984): 5–7.
Dynes, Wayne, Warren Johansson, and John Lauritsen. *Homosexuality, Intolerance, and Christianity: A Critical Examination of John Boswell's Work*. New York: Scholarship Committee, Gay Academic Union, 1981.
Economou, George D. *The Goddess Natura in Medieval Literature*. Cambridge: Harvard University Press, 1972.
———. "The Two Venuses and Courtly Love." In *Pursuit of Perfection: Courtly Love in Medieval Literature*, ed. Joan M. Ferrante and George D. Economou, 17–49. Port Washington, N.Y.: National University Publications of Kennikat Press, 1975.
Edwards, Robert R., and Stephen Spector. "Introduction." In *The Olde Daunce: Love, Friendship, Sex and Marriage in the Medieval World*, ed. Robert R. Edwards and Stephen Spector, 1–13. Albany: State University of New York Press, 1991.
Elon, Amos. "Report from Vienna." *New Yorker* (May 13, 1991), 92–102.
Erickson, Carrolly. *The Medieval Vision: Essays in History and Perception*. New York: Oxford University Press, 1976.
Eucharistic Vessels of the Middle Ages. Cambridge, Mass.: Busch Reisinger Museum, 1975.
Farley, Margaret A., R.S.M. "Fragments for an Ethic of Commitment in Thomas Aquinas." In *Celebrating the Medieval Heritage: A Colloquy on the Thought of Aquinas and Bonaventure*, ed. David Tracy. *Journal of Religion* 58 supp. (1978): 135–55.
Finkelstein, Dorothee Metlitski. "The *Pearl*-Poet as Bezalel." *Mediaeval Studies* 35 (1973): 413–32.
Fleming, John V. "Moral Reputation of the *Roman de la Rose* before 1400." *Romance Philology* 18 (1965): 430–35.
———. *Reason and the Lover*. Princeton: Princeton University Press, 1984.
———. *The Roman de la Rose: A Study in Allegory and Iconography*. Princeton: Princeton University Press, 1969.
Foucault, Michel. "The Battle for Chastity." In *Western Sexuality: Practice and Precept in Past and Present Times*, ed. Philippe Ariès and André Béjin, 14–25. Oxford: Basil Blackwell, 1985.

———. *The Use of Pleasure.* Vol. 2 of *The History of Sexuality.* Trans. Robert Hurley. New York: Pantheon Books, 1978.

Frantzen, Allen J. "The Disclosure of Sodomy in *Cleanness.*" *PMLA* 111, no. 3 (1996): 451–64.

———. "*The Pardoner's Tale,* the Pervert, and the Price of Order in Chaucer's World." In *Class and Gender in Early English Literature: Intersections,* ed. Britton J. Harwood and Gillian R. Overing, 131–47. Bloomington: Indiana University Press, 1994.

Freud, Sigmund. "Leonardo da Vinci and a Memory of His Childhood." [1910] In *Five Lectures on Psycho-Analysis, Leonardo da Vinci, and Other Works,* 59–137. Vol. 11 of *The Standard Edition of the Complete Psychological Works of Sigmund Freud.* Trans. and gen. ed. James Strachey. London: Hogarth Press, 1957.

———. "Psycho-Analytic Notes on an Autobiographical Account of a Case of Paranoia (Dementia Paranoides)." [1911] In *The Case of Schreber, Papers on Technique, and Other Works,* 3–82. Vol. 12 of *The Standard Edition of the Complete Psychological Works of Sigmund Freud.* Trans. and gen. ed. James Strachey. London: Hogarth Press, 1958.

Gallop, Jane. *Thinking through the Body.* New York: Columbia University Press, 1988.

Georgianna, Linda. *The Solitary Self: Individuality in the* Ancrene Wisse. Cambridge: Harvard University Press, 1981.

Gilbert, Arthur N. "Conceptions of Homosexuality and Sodomy in Western History." *Journal of Homosexuality* 6, no. ½ (1980/81): 57–68.

Ginzberg, Louis. *Legends of the Bible.* Philadelphia: Jewish Publication Society, 1992.

Glenn, Jonathan A. "Dislocation of *Kynde* in the Middle English *Cleanness.*" *The Chaucer Review* 18, no. 1 (1983): 77–91.

Goodich, Michael. *The Unmentionable Vice: Homosexuality in the Later Medieval Period.* Santa Barbara, Calif.: Ross-Erikson, 1979.

Gradon, Pamela. *Form and Style in Early English Literature.* London: Methuen, 1971.

Green, Richard Hamilton. "Alan of Lille's *De planctu naturae.*" *Speculum* 31 (1956): 649–74.

Greenberg, David. *The Construction of Homosexuality.* Chicago: University of Chicago Press, 1988.

Gross, Gregory W. "Trade Secrets: Chaucer, the Pardoner, the Critics." *Modern Languages Studies,* 25, no. 4 (1995): 1–36.

Grunzwig, Walter. Review of *Die Stumme Sunde: Homosexualitat in Mittelalter, mit einem Textanhang. (The Silent Sin: Homosexuality in the Middle Ages, with a Textual Appendix),* by Brigitte Spreitzer. *Journal of the History of Homosexuality* 1, no. 1 (1990): 151.

Halley, Janet E. "Textual Intercourse: Anne Donne, John Donne, and the Sexual Poetics of Textual Exchange." In *Seeking the Woman in Late Medieval and Renaissance Writings: Essays in Feminist Contextual Criticism,* ed. Sheila Fisher and Janet E. Halley, 187–206. Knoxville: University of Tennessee Press, 1989.

Halperin, David M. *One Hundred Years of Homosexuality: And Other Essays on Greek Love.* London: Routledge, 1990.

———. "Sex before Sexuality: Pederasty, Politics, and Power in Classical Athens." In *Hidden from History: Reclaiming the Gay and Lesbian Past,* ed. Martin Duberman,

Martha Vicinus, and George Chauncey, Jr., 37–53. New York: New American Library, 1989; London: Penguin, 1991.

Hanning, Robert W. "Sir Gawain and the Red Herring: The Perils of Interpretation." In *Acts of Interpretation: The Text in Its Contexts, 700–1600—Essays on Medieval and Renaissance Literature in Honor of E. Talbot Donaldson*, ed. Mary J. Carruthers and Elizabeth D. Kirk, 5–23. Norman, Okla.: Pilgrim Books, 1982.

Hansen, Elaine Tuttle. "The Feminization of Men." In *Seeking the Woman in Late Medieval and Renaissance Writings: Essays in Feminist Contextual Criticism*, ed. Sheila Fisher and Janet E. Halley, 51–70. Knoxville: University of Tennessee Press, 1989.

Harwood, Britton J., and Gillian R. Overing. "Foreword." In *Class and Gender in Early English Literature: Intersections*, ed. Britton J. Harwood and Gillian R. Overing, vii-xiii. Bloomington: Indiana University Press, 1994.

Heilbrun, Carolyn G. *Toward a Recognition of Androgyny*. New York: Alfred A. Knopf, 1973.

Henderson, George. *Gothic*. Baltimore: Penguin Books, 1967.

Herman, Gerald. "The 'Sin against Nature' and Its Echoes in Medieval French Literature." *Annuale Mediaevale* 17 (1976): 70–87.

Heyward, Carter. *Touching Our Strength: The Erotic as Power and the Love of God*. San Francisco: Harper & Row, 1989.

Heyworth, P. L. "Jocelin of Brakelond, Abbot Samson, and The Case of William the Sacrist." In *Middle English Studies: Presented to Norman Davis in Honour of His Seventieth Birthday*, ed. Douglas Gray and E. G. Stanley, 175–94. Oxford: Clarendon Press, 1983.

Hicks, Eric. *Le Debat sur le* Roman de la Rose. Paris: Librairie Champion, 1977.

Hill, Jillian M. L. *The Medieval Debate on Jean de Meung's* Roman de la Rose: *Morality versus Art*. Studies in Medieval Literature 4. Lewiston, N.Y.: Edwin Mellen Press, 1991.

Hill, Thomas D. Review of *Reason and the Lover*, by John V. Fleming. *Speculum* 60, no. 4 (October 1985): 973–77.

Hinnebusch, William A., O.P. *The History of the Dominican Order: Intellectual and Cultural Life to 1500*. Vol. 2. New York: Alba House, 1973.

Hooks, Bell. *Yearning: Race, Gender, and Cultural Politics*. Boston: South End Press, 1990.

Hudson, Harriet E. "Construction of Class, Family, and Gender in Some Middle English Popular Romances." In *Class and Gender in Early English Literature: Intersections*, ed. Britton J. Harwood and Gillian R. Overing, 76–94. Bloomington: Indiana University Press, 1994.

Huizinga, Johan. *Homo Ludens, A Study of the Play-Element in Culture*. Boston: Beacon Press, 1955.

———. *The Waning of the Middle Ages*. London: St. Martin's Press, 1949; New York: Anchor Books, 1954.

Hult, David F. *Self-Fulfilling Prophecies: Readership and Authority in the First* Roman de la Rose. Cambridge: Cambridge University Press, 1986.

The International Style: The Arts in Europe around 1400. Baltimore: Walters Art Gallery, 1962.

Jaeger, C. Stephen. *The Origins of Courtliness: Civilizing Trends and the Formation of Courtly Ideals, 939–1210*. Philadelphia: University of Pennsylvania Press, 1985.

Johnson, Lynn Staley. *The Voice of the* Gawain-*Poet*. Madison: University of Wisconsin Press, 1984.

Jolliffe, P. S. *A Checklist of Middle English Prose Writings of Spiritual Guidance*. Toronto: Pontifical Institute of Medieval Studies, 1974.

Kane, George. "Chaucer, Love Poetry, and Romantic Love." In *Acts of Interpretation: The Text in Its Contexts, 700–1600—Essays on Medieval and Renaissance Literature in Honor of E. Talbot Donaldson*, ed. Mary J. Carruthers and Elizabeth D. Kirk, 237–55. Norman, Okla.: Pilgrim Books, 1982.

Kaplan, Aryeh. *Jewish Meditation: A Practical Guide*. New York: Schocken Books, 1985.

Kean, P. M. *The* Pearl: *An Interpretation*. New York: Barnes and Noble, 1967.

Keen, Maurice. *The Laws of War in the Late Middle Ages*. London: Routledge & Kegan Paul, 1965.

Keiser, Elizabeth B. "The Festive Decorum of *Cleanness*." In *Chivalric Literature: Essays on Relations between Literature and Life in the Later Middle Ages*, ed. Larry D. Benson and John Leyerle, 63–75. Kalamazoo, Mich.: Medieval Institute Publications, 1980.

———. "Perfection and Experience: The Celebration of Divine Order and Human Sensibility in *Cleanness* and *Patience*." Ph.D. diss. Yale University, 1972.

Kelly, Henry Ansgar. *Love and Marriage in the Age of Chaucer*. Ithaca: Cornell University Press, 1975.

Kelly, T. D., and John T. Irwin. "The Meaning of *Cleanness*: Parable as Effective Sign." *Medieval Studies* 35 (1972): 32–60.

Kirk, Elizabeth D. "The Anatomy of a Mourning: Reflections on the *Pearl*-Dreamer." In *The Endless Knot: Essays in Old and Middle English in Honor of Marie Borroff*, ed. M. Teresa Tavormina and R. F. Yeager, 215–25. Cambridge, Eng.: D. S. Brewer, 1995.

———. *The Dream Thought of* Piers Plowman. New Haven: Yale University Press, 1972.

———. "'Paradis Stood Formed in Hire Yen': Courtly Love and Chaucer's Re-Vison of Dante." In *Acts of Interpretation: The Text in Its Contexts, 700–1600—Essays on Medieval and Renaissance Literature in Honor of E. Talbot Donaldson*, ed. Mary J. Carruthers and Elizabeth D. Kirk, 257–77. Norman, Oklahoma: Pilgrim Books, 1982.

———. "'Wel Bycommes Such Craft upon Cristmasse': The Festive and the Hermeneutic in *Sir Gawain and the Green Knight*." *Arthuriana* 4, no. 2 (summer 1994): 93–137.

———. "'Who Suffreth More than God?': Narrative Redefinition of Patience in *Patience* and *Piers Plowman*." In *The Triumph of Patience*, ed. Gerald J. Schiffhorst, 88–104. Orlando: University Presses of Florida, 1978.

Knight, Stephen. "The Social Function of the Middle English Romances." In *Medieval Literature: Criticism, Ideology, and History*, ed. David Aers, 99–122. Brighton: Harvester Press, 1986.

Knowles, David. *The Evolution of Medieval Thought*. New York: Random House, 1962.

Kristeva, Julia. *Powers of Horror: An Essay on Abjection*. Trans. Leon S. Roudiez. New York: Columbia University Press, 1982.

Krochalis, Jeanne. "Alain de Lille, *De planctu naturae*: Studies Toward an Edition." Ph.D. diss., Harvard University, 1973.

Kruger, Steven F. "Claiming the Pardoner: Toward a Gay Reading of Chaucer's Pardoner's Tale." *Exemplaria* 6, no. 1 (1994): 115-39.

Lawton, David. "Middle English Alliterative Poetry: An Introduction." In *Middle English Alliterative Poetry and Its Literary Background: Seven Essays*, ed. David Lawton, 1-19. Cambridge, Eng.: D. S. Brewer, 1982.

Luria, Maxwell. *A Reader's Guide to the* Roman de la Rose. Hamden, Conn.: Archon Books, 1982.

Luttrell, Claude. "The Figure of Nature in Chretien de Troyes." *Nottingham Medieval Studies* 17 (1973): 3-16.

McAlpine, Monica. "The Pardoner's Homosexuality and How It Matters." *PMLA* 95, no. 1 (1980): 8-22.

McEntire, Sandra J. *The Doctrine of Compunction in Medieval England: Holy Tears*. Lewiston, N.Y.: Edwin Mellen Press, 1990.

McNamara, Jo Ann. "The *Herrenfrage*: The Restructuring of the Gender System, 1050-1150." In *Medieval Masculinities: Regarding Men in the Middle Ages*, ed. Clare A. Lees with Thelma Fensler and Jo Ann McNamara, 3-30. Minneapolis: University of Minnesota Press, 1994.

McNeill, John. *The Church and the Homosexual*. 3d ed. Boston: Beacon Press, 1988.

Mann, Jill. *Chaucer and Medieval Estates Satire: The Literature of Social Classes and the "General Prologue" to the "Canterbury Tales."* Cambridge: Cambridge University Press, 1973.

———. *Geoffrey Chaucer*. New York: Harvester, 1991.

Marchello-Nizia, Christiane. "Amour Courtois, Societé Masculine et Figures du Pouvoir." *Annales: Economies, Societés, Civilisations* 36, no. 6 (1981): 969-81.

Marti, Kevin. *Body, Heart, and Text in the Pearl-Poet*. Studies in Medieval Literature 12. Lewiston, N.Y.: Edwin Mellen Press, 1991.

Mathew, Gervase. *The Court of Richard II*. London: John Murray, 1968.

Mazzeo, Joseph A. *Renaissance and Revolution: Backgrounds to Seventeenth-Century Literature*. New York: Random House, 1967.

Means, Michael H. "The Homiletic Structure of *Cleanness*." *Studies in Medieval Culture* 5 (1975): 165-72.

Moi, Toril. "Desire in Language: Andreas Capellanus and the Controversy of Courtly Love." In *Medieval Literature: Criticism, Ideology, and History*, ed. David Aers, 11-57. New York: St. Martins, 1986.

Morse, Charlotte C. "The Image of the Vessel in *Cleanness*." *University of Toronto Quarterly* 11, no. 3 (1971): 202-16.

———. *The Pattern of Judgment in the* Queste *and* Cleanness. Columbia: University of Missouri Press, 1978.

Nicholls, Jonathan W. *The Matter of Courtesy: A Study of Medieval Courtesy Books and the* Gawain-Poet. Woodbridge, Eng.: D. S. Brewer, 1985.

Nichols, Stephen G. "An Intellectual Anthropology of Marriage in the Middle Ages." In

The New Medievalism, ed. Marina S. Brownlee, Kevin Brownlee, and Stephen G. Nichols, 70–95. Baltimore: Johns Hopkins University Press, 1991.

Niebuhr, H. Richard. *Faith on Earth: An Inquiry into the Structure of Human Faith.* Ed. Richard R. Niebuhr. New Haven: Yale University Press, 1989.

Noonan, John T., Jr. *Contraception: A History of Its Treatment by the Catholic Theologians and Canonists.* New York: New American Library, 1967.

———. "Marital Affection in the Canonists." In *Studia Gratiana Post Octavia Decreti Saecularia* XII, ed. Joseph Forchiella and Alph M. Stickler, vol 2, *Collectanea Stephan Kuttner,* 481–509. Rome: Institut Gratianum Bononiae, 1967.

Oberman, Heiko A. "Some Notes on the Theology of Nominalism with Attention to Its Relation to the Renaissance." *Harvard Theological Review* 53 (January 1960): 47–76.

O'Mara, Philip F. "Holcot and the *Pearl*-Poet," pt. 2. *Chaucer Review* 27, no. 1 (1992): 97–106.

———. "Robert Holcot's 'Ecumenism' and the Green Knight," pt. 1. *Chaucer Review* 26, no. 4 (1992): 329–42.

Owst, G. R. *Literature and Pulpit in Medieval England.* Oxford: Basil Blackwell, 1961.

Padgug, Robert A. "Sexual Matters: On Conceptualizing Sexuality in History." In *Passion and Power: Sexuality in History,* ed. Kathy Peiss and Christina Simmons with Robert A. Padgug, 14–31. Philadelphia: Temple University Press, 1989.

Page, Christopher. "The English *A Capella* Renaissance." *Early Music* (August 1993): 453–70.

Pantin, W. A. *The English Church in the Fourteenth Century.* Toronto: University of Toronto Press, 1980.

Patterson, Lee. *Chaucer and the Subject of History.* Madison: University of Wisconsin Press, 1991.

———. "'For the Wyves Love of Bathe': Feminine Rhetoric and Poetic Resolution in the *Roman de la Rose* and the *Canterbury Tales.*" *Speculum* 58 (1983): 656–95.

———. *Negotiating the Past: The Historical Understanding of Medieval Literature.* Madison: University of Wisconsin Press, 1987.

Payer, Pierre J. *The Bridling of Desire: Views of Sex in the Later Middle Ages.* Toronto: University of Toronto Press, 1993.

———. *Sex and the Penitentials: The Development of a Sexual Code, 550–1150.* Toronto: University of Toronto Press, 1984.

Pearsall, Derek A. "The Alliterative Revival: Origins and Social Backgrounds." In *Middle English Alliterative Poetry and Its Literary Background: Seven Essays,* ed. David Lawton, 34–53. Cambridge, Eng.: D. S. Brewer, 1982.

———. *Old and Middle English Literature.* London: Routledge & Kegan Paul, 1977.

Pieper, Josef. *The Four Cardinal Virtues: Prudence, Justice, Fortitude, Temperance.* Notre Dame, Ind.: University of Notre Dame Press, 1966.

Poirion, Daniel. *Le Roman de la Rose.* Paris: Hatier, 1973.

Potkay, Monica Brzezinski. "*Cleanness*'s Fecund and Barren Speech Acts." *Studies in the Age of Chaucer* 17 (1995): 99–109.

Quilligan, Maureen. "Words and Sex: The Language of Allegory in the *De planctu naturae,* the *Roman de la Rose,* and Book III of *The Faerie Queene.*" *Allegoria* 2 (1977): 195–216.

Relihan, Joel C. *Ancient Menippean Satire*. Baltimore: Johns Hopkins University Press, 1993.

Rich, Adrienne. "Compulsory Heterosexuality and Lesbian Existence." In *Feminist Literary Theory: A Reader*, ed. Mary Eagleton, 22–28. Oxford: Basil Blackwell, 1986.

Ricoeur, Paul. *The Symbolism of Evil*. Trans. Emerson Buchanan. New York: Harper & Row, 1967.

Salter, Elizabeth. "The Alliterative Revival." *Medieval Philology* 64 (1966–67): 146–50, 233–37.

Sartre, Jean-Paul. *Anti-Semite and Jew*. Trans. George J. Becker. New York: Schocken Books, 1948.

Scaglione, Aldo D. *Knights at Court: Courtliness, Chivalry, and Courtesy from Ottonian Germany to the Italian Renaissance*. Berkeley: University of California Press, 1991.

———. *Nature and Love in the Late Middle Ages*. Berkeley: University of California Press, 1963.

Scarry, Elaine. *The Body in Pain: The Making and Unmaking of the World*. Oxford: Oxford University Press, 1985.

Schmidt, A. V. C. "*Kynde Craft* and the *Play of Paramorez*: Natural and Unnatural Love in *Purity*." In *Genres, Themes and Images in English Literature*, ed. Piero Boitani and Anna Torti, 105–24. Tübingen: Gunter Narr Verlag, 1988.

Schmidt, Charles. *Histoire littéraire de l'Alsace à la fin du XVe et au commencement du XVIe siècle* (Reprografischer Nachdruck des Ausg. Paris 1879). Vol. 1. Hildesheim: Golms, 1966.

Schnapp, Jeffrey T. "Dante's Sexual Solecisms: Gender and Genre in the *Commedia*." In *The New Medievalism*, ed. Marina S. Brownlee, Kevin Brownlee, and Stephen G. Nichols, Jr., 201–25. Baltimore: Johns Hopkins University Press, 1991.

Schreiber, Earl G. "The Structures of *Clannesse*." In *The Alliterative Tradition in the Fourteenth Century*, ed. Bernard Levy and Paul Szarmach, 131–52. Kent, Ohio: Kent State University Press, 1981.

Sedgwick, Eve Kosofsky. *Epistemology of the Closet*. Berkeley: University of California Press, 1990.

Spearing, A. C. *The Gawain-Poet: A Critical Study*. Cambridge: Cambridge University Press, 1970.

———. *Medieval Dream Poetry*. Cambridge: Cambridge University Press, 1976.

———. *The Medieval Poet as Voyeur: Looking and Listening in Medieval Love Narratives*. Cambridge: Cambridge University Press, 1993.

———. *Readings in Medieval Poetry*. Cambridge: Cambridge University Press, 1987.

Spector, Stephen. "Anti-Semitism and the English Mystery Plays." In *The Drama in the Middle Ages: Comparative and Critical Essays*, ed. Clifford Davidson, C. J. Gianakaris, and John H. Stroupe, 328–41. New York: AMS Press, 1982.

———. "Empathy and Enmity in the *Prioress's Tale*." In *The Olde Daunce: Love, Friendship, Sex and Marriage in the Medieval World*, ed. Robert R. Edwards and Stephen Spector, 211–28. Albany: State University of New York Press, 1991.

Stanbury, Sarah. *Seeing the Gawain-Poet: Description and the Act of Perception*. Philadelphia: University of Pennsylvania Press, 1991.

Stanton, Domna C. "Introduction: The Subject of Sexuality." In *Discourses of Sexuality*, ed. Domna C. Stanton, 1–46. Ann Arbor: University of Michigan Press, 1992.

Steinberg, Leo. *The Sexuality of Christ in Renaissance Art and Modern Oblivion*. New York: Pantheon, 1983.

Storey, R. L. *Thomas Langley and the Bishopric of Durham*. London: S.P.C.K., 1961.

Stow, George B. "Richard II in Thomas Walsingham's Chronicles." *Speculum* 59 (1984): 68–102.

Tentler, Thomas N. *Sin and Confession on the Eve of the Reformation*. Princeton: Princeton University Press, 1977.

Trumbach, Randolph. "The Birth of the Queen: Sodomy and the Emergence of Gender Equality in Modern Culture, 1660–1750." In *Hidden from History: Reclaiming the Gay and Lesbian Past*, ed. Martin Duberman, Martha Vicinus, and George Chauncey, Jr., 129–40. New York: New American Library, 1989; London: Penguin, 1991.

Tuck, Anthony. *Richard II and the Nobility*. London: Edward Arnold, 1973.

Turner, James Grantham. *One Flesh: Paradisal Marriage and Sexual Relations in the Age of Milton*. Oxford: Oxford University Press, 1987.

Tuve, Rosemond. *Allegorical Imagery: Some Medieval Books and Their Posterity*. Princeton: Princeton University Press, 1966.

Twomey, Michael W. "*Cleanness*, Peter Comestor, and the *Revelationes Sancti Methodii*." *Mediaevalia* 11 (1985): 203–17.

——. "The Sin of *Untrawþe* in *Cleanness*." In *Text and Matter: New Critical Perspectives of the Pearl-Poet*. Ed. Robert J. Blanch, Miriam Youngerman Miller, Julian N. Wasserman, 117–45. Troy, N.Y.: Whitston Publishing, 1991.

Valency, Maurice. *In Praise of Love: An Introduction to the Love-Poetry of the Renaissance*. New York: Macmillan, 1958.

Vantuono, William. Review of *Pattern of Judgment in the* Queste *and* Cleanness, by Charlotte C. Morse. *Studies in the Age of Chaucer* 1 (1979): 177–83.

Vitto, Cindy L. "Feudal Relations and Reason in *Cleanness*." In *The Rusted Hauberk: Feudal Ideals of Order and Their Decline*, ed. Liam O. Purdon and Cindy L. Vitto, 5–28. Gainesville: University Press of Florida, 1994.

Weber, Sarah Appleton. *Theology and Poetry in the Medieval English Lyric: A Study of Sacred History and Aesthetic Form*. Columbus: Ohio State University Press, 1969.

Wallace, David. "*Cleanness* and the Terms of Terror." In *Text and Matter: New Critical Perspectives of the* Pearl-Poet. Ed. Robert J. Blanch, Miriam Youngerman Miller, Julian N. Wasserman, 117–45. Troy, N.Y.: Whitston Publishing, 1991.

Wetherbee, Winthrop. "The Function of Poetry in the *De planctu naturae* of Alain de Lille." *Traditio* 25 (1969): 87–112.

——. "The Literal and the Allegorical: Jean de Meun and the *De planctu naturae*." *Medieval Studies* 33 (1971): 264–91.

——. *Platonism and Poetry in the Twelfth Century: The Literary Influence of the School of Chartres*. Princeton: Princeton University Press, 1972.

Wheeler, Bonnie. "The Masculinity of King Arthur: From Gildas to the Nuclear Age." *Quondam et Futurus: A Journal of Arthurian Interpretations* 2, no. 4 (1992): 1–26.

Wilder, Amos Niven. *Theopoetic: Theology and the Religious Imagination*. Philadelphia: Fortress Press, 1976.

Williams, D. J. "Alliterative Poetry in the Fourteenth and Fifteenth Centuries." In *The New History of Literature,* vol. 1, *The Middle Ages,* ed. W. F. Bolton, 119–67. New York: Peter Bedrick Books, 1987.

———. "A Literary Study of the Middle English Poems *Purity* and *Patience.*" Ph.D. diss., Oxford University, 1965.

Wilson, Edward. *The* Gawain-*Poet.* Leiden: E. J. Brill, 1976.

Wittgenstein, Ludwig. *Philosophical Investigations.* Trans. G. E. M. Anscombe. New York: Macmillan, 1953.

Zavadil, J. B. "A Study of Meaning in *Patience* and *Cleanness.*" Ph.D. diss. Stanford University, 1962.

Ziolkowski, Jan. *Alan of Lille's Grammar of Sex: The Meaning of Grammar to a Twelfth-Century Intellectual.* Cambridge: Medieval Academy, 1985.

Index

Aesthetic ethics: God and self in relation, 37, 79, 103, 111; good as beautiful, 12, 18, 22, 29, 40, 105, 120, 170, 223, 259*n*2; inner and outer beauty, 27–29, 141, 149, 230*n*16; vs. obedience, 106, 239–40*n*33. *See also* Temperance; Thomas Aquinas

Alain de Lille: *Anticlaudianus*, 243*n*5, 259*n*2; *Complaint of Nature*, 10–12, 71–92, 242–46*nn*128–32 passim, 136, 144, 254*n*8, 257*n*19, 258*n*28; marriage sermons, 59, 76; *Sermones de peccatis capitalibus*, 235*n*9

—*Complaint*, characters in: Antigamus/Antigenius, 80, 83, 91, 244*n*14, 245–46*n*24; Cupid, 77, 82, 91, 243–44*n*11, 245–46*n*24; Genius, 88–91, 243*n*10, 245*n*23, 245–46*n*24; Hymen/Marriage, 87–88, 92, 144, 243–44*n*11, 245–46*n*24, 250*n*8; Jocus, 80–82, 245–46*n*24; Nature, 11, 71–92 passim, 117, 121–22, 128, 245*n*23; Orpheus, 129–30; Venus, 72–85, 91–92, 130–31, 244*n*15, 245–46*n*24

—*Complaint*, hetero/homosexual opposition in: 130–32

Albertus Magnus, 247*nn*5, 9

Allegorization: feasts, typological, 206, 210, 231*n*20, 265–66*n*27, 279*n*3; relation between earthly/heavenly love in *Cleanness* debated, 67, 173, 240–41*nn*34, 35, 36, 260–61*nn*5, 6; wedding garment, 35–36, 38. *See also* Alain de Lille, *Complaint*, characters in; Biblical passages discussed; Dualism; Idolatry/sacrilege; Jean de Meun: *Roman*; Sodomy; Vessels

Alliterative revival, 6, 9, 19, 21, 227*n*2

Alter, Robert, 259*n*30

Ambrose, 141*n*3

Anderson, J. J., 36

Andreae, John, 61–62

Andreas Capellanus, 147, 255nn14, 15
Andrew, Malcolm, and Ronald Waldron, 17, 24, 83–84, 209, 236n17, 265n25
Anti-semitism, medieval, 199, 258–59n29; modern, 157
Aquinas, Thomas. *See* Thomas Aquinas
Arden, Heather, 124
Aristotle: craft vs. noble work, 244n15; ethics, 12, 31, 93, 108–10, 228n7, 249n19; epistemology, 249n15; good as beautiful, 12; mean, 30
Artesanus, 100
Augustine of Hippo: critical of ostentatious drabness, 34; goods of marriage, 245n22; intention, role of, 61, 63, 96; lower loves, rejection of, 260n5; lust as sacrilege, 102, 248n12; pervasiveness of his doctrine, 140, 246n2; pessimism of, 31, 140, 246n1; physical perfection lost in Fall, 152; privacy in sex, 240n35; sex/food, 96; sin against nature, 103, 236n19, 248n12

Babees Book, 266n30
Baldwin, Anna P., 266n27
Baldwin, John W., 63–64, 245n20
Baptism, 18, 199, 215, 220, 268n37
Barber, Richard, 27
Barnie, John, 49
Beckwith, Sarah, 180–81, 190–91, 266nn28, 29, 32
Bennett, Michael J., 226n6, 227n2
Benson, Larry D., 234n6, 255n15
Bernard of Clairvaux, 237n21, 240n35
Bernard Silvestris: on Genius, 89–90; on Nature, 242n1; on Venus, 243–44n11
Bezalel, 228n5, 269n2
Biblical characters. *See Cleanness*, biblical characters in; Homosocial bonding
Biblical passages discussed: 1 Cor. 1:6–9, 258n25; 2 Enoch 10:34, 233–34n3; Ephesians 5:3–12, 236n19; Lk. 14:16–24/Matt. 22:14, 40, 269n3; Matt. 5:3–10 (Beatitudes), 18, 37, 217; 2 Peter 2:13, 268n38; 2 Peter 2:20–21, 199; 2 Peter 2:4, 10, 47, 235n10; Romans 1:18–27, 42, 143, 208, 232–33n3; Song of Songs, 173, 260n6; Wisdom of Solomon 10:1–7, 19:18ff, 47, 235nn10, 14
Bloch, R. Howard, 81–82
Book of the Knight of the Tower, 32, 231nn19, 20
Bossi, Egidio, 241n38
Boswell, John, 86–87, 136, 235n8, 236n18, 246–47nn5, 7
Bowers, John M. 226n6, 227n2
Braswell, Mary Flowers, 271n13
Brewer, Derek S., 265n25
Brinton, Thomas, 49
Brundage, James, 70, 241n38, 251n13
Bullough, Vern, 49
Burns, E. Jane, 255n12, 255–56n16

Cadden, Joan, 63, 239n31, 251–52n13
Calabrese, Michael A., 257n19; and Eric Eliason, 4–5, 8, 57–58, 225nn2, 3, 242n41, 268n36
Cantor, Peter. *See* Peter the Cantor
Chaucer, Geoffrey: *Book of the Duchess*, 148; *Parliament of Fowls*, 72, 242n2; —*Canterbury Tales*: General Prologue, 148, 149, 244n12; *Monk's Tale*, 269n4; *Pardoner's Tale*, 148, 236n20, 256–57n19, 270n6; *Parson's Tale*, 47, 55; *Prioress's Tale*, 157, 258–59n29; *Wife of Bath's Prologue*, 23, 119
Chopinel. *See* Jean de Meun
Chretien de Troyes, 170n2, 259
Christ: conception and nativity of, 106, 184–86, 262n17, 263nn19, 20; courtesy of, 264n23, 265nn25, 26; as courtly beloved (lady), 12, 168–73 passim, 184–85, 191, 253n4, 266n27, 271n15; as courtly exemplar (lord), 12, 184–90 passim, 264n23, 265n26; as healer, 186–87, 196; (homo)erotic attraction to, 168–69, 192–93; as king

of Nature, 186, 189; as mother, 169, 192; as Wisdom, 260*n*5
—crucifixion imagery: absence of in *Cleanness* 12, 168–69, 261*n*11, 265–66*n*27; and penitential subjectivity, 191, 195–99 passim; presence of in *Pearl* and *Sir Gawain* 194–95; sacred/profane interpenetration, 168–69, 180–81, 187, 191, 261–62*n*12
Christine de Pisan, 114, 250*nn*4, 6, 263*n*19
Cicero, 253*n*3
Clanvowe, John, 263–64*n*17
Cleanness: affirmative didactic aim of, 17; coherence of, 201–02, 214–16. 222–24; innovative ethic of, 19–20, 223–24, 228*n*8; structure of, 21, 37, 39, 232*n*1, 269*n*5; summary of, 18–19
—biblical characters in: Abraham, 53, 166, 176, 183, 215; Adam, 70, 87, 151–52, 174, 232*n*1, 233*n*4, 234*n*6, 270*n*11; angels visiting Sodom, 6–7, 153–55, 257*n*22, 261*n*9; antediluvian men 151–52; Belshazzar, 214, 270*n*11; Daniel, 205, 209, 212, 214–16, 270*n*10; Eve, 70, 87, 174, 232*n*1, 233*n*4, 234*n*6, 263*n*20; Lot, 153–55, 160–64; Lot's daughters, 155, 160, 162–63, 175, 225*n*3, 259*n*31; Lot's wife, 64–65, 214; Mary, 252*n*1, 263*n*20; Nebuchadnezzar, 214, 270*n*11; Noah, 152, 176–77, 182–83, 257*n*21; Sarah, 106, 175; Satan/Lucifer, 174, 232*n*1, 270*n*11; Sodom, men of, 2, 5–6, 56–57, 152–64; Solomon, 20, 202, 204, 205, 207, 209, 269*n*2; Zedekiah, 202–09 passim, 213–14, 270*n*10. See also Christ; God; Homosocial bonding
—genre of: biblical paraphrase, 20, 40, 227*n*3; chronicle, 202, 207, 268–69*n*1; homily, 19–20, 24, 228*n*8; penitential treatise, 35–36, 267–68; romance, 54, 66, 195, 198, 268–69*n*1. See also Marriage sermons; Penance

—phrases/words discussed: *ayþeroþer welde*, 85; *controeued agayn kynde*, 55; *clene/clannesse*, 14, 22–26, 229*n*10; *clene layk*, 22, 72; Clopyngnel's *clene rose*, 113–15, 168, 172–73, 250*n*5; *crafte*, 25; *doole alþerswettest*, 83–84; *drwry*, 68, 79; *fayre formez*, 17, 21, 29; *femmalez wyse*, 65, 69, 112, 159, 239*n*32; *fetyse of a fayre forme*, 29; *fre þewes*, 22, 167, 259*n*1; *fylþe of þe flesch*, 10, 18, 19, 41–47, 54–57; *gropande*, 166; *honeste*, 26–28, 68, 230*n*15, 265*n*26; *kynde crafte*, 22, 65–70, 83, 95, 101, 161, 164, 230*n*12; *luf-lowe* 79, 84; *make*, 252*n*1; *play of paramorez*, 53, 65–70, 83, 101, 110, 166, 171, 244*n*12; *portrayed hit myseluen*, 79, 240*n*35, 244*nn*12, 13, 250*n*8; *quoynt/quoyntise* (*coyntise*), 39, 231–32, 265*n*25, 271*n*15; *unstered wyth syȝt*, 79, 240*n*35; *usen*, 202, 251, 267*n*11
Cleanness-poet, milieu and audience: aristocratic household environment, 183–84, 227*n*2; audience, speculation about, 19, 20, 44, 51–52, 230*n*16; homosocial milieu of, 226*n*6; intellectual milieu of, 10, 53–54, 228*n*4. See also Cotton Nero A.x., Art.3 Poems; Homophobia; Theopoetic vision
Clopyngnel. See Jean de Meun
The Cloud of Unknowing, 228*n*5, 240*n*35
Cocks, Joan, 138, 253*n*2
Coleman, Janet, 227–28*n*3
Comestor, Peter, 42, 100, 232–33*n*3
Compulsory heterosexuality, 14, 70. See also Heterosexism
Coote, Stephen, 234*n*4
Cotton Nero A.x, Art.3 Poems: 1, 216–23 passim; common authorship 13, 216, 242*n*3, 271*n*14. See also *Patience*; *Pearl*; *Sir Gawain and the Green Knight*

Courtliness: criticized, 105, 107–08, 141–51 passim; emergence of, 139, 141, 145–46, 253n3, 255nn11, 14; legitimation of, 2, 8–10, 19–22, 24, 29–36 passim, 226n6, 228n2, 266n30, 275nn25, 26; *sprezzatura*, 190, 265n24. *See also* Aesthetic ethics; *Cleanness*-poet; Christ; Decorative aesthetic; Loveplay; Magnificence; Romance; Temperance
—dress and deportment: in *Book of the Knight of the Tower*, 32–33, 231n20; in *Canterbury Tales, General Prologue*, 149; in *Cleanness* 18–19, 27–28, 32–36 passim, 39, 154, 162, 202, 210, 222; in *The Merchant of Paris*, 34–35; in *Pearl*, 194, 230n16; polemics against, 108, 142–45, 150, 253–54n6; in *Roman*, 144; in *Sir Gawain*, 142; in *On Temperance*, 32–33, 107–08. *See also* Decorative aesthetic
Crane, Susan, 147, 254n8, 255n13, 256n16, 258n28
Crompton, Louis, 101, 248n10

Damian, Peter, 14, 235n13, 247–48n8
Dante, 256n17
Davenport, William A. 21, 39–40, 58, 241–42n41, 262n15
D'Avray, D. C., 238n26; and M. Tausche, 62, 238nn26, 28
Decorative aesthetic: 253n5; courtly poetic style, 20–21, 182, 185–86, 197, 209, 227n2; gratuitous artifice, 21, 107–08, 228nn5, 6, 253n5; Late Gothic architecture and artifacts 228–29n9, 263n19; liturgical craft and furnishings, 20–21, 25–27, 186, 263n19, 269n2. *See also* Vessels; Courtliness, dress and deportment
Deguilleville, Guillaume, 114
Denley, Marie, 190, 265n26, 266n30
Dinshaw, Carolyn, 8–9, 68, 226n6, 240n35, 245n19
Dionysius, 30

Dollimore, Jonathan, 150, 158, 164
Douglas, Jane Dempsey, 237n22
Douglas, Mary, 179–81
Downing, Christine, 164
Dronke, Peter, 250n8
Dualism: active/passive, 64, 74; form/matter, 89–90, 245n23; masculine/feminine, 59–60, 74–75, 83, 85–86, 89–90, 104, 223; mind/body, 173, 260n5; reason/sensuality, 138; soul/body, 31, 61, 104, 260–61n6; spirit/flesh, 39, 54, 59–60, 61, 64, 65, 137, 240n34. *See also* Hetero/homosexual opposition; Homosexual relations, male; Masculine
Duby, Georges, 254–55nn8, 10, 263n19
Durandus of St. Pourcain, 239n28
Dymmok, Roger, 228n7
Dynes, Wayne, 14, 143, 156; and Warren Johansson, 257–58n25

Economou, George D., 80, 242n1, 243n7, 243–44n11, 245–46n24
Edward II, 150
Edward III, 262n13
Effeminacy. *See* Courtliness; Homosexual relations, male
Eliason, Eric. *See* Calabrese, Michael A.
Elon, Amos, 157
Eneas, 254n8, 258n28
Epic. *See* Romance; Rhetoric
Erickson, Carolly, 263–64n21
Ethics. *See* Aesthetic ethics; Dualism; Heterosexual ethics; Magnificence; Nature; Nominalism; Temperance
Eucharist: laity's decorum, 231n20; lay devotion to, 191, 266n29; and lovemaking, 140, 193; pearl as wafer, 198, 267n35; priestly decorum, 24–26, 187; typological feast, 265–66n27, 231n20

Farley, Margaret A., R.S.M., 96
Female/feminine: commodification of women, 155, 160, 162–63, 255n3,

259n31; Eve as archetype, 3, 70, 137; in male homosocial bonding, 162; status of women, 55, 59, 135, 146–47, 155n12, 175, 183, 252–53n2, 255n12. *See also* Christ; Courtliness; Dualism; Homosexual relations, male
— and sexual desire: allegorized as feminine, 137–140 passim; celebrated in *Cleanness*, 16, 135; "flesh" not equated with female desire in *Cleanness*, 69–70; homosexual relations, 69–70, 100, 241n38; in *Complaint*, 77–79, 85, 131, in *Roman*, 117–20, 123–24, 127; Sodomites in *Cleanness* as having female desires, 159, 164; and "two seed" theory of conception, 251–52n13. *See also* Alain de Lille, *Complaint*, characters in; Christ; Courtliness; Dualism; Homosexual relations, male; Jean de Meun, *Roman*, characters in; Romance
Filth of the flesh: definition by example in *Cleanness*, 41–47, 99. See also *Cleanness*, phrases/words discussed; Homosexual relations, male; Sodomy
Finkelstein, Dorothee Metlitski, 228n5, 244n13, 269n2
Fleming, John V., 115, 250n5, 251n11, 260n5
Flood (biblical): animals in ark, pleasure of, 95, 182, 262n14; caused by sodomy, 42, 45–48, 70, 100; caused by transgressive female sexuality, 70, 100; causes debated, 232–34nn2, 3, 4, 235n11, 257n20; *Cleanness* omits rainbow, 261n11; God's vulnerability in, 167, 174, 176–79, 182–83. *See also* Homosocial bonding
Foucault, Michel, 237, 255n13
Francis of Assisi, 218
Frantzen, Allen J., 6–8, 53, 236n18, 237n24, 240n35, 241n38
Freud, Sigmund, 157–58, 164, 253n4

Gautier de Coincey, 24
Geiler, Jean, 56, 237n22

Gender symbolics. *See* Dualism; Female/feminine; Masculine
Gerson, Jean, 47, 62, 63, 114, 241n38, 250nn4, 6
Gilby, Thomas, O.P., 94, 246n1
Glenn, Jonathan A., 233n4, 257n22
God: anthropomorphism, 48, 103, 178, 181–82, 261n9; as artist/Creator, 2–3, 10, 73, 174–75, 181, 190, 207; beauty of, 29–30, 105; as courtly lord, 26–28, 33, 38, 40, 174–75; inner conflicts of, 40, 178, 213; as love in Trinity, 79, 240n35, 240–42n36, 244n12, 250n8; as masculine/feminine, 79, 240–41n36, 244n13; as patriarchal authority, 64–65, 212, 239–40n33; power of, 39, 106, 203, 215; as teacher, 68, 73, 7879, 83–84, 181; vulnerability of, 24–25, 43, 103, 175, 190, 203. *See also* Aesthetic ethics; Homosocial bonding; Nature
— sacred/profane: anthropological approach to filth, 178–84 passim; cosmogonic myth/ritual, 179, 18284; purity/defilement, 22–23, 177, 187, 230; transforming power of interpenetration of, 169, 203, 213. *See also* Beckwith, Sarah; Christ, crucifixion imagery; Douglas, Mary; Spearing, A. C.
— vengeance of: and anguish, 270n11; and divine courtesy/artistry, 49, 182–84, 262n15; vs. "filth of the flesh" as contrasted with evil generally, 18–19, 42–48 passim, 181–82; in Last Judgment, 206, 210, 269n3, 271n12; as passionless, 103, 248n13, 261n7; and warfare, 174, 261n8
Goldin, Frederic, 255–56n16
Gollancz, Sir Israel, 231n19, 232n1, 235n14, 250n5
Goodich, Michael, 145, 233n3, 235n11
Gower, John, 105, 242n2
Green, R. H., 243n8
Greenberg, David, 237n21
Grilandus, Paulus, 241n38

Gross, Gregory W., 257*n*19, 270*n*6
Guibertus de Tonaco, 62
Guillaume de Lorris: courtly lover's grooming, 144; initial author of *Roman*, 114–17, 249–50*n*2, 250*n*3

Hali Maidenhead, 44
Halley, Janet, 259*n*31
Halperin, David M., 156, 245*n*21, 258*n*27
Hanning, Robert W., 142, 253*n*5, 265*n*26
Hansen, Elaine Tuttle, 256*n*16
Haring, Nikolaus, 242–43*n*5
H. D. [Hilda Doolittle], 264*n*3
Henderson, George, 20
Hermeneutic: *Cleanness*-poet's, 43–44, 217; of desire, 16; feminist, 90, 122, 126–27; key to *Roman*, 115, 125–26; patriarchal, 65; risks, 58–59; of suspicion, 16, 90, 225*n*3
Hetero/homosexual opposition, 3–4, 8–9, 16, 86 87, 132–33, 157–59, 163–164, 199, 226*n*6
Heterosexism: definition, 14; denial of virginity/celibacy in *Roman*, 129–131; evident in *Complaint*'s mystique of marriage, 87–88, 91–92; insemination of Rose by Lover celebrated as human creativity, 126; in literary criticism, 15–16, 58, 70, 241–42*n*41; medieval development of homophobic discourse in relation to courtly heterosexism, 16, 86, 111–12, 226*n*6; procreative desire universalized in 90, 96, 247*n*6. *See also* Homophobia; Homosexual relations, male
Heterosexual Ethics: degree of control required over appetite debated, 59–60, 237–39*nn*25–30; limits of matrimony, 62–63; marital debt, 61; pleasure illicit without reproductive aim, 63. *See also* Dualism; Loveplay; Temperance; Thomas Aquinas
Heyward, Carter, 223

Heyworth, P. C., 55, 236*n*15
Hill, Thomas D., 251*n*11
History: divergent patterns of within *Cleanness*, 194–95, 199–200, 201–216 passim; Jewish, literal, important to Christian, 217; Nature, Law, Grace, Ages of, 269–70*n*5, 270–71*n*11; as order of secondary causality, 203, 206–7; of redemption vs. cosmogonic renewal, 183–84, 191, 194–95, 218. *See also* Allegorization; Christ; Flood (biblical); Sodom, destruction of; Theopoetic vision; Vessels
Holcot, Robert, 231*n*18, 243*n*5
Holthausen, Ferdinand, 232*n*3
Homophobia: *Cleanness*-poet's, 42, 151, 164; definitions, 14; degrees, 115; "gay genocide," 101, 248*n*10; political scandalizing in rhetoric of, 150; theories of causes, 86, 133, 151, 157–59, 164, 226*n*6, 236–37*n*21. *See also* God, vengeance; Homosexual relations, male; Homosocial bonding
Homosexuality, 13, 226*n*8, 258*n*27. *See also* Homosexual relations, male
Homosexual relations, male: definition, 13, 226*n*8; desired by certain type(s), 146*n*5, 258*n*7; group identity, 257–58,n25; 258*n*28; masked by/projected into love of courtly lady, 254–55*n*10; ranked with other unnatural lusts, 70, 100–01, 247*n*8, 247 48*n*9, 248*n*11; theories of causes, 236*n*21, 241*n*38, 246–47*n*5. *See also* Hetero/homosexual opposition; Homophobia; Homosocial bonding; Sodomy
—denounced as: boorishly unfeminine and brutal, 236–27, 148, 151–59; as effeminate and emasculating, 85–86, 142–45, 254*n*8; imitations of heterosexual courtship 154*n*8; motivated by greed, 254*n*8; *on femmalez wyse*, 65, 69, 112, 159, 239*n*32
Homosocial bonding: between angels

and Lot, 153–55; between Christ and man, 68–69, 169; between God and Abraham, 166, 176, 183, 215; between God and man, 9, 12, 38, 136, 151, 162, 165–67, 176–77, 205; between God and Noah, 152, 176–77, 182–83, 257*n*21; and homoerotic/homosexual, 144, 165, 169, 254*n*8, 254–55*n*10; less evident in final exemplum 212–213; suppression of homosexual, 158, 162–64, 165, 169, 199, 226*n*6, 259*n*31. *See also* Hetero/homosexual opposition; Homophobia

Huchet, Jean-Charles, 253*n*4
Huizinga, Johan, 228*n*6
Hult, David, 250*n*3

Idolatry/sacrilege: (figuratively) as adultery, 269–70*n*5; as lust, 248*n*12; as sin after penance, 200, 202, 207; as sodomy, 13, 57, 270*n*6; as unnatural lust 102–03
—literal. *See* Vessels
Irenaeus, 264*n*33
Irigaray, Luce, 259*n*31
Irwin, John T. *See* Kelly, T. D.

Jaeger, Stephen, 141, 144–45, 147, 255*nn*11, 14, 257*n*23
James of Milan, 192
Jean de Meun, 10–12, 113–33 passim, 165–200 passim, 207, 243*n*10, 257*n*19; author of *Roman* continuation, 13–14, 249–50*nn*2, 3; cited as "Clopyngnel" (Chopinel) by *Cleanness*-poet, 113–15, 171–73. *See* Christine de Pisan; Guillaume de Lorris
—*Roman*, characters in: Fair Welcoming, 116, 124, 172; Friend (Ami), 172–73, 259*n*3, 259–60*n*4; Genius, 121–23, 128–32, 243*n*10; God of love/Cupid, 114–26 passim; Lover, 117–27 passim, 172–73, 249–50*n*2; Nature, 11, 116, 118–32 passim; Orpheus, 129–30; Reason, 116–31 passim, 205, 260*n*5; Rose, the, 12, 114, 116, 121–27 passim, 171; Venus, 114, 116

Johansson, Warren. *See* Dynes, Wayne
Johnson, Lynn Staley, 257*n*24, 271*n*12
Julian of Norwich, 264*n*3

Kaplan, Aryeh, 79
Kean, P. M., 268*n*37
Keiser, Elizabeth B., 241*n*41, 249*n*17
Kelly, T. D., and John T. Irwin, 64–65, 266*n*27, 269*n*3
Kempe, Margery, 192
Kirk, Elizabeth D., 271*nn*16, 17
Knight, Stephen, 253*n*5
Knowles, David, 29, 231*n*17
Krochalis, Jeanne, 242*n*4, 243*n*5
Kruger, Steven F., 256–57*n*19

Leo IX, Pope, 235*n*13
Lollards, 51, 55–56, 148, 235–36*n*15, 236–37*n*21, 256*n*18, 266*n*29
Love, Nicholas, 193, 266*n*29
Loveplay: marriage as unnecessary for, 67, 119, 240*n*34; absence of reproductive justification for in *Cleanness*, 5, 67, 107; affirmed by Reason in *Roman*, 118–19; denounced by Nature in Alain, 78–85; licit aim for animals in ark, 95; lovetalk, 68–69, 82–84, 107, 109, 125–27; mutuality of as it bears on patriarchal norms, 68–70, 85–86, 95–96, 118–19; not part of animals' pleasure in for Thomas, 107, 248–49*n*16. *See also* Allegorization; Decorative aesthetic

Magnificence, 21, 228*n*7, 249*n*17, 270*n*8
Male bonding. *See* Homosocial bonding; Homosexual relations, male; Masculine
Mandeville's Travels, 20, 49, 269*n*2
Mann, Jill, 24, 256*n*16

Marriage sermons, 59–60, 238n26, 238–9n27, 239nn29–30
Martianus Capella, 250n8
Masculine: antithetical exemplars of in *Cleanness*, 151–59; chivalric ideal violated, 203; patriarchal fatherhood as ideal, 91; symbolic superiority, 59–60, 74–75, 83, 85 86, 89–90, 104. See Christ; God; Hetero/homosexual opposition; Homosexual relations, male; Homosocial bonding
—courtier ideal (romance). See Courtliness; Romance
—warrior ideal (epic). See Romance
Mathew, Gervase, 27, 151, 230n27
McAlpine, Monica, 144, 154, 256n19
McEntire, Sandra J., 266n27
McNeill, John, 246n5
Means, Michael H., 268n36
Medical discourse on sexuality, 84, 239n31, 247n9, 251–52n13
Menner, Robert J., 232n1
Merchant of Paris, 34–35
Metlitski Finkelstein, Dorothee. See Finkelstein, Dorothee Metlitski
Moi, Toril, 147
Morse, Charlotte C., 42, 68, 223–24, 232n2, 260n6, 269nn3, 5, 270n6, 270–71n11
Myrc, John, 236n20

Nature: age of, 260n6, 269n5, 270n11; as artful, 70, 182, 262n14; sins of lust against, 70; sodomy as "the sin against," 99, 128, 226n7; 236n18, 252n14
—order of: modern redefinition of, 110, 270n11; as natural law, 95–99; as primary basis for secondary order of reason, 97–99; as secondary causality in relation to God's primary causality, 92, 106, 111; and self's nature, 96. See also Ulpian
—personification as heterosexual ethical norm: in Bernard Silvestris, 242n1; in Chaucer, 72; in Gower, 242n2. See also Alain de Lille; Jean de Meun
Nicholas of Lyra, 232n2, 236n19
Niebuhr, H. Richard, 195, 266n31
Nominalism, 231n17; order of secondary causes and God's sovereignty, 105–06
Noonan, John T., 96–97, 108–10, 238, 247–48n9, 249n20

Oberman, Heiko A., 106
Occam, William. See William of Occam
O'Mara, Philip F., 231n18
Orderic Vitalis, 142, 253–54n6
Ovid, 129–30, 234n5, 252n18, 260n4
Owst, G. R., 60, 238n26

Page, Christopher, 23
Patience 1; Beatitudes in, 216–17; courtliness compared to *Pearl* and *Sir Gawain*, 216–23; more theologically complex than *Cleanness*, 13; shifts toward costliness of redemption, 222–23, 271n15
Patterson, Lee, 15, 252n17
Payer, Pierre J., 63, 230n28, 234–35n8, 238–39n28, 239nn29, 30
Pearl, 1; clothing in, 230n16; compared to *Cleanness* and *Sir Gawain*, 216–223 passim; costliness of redemption in, 222–23; courtly ethos as vehicle for religious imagination in, 216–22; Eucharist in, 21–22; focus on fallibility and suffering, 220–21; incarnation/crucifixion in, 194; more theologically complex than *Cleanness*, 13
Pearsall, Derek A., 20, 227n2
Penance: absence of guilt psychology, 39, 264n23; as annual requirement, 60, 198–200; deficient images of in *Cleanness*, 195–200; definition, 198; means for sexual control, 6–7, 60–63, 246n5; Nebuchadnezzar as model, 214–16, 271n13. See also Christ, crucifixion imagery; *Cleanness*, genre of
Peter the Cantor, 49–50, 53

Philip Augustus, 258n25
Pieper, Josef, 248–49n16
Piers Plowman, 268n36
Potkay, Monica Brzezinski, 233n4
Pseudo-Methodian *Revelationes*, 42, 100, 233n3

Rhetoric: celebrative, 20; circumlocution/*periphrasis* ("unnameable sin"), 44–47, 54–59; coercion in troubadour lyric, 255n12; conventions of, in homophobic texts, 148; *ekphrasis*, 20, 228n8; *facetia*, 257n23; hyperbole, 84; linked praise and revulsion in, 40, 53; ornate, 21; oxymoron, 82–83, 117; pleasure of the text (sexual and rhetorical), 54, 80–86, 111–12, 140; polemic, clerical (anti-courtly), 141 51 passim, 210; puns, 54, 84, 237n24
—irony: *Cleanness*-poet's response to, 114–15, 173; in Alain, 76, 81; in *Roman*, 11, 243n8; lack of in Nativity account, 186
—metaphor: concreteness of vehicle in *Cleanness*, 14, 38, 57, 99; grammatical, 74–75, 243nn8, 4; invites affective response, 14, 22–24; legal vs. erotic, 239n33; logic as metaphor/trope, 81
—parody/satire: courtly (lyric) idiom, paradoxical use of, 140, 161; of epic virtues, 151–52; ethos of mutuality/refinement parodied in Jean's *Roman*, 127; Menippean, 81; misogynous/Ovidian, 127, 172; sermon parody, 129
Rich, Adrienne, 14
Richard II, 150, 226n6, 227n2, 230n16, 262n17
Richard Coeur de Lion, 258n25
Robert of Courson, 239n28
Robert of Flamborough, 236n18
Rolle, Richard, 267n34
Romance: absence of procreative ethic in, 117; and "feminized" male, 134–64 passim; love and reason in, 116, 147;

marriage de-emphasized in, 117; Nebuzaradan violates chivalric ideal, 203; romance plot, 54, 253n4; woman and feminine in, 124–25, 141, 146, 253n4, 256n16. *See also* Aesthetic ethics; Courtliness; Female/feminine; Masculine; Rhetoric
—and epic: aggressiveness of Sodomites in relation to, 158; Christ more courtier than warrior, 170; courageous action dominant value in epics, 174; God not entirely warrior nor courtier, 212; Lot and, 154; role of female audience in, 146; satiric exaggeration of epic values, 151–53; transition from epic to romance, 9, 139, 141, 147, 153; virtues of hospitality with respect to, 154
Romance of the Rose. *See* Guillaume de Lorris; Jean de Meun
Root, Robert K., 269n4
Ross, Anthony, O.P., 246n1
Rubin, Gayle, 259n31

Sacrilege. *See* Idolatry/sacrilege
Salter, Elizabeth, 227n2
Sartre, Jean Paul, 157
Schmidt, A. V. C., 4, 41–42, 68, 69, 240–41nn34, 35, 36, 37
Schmidt, Charles, 56
Schnapp, Jeffrey T., 168
Schreiber, Earl G., 233–34n4
Sedgwick, Eve, 101, 144–45, 226n8, 248n10
Sir Gawain and the Green Knight: 1; epic and romance in, 142, 253n5; "feminized" male legitimated in, 148; "love talk" in, 68, 245n19; reflects Alliterative Revival aristocracy, 19, 184; reflects homosocial milieu, 226n6; relation of aesthetic to ethical in, 9–10; style of castle, 229n9; theological and ethical complexity of, 13, 194, 234n6, 265n26
Sodom, destruction of: 101, 225nn1, 4; 248n10. *See also* Flood (biblical)

298 Index

—Dead Sea landscape in *Cleanness:* emblematic of sodomy's sterility, 3, 225*n1;* excremental imagery equates sodomy with anal intercourse, 6–7, 57, 225*n4,* 237*n24;* as positive sign of God's bond with men who share his aesthetic/ethical norms, 52–53; traditional warning against Sodomites' sin, 49–50

Sodomy: allegations of, 49, 51–52, 55–56, 129, 235–236*n15,* 242*n4,* 256*n18;* ambiguity of term, 13, 70, 100, 142, 234–35*n8;* as anal intercourse between males, 233*n3,* 234–35*n8,* 237*n24;* as anal intercourse between male and female, 7; as male couple in a relationship, 56; as male prostitution, 254*n8;* as "unnameable sin," 6, 236*nn19,* 20. *See also* Homosexual relations, male; Nature; Rhetoric

—allegorized as: idolatry, 13, 57, 243*n8;* rupture of divine/human bond of love, 242–43*n8;* spiritual sterility, 64; sterile speech, 57

Spearing, A. C., 26, 135, 230*n13,* 241–42*n41*

Spector, Stephen, 157, 259*n29*

Speculum Sacerdotale, 246*n5*

Stanbury, Sarah, 228

Stow, George B., 150

Style. *See* Decorative aesthetic

Tausche, M. *See* D'Avray, D. C.

Temperance: as the Beautiful, 29*31,* 32–36 passim; and *clannesse,* 29–30, 32–37 passim, 95–96, 99–102, 106–12; on clothing/cosmetics, 34–35, 108; vs. continence, 106, 110; as the honorable (*honestas*), 30–32, 36–37; natural law as procreative sexual norm, 96–103; and pleasure, 93–96, 103*12;* primary and secondary causality, 37; and reason, 30, 94–112; and Reason in Jean, 120; as *savoir faire,* 31; on sex and food, 31–32, 94, 96; and shame/sensitivity to squalor, 37; on touch, 93–94. *See also* Aesthetic ethics; Aristotle; Dualism; Thomas Aquinas

Tentler, Thomas N., 60, 62–63, 70, 100, 238*nn27,* 28, 247–48*n9*

Tetragrammaton, 79, 240–41*n36,* 244*n13*

Theopoetic vision: defined, 2, 10; limitations of, 12–13, 16, 40, 169, 190, 196, 199, 216, 222–24

—innovative elements in: Christ without Crucifixion, 12, 168–69; gender symbolics, 78, 111–12, 135, 169; homophobic wrath, 18, 19, 42–48 passim, 181–82; lovemaking as naturally divine art, 65–70; penance without guilt, 195–200; unique construction of heterosexual/homosexual opposition, 133

Thomas Aquinas: 17–42 passim, 93–112 passim; ethical optimism like *Cleanness*'s vs. Occam, 29, 92, 105–06, 231*n17;* on God's anger as passionless, 103, 248*n13,* 261*n7;* on magnificence, 228*n7,* 270*n8;* role since Counter-reformation, 31; "the vice against nature," 247*n7;* works available in England, 231*n18. See also* Ethics; Homosexual relations; Nature; Sodomy; Temperance

Thomas Walsingham, 150

Trumbach, Randolph, 258*n26*

Tuck, Anthony, 151

Twomey, Michael W., 4, 42, 100, 152, 232–33*n3,* 233–34*n4*

Ulpian, 96

Vantuono, William, 233–34*n4*

Vessels: allegorization of, 38, 49, 269*n3;* description of, 20–21, 204, 208–09, 228–29*n9,* 269*n2;* history of Temple furnishings, 202–07. *See also* Decorative aesthetic

Walafrid Strabo, 235*n*11
Waldron, Ronald. *See* Andrew, Malcolm
Walsingham, Thomas. *See* Thomas Walsingham
Walter de Burgh, 242*n*4
Wetherbee, Winthrop, 83, 86, 88–91, 126
Wheeler, Bonnie, 174
Wilder, Amos Niven, 2
William Marshal, 254–55*n*10
William of Auvergne, 235*n*9
William of Conches, 250*n*8
William of Occam, 105–06
William of St. Thierry, 234*n*5
Williams, D. J., 267–68*n*36
Wilson, Edward, 232*n*1, 265*n*25, 268*nn*38, 1
Wittgenstein, Ludwig, 83

Zavadil, J. B., 268*n*36
Ziolkowski, Jan, 89, 243*nn*8, 10, 244*n*16, 86–87, 132–33, 157–59, 163–164, 199, 226*n*6